# FACTASTIC BOOK OF 1001 LISTS

## Russell Ash

Dallas Cowboys helmet *see*
AMERICAN FOOTBALL AND RUGBY

Light bulb *see*
INVENTIONS

**DORLING KINDERSLEY**
LONDON • NEW YORK • MOSCOW • SYDNEY
www.dk.com

## IMPRINT INFORMATION

### A DORLING KINDERSLEY BOOK
www.dk.com

Produced for Dorling Kindersley by
PAGEOne, Cairn House, Elgiva Lane, Chesham,
Buckinghamshire HP5 2JD

EDITORIAL DIRECTOR  Helen Parker
ART DIRECTOR  Bob Gordon
PROJECT EDITOR  Sarah Watson
EDITOR  Sophie Williams
EDITORIAL CONSULTANT  Jane Yorke
PROJECT ART EDITOR  Chris Clark
DESIGNERS  Melanie McDowell,
Suzanne Tuhrim

FOR DORLING KINDERSLEY
MANAGING EDITOR  Jayne Parsons
MANAGING ART EDITOR  Gill Shaw
PROJECT EDITOR  Maggie Crowley
DTP DESIGNER  Nomazwe Madonko
PRODUCTION  Kate Oliver
PICTURE RESEARCH  Christine Rista
DK PICTURE LIBRARY  Sally Hamilton
JACKET DESIGN  Mark Richards

Published in Great Britain
by Dorling Kindersley Limited, 9 Henrietta Street,
London WC2E 8PS

2 4 6 8 10 9 7 5 3 1

Colour reproduction by GRB Editrice, Italy
Printed in Spain by Artes Graficas Toledo, S. A.
D. L. TO: 1268 - 1998

# CONTENTS

# FACTASTIC
# BOOK OF
# 1001
# LISTS

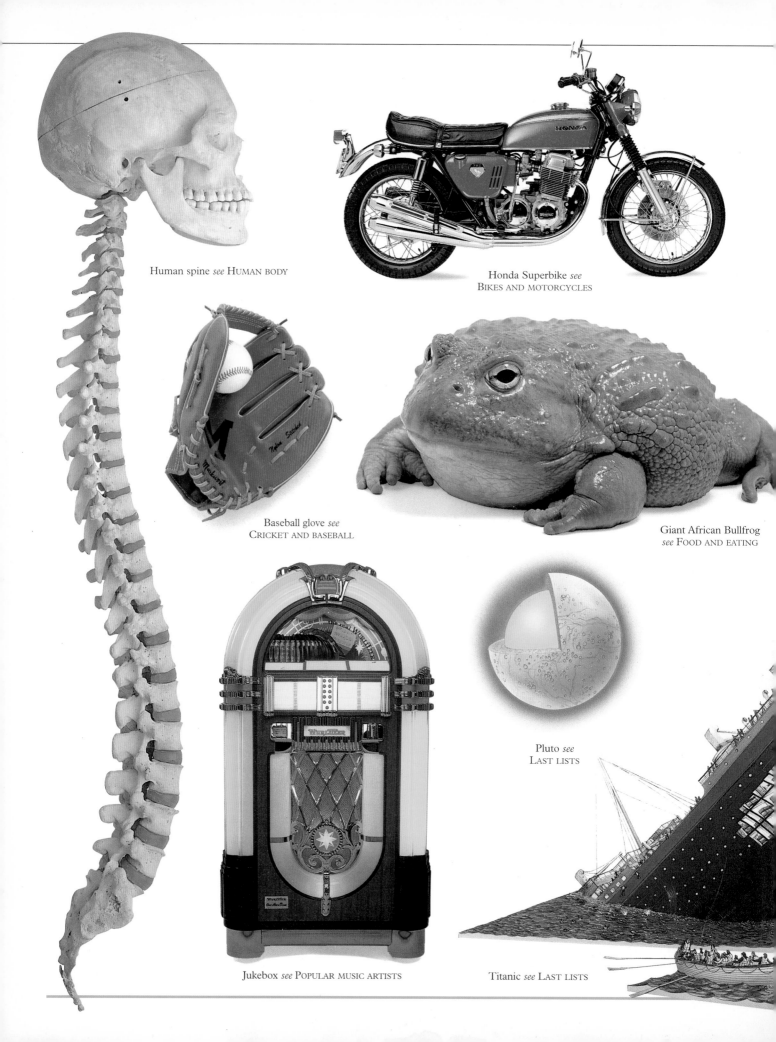

Human spine *see* HUMAN BODY

Honda Superbike *see*
BIKES AND MOTORCYCLES

Baseball glove *see*
CRICKET AND BASEBALL

Giant African Bullfrog
*see* FOOD AND EATING

Pluto *see*
LAST LISTS

Jukebox *see* POPULAR MUSIC ARTISTS

Titanic *see* LAST LISTS

# INTRODUCTION

**Why lists?** Every day of our lives the media bombards us with information through print, TV, CD-ROMs, and the Internet. Lists enable us to make sense of what might otherwise be a mass of data and figures that no one has time to absorb, and provide us with summaries of important events. They help to simplify or organize information in a form that we can easily digest and remember.

**What sort of lists?** In this book I have brought together 1,001 lists of all sorts, biggests and fastests, firsts and lasts, checklists, and lists of milestone events. Each list is easily identifiable by the coloured band at the top. I call them factastic because they are facts, and many of them are also fantastic, a mixture of serious and fun. This is not a book of "bests" and "worsts", which contain someone's personal opinion. The only bests here are bestsellers, and the worsts are worst disasters, all of which can be measured.

**Who says so?** My main source of data is my own library of reference books. I also use specialized library collections and, increasingly, information that is available on

CD-ROM and the Internet. I make a lot of use of "official" sources, such as the United Nations and sports governing bodies, as well as commercial organizations and research groups, many of whose publications are not easily available to the public. The best source of all are private individuals who are happy to share their specialist knowledge – particularly on the Internet.

**How accurate are these lists?** Like all reference book compilers, I strive to be 100 per cent accurate, but it can be difficult: sources often disagree as to even basic figures, such as the areas and populations of countries, and even the height of Mount Everest can appear to change, as new survey methods are used. In addition, lists change all the time. By the time you read this, certain sports records may have been broken, and long-running shows will have run for even longer – or perhaps closed!

**New ideas?** If you have any factastic ideas for lists please send them to me and I'll try to include them in the next book! Equally, if you have any corrections to my lists, you can contact me on our World Wide Web site at www.dk.com (where you will also find details of other DK books), e-mail me direct at ash@pavilion.co.uk, or write to me at the publishers' address. And remember – if you enjoy this book, look out for my annual,

The Top 10 of Everything!

# SPACE

# THE UNIVERSE

## EVOLUTION OF THE UNIVERSE

**THE BIG BANG** Many scientists believe that the Universe was created by a huge explosion called the Big Bang, which occurred 15,000 million years ago.

**THE FIRST ATOMS** Within minutes of the Big Bang the first atoms, the basis of all matter, were formed.

**THE FIRST MOLECULES** After about 10,000 years, temperatures of more than 10,000 million degrees forced atomic particles to come together to form the gases hydrogen and helium.

**GASES FORM STRANDS** About 700,000 years after the Big Bang, gases in space started to form into strands.

**GASES FORM NEBULAE** About 1,000 million years after the Big Bang, the strands of gases swirled together to form clouds of dust and gas called nebulae.

**THE FIRST STARS** As the clumps of dust and gas in a nebula were drawn together by their own gravity, the increasing pressure made gases at the centre very hot. Once the core reached 10 million °C (18 million °F), nuclear reactions occurred and the first stars were born.

**BIRTH OF THE FIRST GALAXIES** About 1,500 million years after the Big Bang, the first galaxies were formed as spinning clouds of stars, dust, and gas.

**CONTINUALLY EXPANDING UNIVERSE** Scientists have proved that the galaxies of the Universe are moving farther and farther apart. This means that the Universe is getting bigger and bigger.

**THE BIG CRUNCH** Most scientists believe that the Universe will expand only so far. Once the energy from the Big Bang is used, it will fall inwards to a Big Crunch.

## SPACE WORDS

**ASTEROID** Chunks of rock of varied size that are found mainly between Mars and Jupiter.

**BLACK HOLE** Formed when a star more than three times as heavy as the Sun collapses at the end of its life, and becomes more compact and dense. This black hole drags in material and nothing, not even light, can escape its gravity.

**COMET** An object composed of snow and dust that orbits the Sun. If a comet approaches the Sun, it forms a tail of gas and dust particles.

**CONSTELLATION** A group of stars around which astronomers have drawn imaginary lines to form a memorable image, for example, a horse.

**GALAXY** An enormous collection of stars. The Universe has about 100,000 million galaxies. The Earth is just one star in the Milky Way galaxy.

**GRAVITY** The invisible force that attracts two masses to each other. It holds the Solar System and galaxies together.

**METEOR** A piece of dust that falls off speeding comets and forms showers, or "shooting stars".

**MOON** A ball of rock that spins on its own axis as well as orbiting a planet. All the planets have moons except Venus and Mercury.

**NEBULA** A cloud of dust and gas in space.

**NEUTRON STAR** A star that has collapsed into a super-dense form of matter. Some neutron stars are seen as pulsars.

**PULSAR** A neutron star that emits pulses of radiation towards Earth as it spins (like a lighthouse). It gets its energy from rotation.

**QUASAR** Thought to be the most distant and luminous objects in the universe, quasars are probably the cores of the first galaxies to be formed.

**STAR** A spinning ball of hot, luminous gas, which releases energy through nuclear reactions.

**SUPERNOVA** The explosion of a large star, which may briefly produce more light than a galaxy.

## GALAXY FACTS

**TYPES OF GALAXY** There are three types of galaxy: spiral, elliptical, and irregular.

**SPIRAL GALAXIES** These are disc-shaped and contain young and old stars.

**ELLIPTICAL GALAXIES** These are the most common type of galaxy and are made up of flat, round collections of old stars.

**IRREGULAR GALAXIES** These do not form a specific shape, and are rare.

**OUR GALAXY** The Sun is only one of 100–200 billion stars in the Milky Way galaxy, which is 100,000 light-years in diameter.

**NEAREST GALAXY** Andromeda is our nearest neighbouring galaxy – 2.2 million light-years away from the Milky Way. It contains 300 billion stars and is 180,000 light-years wide.

**LARGEST GALAXY** The central galaxy of the Abell 2029 galaxy cluster is 5.6 million light-years wide – 80 times wider than ours.

**BRIGHTEST GALAXY** The galaxy known as IRAS F10214+4724 is 300,000,000,000,000 times brighter than the Sun!

## MOST COMMON ELEMENTS

| ELEMENT | PERCENTAGE |
|---|---|
| Hydrogen | 73.90 |
| Helium | 24.00 |
| Oxygen | 1.07 |
| Carbon | 0.46 |
| Neon | 0.14 |
| Iron | 0.12 |
| Nitrogen | 0.10 |
| Silicon | 0.06 |
| Magnesium | 0.05 |
| Sulphur | 0.04 |

**DID YOU KNOW?** The elements hydrogen and helium together comprise almost 98 per cent of all matter in the Universe.

## DISTANCES IN THE UNIVERSE

| Body | Time taken for light from these bodies to reach Earth |
|---|---|
| Moon | 1.26 sec |
| Sun | 8 min 17 sec |
| Pluto (farthest planet) | 5 hr 20 min |
| Nearest star | 4.22 years |
| Most distant star in our galaxy | 62,700 years |
| Nearest body outside our galaxy | 174,000 years |
| Furthest visible star | 2,309,000 years |
| Most distant known quasar | 13,200,000,000 years |
| Edge of universe | 14,000,000,000 years |

## BRIGHTEST STARS FROM EARTH

| Star | Constellation |
|---|---|
| Sun | Solar System |
| Sirius | Canis Major |
| Canopus | Carina |
| Alpha Centauri | Centaurus |
| Arcturus | Boötes |

**DID YOU KNOW?** This is a list of the brightest stars as viewed from Earth. Sirius, which has a diameter of 1,450,000 km (900,988 miles) is, in fact, more than 24 times brighter than the Sun, but its distance from the Earth puts it in second place.

**DID YOU KNOW?** Proxima Centauri is the closest star to Earth, but it is too small to be seen without a telescope!

**AMAZING FACT!** The temperature on the surface of the Sun is about 5,500°C (9,932°F)!

## ALL 88 CONSTELLATIONS

ANDROMEDA (princess) • ANTLIA (air-pump) • APUS (bird-of-paradise) • AQUARIUS (water-bearer) • AQUILA (eagle) • ARA (altar) • ARIES (ram) • AURIGA (charioteer) • BOÖTES (herdsman) • CAELUM (chisel) • CAMELOPARDALIS (giraffe) • CANCER (crab) • CANES VENATICI (hunting dogs) • CANIS MAJOR (big dog) • CANIS MINOR (little dog) • CAPRICORN (goat) • CARINA (keel) • CASSIOPEIA (seated lady) • CENTAURUS (centaur) • CEPHEUS (king) • CETUS (sea monster) • CHAMELEON • CIRCINUS (compass) • COLUMBIA (dove) • COMA BERENCIES (Bernice's hair) • CORONA AUSTRINA (southern crown) • CORONA BOREALIS (northern crown) • CORVUS (crow) • CRATER (cup) • CRUX (cross) • CYGNUS (swan) • DELPHINUS (dolphin) • DORADO (swordfish) • DRACO (dragon) • EQUULEUS (colt) • ERIDANUS (river) • FORNAX (furnace) • GEMINI (twins) • GRUS (crane) • HERCULES (hero) • HOROLOGIUM (clock) • HYDRA (sea serpent) • HYDRUS (water snake) • INDUS (North American) • LACERTA (lizard) • LEO (lion) • LEO MINOR (lion cub) • LEPUS (hare) • LIBRA (scales) • LUPUS (wolf) • LYNX (lynx) • LYRA (lyre) • MENSA (table) • MICROSCOPIUM (microscope) • MONOCEROS (unicorn) • MUSCA (fly) • NORMA (carpenter's square) • OCTANS (octant) • OPHIUCHUS (serpent holder) • ORION (hunter) • PAVO (peacock) • PEGASUS (winged horse) • PERSEUS (hero) • PHOENIX • PICTOR (easel) • PISCES (fishes) • PISCIS AUSTRINUS (southern fish) • PUPPIS (stern) • PYXIS (sailor's compass) • RETICULUM (net) • SAGITTA (arrow) • SAGITTARIUS (archer) • SCORPIO (scorpion) • SCULPTOR • SCUTUM (shield) • SERPENS (snake) • SEXTANS (sextant) • TAURUS (bull) • TELESCOPIUM (telescope) • TRIANGULUM (triangle) • TRIANGULUM AUSTRALE (southern triangle) • TUCANA (toucan) • URSA MAJOR (large bear) • URSA MINOR (small bear) • VELA (sail) • VIRGO (virgin) • VOLANS (flying fish) • VULPECULA (little fox)

## STAR FACTS

**HOW A STAR IS BORN** All stars begin as vast clouds of dust and gas. As this cloud collapses under gravity, parts contract into clumps called protostars, which spin and flatten into discs. Nuclear reactions begin, dust is blown away, and the star is born. It radiates energy and starts to shine, as it gradually burns up.

**CLOSEST STAR** The closest star to the Earth is the Sun, which is 149.6 million km (92.9 million miles) away.

**HEAVIEST STAR** The variable Eta Carinae, 9,100 light-years away in the Carinae Nebula, is 200 times heavier than our own Sun.

**LARGEST STAR** The diameter of the supergiant Betelgeux (the top left star of the Orion constellation) is about 700 million km (400 million miles) – about 500 times that of the Sun.

**SMALLEST STAR** The white dwarf L362-81 has an estimated diameter of just 5,632 km (3,500 miles) – almost 50 times smaller than the Sun.

**BRIGHTEST SUPERNOVA** First seen in 1993, the supernova 1993 J in the galaxy M81 is the brightest to have appeared in the northern sky for 20 years.

**SUPERNOVA ENERGY** The energy released by a supernova in one minute is equivalent to the total energy radiated by the Sun in 900 million years.

**HOW A STAR DIES** The life of a star ends in either a supernova explosion or a planetary nebula.

## COMET FACTS

**WHAT IS A COMET?** Billions of icy lumps called comets fly around the Solar System. Some are knocked onto a path towards the Sun, which melts the lump so it becomes a large head and a long, streaky tail. As comets travel, they shed dust, seen from Earth as meteors.

**FIRST COMETS** In ancient times, people did not know what comets were. Their sudden appearance made superstitious people regard them as omens.

**SHOEMAKER-LEVY** In 1993, Comet Shoemaker-Levy passed close to Jupiter and was broken into fragments by Jupiter's immense gravity. During July 1994, these fragments crashed into Jupiter, causing a series of huge explosions in Jupiter's atmosphere.

**ENCKE'S COMET** Encke is the comet that appears the most frequently. It returns every 3.3 years. It is named after German astronomer Johann Encke (1791–1865), who studied its orbit.

**HALLEY'S COMET** Named after the English scientist Edmond Halley, (1656–1742), this comet was first seen in ancient times. Halley became the first to show that some comets return regularly because they follow predictable orbits that bring them close to the Sun. Halley predicted that the comet he saw in 1682 would return in 1759.

**HALE-BOPP** One of the brightest comets seen in recent years, Hale-Bopp came nearest to Earth on 22 March 1997, when it was viewed by millions.

# THE SOLAR SYSTEM

## SUN FACTFILE

**DIAMETER** At its equator, the Sun is 1,391,980 km (865,121 miles).

**DISTANCE FROM EARTH** The Sun is estimated to be 149,680,000 km (93,026,724 miles) away.

**SUN'S SURFACE** Magnified, the Sun's surface looks grainy. These grains are columns of gas, each 1,000 km (620 miles) wide – the size of France! The columns flare at 5-minute intervals!

**TEMPERATURE** The core of the Sun reaches a temperature of 15,400,000°C (27,720,000°F)!

**SURFACE AREA** The Sun's surface area covers 6,088,575,000,000 sq km (2,350,982,700,000 sq miles)!

**ENERGY OUTPUT** The Sun's hydrogen core works like a nuclear reactor – converting hydrogen to helium at a rate of 600 million tonnes (590 million tons) every second. In doing this, the Sun loses four million tonnes of its mass per second. In the same time, it gives out 35 million times as much electricity as the USA uses in a year!

**SOLAR PROMINENCE** Sometimes gigantic jets of flaming gas shoot off the surface of the Sun, stretching thousands of kilometres (miles) into space. The energy released from these prominences, or flares, can be a million million times that of the first nuclear bomb!

**LIGHT** Just 1 sq m (10.8 sq ft) of the Sun's surface shines as brightly as 600,000 100-watt light bulbs!

**DON'T TRY IT YOURSELF! Never** look directly at the Sun, even through a camera or with sunglasses, because it could damage your eyes.

**TRY IT YOURSELF!** You can cover the Moon in the sky with a coin held at arm's length. In fact, it is a quarter the diameter of the Earth – nearly as big as Australia!

## MOON DATA

**SIZE** Earth's Moon has a diameter of 3,477 km (2,161 miles).

**AGE** Like Earth, the Moon is an incredible 4.6 billion years old!

**DISTANCE FROM EARTH** The Moon is 384,400 km (238,866 miles) away.

**SURFACE TEMPERATURE** Ranges from -155°C to 105°C (-247°F to 221°F).

**SURFACE** The Moon is littered with craters formed by meteorites and dark seas of solidified lava from billions of years ago.

**MOON MISSIONS** Neil Armstrong and Edwin E. "Buzz" Aldrin, from the USA, landed in 1969 in Apollo XI. There have been six landings in total with 12 astronauts. Since there is no air or water on the Moon, the tracks of the astronauts will remain there forever.

**BLUE MOON** In 1950, the Moon appeared to turn blue after a forest fire in Canada threw up smoke particles.

## ASTEROID FACTS

**WHAT IS AN ASTEROID?** Sometimes called "minor planets", asteroids are lumps of rock that orbit the Sun.

**TOTAL MASS** The total mass of all asteroids is less than that of the Moon!

**FIRST FOUND AND LARGEST** Ceres was discovered in 1801 and is the largest asteroid. It is 936 km (582 miles) wide.

**DO THEY COME NEAR EARTH?** On average, a 0.4-km (0.25-mile) diameter asteroid hits Earth every 50,000 years. In 1991, one came within 170,600 km (106,000 miles) of Earth!

**ASTEROID DISASTER** An asteroid that collided with Earth 65 million years ago may have caused dinosaur extinction.

## ASTEROID NAMES

Every asteroid is numbered in the order of its discovery. The discoverer usually calls it after whatever they choose.

**1652** Hergé, the creator of the popular Belgian comic strip *Tintin*.

**2309** Mr Spock, after a ginger cat!

**2865** (Stan) Laurel, comedy star.

**3534** Sax, in honour of Adolphe Sax, inventor of the saxophone.

**4147** Lennon, musician, The Beatles.

**5050** Doctor Watson, after the friend of fictional detective Sherlock Holmes.

**5405** Neverland, after the fantasy island in children's story *Peter Pan*.

## COMPARATIVE WEIGHTS

Gravity is a force that pulls objects together. The heavier and farther apart objects, such as planets, are, the stronger the gravitational pull will be. If you weigh 50 kg (110 lb) on Earth, this is what you will weigh elsewhere in space thanks to gravity:

| PLANET/STAR | WEIGHT | |
| --- | --- | --- |
| | KG | LB |
| Pluto | 3.3 | 7.3 |
| Moon | 8.5 | 18.7 |
| Mercury | 13.5 | 29.8 |
| Mars | 18.5 | 40.8 |
| Venus | 43.0 | 94.8 |
| Uranus | 46.0 | 101.4 |
| Earth | 50.0 | 110.0 |
| Saturn | 58.5 | 128.9 |
| Neptune | 72.0 | 158.7 |
| Jupiter | 132.0 | 291.0 |
| Sun | 1,390.0 | 3064.4 |

**DID YOU KNOW?** The Moon's gravity is less than Earth's because it is smaller than Earth. On Earth, an astronaut weighs 135 kg (298 lb); on the Moon he weighs 22 kg (48 lb)!

## THE NINE PLANETS

| PLANET | DISTANCE FROM SUN | | LENGTH OF ORBIT | DIAMETER | | MOONS |
| --- | --- | --- | --- | --- | --- | --- |
| | MILLION KM | MILLION MILES | | KM | MILES | |
| Mercury | 57.9 | 36.0 | 87.97 days | 4,878 | 3,031 | 0 |
| Venus | 108.2 | 67.2 | 224.70 days | 12,104 | 7,520 | 0 |
| Earth | 149.7 | 93.0 | 365.30 days | 12,756 | 7,296 | 1 |
| Mars | 227.9 | 141.6 | 687.00 days | 6,794 | 4,217 | 2 |
| Jupiter | 778.3 | 483.6 | 11.86 years | 142,984 | 88,846 | 16 |
| Saturn | 1,427.0 | 886.0 | 29.46 years | 120,536 | 74,898 | 18 |
| Uranus | 2,871.0 | 1,784.0 | 84.01 years | 51,118 | 31,763 | 15 |
| Neptune | 4,497.0 | 2,794.0 | 164.80 years | 49,528 | 30,775 | 8 |
| Pluto | 5,914.0 | 3,675.0 | 247.70 years | 2,284 | 1,419 | 1 |

## NAMING THE PLANETS

| PLANET | NAME MEANING |
| --- | --- |
| Mercury | Roman messenger of gods |
| Venus | Roman goddess of love |
| Earth | Land |
| Mars | Roman god of war |
| Jupiter | Chief god of the Romans |
| Saturn | Roman god of farming |
| Uranus | First Greek sky god |
| Neptune | Roman god of water |
| Pluto | Roman god of underworld |

## PLANET FACTS

**MERCURY** This planet, the nearest to the Sun, has the greatest temperature extremes, ranging from -200°C (-328°F) to 430°C (806°F). On Mercury, which has much weaker gravity than Earth, an athlete could leap over an elephant!

**VENUS** The closest planet to Earth, Venus could not be more different. Its inhospitable atmosphere is very hot, dense, and acidic.

**EARTH** This is the only planet that can support life because it has the right balance of water, light, and air.

**MARS** This red planet is completely free of water, but dry riverbeds suggest that water once flowed on the planet.

**JUPITER** This fast-spinning planet is bigger than all the others put together! On Earth, a flea can jump 33 cm (13 in), but on Jupiter, where gravity is 2.6 times that on Earth, the flea could jump only 13 cm (5 in).

**SATURN** A giant planet, Saturn is surrounded by rings of icy rock and dust. These rings are 200 m (656 ft) thick, and more than 270,000 km (167,800 miles) in diameter.

**URANUS** Named after Uranus, the first Greek sky god, this planet is one of the coldest, with an average temperature of -223°C (-369°C). It is made mainly of hydrogen, and has a barren landscape apart from frozen methane clouds. It is surrounded by dark rings.

**NEPTUNE** Pictures of Neptune taken by the *Voyager* probe show that it is a blue planet, with icy clouds of methane very similar to those on Uranus. It has a Great Dark Spot, a giant storm where winds blows at 2,000 km/h (1,240 mph).

**PLUTO** The smallest, darkest, and coldest planet, Pluto was discovered in 1930 by American farmer Clyde Tombaugh (1906–1997).

## TEN LARGEST PLANETARY MOONS

| MOON | ORBITS | DIAMETER | |
| --- | --- | --- | --- |
| | PLANET | KM | MILES |
| Ganymede | Jupiter | 5,269 | 3,274 |
| Titan | Saturn | 5,150 | 3,200 |
| Callisto | Jupiter | 4,820 | 2,995 |
| Io | Jupiter | 3,632 | 2,257 |
| Moon | Earth | 3,475 | 2,159 |
| Europa | Jupiter | 3,126 | 1,942 |
| Triton | Neptune | 2,750 | 1,708 |
| Titania | Uranus | 1,580 | 982 |
| Rhea | Saturn | 1,530 | 951 |
| Oberon | Uranus | 1,516 | 942 |

**DID YOU KNOW?** One of Jupiter's moons, Europa, has a surface of ice that measures at least 97 km (60 miles) thick! Another, Io, was investigated by the 1979 *Voyager* probe, sent to observe the moon. It showed that Io experiences volcanic eruptions that hurl sulphur 300 km (186 miles) high!

## HOTTEST PLANETS

| PLANET | HIGHEST TEMPERATURE | |
| --- | --- | --- |
| | °C | °F |
| Venus | +464 | +868 |
| Mercury | +430 | +806 |
| Earth | +60 | +140 |

**DID YOU KNOW?** These three planets are the only ones above freezing!

## COLDEST PLANETS

| PLANET | LOWEST TEMPERATURE | |
| --- | --- | --- |
| | °C | °F |
| Pluto | -230 | -382.0 |
| Uranus | -223 | -369.4 |
| Mercury | -200 | -328.0 |
| Neptune | -220 | -364.0 |
| Saturn | -160 | -256.0 |

# SPACE EXPLORATION

## EARLY ASTRONOMERS

**EUDOXUS OF CNIDUS (408–355 BC)** According to Greek thinker Eudoxus, the Earth was at the centre of the Universe.

**PTOLEMY (c.AD 120–180)** Greek astronomer Ptolemy compiled a book called the *Almagest*, which provided the basis of scientific astronomy for more than 1,000 years.

**AL-SUFI (903–986)** A Persian nobleman and one of the leading astronomers of his time, Al-Sufi listed the position and brightness of more than 1,000 stars, in his *Book of Fixed Stars*.

**NICOLAUS COPERNICUS (1473–1543)** Copernicus was a Polish monk who wrote a book in which he stated that the Sun was at the centre of the Universe.

**GALILEO GALILEI (1564–1642)** Italian scientist Galileo discovered Jupiter's four largest moons, supporting the theory that the Sun is the centre of the Universe.

**JOHANNES KEPLER (1571–1630)** German astronomer Kepler established three laws ruling planetary movement.

**ISAAC NEWTON (1642–1727)** This English scientist's theory of gravity explained why planets orbit the Sun.

**WILLIAM HERSCHEL (1738–1822)** German-born Herschel found Uranus and four of its moons.

## ASTRONOMY MILESTONES

**1543** Nicolaus Copernicus (1473–1543) shows that Sun is centre of the Solar System.

**1608** First telescope invented by Dutch scientist Hans Lippershey (1570–1619).

**1609** German Johannes Kepler (1571–1630) describes laws of planetary motion.

**1668** Isaac Newton (1642–1727) builds first reflecting telescope.

**1705** British Edmond Halley (1658–1742) predicts return of Halley's comet in 1758.

**1781** German musician William Herschel (1738–1822) discovers Uranus.

**1801** First asteroid, Ceres, discovered by Italian Giuseppe Piazzi (1746–1826).

**1846** German Johann Galle (1812–1910) discovers Neptune.

**1905** German physicist Albert Einstein (1879–1955) proposes the theory of relativity.

**1924** British Edwin Hubble (1889–1953) discovers galaxies beyond the Milky Way.

**1924–1930** "Big Bang" theory formulated independently by Belgian Abbé Lemaitre (1894–1966) and Russian A. Friedmann (1888–1925).

**1930** Clyde Tombaugh (USA, 1906–1997) discovers Pluto.

**1932** US engineer Karl Jansky (1905–1950) picks up first radio waves from outside Earth.

**1949** 3K cosmic background radiation, believed to be remains of Big Bang, is discovered by Americans Arno Penzias (b.1933) and Robert Wilson (b.1936).

**1967** Discovery of pulsars by British astronomer Jocelyn Bell (b.1943).

**1986** *Giotto* space probe sends back first pictures of a comet's nucleus.

**1990** Hubble space telescope is launched above Earth's atmosphere.

**1994** People on Earth see comet Shoemaker-Levy crashing into Jupiter.

**1995** *Galileo* probe reaches Jupiter.

## PROBLEMS OF SPACE TRAVEL

**WEIGHTLESSNESS** Away from the Earth's gravity, objects float unless they are fixed, and injuries may result.

**EATING** Astronauts eat about 70 per cent less in space than on Earth. They can choose from an extensive menu of preserved foods.

**ILLNESS** Viruses, such as colds, spread quickly in the confines of the cabin. Astronauts exercise to overcome motion sickness and muscle-wasting.

**TOILETS** Early astronauts wore nappies, but toilets with hand and toe holds are installed on modern space stations. The waste is shredded by machine, and dumped into space.

**SHAVING** Astronauts must shave with foam, or an electric razor with vacuum attachment to suck away whiskers, which can jam equipment.

**BURPING AND FARTING** Burping in space often brings up vomit, which floats around the cabin in globules. In the confined area, farts are antisocial!

## SPACE JUNK

Junk left in space does not decay and can pose a threat to spacecraft. It includes the following:

• "Dead" satellites

• Tools and equipment lost during spacewalks

• Chunks of discarded booster rockets

• The descent stages of six *Apollo* modules

• Three Lunar Rover vehicles left on the Moon

## COUNTRIES WITH MOST SPACEFLIGHT EXPERIENCE

| COUNTRY | ASTRONAUTS | DURATION OF MISSIONS | | | |
|---|---|---|---|---|---|
| | | DAYS | HR | MIN | SEC |
| USSR/Russia | 85 | 13,094 | 2 | 7 | 17 |
| USA | 234 | 5,768 | 3 | 44 | 1 |
| Germany | 9 | 298 | 11 | 30 | 13 |
| France | 7 | 137 | 20 | 8 | 27 |
| Kazakhstan | 2 | 133 | 21 | 6 | 15 |

**DID YOU KNOW?** Up until 1 January 1998, Soviet and Russian cosmonauts accounted for 66 per cent of the total time spent by humans in space, largely through the long-duration stays on board the *Mir* space station, which has been occupied since 1986.

## ASTRONAUT RECORDS

| RECORD | ASTRONAUT | COUNTRY | DATE | SPACECRAFT/ SPACE STATION |
|---|---|---|---|---|
| First to orbit Earth | Yuri Gagarin | USSR | 1961 | *Vostok I* |
| First woman in space | Valentina Tereshkova | USSR | 1963 | *Vostok 6* |
| First spacewalker | Alexei Leonov | USSR | 1965 | *Voskhod 2* |
| First man on Moon | Neil Armstrong | USA | 1969 | *Apollo 11* |
| Most experienced spaceman | Valeri Polyakov | USSR | 1988 | *Mir* space station |
| Longest spacewalk | Thomas Akers Richard Hieb Pierre Thut | USA | 1992 | *STS-49* |
| Most experienced spacewoman | Shannon Lucid | USA | 1996 | *STS-76 Atlantis, Mir* space station *STS-79 Atlantis* |

**AMAZING FACT!** Leonov's first spacewalk almost ended in disaster, when his spacesuit "ballooned". He was unable to return through the air lock into the capsule until he reduced pressure in his suit to a dangerously low level.

## SPACE EXPLORATION MILESTONES

**1926** US engineer Robert Goddard designs and launches first liquid-fuelled rocket.

**1942** First German V2 rockets tested against Britain in World War II.

**1957** First satellite *Sputnik 1* (USSR) in orbit.

**1958** NASA (National Aeronautics and Space Administration) founded; first US satellite, *Explorer 1*.

**1961** First humans in space: Yuri Gagarin, of the USSR, and Alan Shepard, of the USA. Gagarin is also the first man to orbit Earth.

**1963** Valentina Tereshkova of the USSR is the first woman launched into space. First spacewalk achieved by Alexei Leonov of the USSR.

**1969** First manned Moon landing (*Apollo 11*, USA). Neil Armstrong is first to walk on Moon.

**1970** *Venera 7* is first probe to land on another planet, Venus.

**1986** *Mir* space station becomes operational; *Voyager 2* observes Uranus.

**1996** *Galileo* mini probe is first to enter the atmosphere of a giant planet.

**1997** US *Pathfinder* lands on Mars.

## FIRST IN-FLIGHT SPACE FATALITIES

**1967** Launched on 24 April, Soviet spaceship *Soyuz 1* had technical problems during its 18th orbit. The capsule parachute tangled and it crash-landed near Orsk in the Ural Mountains, killing astronaut Viktor Komarov.

**1971** After a then record 23 days in space, on 29 June, the Soviet *Soyuz 9*'s capsule depressurized. Although it landed intact, all three cosmonauts – Georgi Gobrovolsky, Vladislav Volkov, Viktor Patsayev – who were not wearing spacesuits – were found to be dead.

**1986** On 28 January, *Challenger STS-51-L*, the USA's 25th Space Shuttle mission, exploded on take-off from Cape Canaveral, Florida, USA, killing astronauts Gregory Jarvis, Christa McAuliffe, Ronald McNair, Ellison Onizuka, Judith Resnik, Francis Scobee, and Michael Smith. The disaster was watched by thousands on the ground and millions on worldwide television. It prompted a full review of the engineering problems and revision of the safety methods undertaken. It was not until 29 September 1988 that the next Space Shuttle, *Discovery STS-26*, was successfully launched.

## ANIMALS IN SPACE

**DOGS** Early Soviet space experiments involved launching several dogs into space, including Laika, a female Samoyed husky, launched in 1957.

**MICE** In 1958, two mice called Laska and Benjy became the first living creatures the USA sent into space.

**CHIMPANZEES** The USA launched Ham, a male chimpanzee, on a pre-manned flight test in 1961.

**CAT** In 1963, a cat called Félicette was launced in a suborbital flight in a French *Veronique* rocket.

**SPIDERS** Two spiders, Anita and Arabella, took part in experiments in the USA's *Skylab 3*, 1973, to see whether they could spin their webs in zero gravity.

**JELLYFISH** Apart from bacteria, the largest group of creatures in space was the 2,478 jellyfish on Space Shuttle *STS–40* in 1991.

# THE EARTH

## ROCKS and MINERALS

### GEOLOGICAL TIMECHART

Geologists divide the Earth's history into three different time spans called eras, periods, and epochs. Eras are the longest, and epochs the shortest. Each interval marks a particular stage in our planet's history.

**mya** = millions of years ago

| ERA | PERIOD | EPOCH | MYA | EVENTS |
|-----|--------|-------|-----|--------|
| CENOZOIC | Quaternary | Holocene | 0.01 | Humans farm and develop technology. |
| | | Pleistocene | 1.6 | Ice ages. *Homo sapiens* evolves. Sabre-toothed cats and mammoths die out. |
| | Tertiary | Pliocene | 5.3 | Many modern mammals appear. |
| | | Miocene | 23 | Deer-like hoofed mammals flourish. First hominids (human-like primates). |
| | | Oligocene | 34 | First human-like creatures appear. Hunting birds thrive. |
| | | Eocene | 53 | Mammals grow larger. Primates evolve. |
| | | Palaeocene | 65 | Mammals, insects, and flowering plants flourish. |
| MESOZOIC | Cretaceous | | 135 | First flowering plants. Mass extinction of dinosaurs at end of period. |
| | Jurassic | | 205 | Dinosaurs flourish. First birds evolve. |
| | Triassic | | 250 | Dinosaurs and mammals appear. |
| PALAEOZOIC | Permian | | 300 | Reptiles diversify. Conifers replace tree ferns. |
| | Carboniferous | | 345 | Swampy forests. First reptiles. |
| | Devonian | | 410 | Age of sharks and fish. Insects and amphibians appear. Giant tree ferns. |
| | Silurian | | 438 | First jawed fish and giant scorpions. Small land plants colonize shore. |
| | Ordovician | | 510 | First crustaceans and early jawless fish. Coral reefs form. |
| | Cambrian | | 570 | First molluscs and trilobites. |
| | Precambrian | | 4,650+ | First single-celled life forms. |

**! MEMORY TIP!** Remember the order of the periods and epochs, from Cambrian up to Pleistocene, with the following phrase: **C**hina **o**wls **s**eldom **d**eceive **c**lay **p**igeons. **T**hey **j**ust **c**hase **p**ast **e**ach **o**ther **m**aking **p**reposterous **p**uns.

### ROCK TYPES

All rocks fit into one of the following three categories:

**IGNEOUS** Igneous rocks form as molten magma or lava solidifies. The oldest igneous rocks date back at least 3.6 billion years, while the youngest are still forming.

**SEDIMENTARY** About 75 per cent of the Earth's surface is covered with thin layers of debris. These sediments settle on the beds of oceans, lakes, and rivers, and are compacted over millions of years to form sedimentary rock.

**METAMORPHIC** When rocks are baked by the heat of molten magma or squeezed by the movements of vast tectonic plates, they are transformed into new, metamorphic rocks.

### AMAZING METEORITE FACTS

**WHAT IS A METEORITE?** Lumps of rock called meteoroids that move around in space sometimes fall to Earth as meteorites.

**LARGEST IN THE WORLD** The Hoba meteorite was found on a farm in Grootfontein, South Africa, in 1920. It is a 2.73 x 2.43-m (9 x 8-ft) slab of 82 per cent iron and 16 per cent nickel.

**LARGEST ON EXHIBITION** Named *Ahnighito*, or "the tent", by local Inuit, this meteorite was found in 1897 at Cape York in Greenland by US explorer Robert Peary. Weighing 30 tonnes (30.4 tons) – as much as six bull elephants – it is in the New York Museum of Natural History.

**HOW OFTEN DO THEY FALL?** It has been calculated that about 500 meteorites fall to Earth every year, although many fall in the sea and in unpopulated areas.

**WHAT IS THE RISK OF BEING STRUCK?** There is no recorded case of a person being killed by a meteorite, although animals are occasional victims. In the USA, it is estimated that one meteorite death could occur every 9,300 years.

## LAYERS OF THE EARTH

**OCEANIC CRUST** This layer of rock has an average thickness of 3.2 km (2.2 miles). It lies under the ocean floor.

**CONTINENTAL CRUST** Lying beneath the continents, this layer is older than the oceanic crust, and is 60 km (44 miles) thick.

**MANTLE** This layer of hot, often molten, rock is 2,865 km (1,780 miles) thick.

**OUTER CORE** At 2,260 km (1,404 miles) thick, the outer core of molten nickel and iron gives the Earth its magnetic field.

**INNER CORE** At the centre of the Earth, the solid, inner core is 1,222 km (759 miles) thick.

## BASIC ELEMENTS OF ROCK

About 99 per cent of all rocks contain the eight main elements in the Earth's crust.

| ELEMENT | PERCENTAGE OF EARTH'S CRUST |
|---|---|
| Oxygen | 46.5 |
| Silicon | 28.9 |
| Aluminium | 8.3 |
| Iron | 4.8 |
| Calcium | 4.1 |
| Potassium | 2.4 |
| Sodium | 2.3 |
| Magnesium | 1.9 |

## BIRTHSTONES

Some birthstones are linked with the months of the year.

| | |
|---|---|
| January | Garnet |
| February | Amethyst |
| March | Aquamarine |
| April | Diamond |
| May | Emerald |
| June | Pearl |
| July | Ruby |
| August | Peridot |
| September | Sapphire |
| October | Opal |
| November | Topaz |
| December | Turquoise |

## ROCKS AND MINERALS

**ROCKS** Three types of rock are found on Earth: igneous, sedimentary, and metamorphic. Within each type, rocks can be further identified by their colour, structure, and texture.

*Examples* Granite and marble

**MINERALS** These natural, non-living substances grow from elements in the Earth and are shaped by temperature and pressure. They can be identified by their hardness, specific gravity, colour, and the symmetry of their crystals.

*Examples* Sulphur and copper

**CRYSTALS** Derived from the Greek word *kryos* meaning cold, crystals are formed from molten or dissolved minerals. Crystal symmetry or shape is grouped into six main shapes or "systems": monoclinic, triclinic, trigonal/hexagonal, cubic, orthorhombic, and tetragonal.

*Examples* Quartz and pyrite

**GEMSTONES** These are minerals whose colour, rarity, or hardness makes them valuable. There are 100 types of gems.

*Examples* Diamond and ruby

## MOHS' SCALE

**DID YOU KNOW?** German mineralogist Friedrich Mohs (1773–1839) devised a rating system for minerals, known as Mohs' scale. It defines the hardness or the ability of a mineral to resist scratching. A mineral with a high Mohs' score can scratch any material with a lower rating.

| HARDNESS | | SCRATCH TOOL | MINERAL |
|---|---|---|---|
| 10 | Very hard | Steel file | Diamond |
| 9 | Very hard | Steel file | Corundum |
| 8 | Very hard | Steel file | Topaz |
| 7 | Very hard | Steel file | Quartz |
| 6 | Hard | Heavy penknife | Orthoclase |
| 5 | Hard | Heavy penknife | Apatite |
| 4 | Semi-hard | Window glass | Fluorite |
| 3 | Soft | Copper wire or coin | Calcite |
| 2 | Soft | Fingernail | Gypsum |
| 1 | Very soft | Fingernail | Talc |

## FAMOUS ROCKS

**ULURU** Looming up from the Australian desert, this giant block of red sandstone, once known as Ayers Rock, is the world's largest free-standing rock. It is more than 2.4 km (1.5 miles) long, 348 m (1,142 ft) high, and has a perimeter of 9.4 km (5.8 miles). Uluru, meaning "great pebble", is the name given to the rock by Aboriginal Australians, for whom it is sacred.

**BLACK STONE OF MECCA** The Black Rock is located in the Eastern corner of the Ka'ba, the Great Mosque in Mecca, Islam's holiest shrine. According to legend, it was once white, but by absorbing the sins of the countless pilgrims who touch it, it has turned black.

**DEVIL'S TOWER** The tallest rock formation in the USA, this giant monolith is visible from 160 km (100 miles) away. Its fluted columns rise 265 m (865 ft) high into the sky.

**BALANCING ROCKS OF EPWORTH** Just outside Harare, Zimbabwe, granite boulders teetering on top of each other have been formed by erosion from an ancient mass of granite. The rocks will sway from side to side, but always return to their original position.

**GIANT'S CAUSEWAY** Said to have been built by Irish giant Finn MacCool in pursuit of his Scottish counterpart Finn Gall, this rock formation in Northern Ireland, UK, comprises 40,000 rock columns which range from sea level to 6 m (18 ft) high. From overhead, they look like paving stones, many of which are perfect hexagons.

**ROCK OF GIBRALTAR** This long, steep mountain lies in the British colony of Gibraltar at the southernmost tip of Spain. At 426 m (1,396 ft) high and 4 km (2.25 miles) long, it is known as one of the Pillars of Hercules. The other Pillar of Hercules is the Jebel Musa in Africa, which lies opposite at the narrowest point of the Strait of Gibraltar.

# PHYSICAL FEATURES

## HIGHEST MOUNTAINS

All 35 of the highest mountains in the world are found in the Himalaya-Karakoram range in Asia.

| MOUNTAIN | COUNTRY | HEIGHT | |
|---|---|---|---|
| | | M | FT |
| Everest | Nepal/Tibet | 8,846 | 29,022 |
| K2 | Kashmir/China | 8,611 | 28,250 |
| Kangchenjunga | Nepal/Sikkim | 8,598 | 28,208 |
| Lhotse | Nepal/Tibet | 8,501 | 27,890 |
| Makalu I | Nepal/Tibet | 8,470 | 27,790 |
| Dhaulagiri I | Nepal | 8,172 | 26,810 |
| Manaslu I | Nepal | 8,156 | 26,760 |
| Cho Oyu | Nepal | 8,153 | 26,750 |
| Nanga Parbat | Kashmir | 8,126 | 26,660 |
| Annapurna I | Nepal | 8,078 | 26,504 |

**DID YOU KNOW?** On 29 May 1953, Edmund Hillary from New Zealand and Sherpa Tenzing Norgay from Nepal became the first people to reach the summit of Mount Everest.

## LONGEST CAVE SYSTEMS

| CAVE SYSTEM | COUNTRY | LENGTH M | FT |
|---|---|---|---|
| Mammoth cave system | USA | 560,000 | 1,837,270 |
| Optimisticeskaja | Ukraine | 178,000 | 583,989 |
| Hölloch | Switzerland | 137,000 | 449,475 |
| Jewel Cave | USA | 127,000 | 416,667 |
| Siebenhengsteholensystem | Switzerland | 110,000 | 360,892 |

**AMAZING FACT!** The Mammoth cave system is longer than the world's longest glacier, and even longer than the length of all the tunnels of the London underground tube system. The opening was discovered in 1799 by a hunter chasing a bear. Once a source of saltpetre, an ingredient of gunpowder, the caves became a major tourist attraction. The Mammoth Cave National Park was established in 1941.

## LONGEST MOUNTAIN RANGES

| RANGE | LOCATION | LENGTH | |
|---|---|---|---|
| | | KM | MILES |
| Andes | South America | 7,242 | 4,500 |
| Rocky Mountains | North America | 6,035 | 3,750 |
| Himalayas/Karakoram/ Hundu Kush | Asia | 3,862 | 2,400 |
| Great Dividing Range | Australia | 3,621 | 2,250 |
| Trans-Antarctic Mountains | Antarctica | 3,541 | 2,200 |
| Brazilian East Coast Range | Brazil | 3,058 | 1,900 |
| Sumatran/ Javan Range | Sumatra, Java | 2,897 | 1,800 |
| Tien Shan | China | 2,253 | 1,400 |
| Eastern Ghats | India | 2,092 | 1,300 |
| Altai | Asia | 2,012 | 1,250 |
| Central New Guinean Range | Papua New Guinea | 2,012 | 1,250 |
| Urals | Russia | 2,012 | 1,250 |

**DID YOU KNOW?** The longest undersea mountain range, the Mid-Atlantic Ridge, is 11,265 km (7,000 miles) long.

## EARTH'S LOWEST POINTS

**DEAD SEA** Lying between Israel and Jordan, the Dead Sea's shore is the lowest exposed ground below sea level, at 400 m (1,312 ft). The sea bed actually reaches 728 m (2,388 ft) below sea level. If there was a flight of stairs to take you back up to sea level, you would have to climb about 2,000 steps.

**TURFAN DEPRESSION** China's Turfan Depression is the second lowest point in the world, at 154 m (505 ft) below sea level.

**QATTARA DEPRESSION** The world's third lowest point is Egypt's Qattara Depression, at 133 m (436 ft) below sea level. It is on the Mediterranean coast, near the Libyan border.

## ISLAND RECORDS

| RECORD | ISLAND | MEASUREMENTS |
|---|---|---|
| Largest island | Greenland (Kalaatdlit Nunaat) | 2,175,600 sq km (840,070 sq miles) |
| Smallest island country | Nauru (Pacific Ocean) | Nauru has an area of 21.2 sq km (8.2 sq miles) |
| Remotest island | Bouvet Island | 1,700 km (1,056 miles) from Queen Maud Land, east Antarctica |
| Longest island arc | Indonesia | Covers 8 million sq km (3 million sq miles) |
| Highest island | Irian Jaya | Mount Jaya in Irian Jaya rises 5,030 m (16,500 ft) |

**AMAZING FACT!** Although Australia looks to be the largest island on the map, it is actually regarded worldwide as a continental landmass, and not an island. It has an area of 7,618,493 sq km (2,941,517 sq miles), which is three times the size of Greenland.

## HIGHEST ACTIVE VOLCANOES

| VOLCANO | LOCATION | LATEST ACTIVITY | HEIGHT M | FT |
|---|---|---|---|---|
| Guallatiri | Chile | 1987 | 6,060 | 19,882 |
| Láàscar | Chile | 1991 | 5,990 | 19,652 |
| Cotopaxi | Ecuador | 1975 | 5,897 | 19,347 |
| Tupungatito | Chile | 1986 | 5,640 | 18,504 |
| Popocatépetl | Mexico | 1995 | 5,452 | 17,887 |
| Ruiz | Colombia | 1992 | 5,400 | 17,716 |
| Sangay | Ecuador | 1988 | 5,230 | 17,159 |
| Guagua Pichincha | Ecuador | 1988 | 4,784 | 15,696 |
| Purace | Colombia | 1977 | 4,755 | 15,601 |
| Kliuchevskoi | Russia | 1995 | 4,750 | 15,584 |

**DID YOU KNOW?** In 1985 and 1987, Guallatiri, the southernmost volcano in the Andes, ejected whitish-yellow fumes up to 500 m (1,648 ft) high every half an hour.

## LARGEST METEORITE CRATERS

| CRATER | WIDTH KM | MILES |
|---|---|---|
| Sudbury, Ontario, Canada | 140 | 87 |
| Vredefort, South Africa | 140 | 87 |
| Manicouagan, Quebec, Canada | 100 | 62 |

**DID YOU KNOW?** Recently, by using photographs taken from space, many new possible astroblemes (impact sites) have been discovered, including a massive site in Prague, Czech Republic, which measures 320 km (199 miles).

## DEEPEST CAVES

| CAVE SYSTEM | LOCATION | M | FT |
|---|---|---|---|
| Réseau Jean Bernard | France | 1,602 | 5,256 |
| Lampreschtsofen | Austria | 1,535 | 5,036 |
| Gouffre Mirolda | France | 1,520 | 4,987 |
| Shakta Pantjukhina | Georgia | 1,508 | 4,947 |
| Sistema Huautla | Mexico | 1,475 | 4,839 |

## LARGEST DESERTS

**SAHARA** North Africa's Sahara Desert is the world's largest, covering 9,000,000 sq km (3,500,000 sq miles). This hot, sandy desert is rapidly encroaching on grazing land.

**AUSTRALIAN** The Australian Desert covers 3,800,000 sq km (1,470,000 sq miles), but is made up of smaller desert regions – the Gibson, Simpson, and Great Sandy Desert.

**ARABIAN** The Arabian Desert covers 1,300,000 sq km (502,000 sq miles) of southwest Asia. Part of this desert is the Empty Quarter, a vast expanse of sand, which covers 647,500 sq km (250,000 sq miles).

**GOBI** Central Asia's barren Gobi Desert covers 1,036,000 sq km (400,000 sq miles). It has scorching summers and bitterly cold winters. Its name comes from *kobi*, the Mongolian word for desert. The Chinese call it *shamo*, or "sandy sea".

**KALAHARI** Covering 520,000 sq km (201,000 sq miles), an area larger than France, the Kalahari, in southern Africa, is the fifth largest desert. Its name comes from a local word that means torture, or suffering, but the Boer (Dutch) settlers called it *Bosjeveld*, or "thorn field".

# RIVERS and LAKES

## WORLD'S LONGEST RIVERS

| RIVER | COUNTRIES | LENGTH KM | MILES |
|---|---|---|---|
| Nile | Tanzania, Uganda, Sudan, Egypt | 6,670 | 4,145 |
| Amazon | Peru, Brazil | 6,448 | 4,007 |
| Yangtze–Kiang | China | 6,300 | 3,915 |
| Mississippi–Missouri–Red Rock | USA | 5,971 | 3,710 |
| Yenisey–Angara–Selenga | Mongolia, Russia | 5,540 | 3,442 |
| Huang He (Yellow River) | China | 5,464 | 3,395 |
| Ob'–Irtysh | Mongolia, Kazakhstan, Russia | 5,410 | 3,362 |
| Zaïre (Congo) | Angola, Congo, Democratic Republic of the Congo | 4,700 | 2,920 |
| Lena–Kirenga | Russia | 4,400 | 2,734 |

**DID YOU KNOW?** The River Nile could stretch all the way from New York, USA, to Berlin, Germany! The source of the river, Lake Victoria, Central Africa, was identified in 1858 by British explorer John Hanning Speke (1827–1864).

## LARGEST LAKES

| LAKE | LOCATION | APPROX. AREA SQ KM | SQ MILES |
|---|---|---|---|
| Caspian Sea | Azerbaijan/Iran/Kazakhstan/Russia/Turkmenistan | 371,000 | 143,205 |
| Superior | Canada/USA | 82,414 | 31,820 |

**DID YOU KNOW?** Lake Superior, one of the group of famous Great Lakes in eastern North America, is the world's largest freshwater lake!

| Lake | Location | Sq km | Sq miles |
|---|---|---|---|
| Victoria | Kenya, Tanzania, Uganda | 68,800 | 26,570 |
| Huron | Canada, USA | 59,596 | 23,010 |
| Michigan | USA | 58,016 | 22,400 |
| Aral Sea | Kazakhstan, Uzbekistan | 40,000 | 15,444 |
| Tanganyika | Burundi, Tanzania, Congo, Zambia | 32,900 | 13,860 |
| Great Bear | Canada | 31,790 | 12,270 |
| Baikal | Russia | 30,500 | 11,775 |

**DID YOU KNOW?** Lake Baikal (or Baykal), Siberia, has a depth of up to 1.63 km (1.02 miles) in parts and contains one-fifth of the world's fresh water.

| Lake | Location | Sq km | Sq miles |
|---|---|---|---|
| Great Slave | Canada | 28,440 | 10,980 |

## AMAZING RIVERS

**GREATEST OUTFLOW** The River Amazon, Brazil, discharges 10.5 cubic km (2.5 cubic miles) of water a minute into the Atlantic Ocean. That is enough for everyone in the world to have a bath every 44 minutes, allowing 80 litres (17.5 gallons) per bath.

**LARGEST RIVER DELTA** A delta is a wide, flat floodplain where a river becomes blocked with sediment and splits into many separate streams. The largest is the Ganges and Brahmaputra delta, which covers about 75,000 sq km (30,000 sq miles) – Sri Lanka could fit into this with room to spare!

**LONGEST EUROPEAN RIVER** The River Volga, Russia, flows for a distance of 3,531 km (2,194 miles).

**LONGEST AUSTRALASIAN RIVER** Australia's Murray River travels 2,589 km (1,609 miles)!

**DID YOU KNOW?** All rivers receive their water from rain or melting snow.

## RIVER TYPES

**PERENNIAL** Usually found in temperate and tropical areas, perennial rivers flow year round. Although in mountain areas, such as the Rockies, river levels vary greatly between winter and summer, the river never dries up.

**EPHEMERAL** Many desert rivers are ephemeral. These rivers are usually dry and hardly ever have water flowing in them. The Todd River in central Australia is an ephemeral river.

**SEASONAL** Found in many areas of the Mediterranean, seasonal rivers are only full for part of the year. Often, they are rocky streams that flow in the winter and are bone dry during the summer.

## AMAZING LAKES

**LARGEST MAN-MADE RESERVOIR** Owen Falls, in Uganda, has a volume of 205 cubic km (49 cubic miles). Completed in 1954, it generates hydroelectricity by waterfalls driving turbines.

**LARGEST AUSTRALASIAN LAKE** Australia's Lake Eyre has an area of 9,323 sq km (3,600 sq miles). It loses a lot of water by evaporation due to the heat of the sun. This process leaves the lake very salty.

**OLDEST LAKE** While most lakes are short-lived geological features, lasting only a few hundred thousand years, Lake Baikal, in Siberia, is 25 million years old.

**LARGEST SOUTH AMERICAN LAKE** Lake Titicaca, which sits in both Peru and Bolivia, has an area of 8,288 sq km (3,200 sq miles).

**DID YOU KNOW?** Lake Geneva will be filled in by sediment from the River Rhone and disappear in approximately 40,000 years!

## HIGHEST WATERFALLS

| WATERFALL | LOCATION | TOTAL DROP | |
|---|---|---|---|
| | | M | FT |
| Angel Falls | Venezuela | 979 | 3,212 |
| Tugela | South Africa | 947 | 3,107 |
| Utigård | Norway | 800 | 2,625 |
| Mongefossen | Norway | 774 | 2,540 |
| Yosemite | USA | 739 | 2,425 |
| Østre Mardøla Foss | Norway | 656 | 2,152 |
| Tyssestrengane | Norway | 646 | 2,120 |
| Cuquenán | Venezuela | 610 | 2,000 |
| Sutherland | New Zealand | 580 | 1,904 |
| Kjellfossen | Norway | 561 | 1,841 |

**AMAZING FACT!** The longest single drop in the Angel Falls is 807 m (2,648 ft) – twice the height of the Eiffel Tower, France!

## FRESHWATER ISLANDS

We think of islands as being in seas, and surrounded by sea water, but some are found in rivers and lakes, with fresh water around them. Here are six of the largest:

**MARAJÓ** Found at the mouth of the River Amazon, Brazil, Marajó has an area of 48,000 sq km (18,500 sq miles).

**BANANAL** Bananal Island, River Araguaia, Brazil, measures 20,000 sq km (7,720 sq miles).

**MANITOULIN** The island of Manitoulin, in Lake Huron, Canada, has an area of 2,766 sq km (1,068 sq miles).

**ROYALE** Surrounded by Lake Superior, USA and Canada, Royale is 544 sq km (210 sq miles).

**SAINT JOSEPH** Saint Joseph, Lake Huron, has an area of 365 sq km (141 sq miles).

**DRUMMOND** Also surrounded by Huron, Drummond covers 352 sq km (136 sq miles).

## INLAND WATER FACTS

**LONGEST CANAL** The Suez Canal links the Mediterranean with the Red Sea and stretches 174 km (108 miles).

**MOST CANALS** The Netherlands has 8,000 km (4,971 miles) of canals.

**OLDEST CANALS** These were built in Sumer (now Iraq) around 4000 BC.

**WHAT IS A FJORD?** In regions where deep valleys have been scoured by glaciers, the sea level often rises and floods the valleys, forming fjords.

**LONGEST FJORD** Nordvest Fjord, Greenland, extends for 313 km (194 miles) inland.

## GLACIER FACTS

**HOW ARE GLACIERS MADE?** Layers of snow build up over years, turning into an icy mass called a firn. Eventually the firn becomes an ice cap and gravity forces it to flow down to lower ground.

**LONGEST GLACIER** Antarctica's Lambert-Fisher glacier is the longest in the world, at 515 km (320 miles) in length. It is 3.5 km (2.2 miles) deep and 64 km (40 miles) wide. It was discovered as recently as 1956.

**MOST GLACIATED REGIONS** More than one-tenth of the Earth's surface is permanently covered with ice. About 90 per cent of this occurs in Antarctica. The South Polar region has 12,588,000 sq km (4,610,610 sq miles) of permanent snow and ice.

**AVERAGE GLACIER FLOW** Many of the world's glaciers begin high up in the mountains, and flow at a rate of 2 m (7 ft) per day.

## THE GREAT LAKES

The Great Lakes are a group of freshwater lakes in North America.

**SUPERIOR** The farthest north, Superior covers 82,414 sq km (31,820 sq miles).

**ONTARIO** At 19,477 sq km (7,520 sq miles), Ontario means "beautiful lake".

**HURON** Named by French settlers, Lake Huron covers 59,596 sq km (23,010 sq miles).

**MICHIGAN** The only great lake contained in the USA, Michigan measures 58,016 sq km (22,400 sq miles).

**ERIE** Lake Erie covers 25,719 sq km (9,930 sq miles). Its name comes from the Iroquois "erie" meaning "cat".

**MEMORY TIP!** Think of **HOMES** to remember the Great Lakes: **H**uron, **O**ntario, **M**ichigan, **E**rie, **S**uperior.

# OCEANS and SEAS

## OCEANS AND SEAS

| NAME | APPROXIMATE AREA | |
|---|---|---|
| | SQ KM | SQ MILES |
| Pacific Ocean | 166,240,000 | 64,185,629 |

**! DID YOU KNOW?** The Pacific Ocean contains more water than all the world's other seas and oceans put together!

| NAME | SQ KM | SQ MILES |
|---|---|---|
| Atlantic Ocean | 86,560,000 | 33,421,006 |
| Indian Ocean | 73,430,000 | 28,351,484 |
| Arctic Ocean | 13,230,000 | 5,108,132 |
| Arabian Sea | 3,864,000 | 1,492,000 |
| South China Sea | 2,974,600 | 1,148,499 |
| Caribbean Sea | 2,753,000 | 1,062,939 |
| Mediterranean Sea | 2,510,000 | 969,116 |
| Bering Sea | 2,261,000 | 872,977 |
| Bay of Bengal | 2,173,000 | 839,000 |
| Gulf of Mexico | 1,542,985 | 595,749 |
| Sea of Okhotsk | 1,527,570 | 589,798 |
| East China Sea | 1,249,150 | 482,299 |
| Sea of Japan | 1,012,945 | 391,100 |
| Andaman Sea | 797,700 | 307,993 |
| Hudson Bay | 730,380 | 282,001 |
| North Sea | 575,300 | 222,124 |
| Red Sea | 437,700 | 168,996 |

**! DID YOU KNOW?** Most oceans are about 3.5 per cent salt, but the Red Sea is 4.2 per cent salt.

| NAME | SQ KM | SQ MILES |
|---|---|---|
| Black Sea | 436,400 | 168,495 |
| Baltic Sea | 414,400 | 160,000 |
| Caspian Sea | 371,800 | 143,552 |
| Yellow Sea | 294,000 | 113,514 |
| Persian Gulf | 238,790 | 92,197 |
| Gulf of California | 162,000 | 62,548 |
| Irish Sea | 103,600 | 40,000 |
| English Channel | 89,900 | 34,710 |

**! AMAZING FACTS!** The world's oceans and seas together make up 94 per cent of all the water on Earth! • The Atlantic Ocean grows by 2.5 cm (1 in) every year, and it sinks about 10 cm (4 in) every 100 years! • The oldest parts of the ocean floor are about 200 million years old! • The Persian Gulf, in the Indian Ocean, is the warmest sea. • The highest tides occur in Canada's Bay of Fundy, rising more than 15 m (49 ft)!

## WAVE HEIGHT SCALE

This wave height scale describes the sort of waves that sailors might encounter at sea. Wave height varies according to wind speed, and the higher ranges may prove dangerous, especially to small boats.

| CODE | DESCRIPTION | HEIGHT RANGE | |
|---|---|---|---|
| | | M | FT |
| 0 | Glassy | 0 | 0 |
| 1 | Calm | 0–0.3 | 0–1 |
| 2 | Rippled | 0.3–0.6 | 1–2 |
| 3 | Choppy | 0.6–1.2 | 2–4 |
| 4 | Very choppy | 1.2–2.4 | 4–8 |
| 5 | Rough | 2.4–4 | 8–13 |
| 6 | Very rough | 4–6 | 13–20 |
| 7 | High | 6–9 | 20–30 |
| 8 | Very high | 9–14 | 30–45 |
| 9 | Ultra high | 14+ | 45+ |

**! DID YOU KNOW?** When the waves in an ocean or sea form white frothy tips, they are called "white horses".

## ELEMENTS IN SEAWATER

The world's oceans and seas contain various minerals. Rain dissolves minerals from rocks, and washes them into the oceans. The most abundant are sodium and chlorine, which together form salt (sodium chloride).

| ELEMENT | AVERAGE PERCENTAGE |
|---|---|
| Chlorine | 55.29 |
| Sodium | 30.79 |
| Magnesium | 3.66 |
| Sulphur | 7.94 |
| Calcium | 1.19 |
| Potassium | 1.13 |

**! AMAZING FACT!** The total amount of salt in the world's oceans and seas would cover Europe to a depth of 5 km (3 miles).

## UNDERWATER FEATURES

**HIGHEST UNDERWATER SEAMOUNT** The Great Meteor Tablemount in the north Atlantic Ocean is a huge submerged mountain – the tallest underwater mountain in the world. It was formed from a volcano erupting on the sea bed. The mountain measures 4,000 m (13,123 ft) high and is more than 100 km (62 miles) wide at its base.

**LONGEST OCEAN MOUNTAIN RANGE** The Atlantic Ocean's Mid-Atlantic Ridge is a line of rocks that marks the point where two of the Earth's tectonic plates meet. It stretches 11,265 km (7,000 miles) from a point north of Iceland to Bouvet Island in the South Atlantic Ocean. Some of its mountains are 4,000 m (13,123 ft) high.

**TALLEST MOUNTAIN RISING FROM THE OCEAN** Mauna Kea rises up 10,205 m (33,480 ft) from the floor of the Pacific Ocean to form the island of Hawaii. It is the world's tallest mountain from base to peak.

**DEEPEST SUBMARINE CANYON** A canyon 1,800 m (5,906 ft) deep is found 40 km (25 miles) south of Esperance, Australia. It is even deeper than the Grand Canyon in the USA!

**BLACK SMOKERS** Smokers are tall towers of mineral deposits that form on the ocean floor. Occurring in areas of volcanic activity, they erupt jets of hot water every few minutes. They were first discovered in 1977 by marine biologists in the American submersible, *Alvin*.

**! AMAZING FACT!** Legend has it that a fantastic city called Atlantis once existed in the centre of the Atlantic Ocean. It was apparently destroyed by an earthquake, and lost beneath the surface forever.

## SEA ICE FACTS

**WHEN DOES THE SEA FREEZE?** Oceans and seas freeze over only when the temperature falls below -1.9°C (28°F).

**LARGEST ICEBERG** The biggest iceberg recorded was over 335 km (208 miles) long and 97 km (60 miles) wide – an area three times as big as Cyprus!

**HOW OLD ARE ICEBERGS?** Scientists estimate that the average age of the ice that forms icebergs is 5,000 years!

**TALLEST ICEBERG** A 167-m (550-ft) iceberg was seen off Greenland in 1958.

**LONGEST GLACIER** The Lambert-Fisher Ice Passage, in Antarctica, extends for a distance of 515 km (320 miles).

**FASTEST-MOVING GLACIER** Greenland's Quarayaq glacier flows as fast as 20–24 m (65–80 ft) every day!

**DID YOU KNOW?** Only about 12 per cent of an iceberg is visible above the surface of the water – the rest is hidden below the surface.

## DEEPEST DEEP-SEA TRENCHES

| TRENCH | OCEAN | DEEPEST POINT M | FT |
|---|---|---|---|
| Marianas | Pacific | 10,924 | 35,837 |
| Tonga | Pacific | 10,800 | 35,430 |
| Philippine | Pacific | 10,497 | 34,436 |
| Kermadec | Pacific | 10,047 | 32,960 |
| Bonin | Pacific | 9,994 | 32,786 |
| New Britain | Pacific | 9,940 | 32,609 |
| Kuril | Pacific | 9,750 | 31,985 |
| Izu | Pacific | 9,695 | 31,805 |
| Puerto Rico | Atlantic | 8,605 | 28,229 |
| Yap | Pacific | 8,527 | 27,973 |
| Japan | Pacific | 8,412 | 27,599 |
| South Sandwich | Atlantic | 8,325 | 27,313 |

**AMAZING FACT?** Eight of the deepest ocean trenches would be deep enough to submerge Mount Everest!

## DEEPEST OCEANS AND SEAS

| OCEAN/SEA | GREATEST DEPTH M | FT |
|---|---|---|
| Pacific Ocean | 10,924 | 35,837 |

**DID YOU KNOW?** The deepest point in the deepest ocean is close to 11 km (6.8 miles) down, almost 29 times the height of the Empire State Building!

| | | |
|---|---|---|
| Atlantic Ocean | 9,219 | 30,246 |
| Indian Ocean | 7,455 | 24,460 |
| Caribbean Sea | 6,946 | 22,788 |
| Arctic Ocean | 5,625 | 18,456 |
| South China Sea | 5,016 | 16,456 |
| Bering Sea | 4,773 | 15,659 |
| Mediterranean Sea | 4,632 | 15,197 |
| Gulf of Mexico | 3,787 | 12,425 |
| Japan Sea | 3,742 | 12,276 |

**DID YOU KNOW?** The Arctic Ocean has an average depth of only 1,205 m (3,953 ft), making it the shallowest ocean in the world. It is frozen solid for most of the year.

## MOST RECENT UNDERWATER DESCENT RECORDS

| PERSON | COUNTRY | SUBMARINE | LOCATION | DATE | DEPTH M | FT |
|---|---|---|---|---|---|---|
| William Beebe Otis Barton | USA | Bathysphere | Bermuda | 15 August 1934 | 923 | 3,028 |
| Otis Barton | USA | Benthoscope | Santa Cruz, USA | 16 August 1949 | 1,372 | 4,500 |
| Georges Houot and Pierre Willm | France | *F.R.N.S. 3* bathyscaphe | Toulon, France | 12 August 1953 | 1,550 | 5,085 |
| Georges Houot and Pierre Willm | France | *F.R.N.S. 3* bathyscaphe | Cap Ferrat, France | 14 August 1953 | 2,100 | 6,890 |
| Auguste and Jacques Piccard | France | *Trieste* bathyscaphe | Ponza, Italy | 30 September 1953 | 3,150 | 10,335 |
| Georges Houot and Pierre Willm | France | *F.R.N.S. 3* bathyscaphe | Dakar, Senegal | 14 February 1954 | 4,050 | 13,287 |
| Jacques Piccard and Donald Walsh | Switzerland USA | *Trieste 2* bathyscaphe | Marianas Trench, Pacific Ocean | 14 November 1959 | 5,669 | 18,600 |
| Jacques Piccard and Donald Walsh | Switzerland USA | *Trieste 2* bathyscaphe | Marianas Trench, Pacific Ocean | 7 January 1960 | 7,315 | 24,000 |
| Jacques Piccard and Donald Walsh | Switzerland USA | *Trieste 2* bathyscaphe | Marianas Trench, Pacific Ocean | 23 January 1960 | 10,916 | 35,814 |

**DID YOU KNOW?** Because the Marianas Trench is the deepest known place in the world's oceans, the 1960 descent of the *Trieste 2* to its lowest point set a record that can never be broken. Scientists on board travelled in an observation capsule with thick walls to withstand the pressure.

**AMAZING FACT!** Joint record-holder Jacques Ernest Jean Piccard (b.1922) is the son of Auguste. As well as their ocean descent records, three members of the Piccard family – Auguste (1884–1962), his twin brother Jean Félix (1884–1963), and Jean's wife Jeanette (1895–1981) – set balloon altitude records!

# WEATHER

## WEATHER RECORDS

**WINDIEST PLACE** In Port Martin, Antarctica, the wind speed averaged 105 km/h (65 mph) for a whole month.

**BIGGEST HAILSTONES** On 3 September 1970, hailstones weighing 760 g (1 lb 11oz) and the size of tenpin bowling balls fell on Kansas, USA.

**BIGGEST SNOWFALL** Single snowstorms have resulted in almost 5 m (16 ft) of snow – the equivalent of three adults standing on each others' shoulders! However, the greatest snowfall ever occurred in Paradise, Mount Rainier, USA, between February 1971 and February 1972, when 31 m (102 ft) of snow fell!

**DRIEST PLACE** Chile's Atacama Desert is so dry that it receives an average rainfall of only 0.51 mm (0.02 in) per year.

**MOST RAINY DAYS** Hawaii's Mount Wai-'ale-'ale experiences up to 350 days of rain per year.

**RAINING FROGS** Although, as yet, there are no reports of any cats and dogs falling from the sky, the people of Trowbridge, UK, were amazed and bewildered when there was a downpour of live frogs! Strong winds had sucked them up from local ponds and rivers.

**MOST THUNDERY DAYS** Thunder occurs on 200–250 days of the year in Java, Indonesia and also around Lake Victoria, Africa.

**SUNNIEST PLACE** In the Eastern Sahara Desert, Africa, the Sun shines for 97 per cent of the time.

**LEAST SUNSHINE** At the North Pole, the freezing cold winters last 182 days during which the Sun never shines.

**DID YOU KNOW?** In any one day, there may be 44,000 storms over the Earth!

**TRY IT YOURSELF!** To find out how far away a storm is, count slowly between the flash and the rumble. Every three is a kilometre; each five is a mile.

### HIGHEST RECORDED RAINFALL

| TOWN | COUNTRY | RECORD RAINFALL | |
| --- | --- | --- | --- |
| | | MM | IN |
| Cherrapuni | India | 10,795 | 425 |
| Andagoya | Colombia | 7,137 | 281 |
| Pago Pago | Samoa | 4,928 | 194 |
| Moulmein | Burma | 4,826 | 190 |
| Tabing | Indonesia | 4,445 | 175 |
| Monrovia | Liberia | 4,420 | 175 |

**TRY IT YOURSELF!** If you are caught in a thunderstorm, to avoid being struck by lightning, crouch down low and keep your feet together. Keep away from trees.

### RECORD HIGH TEMPERATURES

| TOWN | COUNTRY | HIGHEST TEMPERATURE | |
| --- | --- | --- | --- |
| | | °C | °F |
| Arouane | Mali | 54.4 | 130 |
| Abadan | Iran | 52.8 | 127 |
| Cloncurry | Australia | 52.8 | 127 |
| Wadi Halfa | Sudan | 52.8 | 127 |
| Aswan | Egypt | 51.1 | 124 |
| Fort Flatters | Algeria | 51.1 | 124 |
| Mosul | Iraq | 51.1 | 124 |
| Cufra | Libya | 50.0 | 122 |
| Gabes | Tunisia | 50.0 | 122 |

### RECORD COLD TEMPERATURES

Although it is not a country, but a dependency of Denmark, Greenland is included in this list as the town of Eismitte is the world's oldest inhabitable place.

| TOWN | COUNTRY/ DEPENDENCY | COLDEST TEMPERATURE | |
| --- | --- | --- | --- |
| | | °C | °F |
| Eismitte | Greenland | -64.8 | -85 |
| Yakutsk | Russia | -64.3 | -84 |
| Fairbanks | USA | -54.4 | -66 |
| Aklavik | Canada | -52.2 | -62 |
| Ulan Bator | Mongolia | -44.4 | -48 |

### CONTINENTAL HIGHS

| CONTINENT | TEMPERATURE | |
| --- | --- | --- |
| | °C | °F |
| Africa | 57.8 | 136 |
| North America | 56.7 | 134 |
| Asia | 53.9 | 129 |
| Australasia and Oceania | 53.3 | 128 |
| Europe | 50.0 | 122 |
| South America | 48.9 | 120 |
| Antarctica | 14.4 | 58 |

**DID YOU KNOW?** The sizzling temperature that tops this list was recorded in Azizia, Libya, Africa in 1922.

### CONTINENTAL LOWS

| CONTINENT | TEMPERATURE | |
| --- | --- | --- |
| | °C | °F |
| Antarctica | -89.2 | -128.6 |
| Australasia and Oceania | -22.2 | -8 |
| South America | -32.7 | -27 |
| Europe | -54.9 | -67 |
| Asia | -67.7 | -90 |
| North America | -62.7 | -81 |
| Africa | 23.9 | -11 |

**DID YOU KNOW?** No-one lives in Antarctica as the climate is so harsh, but visiting scientists work in research stations.

## BEAUFORT SCALE FOR MEASURING WIND SPEED

The Beaufort scale, which was introduced in 1806 by British Admiral Sir Francis Beaufort (1774–1857), describes the effects of wind on land and sea. The scale is divided into a series of values, known as forces, from 0 for total calm to 12 and above for hurricanes. Each value represents a specific range and classification of wind speeds with accompanying descriptions of the effects on surface features.

| FORCE | DESCRIPTION | SPEED | | CHARACTERISTICS |
|---|---|---|---|---|
| | | KM/H | MPH | |
| 0 | Calm | 1.6 | 1 | Smoke rises vertically; sea surface is mirror smooth |
| 1 | Light air | 1.7–5 | 1–3 | Rising smoke indicates the direction of the wind |
| 2 | Slight breeze | 6–12 | 4–7 | Wind can be felt on the face and leaves rustle in trees |
| 3 | Gentle breeze | 13–20 | 8–12 | Wind extends a light flag |
| 4 | Moderate wind | 21–30 | 13–18 | Loose paper blows around; frequent whitecaps at sea |
| 5 | Fresh wind | 31–39 | 19–24 | Small trees sway |
| 6 | Strong wind | 40–50 | 25–31 | Wind whistles in telephone wires; some spray on the surface of the ocean |
| 7 | High wind/ near gale | 51–61 | 32–38 | Large trees sway |
| 8 | Gale | 62–74 | 39–46 | Twigs break from trees; long streaks of foam appear on the surface of the sea |
| 9 | Strong gale | 75–87 | 47–54 | Branches break from trees |
| 10 | Whole gale/ storm | 88–102 | 55–63 | Trees uprooted; sea takes on a white appearance |
| 11 | Severe storm | 103–116 | 64–72 | Widespread damage |
| 12+ | Hurricane | 117–132 | 73–82 | Structural damage on land; storm waves at sea |

## CLOUD LAYERS

**STRATUS** The lowest of all clouds, stratus form below 450 m (1,456 ft) and often hide hills and tall skyscrapers with fog.

**CUMULUS** Puffy cumulus clouds are grey at the bottom and brilliant white on top and form between 450–2,000 m (1,476–6,562 ft).

**STRATOCUMULUS** These clouds are recognizable by a low sheet of grey or white lumpy clouds, forming at 450–2,000 m (1,476–6,562 ft) high.

**CUMULONIMBUS** When there is a heavy shower, thunderstorm, or tornado, blame these massive, dark cumulonimbus clouds. They stretch as high as 450–2,000 m (1,476–6,562 ft).

**NIMBOSTRATUS** Thick, multi-layered clouds, nimbostratus bring only rain and snow. They form at 900–3,000 m (2,953–9,843 ft) above the ground.

**ALTOSTRATUS** Forming a thin, watery layer 2,000–7,000 m (6,562–22,966 ft) above the ground, altostratus clouds make a coloured ring around the Sun and Moon.

**CIRRUS** The highest in the sky, wispy cirrus clouds are 5,000 m (16,404 ft) higher than Mount Everest. They drift above us at between 5,000–13,500 m (16,404–44,291 ft).

**CIRROCUMULUS** Also at 5,000–13,500 m (16,404–44,291 ft), cirrocumulus clouds are made of icy particles and resemble fish-scales in appearance – hence the phrase "a mackerel sky".

**DID YOU KNOW?** The highest thunderclouds in the sky are black flat-topped cumulonimbus, which loom above us at 16 km (10 miles) high. They often bring hail showers or tornadoes.

## HOW FAR CAN YOU SEE?

**EXTREMELY CLEAR** In good, clear conditions, you can see for more than 50 km (31 miles).

**LIGHT HAZE** In a light haze or mist, visibility is reduced to about 10 km (6 miles) – a vast difference from a clear day.

**LIGHT FOG** Ground level cloud or light fog drastically reduces the distance you can see to only about 1 km (0.6 miles).

**VERY DENSE FOG** Extremely dense fog is a hazard to transport, especially road-users, but it is possible to see up to 15 m (50 ft). Fortunately, fog that, as in the expression, is so thick that you "can't see your hand in front of your face" is exceptionally rare.

**DID YOU KNOW?** Some people use the expression "a pea souper" to describe a very dense fog – comparing it to thick pea soup!

# NATURAL DISASTERS

## WORST AVALANCHES AND LANDSLIDES OF THE 20TH CENTURY

| LOCATION | INCIDENT | DATE | ESTIMATED NUMBER KILLED |
|---|---|---|---|
| Yungay, Peru | Landslide | May 1970 | 17,500 |
| Italian Alps | Avalanche | December 1916 | 10,000 |
| Huarás, Peru | Avalanche | December 1941 | 5,000 |
| Nevada Huascaran, Peru | Avalanche | January 1962 | 3,500 |
| Medellin, Colombia | Landslide | September 1987 | 683 |
| Chungar, Peru | Avalanche | March 1971 | 600 |

**DID YOU KNOW?** This list includes only incidents where deaths occurred as a direct result of the avalanche or landslide itself, rather than by flooding or earthquakes. The worst incident of all was the destruction of Yungay in Peru, which was part of a much larger cataclysm that left up to 70,000 dead. Following an earthquake and flooding, the town was wiped out by an avalanche that left 2,500 survivors out of a population of 20,000.

## MOST DESTRUCTIVE FLOODS AND STORMS OF THE 20TH CENTURY

| LOCATION | DATE | ESTIMATED NUMBER KILLED |
|---|---|---|
| Huang He River, China | August 1931 | 3,700,000 |
| Bangladesh | November 1970 | 300–500,000 |
| Henan, China | September 1939 | 200,000 |
| Chang Jiang River, China | September 1911 | 100,000 |
| Bengal, India | November 1942 | 40,000 |

**DID YOU KNOW?** The Earth's surface is made up of "plates" that move constantly but very slowly. When two plates collide, pressure builds up and the result is an earthquake.

## HURRICANE NAMES

| 1998 | 1999 | 2000 | 2001 | 2002 | 2003 |
|---|---|---|---|---|---|
| Alex | Arlene | Alberto | Allison | Arthur | Ana |
| Bonnie | Bret | Beryl | Barry | Bertha | Bill |
| Charley | Cindy | Chris | Chantal | Cristobal | Claudette |
| Danielle | Dennis | Debby | Dean | Dolly | Danny |
| Earl | Emily | Ernesto | Erin | Edouard | Erika |
| Frances | Floyd | Florence | Felix | Fay | Fabian |
| Georges | Gert | Gordon | Gabrielle | Gustav | Grace |
| Hermine | Harvey | Helene | Humberto | Hanna | Henri |
| Ivan | Irene | Isaac | Iris | Isidore | Isabel |
| Jeanne | José | Joyce | Jerry | Josephine | Juan |
| Karl | Katrina | Keith | Karen | Kyle | Kate |
| Lisa | Lenny | Leslie | Lorenzo | Lili | Larry |
| Mitch | Maria | Michael | Michelle | Marco | Mindy |
| Nicole | Nate | Nadine | Noel | Nana | Nicholas |
| Otto | Ophelia | Oscar | Olga | Omar | Odette |
| Paula | Philippe | Patty | Pablo | Paloma | Peter |
| Richard | Rita | Rafael | Rebekah | Rene | Rose |
| Shary | Stan | Sandy | Sebastien | Sally | Sam |
| Tomas | Tammy | Tony | Tanya | Teddy | Teresa |
| Virginie | Vince | Valerie | Van | Vicky | Victor |
| Walter | Wilma | William | Wendy | Wilfred | Wanda |

This is a list of the agreed names given to hurricanes, or tropical cyclones, in the order in which they occur in the Atlantic, the USA, and the Caribbean. The lists are reused every six years, so the 1998 list will be reused in 2004.

## GREAT VOLCANIC ERUPTIONS

**VESUVIUS, ITALY** In AD 79, Mount Vesuvius erupted, engulfing and preserving the Roman cities of Herculaneum and Pompeii. As many as 20,000 people lost their lives.

**LAKI, ICELAND** Iceland is highly volcanic but as it is thinly populated, eruptions seldom result in major loss of life. However, when the Laki volcanic ridge erupted in 1783, it engulfed villages in a river of lava 80 km (50 miles) long and 30 m (100 ft) deep, releasing poisonous gases that killed about 9,350 people.

**TAMBORA, INDONESIA** The eruption of Tambora in 1815 killed about 10,000 islanders outright, with a further 82,000 dying later from disease and the famine caused by the destruction of crops. No other volcano has caused such a loss of human life.

**KRAKATOA, SUMATRA** After a series of eruptions in August 1883, the island of Krakatoa exploded with a tremendous bang that was recorded 4,800 km (3,000 miles) away. Officially 36,417 people were killed, but some sources put the fatalities at 200,000.

**MONT PELÉE, MARTINIQUE** After lying dormant for centuries, in 1902 Mont Pelée burst apart, showering the island with molten lava, ash, and gas, and destroying all life.

## EARTHQUAKE RECORDS

**WORST EVER** If historical records are to be believed, an earthquake affecting the Middle East and North Africa in 1202 killed as many as 1,000,000 people.

**WORST 20TH-CENTURY** In 1920, an earthquake and resulting landslides in Kansu Province, China, left 180,000 dead.

**LONGEST-LASTING** Most earthquakes last less than a minute and there are no accurate records of durations of many. However, an earthquake in 1964, in Alaska, USA, lasted five minutes, and killed 131 people.

**MOST POWERFUL** In 1906, an earthquake 322 km (200 miles) off the Colombian coast measured 8.9 on the Richter scale.

## WORST DISASTERS

**FAMINE** A famine in China in 1959–1961 is believed to have killed at least 30,000,000 people. Just ten years later, in 1969–1971, another famine caused a further 20,000,000 deaths.

**FIRE** The Peshtigo forest fire, which broke out in Wisconsin, USA, in 1871 resulted in 2,682 deaths. Bush fires in Australia, in 1983, devastated vast areas of Victoria and destroyed seven towns and 2,000 homes.

**HAILSTONES** In 1888, in Moradabad and Beheri, India, 246 people and more than 1,600 sheep and goats were killed by hailstones as big as cricket balls.

**TORNADO** In 1989, a tornado at Shaturia, Bangladesh, left around 1,300 people dead and 50,000 homeless.

**TSUNAMI** In 1960, the combined effect of a tornado and tsunami, or tidal wave, killed 12,000 Moroccans. A tsunami that hit Papua New Guinea in 1998 is believed to have killed more than 6,000.

## RICHTER SCALE

Invented in 1935 by US seismologist (earthquake expert) Charles F. Richter (1900–1985), the Richter scale is used to indicate the magnitude or strength of an earthquake, based on the size of seismic waves (vibration of the ground). Each level on the scale is ten times higher than the one before it.

**0** Detected by sensitive seismographs

**1** Detected by instruments

**2** Lowest felt by humans

**3** Slight vibration; more than 100,000 a year around the world

**4** Up to 15,000 a year; 4.5 is detected by seismographs worldwide, but causes little damage

**5** 3,000 a year; the 1960 Agadir, Morocco, earthquake was 5.6

**6** 100 a year worldwide

**7** 20 a year; the 1995 Kobe, Japan, earthquake was 7.2

**8** Major destructive earthquakes; average two a year. The 1907 San Francisco, USA, earthquake is estimated at 8.25

**9** No quake higher than 8.9 has been recorded, but 9.0 or even higher is theoretically possible

## MODIFIED MERCALLI SCALE FOR MEASURING EARTHQUAKES

Using a range of I–XII, the Mercalli scale, devised by Italian geologist Giuseppe Mercalli (1850–1914), indicates an earthquake's intensity by observing its effects.

**I** Movement detected by instruments

**II** Felt by people resting

**III** Hanging lights sway

**IV** Windows rattle; parked cars rock

**V** Small objects move; doors swing

**VI** Felt by all; trees sway; objects fall off shelves; window glass shatters

**VII** Difficult to stand; bricks and tiles fall; chimneys crack

**VIII** Hard to steer a car; tree branches snap; chimneys fall

**IX** General panic; ground cracks; damage to underground pipes

**X** Pipes burst; rivers flood; buildings collapse

**XI** Few structures survive; bridges destroyed, large gaps in ground

**XII** Total destruction; waves ripple ground

# LIFE ON EARTH

## CLASSIFICATION

### HOW TO CLASSIFY A SPECIES

Living things are classified according to the features they have in common. This is how a tiger would be classified.

**KINGDOM** Animals (Animalia) A kingdom is the largest grouping in the classification.

**PHYLUM** Chordates (Chordata) A phylum is a major group within a kingdom. It is sometimes called a division in the classification of plants.

**CLASS** Mammals (Mammalia) A class is a major part of a phylum or sub-phylum. A sub-class is a large group within a class.

**FAMILY** Cats (Felidae) A family is a large collection of species that have several features in common.

**GENUS** Big cats (*Panthera*) A genus is a small collection of similar species.

**SPECIES** Tiger (*Panthera tigris*)

### THE FIVE KINGDOMS

All living things are divided into five groups, called kingdoms, based on the different ways in which they work.

**MONERANS** This kingdom includes the single-celled organisms, such as bacteria. Monerans were the first life forms, and there are now more than 5,000 species. The kingdom of Monerans also includes blue-green algae.

**PROTISTS** This kingdom contains simple organisms, most of which have only a single cell. There are at least 65,000 species of protist.

**FUNGI** Fungi, such as mushrooms and toadstools, absorb food that has been made by plants and animals. The kingdom has many thousands of species.

**PLANTS** Plants cannot move. They reproduce by making spores or seeds. The kingdom contains more than 400,000 species.

**ANIMALS** The animal kingdom contains organisms that cannot make their own food and must therefore feed themselves. Most animals are able to move around in search of food, but some spend their adult lives in one place.

### KINGDOM OF MONERANS

| PHYLUM | LATIN NAME | SPECIES |
|---|---|---|
| Typical bacteria | Eubacteria | 5,000 |
| Primitive bacteria | Archaebacteria | 500 |

### KINGDOM OF PROTISTS

| COMMON NAME | PHYLUM | SPECIES |
|---|---|---|
| Algae | Several | 20,000 |
| Amoebas | Sarcodina | 20,000 |
| Flagellates | Zoomastigina | 15,000 |
| Ciliates | Ciliophora | 8,000 |
| Sporozoans | Sporozoa | 5,000 |

### KINGDOM OF FUNGI

| PHYLUM | LATIN NAME | SPECIES |
|---|---|---|
| Sac fungi | Ascomycota | 30,000 |
| Fungi imperfecti | Deuteromycota | 25,000 |
| Club fungi | Basidiomycota | 25,000 |
| Moulds | Zygomycota | 750 |
| Water moulds | Oomycota | 600 |

### KINGDOM OF PLANTS

Most plants are organisms that produce food from sunlight. Most phyla contain non-flowering plants, including the spore- and the cone-bearing phyla. There is only one phylum of flowering plants, which produce flowers, fruits, and seeds.

| PHYLUM | LATIN NAME | SPECIES |
|---|---|---|
| Flowering plants | Angiospermophyta | 250,000 |
| Mosses, liverworts | Bryophyta | 15,000 |
| Ferns | Pteridophyta | 12,000 |
| Club mosses | Lycopodophyta | 1,000 |
| Gymnosperms | Gymnospermophyta | 1,000 |
| Horsetails | Sphenophyta | 15 |

**DID YOU KNOW?** Gymnosperms are non-flowering plants, and include conifers (pine trees) and cycads (palm trees).

### FLOWERING PLANTS

There are more than 250,000 species of flowering plants, of which there are two groups: monocotyledons and dicotyledons.

**MONOCOTYLEDONS** Plants whose seeds have one cotyledon (seed-leaf,) and that have leaves with parallel veins are called monocotyledons. The flower parts are usually in threes, or multiples of three. Examples of monocotyledons are irises, grasses, and orchids.

**DICOTYLEDONS** Plants which have seeds with two cotyledons (seed-leaves), and leaves with a branching network of veins are called dicotyledons. Flower parts are usually in fours or fives, or multiples of these numbers. Many species have woody stems. Examples of dicotyledons are beans, roses, cacti, carrots, and oak trees.

## KINGDOM OF ANIMALS

| PHYLUM | LATIN NAME | SPECIES |
|---|---|---|
| Arthropods | Arthropoda | 1,000,000+ |
| Molluscs | Mollusca | 110,000 |
| Chordates | Chordata | 45,000 |
| Roundworms | Nematoda | 20,000 |
| Segmented worms | Annelida | 18,600 |
| Flatworms, flukes | Platyhelminthes | 15,000 |
| Corals, jellyfish | Cnidaria | 9,500 |
| Sponges | Porifera | 9,000 |
| Echinoderms | Echinodermata | 6,000 |
| Moss animals | Bryozoa | 4,000 |
| Rotifers | Rotifera | 2,000 |
| Spiny-headed worms | Acanthocephala | 1,500 |
| Water bears | Tardigrada | 600 |
| Lampshells | Brachiopoda | 300 |
| Horsehair worms | Nematomorpha | 250 |
| Velvet worms | Onychophora | 100 |
| Comb jellies | Ctenophora | 90 |

## CLASSES OF MOLLUSC

| CLASS | LATIN NAME | SPECIES |
|---|---|---|
| Snails | Gastropoda | 35,000 |
| Mussels, clams | Bivalvia | 15,000 |
| Octopuses, squids | Cephalopoda | 600 |
| Deep-sea limpets | Monoplacophora | 500 |
| Chitons | Polyplacophora | 500 |
| Tusk shells | Scaphopoda | 350 |
| Solenogasters | Aplacophora | 250 |

## CLASSES OF ARTHROPOD

| CLASS | LATIN NAME | SPECIES |
|---|---|---|
| Insects | Insecta | 1,000,000+ |
| Millipedes | Diplopoda | 10,000 |
| Centipedes | Chilopoda | 2,500 |
| Sea spiders | Pycnogonida | 1,000 |
| Horseshoe crabs | Merostomata | 4 |

## ARACHNID ORDERS

Camel spiders • Harvestmen • Micro-whip scorpions • Mites • Pseudoscorpions • Ricinuleids Scorpions • Spiders • Whip scorpions and spiders

## CLASSES OF VERTEBRATE

Animals in the phylum Chordata have a stiff cord running down their bodies. Most are vertebrates (animals with backbones). Sea squirts – a subphyla of about 2,500 species – have a cord, but it is not a true backbone.

| CLASS | LATIN NAME | SPECIES |
|---|---|---|
| Bony fish | Osteichthyes | 20,000 |
| Birds | Aves | 9,000 |
| Reptiles | Reptilia | 6,000 |
| Mammals | Mammalia | 4,600 |
| Amphibians | Amphibia | 4,200 |
| Sharks and rays | Chondrichthyes | 800 |
| Jawless fish | Agnatha | 75 |

## MAMMAL ORDERS

Aardvarks • Bats • Carnivores • Colugos Elephant shrews • Elephants • Even-toed hoofed mammals • Hares, rabbits, pikas Hyraxes • Insectivores • Manatees and dugongs Marsupials • Monotremes • Odd-toed hoofed mammals • Pangolins • Primates • Rodents Seals, sealions, walruses • Sloths, anteaters, armadillos • Tree shrews • Whales and dolphins

## CLASSES OF CRUSTACEAN

Crustaceans are a subphylum of arthropods. There are about 40,000 species.

| CLASS | LATIN NAME | SPECIES |
|---|---|---|
| Crabs, lobsters, shrimps | Malacostraca | 20,000 |
| Copepods | Copepoda | 7,500 |
| Mussel shrimps | Ostracoda | 2,000 |
| Barnacles | Cirripedia | 1,220 |
| Branchiopods | Branchiopoda | 1,000 |
| Spiny sand shrimps | Branchiura | 125 |
| Mystacocarideans | Mystacocarida | 10 |
| Sand shrimps | Cephalocarida | 9 |

## INSECT ORDERS

Ants, bees, wasps • Beetles • Bugs • Butterflies, moths • Caddisflies • Cockroaches • Diplurans Dragonflies • Earwigs • Fleas • Grasshoppers, crickets • Grylloblattids • Lacewings, ant lions Lice • Mayflies • Praying mantises • Proturans Scorpionflies • Silverfish • Springtails • Stick and leaf insects • Stoneflies • Stylopids • Termites Thrips • True flies • Webspinners • Zorapterans

## AMPHIBIAN ORDERS

Caecilians • Frogs, toads Newts, salamanders

## REPTILE ORDERS

Crocodiles, alligators Snakes and lizards • Tuatara Turtles and tortoises

## BONY FISH ORDERS

Carp, characins • Catfish Eels • Flying fish, garfish Herrings, anchovies Perches, cichlids, gobies, wrasses • Salmon, trout

## CARTILAGINOUS FISH ORDERS

Sharks, skates, and rays

## BIRD ORDERS

Albatrosses, petrels, shearwaters • Cranes, rails, coots, bustards • Divers Ducks, geese, swans Eagles, hawks, vultures Emus, cassowaries Frogmouths, nightjars Grebes • Herons, storks, ibises, spoonbills, flamingos Kingfishers, bee-eaters, rollers, hornbills • Kiwis Mousebirds • Ostriches Owls • Parrots Pelicans, gannets, frigate birds, cormorants, anhingas Penguins • Perching birds Pheasants, partridges, grouse, turkeys • Pigeons, doves • Rheas • Sandgrouse Swifts, hummingbirds Tinamous • Trogons, quetzals • Turacos, cuckoos, roadrunners • Waders, terns, gulls, auks • Woodpeckers, barbets, honeyguides, puffbirds, toucans

**DID YOU KNOW?**
Bird species outnumber mammals by two to one.

# TREES and PLANTS

## THE LANGUAGE OF FLOWERS

In the 19th century, flowers and plants were given symbolic meanings, and by choosing which flowers were used in a bouquet, the sender could convey a hidden message.

| PLANT | MEANING |
|---|---|
| Bluebell | Permanence |
| Carnation | Pure love |
| Daffodil | Admiration |
| Forget Me Not | True, lasting love |
| Geranium (scarlet) | Comfort/stupidity |
| Hollyhock | Ambition |
| Lavender | Distrust |
| Poppy | Extravagance |
| Rose | Love |

## MOST FORESTED LANDS

These are the countries with the greatest area of forest and woodland as a percentage of their total land area. With increasing deforestation, the world average of forest area has fallen to about 31 per cent.

| COUNTRY/ DEPENDENCY | PERCENT COVERED BY FOREST |
|---|---|
| Surinam | 92 |
| Papua New Guinea | 91 |
| Solomon Islands | 85 |
| French Guiana (French dependency) | 81 |
| Guyana | 77 |

**DID YOU KNOW?** The least forested large countries in the world are the desert lands of the Middle East and North Africa, such as Libya. Less than 0.5 per cent of the land area of these countries is covered by forest or woodland.

## PLANT PARTS

**LEAF** A leaf traps the energy in sunlight to make food – a process called photosynthesis.

**STEM** The part of a plant that supports the buds, leaves, and flowers, and carries water and nutrients throughout the plant.

**SHOOT** A plant shoot consists of a stem, bud, leaves and flowers. It normally grows towards the light.

**BUD** An undeveloped shoot that is protected by scales. When conditions are favourable, the scales fold back, the bud bursts, and the shoot starts to grow.

**ROOT** The part of a plant that collects water, minerals, and in some, food.

## TOP NON-FOOD CROPS IN THE WORLD

| CROP | USE | ANNUAL PRODUCTION | |
|---|---|---|---|
| | | TONNES | TONS |
| Cotton | Clothing | 19,560,000 | 19,250,952 |
| Tobacco | Cigarettes | 6,968,996 | 6,858,866 |
| Rubber | Tyres, shoes, balls, erasers | 6,826,580 | 6,718,720 |
| Jute | Sacks, rope | 2,786,654 | 2,742,625 |
| Castor beans | Oil | 1,325,251 | 1,304,312 |
| Coir | Mats | 654,390 | 644,051 |
| Flax | Linen | 534,049 | 525,611 |
| Sisal | String | 325,123 | 319,986 |
| Hops | Flavouring beer | 122,188 | 120,257 |

## POISONOUS PLANTS

Many common plants, such as buttercups, are poisonous if they are eaten, because they contain harmful chemicals known as phytotoxins.

**ACONITE** Also called Wolf's Bane or Monkshood, the plant is found in Europe and North America. It can cause death within minutes.

**CURARE** Extracted from the bark of certain trees, it is used by South American Indian tribes to tip their poison arrows.

**DEADLY NIGHTSHADE** Also known as Belladonna, it contains a tiny amount of the poison atropine, enough to kill a child.

**HEMLOCK** Water hemlock and spotted hemlock contain some of the most deadly poisons known, even though carrots, celery, and parsnips belong to the same family!

## STRANGE PLANTS AND TREES

**SEE THE LIGHT** The Japanese fungus *Mycaena lux-coeli* produces phosphorescent enzymes that make it glow like a miniature lantern. It can be seen in the dark from 15 m (50 ft) away.

**DEAD STRANGE** *Rafflesia*, a parasitic plant that grows in the forests of Southeast Asia, has the largest and possibly the smelliest flower in the world. It looks and smells like a lump of decaying flesh, and is visited by swarms of flies, which pollinate the flower while crawling over it.

**DRINK YOUR MILK** The South American milk tree, *Brosimum utile*, belongs to the fig family, and produces a sap which looks, tastes, and is used just like cows' milk!

## PLANT MYTHOLOGY

**ROWAN** Rowan used to be made into garlands, then placed around the necks of pigs to fatten them up.

**OAK** An old rhyme warned that oak trees should be avoided in thunder storms as they were believed to be good conductors of electricity: "Beware the oak, it draws the stroke".

**MISTLETOE** If mistletoe was hung in a house before Christmas, it is believed that a death would occur.

**LAUREL** Laurel has long been associated with victory – soldiers who had won battles wore laurel wreaths.

## TREE RECORDS

**LARGEST FORESTS/MOST COMMON TREES** Russia has 20 per cent of the world's total forest area. The Siberian larch accounts for 38 per cent of the total tree cover in Russia. The huge Tongass National Forest, Sitka, Alaska, which is the largest forest in the USA, occupies some 67,664 sq km (26,125 sq miles), an area almost as large as the whole of Ireland!

**FASTEST-GROWING TREES** A eucalyptus tree in New Guinea grew 10.6 m (35 ft) in 15 months. One in Zimbabwe reached 30.48 m (100 ft) in seven years and one in New Zealand 45.72 m (150 ft) in 15 years.

**SLOWEST-GROWING TREES** *Puya raimondii*, a rare South American evergreen, is one of the slowest to grow and takes the longest to flower – its panicle (flower tuft) appears after 80 to 150 years, after which the plant dies. *Fitzroya*, a Chilean conifer, can take 300 years to reach 20 m (66 ft).

**OLDEST TREE SPECIES** Imprints of leaves of the maidenhair tree (*Ginkgo biloba*) have been found in sedimentary rocks of the Jurassic and Triassic Periods (135–210 million years ago). This means they must have been living at the same time as the dinosaurs.

**LARGEST TREE** The General Sherman giant sequoia in Sequoia National Park, California is 2,535 cm (998 in) in circumference, and 83.8 m (275 ft) tall – the tallest living thing on the planet. It has been calculated that if it were converted into pencils, end to end, they would more than reach round the Equator, a distance of 40,075.02 km (24,901.46 miles)!

**MOST DROUGHT RESISTANT** Africa's baobab tree stores up to 136,000 litres (30,000 gallons) of water in its trunk.

## PLANT RECORDS

**FASTEST-GROWING PLANTS** A *Hesperoyucca whipplei*, a shrub also known as "Our Lord's Candle", grew 3.65 m (12 ft) in 14 days in 1978 – an average of approximately 25 cm (9.8 in) a day. There are also examples of sunflowers growing to 6 m (20 ft) in one season, and some bamboos can spurt by 90 cm (35.4 in) a day, and reach 30 m (98.4 ft) high in three months.

**SLOWEST-GROWING PLANTS** *Dioon edule*, an evergreen shrub found in Mexico that resembles a tree fern, measured just 10 cm (3.9 in) high when it was 120 years old. It grew by 0.76 mm (0.03 in) a year. It is the slowest-growing flowering plant – one aged 1,000 years was only 2 m (6 ft 6 in) high.

**OLDEST PLANT SPECIES** A holly-like bush in Tasmania is thought to have been growing for more than 43,000 years! Various lichens on rocks grow only a few millimetres a century, and may be thousands of years old. The trunk of a vine planted in 1768 at Hampton Court, Middlesex, UK, now measures 2.16 m (7 ft) in diameter.

**LARGEST FRONDS** The Pacific giant kelp seaweed (*Macrocystis pyrifera*) has the largest fronds of any plant. Each one may grow up to 120 m (394 ft) – taller than the Statue of Liberty!

**LARGEST SEED** The huge seed of the coco de mer palm can weigh as much as 25 kg (55 lb) – the equivalent of about 30 coconuts!

## PLANTS NAMED AFTER PEOPLE

**CAMELLIA** Georg Joseph Kamel, a Moravian missionary.

**FREESIA** Friedrich Heinrich Theodor Friese, a German doctor.

**GREENGAGE** Sir William Gage, a British collector.

**MAGNOLIA** Pierre Magnol, a French botanist.

# ANIMAL RECORDS

## MOST INTELLIGENT ANIMALS

Edward O. Wilson, Professor of Zoology at Harvard University, observed animal intelligence, and measured learning performance over a wide range of tasks, taking account of the animal's brain size. Here are his findings:

| | | | |
|---|---|---|---|
| 1 | Human | 9 | Dolphin |
| 2 | Chimpanzee | 10 | Elephant |
| 3 | Gorilla | 11 | Pig |
| 4 | Orang-utan | | |
| 5 | Baboon | | |
| 6 | Gibbon | | |
| 7 | Monkey | | |
| 8 | Smaller toothed whale | | |

**DID YOU KNOW?** A chimpanzee's brain weighs 0.44 kg (0.97 lb).

## ANIMAL RECORDS

**TALLEST ANIMAL** Adult giraffes, from the African savanna, reach an average height of 5.9 m (19.4 ft), including horns of about 15–22 cm (6–9 in).

**LOUDEST INSECT** You can hear the familiar noise of a cicada from 400 m (1,312 ft) away.

**LOUDEST LAND ANIMAL** Howler monkey calls echo through the rainforest for more than 3 km (2 miles).

**HEAVIEST SEA MAMMAL** The blue whale is probably the largest animal ever to have lived, weighing in at 130 tonnes (128 tons) and stretching 33.5 m (110 ft) long.

**TALLEST BIRD** The ostrich, of eastern and southern Africa, is the world's tallest bird, measuring 2.75 m (9 ft) in height, but it cannot fly.

**LOUDEST SEA MAMMAL** Registering up to 188 decibels, the call of the blue whale can be heard by other whales up to 1,600 km (1,000 miles) away.

**LONGEST LAND ANIMAL** The Royal Python grows up to 10.7 m (35 ft).

**HEAVIEST LAND ANIMAL** African elephants are about 7.3 m (24 ft) long and weigh 7,000 kg (14,432 lb).

**SMALLEST PET DOG** A tiny chihuahua weighs as little as 0.45 kg (1 lb).

### SLEEPIEST CREATURES

| ANIMAL | AVERAGE HOURS OF SLEEP PER DAY |
|---|---|
| Koala | 22 |
| Two-toed sloth | 20 |
| Little brown bat | 19 |
| Giant armadillo | 18 |

**DID YOU KNOW?** The shrew has no time for sleep. It must constantly hunt and consume food or it will perish.

## WHAT'S THE BIGGEST?

| CLASS | ANIMAL | LENGTH |
|---|---|---|
| Fish | Whale shark | 18 m (59 ft) |
| Land mammal | African elephant | 4 m (13.1 ft) |
| Sea mammal | Blue whale | 33.5 m (110 ft) |
| Mollusc | Atlantic giant squid | 6.1 m (20 ft) |
| Reptile | Asian saltwater crocodile | 10 m (32 ft) |
| Amphibian | Chinese giant salamander | 1.8 m (5.9 ft) |
| Bird | Ostrich | 2.75 m (9 ft) |
| Crustacean | Japanese spider crab | 2.75 m (9 ft) |
| Arachnid | Indian scorpion | 29.2 cm (11.5 in) |
| Insect | Goliath beetle | 11 cm (4.3 in) |

**AMAZING FACT!** Groups of giant squid live in the Atlantic Ocean. Their eyes alone have a diameter of 50 cm (19.7 in).

## WHAT'S THE SMALLEST?

| CLASS | ANIMAL | LENGTH |
|---|---|---|
| Fish | Dwarf pygmy goby | 8 mm (0.31 in) |
| Mammal | Kitti's hog-nosed bat | 160 mm (6.25 in) |
| Mollusc | *Ammonicera* | A granule of sugar |
| Reptile | Virgin Island gecko | 18 mm (0.75 in) |
| Amphibian | *Psyllophryne didactyla* (frog) | 10.4 mm (0.41 in) |
| Bird | Bee hummingbird | 56 mm (2.2 in) |
| Crustacean | *Alonella* flea | A grain of salt |
| Arachnid | Midget spider | Microscopic |
| Insect | Mymarid wasp | 0.17 mm (0.0067 in) |

**AMAZING FACT!** Bee hummingbirds are so tiny, weighing just 1.6 g (0.056 oz), that they need to eat half their body weight in food every day just to stay alive!

## FASTEST ANIMALS IN THE SEA

| ANIMAL | KM/H | MPH |
| --- | --- | --- |
| Sailfish | 110 | 68 |
| Marlin | 80 | 50 |
| Bluefin tuna | 74 | 46 |
| Yellowfin tuna | 70 | 44 |
| Blue shark | 69 | 43 |
| Wahoo | 66 | 41 |

## FASTEST ANIMALS ON LAND

| ANIMAL | KM/H | MPH |
| --- | --- | --- |
| Cheetah (over short distance) | 105 | 65 |
| Pronghorn antelope | 89 | 55 |
| Mongolian gazelle | 80 | 50 |
| Springbok | 80 | 50 |
| Lion (over short distance) | 80 | 50 |
| Thomson's gazelle | 76 | 47 |

## FASTEST ANIMALS IN THE AIR

| ANIMAL | KM/H | MPH |
| --- | --- | --- |
| Peregrine falcon (diving) | 298 | 185 |
| Golden eagle | 240 | 150 |
| Spine-tailed swift | 171 | 106 |
| Frigate bird | 153 | 95 |
| Spur-winged goose | 142 | 88 |
| Red-breasted merganser | 129 | 80 |

## HOW FAST IS ITS HEART?

| ANIMAL | HEARTBEATS PER MINUTE |
| --- | --- |
| Hummingbird | 1,000+ |
| Bat | 750 |
| Mouse | 500–600 |
| Chicken | 250–300 |
| Cat | 120 |
| Sheep | 75 |
| Human/Cow | 60–80 |
| Horse/Lion | 40 |
| Frog/Camel | 30 |

**DID YOU KNOW?** In sub-zero conditions, a frog's heart rate dips as low as 6–8 beats per minute.

## HOW LONG CAN THEY LIVE?

| TYPE | ANIMAL | YEARS |
| --- | --- | --- |
| Mollusc | Marine clam | 200 |
| Reptile | Giant tortoise | 150 |
| Land mammal | Human | 121 |
| Sea mammal | Killer whale | 90 |
| Fish | European eel | 88 |
| Bird | Andean condor | 72 |
| Crustacean | North American lobster | 50 |
| Amphibian | Common toad | 40 |
| Arachnid | Theraphosid spider | 28 |
| Insect | Queen ant | 18 |

**DID YOU KNOW?** Common male houseflies complete their entire life cycle in just 17 days, giving them the shortest animal lifespan.

## ANIMAL REPRODUCTION RECORDS

**QUICKEST COURTSHIP** After a year or more as a larva, the adult mayfly has one day to find a mate and lay its eggs before it dies.

**GREATEST EGG LAYERS** Tapeworms, which live inside the gut of other animals, release up to a million eggs a day for several years but hardly any survive. The giant clam lays as many as 1,000 million eggs once a year for up to 40 years.

**LONGEST GESTATION** The pregnancy of an Asian elephant lasts 660 days, about 22 months – more than twice that of a human mother.

**SHORTEST GESTATION** The young of the Virginian opossum develop fully in just 12 days.

**LARGEST ANIMAL BABY** Blue whales are 6–8 m (20–26 ft) long and weigh 2–3 tonnes (1.9–2.9 tons) at birth. Every day, the baby drinks 200 litres (360 pints) of its mother's milk.

**MOST PROLIFIC FISH** On average, ocean sunfish lay about 30 million eggs, although one female was found to be carrying 300 million eggs. They do this because so few of the young survive.

**YOUNGEST MAMMAL BREEDER** Female Norway lemmings can breed when they're just 14 days old!

**LARGEST MAMMAL LITTER** Tailless tenrecs from Madagascar may produce up to 31 young in a single birth.

**HEAVIEST BIRDS' NEST** Bald eagles build huge nests. The largest recorded weighed 3 tonnes (2.9 tons) – equal to three cars.

**MOST MAMMAL YOUNG PER YEAR** The prairie vole rears 17 litters in quick succession, bringing up to 150 young into the world.

# MAMMALS

## HOW BIG ARE THE BIG CATS?

The length of tails among members of the cat family varies considerably – it may be as much as 140 cm (55 in) in the case of the leopard, or as little as 8 cm (3 in) in the lynx. The measurements are from the nose to the tip of the tail.

| SPECIES | WHERE FOUND | MAX. LENGTH CM | IN |
|---|---|---|---|
| Tiger | Asia | 330 | 130 |
| Leopard | Asia, Africa | 320 | 126 |
| Lion | Africa, Asia | 280 | 110 |
| Jaguar | North, Central, and South America | 271 | 107 |
| Mountain lion | North, Central, and South America | 245 | 96 |
| Snow leopard | Asia | 240 | 94 |
| Cheetah | Africa, Asia | 220 | 87 |
| Clouded leopard | Asia | 197 | 78 |
| Ocelot | North, Central, and South America | 170 | 67 |
| Lynx | Europe, Asia, North America | 138 | 54 |
| Golden cat | Africa | 138 | 54 |
| Serval | Africa | 125 | 49 |
| Caracal | Africa | 120 | 47 |
| Bobcat | North and Central America | 119 | 47 |
| Wild cat | Europe, Asia | 103 | 41 |
| Pampas cat | South America | 102 | 40 |
| Domestic cat | Worldwide | 97 | 38 |

## MAMMAL HOMES

| MAMMAL | HOME |
|---|---|
| Badger | Earth, sett |
| Beaver | Lodge |
| Bear | Den |
| Fox | Burrow, earth, kennel |
| Hare | Form |
| Otter | Holt |
| Rabbit | Burrow, warren |
| Squirrel | Drey |

## MAMMAL GROUPS

| MAMMAL | GROUP |
|---|---|
| Bats | Colony |
| Bears | Sloth, sleuth |
| Camels | Caravan, flock |
| Cows | Kine |
| Lions | Pride |
| Mice | Nest |
| Monkeys | Troop |
| Pigs | Litter, herd |
| Porpoises | School |
| Tigers | Ambush |
| Wolves | Pack |

## WHAT DO YOU CALL A YOUNG...?

| MAMMAL | YOUNG CALLED |
|---|---|
| Antelope | Calf, kid |
| Bear | Cub |
| Beaver | Kit, kitten |
| Bobcat | Kit, kitten |
| Buffalo | Calf |
| Camel | Calf |
| Cat | Catling, pussy, kit, kitten |
| Cow | Calf, heifer (female only), stirk |
| Deer | Fawn, yearling |
| Dog | Pup, puppy, whelp |
| Donkey | Foal, colt (male), filly (female) |
| Elephant | Calf |
| Elephant seal | Weaner |
| Elk | Calf |
| Fox | Cub, kit, kitten, whelp |
| Giraffe | Calf |
| Goat | Kid |
| Hamster | Kit, kitten |
| Hare | Leveret |
| Hippopotamus | Calf |
| Horse | Foal, yearling, colt (male), filly (female) |
| Kangaroo | Joey |
| Lion | Cub, lionet, whelp |
| Moose | Calf |
| Pig | Farrow, grice, piglet, shoat, suckling |
| Rabbit | Bunny, kit, kitten |
| Seal | Pup |
| Sheep | Cosset, hog, lamb, lambkin |
| Wolf | Cub, whelp |

## BEARS OF THE WORLD

| BEAR | WHERE FOUND | WEIGHT KG | LB | LENGTH CM | IN |
|---|---|---|---|---|---|
| Brown (grizzly) bear | North America, Europe, Asia | 136–390 | 300–860 | up to 290 | 114 |
| Polar bear | Arctic | 200–800 | 440–1,760 | up to 257 | 101 |
| American black bear | North America | 60–300 | 130–660 | 127–191 | 50–75 |
| Sloth bear | Asia | 80–140 | 175–310 | 152–191 | 60–75 |
| Asiatic black bear | Southern Asia | 100–200 | 220–440 | 127–188 | 50–74 |
| Spectacled bear | South America | 70–113 | 150–250 | 152–183 | 60–72 |
| Sun bear | Asia | 27–65 | 60–145 | 122–152 | 48–60 |

**DID YOU KNOW?** The Giant panda bear is usually considered a member of the racoon family, and not a true bear, but it would come eighth in this list, at 122–152 cm (48–60 in) in length.

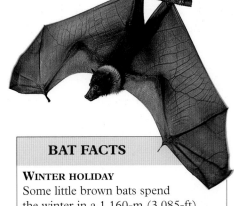

## HOW LONG CAN THEY STAY UNDERWATER?

| MAMMAL | UNDERWATER SURVIVAL (MINS) |
|---|---|
| Human | 1 |
| Polar bear | 1.5 |
| Human pearl diver | 2.5 |
| Sea otter | 5 |
| Platypus | 10 |
| Muskrat | 12 |
| Hippopotamus | 15 |
| Sea cow | 16 |
| Seal | 22 |
| Sperm whale | 112 |

## SMALLEST MAMMALS

| MAMMAL | WEIGHT | | LENGTH | |
|---|---|---|---|---|
| | G | OZ | CM | IN |
| Kitti's hognosed bat | 2.0 | 0.07 | 2.9 | 1.1 |
| Pygmy shrew | 1.5 | 0.05 | 3.6 | 1.4 |
| Pipistrelle bat | 3.0 | 0.11 | 4.0 | 1.6 |
| Little brown bat | 8.0 | 0.28 | 4.0 | 1.6 |
| Masked shrew | 2.4 | 0.08 | 4.5 | 1.8 |
| Southern blossom bat | 12.0 | 0.42 | 5.0 | 2.0 |
| Harvest mouse | 5.0 | 0.18 | 5.8 | 2.3 |
| Pygmy glider | 12.0 | 0.42 | 6.0 | 2.4 |
| House mouse | 12.0 | 0.42 | 6.4 | 2.5 |
| Common shrew | 5.0 | 0.18 | 6.5 | 2.5 |
| Water shrew | 12.0 | 0.42 | 7.0 | 2.8 |
| Bank vole | 15.0 | 0.53 | 8.0 | 3.2 |
| Pygmy possum | 15.0 | 0.53 | 8.5 | 3.4 |

*Ranked by length*

## BAT FACTS

**WINTER HOLIDAY**
Some little brown bats spend the winter in a 1,160-m (3,085-ft) deep zinc mine in New York.

**BLOOD THIRSTY** The vampire bat lives on blood alone. During its brief feeding period, it can consume more than its own body weight in blood.

**ON THE WING** Flying foxes of the Pteropus group are the largest bats in the world, with wingspans of up to 2 m (6.5 ft) across.

**COMPLETELY BATS** During World War II, the US airforce captured millions of bats. They planned to make all the bats carry tiny bombs, fly into buildings, and explode. Fortunately, the war ended before the plan could be put into action!

## AMAZING MAMMALS

**MARSUPIALS** The male red kangaroo can grow to more than 2 m (6.5 ft) tall and 2.5 m (8 ft) in overall length.

**SWIMMERS** A shark's skin is rough enough to be used as sandpaper, and its teeth are literally as hard as steel.

**CAMOUFLAGE** To complete their camouflage, polar bears cover their black noses with their paw as they stalk prey in the snow.

**BURROWERS** The badger has strong front legs and long claws so that it can dig underground burrows up to 20 m (66 ft) long.

**LONGEST LIVING** Humans are the longest-living mammals, but Asian elephants come a close second. The oldest recorded example of the species died at 78 years old.

**LONGEST SLEEPING** The barrow ground squirrel of Alaska, USA, hibernates for nine months at a time.

## MAMMALS WITH THE LONGEST TAILS

**❗DID YOU KNOW?**
The flying squirrel uses its flattened tail as a rudder for steering as it leaps from tree to tree. The tail also acts as an air brake.

| MAMMAL | TAIL LENGTH | |
|---|---|---|
| | CM | IN |
| Asian elephant | 150 | 59 |
| Leopard | 140 | 55 |
| African elephant | 130 | 51 |
| African buffalo | 110 | 43 |
| Giraffe | 110 | 43 |
| Red kangaroo | 110 | 43 |
| Langur | 100 | 39 |

**❗DID YOU KNOW?**
Camels can drink 113 litres (200 pints) of water in half an hour.

# UNDERWATER CREATURES

## REPRODUCTION FACTFILE

**MALE MOTHER** The female seahorse lays her eggs in her partner's pouch. He carries the tiny, developing seahorses until they are ready to be born, between two and six weeks later.

**LARGEST EGG** The whale shark lays an egg about 30 cm (14 in) in length.

**ONE YOUNG** Some sharks give birth to just one pup because the first to develop inside the mother eats all the other eggs!

**MERMAID'S PURSES** Hard, horny "mermaid's purses" found on the sea shore are the dried out egg cases of dogfish, skates, and rays. The embryos grow inside, wriggling out after six to nine months.

**SHARK PUPS** It takes sharks 9–22 months to grow inside their mother, and up to 100 pups can be born at one time.

## DEEP-SEA DIVERS

**BIRDS** Some emperor penguins have been recorded 265 m (870 ft) deep.

**TURTLES** In 1987, a leatherback turtle was fitted with a depth-gauge that recorded 1,200-m (3,937-ft) dives. Turtles may go even deeper for food.

**WHALES** Sperm whales regularly dive to 1,200 m (3,937 ft), and sometimes descend to twice this depth!

**DEEP-SEA FISH** Fish in the brotulid group have been found in deep-sea trenches, such as the Puerto Rico Trench, at 8,300 m (27,230 ft) – almost as deep as Mount Everest is high!

**DID YOU KNOW?** In a record-breaking mission in the bathyscaphe *Trieste*, scientists Jacques Piccard and Donald Walsh observed creatures living as far down as 10,916 m (35,814 ft) in the Marianas Trench, Pacific Ocean.

## LARGEST MARINE MAMMALS

| MAMMAL | LENGTH | | WEIGHT | |
|---|---|---|---|---|
| | M | FT | TONNES | TONS |
| Blue whale | 33.5 | 110.0 | 130.0 | 127.9! |
| Fin whale | 25.0 | 82.0 | 45.0 | 44.2! |
| Right whale | 17.5 | 57.4 | 40.0 | 39.3? |
| Sperm whale | 18.0 | 59.0 | 36.0 | 35.4? |
| Grey whale | 14.0 | 46.0 | 32.7 | 32.18 |
| Humpback whale | 15.0 | 49.2 | 26.5 | 26.08 |
| Baird's whale | 5.5 | 18.0 | 11.0 | 10.8? |
| Southern elephant seal | 6.5 | 21.3 | 3.6 | 3.54 |
| Northern elephant seal | 5.8 | 19.0 | 3.4 | 3.3? |
| Pilot whale | 6.4 | 21.0 | 2.9 | 2.8! |

**DID YOU KNOW?** The herbivorous dugong, a type of sea cow, is the largest mammal to live in inland waters, weighing up to 907 kg (2,000 lb) and measuring 4.1 m (13.5 ft) in length.

**DID YOU KNOW?** The grey whale travels further than any other whale. It swims about 20,000 km (12,500 miles) each year from its winter breeding grounds in Mexico to the Bering Sea.

## SMALLEST MARINE MAMMALS

**SMALLEST WHALE** The pygmy right whale grows to 6.45 m (21 ft) and weighs 3.2 tonnes (3.15 tons) – less than a quarter of the length and under three per cent of the weight of the largest, the blue whale.

**SMALLEST DOLPHIN** There are several contenders for smallest dolphin, one of which is Hector's dolphin, found off New Zealand. It is 1.53 m (5 ft) long, and weighs under 57.27 kg (126 lb).

**SMALLEST SEAL** The rare Galápagos fur seal, reaches a maximum weight of 64 kg (142 lb) and a length of 1.5 m (4 ft 11 in).

**SMALLEST SEA MAMMAL** Found off the western coast of South America, the marine otter weighs a maximum of 4.5 kg (10 lb). It measures only about 1.15 m (3 ft 9 in) long. Marine otters sometimes come ashore, unlike the slightly larger sea otters, which spend their lives in the water.

## FACTASTIC MARINE CREATURES

**SMALLEST MOLLUSC** The gastropod *Ammonicera* is only 1 mm (0.04 in) long.

**LARGEST INVERTEBRATES** Giant squid can grow 15 m (50 ft) long and weigh 2 tonnes (1.9 tons). Imagine coming face to face with 40-cm (15.7-in) wide eyes!

**ITS ELECTRIFYING!** The electric eel, from the Amazon, kills fish with 500-volt shocks from muscles that act like tiny batteries.

**LEAVING A LEG BEHIND** Crabs and other crustaceans can escape danger by simply discarding an injured or trapped limb!

**NO EYES** Some cave-dwelling fish have no eyes because they spend their lives in darkness and don't need them!

**LARGEST CRUSTACEAN** The Japanese spider crab has a leg span of 4 m (13 ft).

**LOBSTER MARCH** Hundreds of spiny lobsters often walk one after another for 100 km (60 miles) in search of an area to settle. They make sounds, which are thought to co-ordinate the journey!

**HEAVIEST CRUSTACEAN** The North Atlantic lobster weighs up to 20 kg (44 lb).

## DANGEROUS UNDERWATER CREATURES

**BLUEFISH** Considered the fiercest fish, the bluefish of the Americas attacks and eats other fish: a 2-kg (5-lb) bluefish can devour a tonne (ton) of fish a year – 500 times its body weight!

**LIONFISH** The fins of this brightly coloured fish contain a deadly poison!

**CONE-SHELL** Found in the South Pacific and Indian Oceans, the poisonous barbs of the cone-shell cause paralysis and death. The geographer cone is the most dangerous.

**SEA WASP** Also known as the box jellyfish, found off the Australian coast, it has 9-m (30-ft) tentacles. Its venom is as powerful as that of a cobra.

**JAPANESE PUFFER** Also known as the maki-maki, or "deadly death puffer fish", certain parts of a Japanese puffer's body contain a nerve poison that, if eaten, can kill a person. There is no known antidote. Despite the danger, they are eaten as a delicacy in Japan. Although chefs are trained to prepare them, 50 people a year die from negligence in the kitchen.

**OCTOPUS** The bites of several species, especially the blue-ringed octopus found off Australia, are dangerous, often causing paralysis.

**SEA URCHIN** If trodden on, several sea urchins cause severe paralysis or death.

**SEA LAMPREY** Not a good ingredient for a fish stew! These eel-like creatures may be poisonous – English king Henry I died after gorging himself on "a surfeit of lampreys".

**PORTUGUESE MAN-OF-WAR** Found in tropical seas, this vicious jellyfish-like creature has 21-m (70-ft) tentacles! It can cause very painful stings that affect the nerves.

**SEA SNAKE** All sea snakes are dangerous, but *Hydrophis belcheri* has a deadly venom that is stronger than that of many land snakes.

**PIRANHA** Living in South America, these fish will strip a human to the bone in minutes!

**STINGRAY** Lurking in most coastal waters, the stingray has a highly venomous spine above its tail. A sting can hinder breathing, but rarely kills.

**DID YOU KNOW?** The teeth of the great white shark are 12 cm (5 in) long. New ones grow forward to replace them as they wear out.

## UNDERWATER LIFESPANS

| ANIMAL | LONGEST IN YEARS |
|---|---|
| Quahog (marine clam) | 200 |
| Deep-sea clam | 100 |
| Killer whale | 90 |
| Sea anemone | 80 |
| Sperm whale | 65 |
| Whale shark | 60 |
| North American lobster | 50 |
| Grey seal | 46 |
| Blue whale | 45 |
| Australian school shark | 32 |
| Californian sea lion | 30 |
| Starfish | 15 |

At the other end of the scale, some fish have lifespans of less than a year, among them the white goby, seahorse, and dwarf pygmy goby.

## BIG FISH RECORDS

**WHALE SHARK** Not only the biggest shark, but also the biggest fish, the gigantic whale shark can grow to a length of 12 m (39 ft)!

**OARFISH** Also called ribbonfish, oarfish are the biggest bony fish, growing up to 9 m (30 ft) long. They live in deep tropical waters.

**EUROPEAN CATFISH** A catfish weighing 363.3 kg (720 lb) was allegedly caught in the 1800s in the Dnieper River, in Russia.

**PLA BUK** Found in the waters of the Mekong River, China, the giant pla buk can weigh as much as 242 kg (553 lb).

**WHITE STURGEON** Caught by a lucky angler in California, USA, in 1983, this huge fish weighed 212.28 kg (468 lb)!

**TRY IT YOURSELF!** You can measure a fish's top swimming speed per second by multiplying its length by ten. So, a trout 15 cm (6 in) long swims at 1.5 m (5 ft) per second!

## HEAVIEST SHARKS

| SPECIES | KG | LB |
|---|---|---|
| Whale shark | 21,000 | 46,297 |
| Basking shark | 14,515 | 32,000 |
| Great white shark | 3,314 | 7,300 |
| Greenland shark | 1,020 | 2,250 |
| Tiger shark | 939 | 2,070 |
| Great hammerhead shark | 844 | 1,860 |
| Six-gill shark | 590 | 1,300 |
| Grey nurse shark | 556 | 1,225 |
| Mako shark | 544 | 1,200 |
| Thresher shark | 500 | 1,100 |

**DID YOU KNOW?** Although whale sharks are huge, you needn't worry, they're not dangerous! Whale sharks eat only plankton and could not swallow a person whole because their throats are only 10 cm (4 in) in diameter.

35

# BIRDS

## ONE AND ONLY BIRDS

**HIBERNATING BIRD** The only bird to hibernate is the North American poor-will (*Phalaenoptilus nuttallii*). During the cold winters, its metabolism slows down and its body temperature drops from 41°C (106°F) to 13°C (55°F).

**POISONOUS BIRD** The only poisonous bird known is the black and orange hooded pitohui (*Pitohui dichrous*) from New Guinea. The poisons it gives off are similar to those secreted by poison-dart frogs.

LANNER FALCON

**DID YOU KNOW?**
Sleek body feathers give the bird the streamlined shape it needs for flight.

**DID YOU KNOW?**
Beneath its body feathers, a bird has soft, fluffy down feathers to keep it warm.

## AMAZING MIGRATIONS

**LONGEST** Each year, the sun-loving Arctic tern flies from the Arctic to the Antarctic and back – a round trip of about 40,000 km (25,000 miles).

**UNLIKELIEST** Even though it weighs only 3.5 g (0.1 oz), the ruby-throated hummingbird flies non-stop for about 800 km (500 miles) from North to South America every autumn. It flies back in the spring.

**YOUNGEST** Left behind by their parents, young shining bronze cuckoos migrate 6,400 km (4,000 miles) from New Zealand to Australia and then on to the Bismarck archipelago.

**DID YOU KNOW?**
A bird's strong, broad wing or flight feathers provide the surface needed to produce lift.

**DID YOU KNOW?**
Long, strong tail feathers help the bird steer, balance, and brake in the air.

## FEATHER FACTS

**WHAT ARE THEY MADE OF?** Feathers are made of dead cells and composed of keratin, the same material as our hair and nails.

**PARTS OF A FEATHER** The shaft of a feather is the rachis; the body is the vane; and the strands are barbs. Barbs have tiny hooks on them called barbules, which cling to each other like Velcro.

**UNLUCKY FEATHERS** Peacock feathers are believed to represent the evil eye, and are considered unlucky in many cultures.

**EDIBLE FEATHERS?** Grebes eat their own feathers. This may help them to digest food by forming pellets that enable them to regurgitate the bones and scales of the fish they eat.

**LONGEST FEATHERS** The tail feathers of the Japanese phoenix fowl, or onagodori, may measure up to 10.6 m (34.7 ft) – the longest of any bird – although these birds cannot fly!

**WHY ARE FLAMINGO FEATHERS PINK?** A flamingo's fishy diet keeps its feathers pink. Flamingos in captivity have to eat a special diet rich in carotene – the orange colouring in carrots – otherwise their feathers turn white!

## BON APPETIT!

Ostriches appear to be indiscriminate in their choice of food. A director of the London Zoological Society, E. G. Boulenger, listed the following objects as having been extracted from the stomach of one unfortunate ostrich at its post-mortem in the 1930s:

| | |
|---|---|
| 1 key | 2 collar studs |
| 1 part of a gold necklace | 1 glove fastener |
| 1 12.5-cm (5-in) piece of wood | 1 bicycle tyre valve |
| 1 part of a comb | 2 handkerchiefs |
| 1 pencil | 1 90-cm (35-in) length of thick string |
| 3 gloves | |
| 1 film spool | 8 coins |

## LARGEST WINGSPANS

| | MAXIMUM WINGSPAN | |
|---|---|---|
| **BIRD** | **M** | **FT** |
| Marabou stork | 4.0 | 13 |
| Albatross | 3.7 | 12 |

**DID YOU KNOW?**
The wingspan of an adult albatross is greater than the length of a small car!

| | | |
|---|---|---|
| Trumpeter swan | 3.4 | 11 |
| Mute swan | 3.1 | 10 |
| Whooper swan | 3.1 | 10 |
| Grey pelican | 3.1 | 10 |
| Californian condor | 3.1 | 10 |
| Black vulture | 3.1 | 10 |
| Great bustard | 2.7 | 9 |
| Kori bustard | 2.7 | 9 |

## LARGEST FLYING BIRDS

| BIRD TYPE | WEIGHT | | |
|---|---|---|---|
| | KG | LB | OZ |
| Great bustard | 20.9 | 46 | 1 |
| Trumpeter swan | 16.8 | 37 | 1 |
| Mute swan | 16.3 | 35 | 15 |
| Albatross | 15.8 | 34 | 13 |
| Whooper swan | 15.8 | 34 | 13 |
| Manchurian crane | 14.9 | 32 | 14 |
| Kori bustard | 13.6 | 30 | 0 |
| Grey pelican | 13.0 | 28 | 11 |
| Black vulture | 12.5 | 27 | 8 |

## BIRD GROUP NAMES

Most of the following names are still used, but some, such as a murmuration of starlings, a murder of crows, and an unkindness of ravens, are now out of fashion.

A bevy of quail

A bouquet of pheasants

A brood of hens

A cast of hawks

A charm of finches

A colony of penguins

A covey of partridges

An exaltation of larks

A flight of swallows

A gaggle of geese

A siege of herons

A skein of geese

A trip of dotterel

A wisp of snipe

## RARE AND ENDANGERED BIRDS

Rare birds are most under threat in places where they are unable to seek refuge, such as on islands like Mauritius, where the dodo became extinct in the 17th century.

| BIRD | COUNTRY | BREEDING PAIRS |
|---|---|---|
| Spix's macaw | Brazil | 1 |
| Cebu flower pecker | Philippines | 1 |
| Hawaiian crow | Hawaii | 5 |
| Black stilt | New Zealand | 12 |
| Echo parakeet | Mauritius | 13 |
| Imperial Amazon parrot | Dominica | 15 |
| Magpie robin | Seychelles | 20 |
| Kakapo | New Zealand | 24 |
| Pink pigeon | Mauritius | 70 |
| Mauritius kestrel | Mauritius | 100 |

**RARE RECOVERY!** The Mauritius kestrel was formerly second rarest bird, but has recovered to more than 100 pairs.

## TEN FASTEST BIRDS

Birds are among the fastest animals on Earth. When diving, peregrine falcons can reach speeds of almost 298 km/h (185 mph). However, most comparisons of air speed in birds rule out diving or wind-assisted flight. This list picks out star performers among medium to large-sized birds (mainly waterfowl), that can hit their top speed without help from wind or gravity.

| BIRD | MAXIMUM RECORDED SPEED | |
|---|---|---|
| | KM/H | MPH |
| Spine-tailed swift | 171 | 106 |
| Frigate bird | 153 | 95 |
| Spur-winged goose | 142 | 88 |
| Red-breasted merganser | 129 | 80 |
| White-rumped swift | 124 | 77 |
| Canvasback duck | 116 | 72 |
| Eider duck | 113 | 70 |
| Teal | 109 | 68 |
| Mallard | 105 | 65 |
| Pintail | 105 | 65 |

**AMAZING FACT!** The speediest of flightless birds is the ostrich, which can run at 72 km/h (45 mph) and can maintain this speed for nearly 20 minutes.

## LARGEST FLIGHTLESS BIRDS

| BIRD | WEIGHT | | | HEIGHT | |
|---|---|---|---|---|---|
| | KG | LB | OZ | CM | IN |
| Ostrich | 156.5 | 345 | 0 | 274.3 | 108.0 |
| Emu | 40.0 | 88 | 3 | 152.4 | 60.0 |
| Cassowary | 33.5 | 73 | 14 | 152.4 | 60.0 |
| Rhea | 25.0 | 55 | 2 | 137.1 | 54.0 |
| Emperor penguin | 29.4 | 64 | 13 | 114.0 | 44.0 |
| Flightless cormorant | 4.5 | 9 | 15 | 95.0 | 37.4 |

## BIRDS' EGGS

**SMALLEST EGGS** The miniscule eggs of the bee hummingbird are as small as peas and weigh just 0.25 g (0.008 oz).

**LARGEST EGGS** Ostrich eggs can measure up to 20 cm (8 in) long and weigh up to 1.65 kg (3.5 lb) – equal to about 24 hens' eggs.

**LARGEST CLUTCH** The grey partridge may lay as many as 19 eggs in a single clutch.

**DID YOU KNOW?** Webbed feet prevent water birds from sinking into the mud.

# INSECTS and SPIDERS

## INSECT RECORDS

**LONGEST** Stick insects are the longest insects! Some measure up to 51 cm (20 in), in length.

**HEAVIEST** A goliath beetle may be as long as 11 cm (4 in), and can weigh 70–100 g (2.5–3.5 oz), almost as heavy as a small apple!

**SMALLEST** Battledore wing fairy flies, a kind of parasitic wasp, measure just 0.21 mm (0.0083 in).

**LONGEST-LIVED** Jewel beetle larvae may live inside wood for 30 years or more before the insect emerges.

**NOISIEST** The mating calls from a male cicada colony can measure 80–100 decibels from 18.28 m (60 ft) – as noisy as heavy traffic!

**TOUGHEST** Snow fleas can live in temperatures of -15°C (-59°F)!

**MOST NUMEROUS** There are about 50,000 springtails per sq m (5,000 per sq ft) of grassland in the world.

## FACTASTIC MOTHS AND BUTTERFLIES

**SO MANY SPECIES** There are at least 170,000 different species of butterflies and moths.

**LARGEST MOTH** The Atlas moth is the largest in the world.

**SMALLEST MOTH** The *Stigmella ridiculosa* moth measures only 2 mm (0.08 in) across.

**SMALLEST BUTTERFLY** The grass jewel butterfly has a wingspan of only 1–1.5 cm (0.39–0.59 in).

**LONG-DISTANCE FLIERS** Butterflies have been tracked travelling 4,828 km (3,000 miles)! Monarch butterflies regularly migrate a distance of 3,000 km (1,864 miles) from Canada and the USA to Mexico.

**AMAZING ANTENNAE** The antennae of male longhorn moths are six times as long as their bodies.

**HUNGRY CATERPILLAR** In its lifetime, a black arches moth caterpillar can eat about 1,000 pine needles and damage another 1,000 at the same time.

## REPRODUCTION RECORDS

**LARGEST EGGS** Malaysian stick insects lay eggs that measure 1.3 cm (0.5 in) in diameter.

**MOST EGGS LAID** The Queen *Macrotermes* termite can lay up to 40,000 eggs per day!

**LONGEST IN EGG** The cerambycid beetle *Saperda carcharia* takes nine and a half months to hatch.

**❗ DID YOU KNOW?**
Butterflies flap their wings about 640 times a minute when flying!

**❗ DID YOU KNOW?**
The female Queen Alexandra birdwing butterfly, of Papua New Guinea, has the largest wingspan of any insect, at 28 cm (11 in)!

## DEADLY SPIDERS

Spiders are the number 1 phobia of many people. Most spiders are harmless, but some species are lethal killers, such as the following examples:

- Black widows
- Brown recluse spiders
- Hobo spider
- Tarantulas
- Banana spider
- Sydney funnel web
- Redback
- White-tailed spider
- Mouse spider

## SPIDER AND SCORPION FACTFILE

**LARGEST SPIDER** The goliath bird-eating spider is 28 cm (11 in) in diameter – as big as a dinner plate!

**SPEEDY SPIDER** Watch out at home – ordinary house spiders can speed at 1.9 km/h (1 mph)!

**LARGEST SPIDER WEB** The orb weaver spider group can make 3-m (10-ft) webs – as large as bedsheets!

**SMALLEST SPIDER WEB** A midget spider weaves the world's tiniest web, at 10 mm (0.39 in) – that's smaller than your fingernail.

**LARGEST SCORPION** *Heterometrus swannerdami* measures 18 cm (7 in) from its pincers to its tail.

**SMALLEST SCORPION** *Microbothus pusillus* is just 13 mm (0.5 in) long.

**MOST POISONOUS SCORPION** The Israeli gold scorpion has the most poisonous sting known.

## HOW LONG DO INSECTS LIVE?

| ANIMAL | LIFESPAN |
| --- | --- |
| Wood-boring beetle | 45 years |
| Jewel beetle | 30 years |
| Periodic cicada | 17 years |
| Indian meal moth | 4 weeks |
| Housefly | 17 days |
| Mayfly | 1 hour |

## THESE ARE NOT INSECTS!

Here are some creatures that are often mistaken for insects: Spiders • Scorpions Crabs • Prawns • Woodlice • Centipedes Millipedes • Worms • Slugs • Snails

## HAVE YOU SEEN...?

You are not likely to come across a Queen Alexandra Birdwing butterfly, as they are the rarest butterflies in the world.

## DANGEROUS INSECTS

**BEES AND HORNETS** Stings may be painful, but multiple stings may cause an allergic reaction, or death. More people are killed by bees than by snakes!

**COCKROACHES** As well as devouring food, cockroaches transmit diseases.

**HARVEST MITES** In some tropical countries, harvest mites transmit typhus to people.

**KISSING BUGS** The bite of these insects spreads Chagas' disease, which kills some 45,000 people a year.

**LOCUSTS** Locusts are responsible for destroying crops, leaving some human populations destitute. It has been estimated that a swarm of 50 billion desert locusts can eat in a day enough food for 500,000 people for a year.

**MOSQUITOES** These insects carry diseases such as malaria, which causes between 1,500,000 and 2,700,000 deaths a year, in tropical countries. Malaria has killed about half of all the human population since the Stone Age.

**TERMITES** Hordes of these demon insects can destroy entire buildings by eating away at the wooden structure.

## FASTEST INSECTS

| INSECT | TOP SPEED | |
| --- | --- | --- |
| | KM/H | MPH |
| Dragonfly | 32.0 | 20.0 |
| Hornet | 21.5 | 13.39 |
| Horsefly | 14.3 | 8.93 |
| Bee | 18.0 | 11.0 |

**DID YOU KNOW?** A bee could travel 4 million miles at 11 km/h (7 mph) on the energy it would obtain from one gallon (4.5 litres) of nectar.

## USEFUL INSECTS

**BEES** Worldwide, bees produce over a million tonnes (0.9 million tons) of honey annually and help to pollinate crops. Beeswax is also used in furniture polish.

**LAC INSECT** This scaled insect secretes a resin which is used to make varnish for furniture and leather goods.

**SILKWORMS** Silkworm larvae are used commercially to make silk. About 40,000 silkmoth cocoons could provide enough silk to circle the earth in a single thread.

**SCALE INSECTS** The crushed bodies of Mexican scale insects produce cochineal, a red food colouring.

## EDIBLE INSECTS

**AUSTRALIA** Aboriginal Australians eat wichety grubs (giant moth caterpillars). They also tap the hollow logs where beetles live to catch beetle larvae.

**CAMBODIA** People sit around campfires at night and attract cicadas by clapping. They then cook them by roasting them on the fires, like sausages on sticks.

**CENTRAL AND SOUTH AMERICA** The wings, heads, and legs of parasol ants are removed, and their bodies are eaten raw or toasted.

**CHINA** Grasshoppers (*Tsa ku meng*) are fried in sesame oil until crisp, then served and eaten like roasted nuts.

**INDIA** To make red ant chutney (*Chindi chutney*), ants are cooked on a fire, then ground into a paste, which is salted, mixed with chillies and baked.

**MEXICO** A delicacy in parts of Mexico is a giant water bug – so huge that it eats frogs! Waterboatmen eggs are served like caviar.

## BEST JUMPERS

**HIGH JUMPER** Fleas can leap 30 cm (12 in) into the air – about 200 times their own height!

**LONG JUMPER** The desert locust, a type of grasshopper, can leap distances of 50 cm (19.5 in) – ten times the length of its body!

## NAMES OF INSECT ORDERS

| INSECT | ORDER | MEANING |
| --- | --- | --- |
| Beetles | Coleoptera | Hard wings |
| Butterflies | Lepidoptera | Scaly wings |
| Midges | Diptera | Two-wings |
| Aphids | Hemiptera | Half wings |
| Grasshoppers | Orthoptera | Straight wings |
| Caddisflies | Trichoptera | Hairy wings |
| Springtails | Collembola | Sticky peg |
| Dragonflies | Odonata | Toothed flies |
| Thrips | Thysanoptera | Fringed wings |
| Lacewings | Neuroptera | Net-veined wings |
| Cockroaches | Blattodea | Insect avoiding light |
| Bark lice | Pscoptera | Milled wings |
| Stick insects | Phasmatodea | Like a ghost |
| Fleas | Siphonaptera | Tube without wings |
| Termites | Isoptera | Equal wings |
| Mayflies | Ephemeroptera | Living for a day |

# AMPHIBIANS and REPTILES

## FROG RECORDS

**OLDEST FROG**  The Stephens Island frog evolved on Earth 170-275 million years ago, and is thought to be the ancestor of all frogs. Discovered in 1917, it is found only in New Zealand.

**SMELLIEST FROG**  The Venezuela skunk frog (*Aromobates nocturnus*), discovered in 1991, deters enemies by releasing a stinky chemical identical to the one that skunks spray as a defence!

POISON-ARROW FROG

**LARGEST FROGS**  The Rana goliath frog, found in the African countries of Cameroon, Democratic Republic of Congo, and Equatorial Guinea, is the largest frog ever known. In 1949, a bullfrog weighing about 3.5 kg (8 lb) and allegedly 1 m (3.3 ft) long was found in Martha Lake, Washington, USA.

**LARGEST TREE FROG**  *Hyla vasta*, found only on Hispaniola, in the Caribbean, is 18 cm (7.1 in) long. It has huge round fingers and toes that grip like superglue.

**LARGEST TOAD**  The bodies of some South American marine toads (*Bufo marinus*) measure 23 cm (9 in) long. They can weigh almost 1.5 kg (3 lb). They come from South America, but have been introduced around the world to control sugar beetles that destroy crops. In Australia, marine toads have been moving south from Queensland, allegedly by stowing away on trucks.

**SMALLEST TOAD**  The East African toad (*Bufo taitanus beiranus*), from Mozambique, rarely grows more than 2.5 cm (1 in) long.

**RECORD EGG-LAYER**  The female marine toad (*Bufo marinus*) can lay as many as 35,000 eggs a year.

## DEFENSIVE FROGS

**DON'T PICK ME UP!**  The dagger frog (*Babini holsti*), found in Okinawa, Japan, has a sharp spiny "thumb" to stab anyone who picks it up!

**DON'T BREATHE ON ME!**  In Germany, spadefoot toads are called the "Knoblauchskrote", or "garlic toads", because of the smelly substance they give off!

**DON'T TOUCH ME!**  Deadly "poison-arrow" frogs from Central and South America include the golden-dart frog, which has enough poison to kill 1,000 people!

## FACTASTIC FROGS

**WHEN IS A FROG A TOAD?**  It is not always easy to distinguish between frogs and toads. Frogs tend to live in water, while toads live on land and breed in water. Technically they all belong to the genus *Rana*, so are all frogs!

**GIGANTIC EGGS**  The male red-eyed tree frog (*Agalychnis callidryas*) is half the size of the female, but her egg cluster is bigger than both of them!

**MALE MIDWIFE**  The male European midwife frog carries 35–50 eggs wrapped around his hind legs. After three weeks, he takes them into the water to hatch.

**LARGE LARVA**  The tadpoles of the paradoxical frog (*Pseudis paradoxus*), from Trinidad and the Amazon, can be 25 cm (10 in) long – three times bigger than the frogs they turn into, which are rarely more than 7.6 cm (3 in).

**SEE-THROUGH FROGS**  Some frogs, such as the African lesser banana frog (*Megalixalus stuhlmanni*), have such transparent flesh that you can see their bones through it.

**THROATY NOISES**  The white-lipped frog, that lives in the Puerto Rican rainforests, communicates by thumping the ground with its throat pouch. This is detected by other frogs up to 5.5 m (18 ft) away.

## FUNNY FROG AND TOAD NAMES

Many frogs have strange common and Latin names:

| COMMON NAME | LATIN NAME |
| --- | --- |
| Catholic frog | *Notaden bennetti* |
| Cricket frog | *Acris gryllus gryllus* |
| Fire-bellied toad | *Bombina bombina* |
| Little green toad | *Bufo debilis* |
| Meadow frog | *Rana pipiens pipiens* |
| Mountain chicken | *Leptodactylus fallax* |
| Mountain chorus frog | *Pseudacris brachyphora* |
| Oregon red-legged frog | *Rana aurora aurora* |
| Peeper | *Hyla crucifer crucifer* |
| Texan cliff frog | *Eleutherodactylus latrans* |
| Warty frog | *Rana tuberculosa* |

## LEAP FROGS

**BEST JUMPER**  Cricket frogs leap 36 times their own length: if a human did this, the record could be 65.8 m (216 ft).

**WORST JUMPER**  The tiny greenhouse frog jumps less than 13 cm (5 in).

## FROG AND TOAD SOUNDS

Not all frogs and toads "ribbit" – according to the American Audubon Society, which, in 1975, published a report to identify frog and toad sounds.

| FROG/TOAD | SOUND |
| --- | --- |
| American toad | Trilling |
| Fowler's toad | Nasal bleat |
| Green frog | Like a plucked banjo string |
| Grey tree frog | Short, harsh trill |
| Leopard and pickerel frogs | Resembles snoring |
| Spring peeper | Like sleigh bells |
| Wood frog | Creaky clatter |

**HAVE YOU EVER HEARD…?**
The carpenter frog, which sounds like a carpenter hammering nails, the pig frog, which grunts like pigs, or the sheep frog, which resembles bleating sheep?

## LIZARD FACTS

**COLOUR CHANGE** Chameleons such as the Parson's chameleon change colour to hide themselves from predators or to show their mood.

**LONG TONGUE** A chameleon has a sticky tongue as long as its body and tail together!

**SMALLEST LIZARD** The Virgin Island gecko is just 18 mm (0.7 in) in length.

**BIGGEST LIZARD** Komodo Dragons, from Indonesia, can grow up to 3 m (10 ft) long.

**WALKING ON WATER** To escape predators, basilisk lizards drop onto water and run across the surface!

## HEAVIEST TURTLES AND TORTOISES

| TURTLE/TORTOISE | MAXIMUM WEIGHT | |
| --- | --- | --- |
| | KG | LB |
| Pacific leatherback turtle | 865 | 1,908 |
| Atlantic leatherback turtle | 454 | 1,000 |
| Green sea turtle | 408 | 900 |
| Aldabra giant tortoise | 408 | 900 |
| Loggerhead turtle | 386 | 850 |
| Galápagos giant tortoise | 385 | 849 |

**DID YOU KNOW?** Aldabra giant tortoises may live 50 years and are probably the longest-lived of their kind!

## TERRIFIC TURTLES

**PREHISTORIC MONSTER** All living turtles would be dwarfed in size by prehistoric monster turtles, such as *Stupendemys geographicus*, which were 3 m (10 ft) long and weighed more than 2,040 kg (4,497 lb).

**EGG DELAY** Some female turtles produce eggs four years after mating!

**TURTLES IN DANGER** In 1947, 40,000 Kemp's Ridley turtles laid eggs on their nesting beach in Mexico. By the mid 1990s, hunting had reduced numbers to less than 5,000.

**DID YOU KNOW?** This harmless Sinaloan milk snake looks like the poisonous coral snake – so predators keep away!

## AMAZING ALLIGATORS AND CROCODILES

**LARGEST CROCODILE** The saltwater crocodile measures up to 10 m (33 ft) long! As well as being the largest, it is the most dangerous of all crocodiles.

**SMALLEST CROCODILE** South America's dwarf caimans hardly ever grow more than 1.5 m (5 ft) long.

**STONE SWALLOWERS** Crocodiles swallow stones! These accumulate in the stomach and help the animal to remain submerged under the water.

**SUPER-SHARP TEETH** Crocodiles and alligators have sharp, pointed teeth for tearing prey apart. As they wear, new teeth appear – as many as 50 new sets in a lifetime.

## LONGEST SNAKES

| SNAKE | MAXIMUM LENGTH | |
| --- | --- | --- |
| | M | FT |
| Reticulated python | 10.7 | 35 |
| Anaconda | 8.5 | 28 |
| Indian python | 7.6 | 25 |
| Diamond python | 6.4 | 21 |
| King cobra | 5.8 | 19 |
| Boa constrictor | 4.9 | 16 |
| Bushmaster | 3.7 | 12 |
| Giant brown snake | 3.4 | 11 |
| Diamondback rattlesnake | 2.7 | 9 |
| Indigo or gopher snake | 2.4 | 8 |

**DID YOU KNOW?** Reports of monster 36.5-m (120-ft) anacondas have been published, but there is no evidence to prove this. Even so, an 8-m (25-ft) anaconda can eat a 2-m (6-ft) caiman; digesting it takes a week!

## TWELVE DEADLY SNAKES

The world's most dangerous snakes, listed here, are all from the poisonous Elapidae family of reptiles, except the rattlesnake, which belongs to Viperidae.

| SNAKE | FOUND IN | DEATH RATE % |
| --- | --- | --- |
| Black mamba | Africa | 95–100 |
| Common krait | Asia | 77–93 |
| Russell's viper | Asia | 30–65 |
| Taipan | Australia | 25–50 |
| Indian cobra | Asia | 33 |
| Cape cobra | Africa | 25 |
| Egyptian cobra | Africa/Asia | unknown |
| Multibanded krait | Asia | unknown |
| King cobra | Asia | 18 |
| Green mamba | Africa | unknown |
| Tropical rattlesnake | C./S. America | 15–25 |
| Tiger snake | Australia | 20 |

**DID YOU KNOW?** The Black mamba, from parts of Africa, is not only a vicious killer, but it is reputed to be the fastest-moving land snake. It is capable of chasing after prey at 14–19 km/h (10–12 mph).

# EXTINCT and ENDANGERED

## MOST ENDANGERED ANIMALS

**YANGTZE RIVER DOLPHIN** Pollution has reduced the number of river dolphins in China to less than 200.

**SIBERIAN TIGER** Hunted for their fur and body parts, tigers are becoming increasingly rare. There are only between 250 and 400 Siberian tigers remaining in their natural habitat.

**MONK SEAL** There are now fewer than 400 Mediterranean monk seals. Their habitats have been polluted by oil, sewage, and industrial chemicals, making survival difficult.

**MOUNTAIN GORILLA** Only 400 gorillas remain in central Africa. Destruction of their forest habitat and hunting to supply the trade in body parts have led to declining numbers.

**GIANT PANDA** There are only about 1,000 pandas left in China. As their forest habitat is destroyed, their supply of food and shelter is reduced.

**JAVAN RHINOCEROS** Only about 70 rhinoceros are left in Java, Indonesia. Their habitat is being destroyed and they are hunted for their tusks.

**BLUE WHALE** About 9,000 blue whales swim in the world's oceans, but they are hunted for trade and suffer from pollution in the oceans.

**ASIAN ELEPHANT** Although 34,000–50,000 elephants remain in Southeast Asia, India, and China, their numbers are rapidly decreasing due to hunting for their ivory tusks, and the destruction of their habitat for farmland and buildings.

**JAGUAR** Poachers hunt the jaguar and its relation, the ocelot, for their attractive, spotted coats. These are then made into coats, shoes, or bags. Most of this killing is illegal, but while demand for these goods is high, it will continue.

**PAMPAS DEER** Large herds once grazed on the pampas of South America, but the introduction of farm mammals has drastically reduced the number of pampas deer.

**KAKAPO** This flightless bird from New Zealand has become endangered because animals such as cats, rats, stoats, and ferrets eat their eggs and young.

 **DID YOU KNOW?** This black rhinoceros is very agile, and despite its hefty weight, it can gallop at 48 km/h (30 mph)!

## THREATS TO WILDLIFE

**HABITAT DESTRUCTION** More and more land is being claimed by humans for planting crops and building settlements and roads.

**POACHING** Many animals are killed for their skins, horns or tusks, and bones. Animal body parts are used in some traditional medicines.

**POLLUTION** Industry and farming can poison wildlife. Chemical spills, drainage, and acid rain can kill river wildlife. Farming pesticides can upset the natural balance and the habitat's food chains.

**NON-NATIVE SPECIES** When humans introduce new animals to a habitat, competition can lead to the demise of some species.

## HOW RARE?

Listed below are the first in a range of categories in which the International Union for the Conservation of Nature places the species of animals and plants that it considers under threat.

**EXTINCT** Used when there are no definite reports of species of animals or plants for 50 years.

**ENDANGERED** Describes species of animals or plants that are in danger of extinction.

**VULNERABLE** Species likely to become endangered unless threats can be removed.

**RARE** Used to describe species that are at risk through low numbers, but are not yet endangered.

**THREATENED** A term for species that are under threat in various different ways.

**COMMERCIALLY THREATENED** Describes species whose survival is threatened by exploitation for commercial purposes.

## EXTINCT ANCIENT ANIMALS

**SABRE-TOOTHED CAT** Also called *Smilodon*, the sabre-toothed cat of North and South America was one of the most ferocious carnivores. It had 15-cm (6-in) front teeth to slice through flesh.

**WOOLLY MAMMOTH** The woolly mammoth lived during the Ice Age in the cold tundra of North America, Europe, and Asia. It stood 3 m (10 ft) tall at the shoulder and had huge ivory tusks.

**FIRST BIRD** *Archaeopteryx* lived 150 million years ago. It is recognized as the first bird, evolving from a small group of meat-eating dinosaurs.

## DINOSAUR RECORDS

**FASTEST CARNIVORE** Coelurosaurs could travel at about 40 km/h (25 mph) when chasing prey.

**LARGEST EGG** Just one of the giant eggs laid by *Hypselosaurus* was about the same volume as 60 chickens' eggs!

**LARGEST BRAIN** Small, speedy meat eaters, such as *Troodon*, had the largest brain in proportion to their size, but were not necessarily the most intelligent.

**SMALLEST BRAIN** *Stegosaurus* had a brain smaller than a walnut.

**SMALLEST CARNIVORE** The tiny, chicken-sized *Compsognathus* was less than 70 cm (28 in) long.

**LARGEST CLAWS** *Therizinosaurus* had the largest claws known, measuring about 90 cm (35 in) long!

**SMALLEST EVER FOUND** *Mussaurus* was only 20 cm (8 in) long. However, because only one skeleton was found, dinosaur experts think that it could have been a hatchling.

**LARGEST FOOTPRINT** Footprints made by a duck-billed dinosaur were 1.3 m (4.25 ft) long and 80 cm (31 in) wide.

**LONGEST SKELETON** The longest complete skeleton found is that of *Diplodocus*, a long-necked sauropod that grew to 26 m (85.25 ft) long. As many as 50 people could stand side by side next to *Diplodocus*!

**BEST DEFENCE** *Ankylosaurus* had a hard bone at the end of its tail that could be swung at an enemy to keep it away.

**LONGEST TAIL** *Barosaurus* had the longest tail, measuring 13 m (43 ft)!

---

**! DID YOU KNOW?**
*Tyrannosaurus rex* had a gigantic mouth, full of huge, serrated teeth, each measuring up to 18 cm (7 in) in length!

---

## DINOSAUR NAMES

**1824** *Megalosaurus*, meaning "great lizard" was named by William Buckland (1784–1856).

**1825** Gideon Mantell (1790–1852), a doctor with an interest in the study of geology, named *Iguanodon*, meaning Iguana tooth, after finding the first *Iguanodon* teeth in 1822. It was among a pile of stones used for road repairs!

**1841** Richard Owen (1804–1892) named *Cladeiodon*, or "branch tooth", and *Cetiosaurus*, meaning "whale lizard", in the same year.

**1850** Gideon Mantell named *Pelorosaurus*, or "monstrous lizard".

**1856** Joseph Leidy (1823–1891) named five dinosaurs in one year, the first being *Deinodon*, or "terrible tooth".

---

**! DID YOU KNOW?**
The carnosaur *Tyrannosaurus rex* was the largest land-based carnivore ever to have walked the Earth, at 14 m (46 ft) long!

---

## LAST SEEN ALIVE

**AUROCHS 1627** This giant wild ox was last recorded in central Europe, after the need for more farmland in western Europe pushed its habitat eastwards. The creature was extensively hunted, and the last died in Jaktorow Forest in Poland.

**AEPYORNIS 1649** Also known as the "elephant bird", the 3-m (10-ft) wingless creature was once a native of the island of Madagascar.

**DODO 1681** Unable to fly and easy to tame, the dodo (meaning "stupid" in Portuguese) was extensively collected by Europeans who discovered it in 1768. British naturalist Benjamin Harry saw the last dodo alive on the island of Mauritius, in the Indian Ocean, in 1681.

**STELLER'S SEA COW 1768** This large marine mammal, one of the creatures that gave rise to the legend of the mermaid, was hunted to extinction.

**PASSENGER PIGEON 1914** The last passenger pigeon, Martha, died aged 29 in Cincinnati Zoo, USA.

---

## LARGEST DINOSAURS EVER DISCOVERED

| YEAR | NAME | DIET | WEIGHT | | LENGTH | |
|------|------|------|--------|--|--------|--|
| | | | TONNES | TONS | M | FT |
| 1985 | *Seismosaurus* | Plants | 56–89 | 55–88 | 30–36 | 98–119 |
| 1972 | *Supersaurus* | Plants | 56 | 55 | 24–30 | 80–100 |
| 1929 | *Antarctosaurus* | Plants | 45–56 | 44–55 | 18–30 | 60–98 |
| 1890 | *Barosaurus* | Plants | Uncertain | | 23–27.5 | 75–90 |

**! DID YOU KNOW?** The dinosaur *Barosaurus* was named "heavy lizard" by US palaeontologist Othniel C. Marsh in 1890. Archaeologists have found its remains in both North America and Africa, proving the existence of a land link between the two continents in Jurassic times, some 205–140 million years ago.

# SCIENCE

## SCIENCE FACTS

### MILESTONES OF SCIENCE

**c.400 BC** Greek philosophers Epicurus and Democritus suggest that matter is made of particles called atoms.

**c.350 BC** Aristotle's study and classification of living things dominates scientific thinking for centuries.

**c.260 BC** Greek scientist Archimedes (287–212 BC) devises the principles of mechanics and invents many devices.

**c.2 BC** Early chemists attempt to turn metals to gold.

**1638** Galileo Galilei (1564–1642) founds mechanics and is the first to use a telescope to explore the planets.

**1661** Robert Boyle (1627–1691) uses theory of moving particles to explain chemical reactions.

**1661** Isaac Newton (1642–1727) develops laws of motion and gravitation.

**1779** Italian physicist Alexander Volta (1745–1827) invents the battery.

**1803** British chemist and physicist John Dalton (1766–1844) proposes modern atomic theory, developing Greek thought.

**1869** Dmitri Mendeleyev (1834–1907) devises the Periodic Table of elements.

**1888** German physicist Heinrich Hertz (1857–1894) creates radio waves.

**1905** Albert Einstein (1879–1955) writes his relativity theories.

**1938** Enrico Fermi (1901–1954) builds a nuclear reactor.

**1960** Laser is invented by Theodore Maiman (b.1927).

### FAMOUS SCIENTISTS

**ISAAC NEWTON (1642–1727)** Developed three laws of motion, a law of gravitation, and made discoveries in light and maths.

**HENRY CAVENDISH (1731–1810)** Discovered hydrogen in 1766.

**WILLIAM HERSCHEL (1738–1822)** Discovered infra-red waves in 1800. He also discovered Uranus and many stars.

**ANTOINE LAVOISIER (1743–1794)** Named oxygen in 1779. Named some of the components of air and water.

**HUMPHREY DAVY (1778–1829)** Discovered potassium, sodium, magnesium, barium, calcium, and strontium during 1807–1808.

**JAMES JOULE (1818–1889)** In 1843, he formulated the relationship between heat, power, and work.

**LOUIS PASTEUR (1822–1895)** Pioneered a rabies vaccine and the pasteurization process.

**JOSEPH LISTER (1827– 1912)** First to use carbolic acid as an antiseptic.

**MAX PLANCK (1858–1947)** Proposed his quantum theory in 1900, stating that energy consists of small units called "quanta".

**MARIE CURIE (1867–1934)** Pioneer of research into radioactivity. She also discovered the elements polonium and radium.

**ALBERT EINSTEIN (1879–1955)** Published the special and general theory of relativity which forms the basis of our ideas about the Universe.

**ALEXANDER FLEMING (1881–1955)** Discovered penicillin in 1928. It was first used in World War II.

### FIELDS OF SCIENCE

**ASTRONOMY** The study of the nature and movement of the objects in the Universe: planets, moons, comets, asteroids, stars, and galaxies.

**BIOLOGY** The study of plants and animals and how they grow, feed, reproduce, and evolve.

**CHEMISTRY** The study of the basic substances, or elements, that are found in the Universe, and how they combine to form complex substances called compounds.

**COSMOLOGY** The study of the structure and origin of the Universe.

**ECOLOGY** The study of the relationships between organisms and their environment.

**ELECTRONICS** A science that deals with electrical signals.

**GENETICS** The study of the genes in the human body and the way that characteristics are inherited.

**GEOLOGY** The study of the shape and structure of the Earth and its physical features.

**MATHEMATICS** The study of numbers, shapes, and quantities.

**MEDICINE** The study of the illnesses and diseases that affect the human body and the search for non-surgical prevention, relief, and cures.

**METEOROLOGY** The study of the weather and the Earth's atmosphere.

**PHYSICS** Investigates energy and matter, the material from which everything is made.

**PHYSIOLOGY** The study of how living organisms and their parts work.

**TECHNOLOGY** The science in which scientific discoveries are put to practical use.

## MATTER FACTS

**LOWEST MELTING POINT** Since Mercury melts at -38.9°C (-38°F), it is liquid at room temperature. Mercury is used in thermometers because it expands as it is heated.

**HIGHEST MELTING POINT** The temperature must be 3,652°C (6,606°F) before carbon will melt – two-thirds as hot as the sun's surface.

**RAREST ELEMENTS** Astatine is the rarest element on Earth; rhodium is the scarcest metal in the world – just 3 tonnes (2.9 tons) are mined every year.

**HEAVIEST METAL** A 33-cm³ (13-in³) cube of osmium weighs 640 kg (1,411 lb) – equivalent to ten people each weighing 64 kg (141 lb), or a small car!

**DID YOU KNOW?** At 0°C (32°F) water becomes solid (ice). Above 100°C (212°F) it turns to gas (steam).

## NEWTON'S LAWS OF MOTION

In 1661, the English physicist developed three laws describing motion:

**FIRST LAW** An object will remain still or continue to travel at the same velocity unless a force acts on it.

**SECOND LAW** The acceleration of an object depends upon its mass and the amount of force acting on it.

**THIRD LAW** When two forces act on each other, they experience equal forces in opposite directions.

## ATOMIC TERMS

**ATOM** The smallest part of an element that can exist. Its nucleus contains protons and neutrons, surrounded by electrons. Everything is made of atoms.

**ELEMENT** A substance in its purest form – it cannot be broken down any further.

**ELECTRON** A particle with a negative electric charge. Found in all atoms.

**NEUTRON** A particle in the nucleus of an atom which has no electric charge.

**PROTON** A particle in the nucleus of an atom with a positive charge.

**NUCLEUS** This is the centre of an atom, and contains protons and neutrons.

**ATOMIC NUMBER** The number of protons in the nucleus of an atom.

**ATOMIC MASS** The mass of an atom in relation to that of a carbon-12 atom.

**DID YOU KNOW?** A proton is about 2,000 times heavier than an electron!

## ELECTRICITY AND ELECTRONICS FACTS

**ELECTRICITY** The name comes from the Greek word "elektron", meaning "amber". The Greeks noticed that when amber was rubbed with a cloth, static electricity made small objects stick to it.

**AMAZING MICROCHIPS** In 1950, nine million transistors would have covered eight football fields. By 1994, this many transistors could be fitted into a single microchip the size of a fingernail!

**ELECTRONICS IN YOUR LIFE** Everyday equipment that relies on electronics to work includes: calculators, car controls, cameras, washing machines, medical scanners, mobile telephones, radar systems, and computers.

**FIBRE-OPTIC CABLES** These very fine cables carry more data than copper ones, transmitting information in light pulses.

**AMAZING FACT!** Computer performance has increased by a factor of one million between 1950 and 1990!

## ACIDS AND ALKALIS

The acid or alkali (or base) content of a substance is measured in pH (potential Hydrogen) on a scale of 0–14. Acids dissolve in water to form sharp-tasting solutions, like lemon juice. Alkalis dissolve in water to form soapy solutions.

| SUBSTANCE | | pH |
|---|---|---|
| Hydrochloric acid | (Acid) | 0 |
| Car battery acid | | 1.0 |
| Lemon juice | | 2.4 |
| Apple | | 3.0 |
| Vinegar | | 4.0 |
| Rainwater | | 5.6 |
| Milk | | 6.6 |
| Pure water | (Neutral) | 7.0 |
| Human blood | | 7.4 |
| Sea water | | 7–8 |
| Baking soda | | 8.5 |
| Ammonia | | 12.0 |
| Caustic Soda | (Alkali) | 14.0 |

## SOUND LEVELS

The decibel (dB) measures sound. Every 10 dB is a tenfold increase in intensity.

| SOUND | dB |
|---|---|
| Silence | 0 |
| Rustle of leaves | 10 |
| Normal conversation, soft music | 30 |
| Quiet countryside, ticking watch | 40 |
| Restaurant, office | 50–60 |
| Busy traffic, loud television | 70 |
| Inside car, underground train | 80 |
| Very loud snore | 88 |
| Roaring lion | 90 |
| Lawnmower, chainsaw, blender | 100 |
| Powerful rock music | 100 |
| Rocket taking off | 130 |

## COLOURS OF THE SPECTRUM

Red • Orange • Yellow • Green • Blue • Indigo • Violet

**MEMORY TIP!** Richard Of York Gained Battles In Vain

# THE ELEMENTS

WHAT'S AN ATOMIC NUMBER?  Every element has a different atomic number, which is the number of protons in the nucleus of one atom of the element.

| ELEMENT | SYMBOL | ATOMIC NUMBER | DISCOVERER | COUNTRY | DATE | DESCRIPTION AND USES |
|---|---|---|---|---|---|---|
| Actinium | Ac | 89 | André Debierne | France | 1899 | Soft silvery radioactive metal: nuclear research |
| Aluminium | Al | 13 | Hans Christian Oersted | Denmark | 1825 | Light silvery metal: aircraft, cars, drink cans, foil |
| Americium | Am | 95 | Glen Seaborg & team | USA | 1945 | Silvery radioactive metal: radiography |
| Antimony | Sb | 51 | Unknown | Unknown | c.1600 BC | Silvery metal: batteries, machine bearings |
| Argon | Ar | 18 | W. Ramsay/Baron Rayleigh | UK | 1894 | Colourless gas: used in metal-making, lamps |
| Arsenic | As | 33 | Albertus Magnus | Germany | c.1250 | Grey poisonous metal: alloys, pesticides, glass-making |
| Astatine | At | 85 | D. R. Corson & team | USA | 1940 | Radioactive non-metal: no practical uses |
| Barium | Ba | 56 | Sir Humphry Davy | UK | 1808 | Soft, silvery-white metal: clinical body imaging |
| Berkelium | Bk | 97 | Glen Seaborg & team | USA | 1949 | Silvery radioactive metal: nuclear research |
| Beryllium | Be | 4 | F. Wöhler/A. A. Bussy | Germany/France | 1828 | Soft, silvery-white metal: alloys for tools |
| Bismuth | Bi | 83 | Unknown | Unknown | c.1500 | Silvery metal: electronics, chemicals, cosmetics |
| Bohrium | Bh | 107 | Peter Armbruster & team | Germany | 1981 | Radioactive metal: no practical uses |
| Boron | B | 5 | Sir Humphry Davy | UK | 1808 | Dark powder: glass, detergents, fireproofing |
| Bromine | Br | 35 | A. Balard/C. Löwig | France/Germany | 1826 | Red liquid: fuel additives, pesticides, photography |
| Cadmium | Cd | 48 | Friedrich Stromeyer | Germany | 1817 | Silvery metal: batteries |
| Caesium | Cs | 55 | Gustav Kirchhoff | Germany | 1860 | Gold metal: glass, radiation equipment |
| Calcium | Ca | 20 | Sir Humphry Davy | UK | 1808 | Soft silvery-white metal: water treating, cement |
| Californium | Cf | 98 | Glen Seaborg & team | USA | 1950 | Silvery radioactive metal: cancer treatment, mining |
| Carbon | C | 6 | Unknown | Unknown | Ancient | Various forms (graphite, diamonds, coal): many uses |
| Cerium | Ce | 58 | Wilhelm Hisinger & team | Sweden | 1803 | Grey metal: alloys, glass, ceramics, lighter flints |
| Chlorine | Cl | 17 | Carl Scheele | Sweden | 1774 | Grey-yellow gas: purifying water |
| Chromium | Cr | 24 | Nicolas-Louis Vauquelin | France | 1797 | Hard blue-white metal: chrome plating |
| Cobalt | Co | 27 | Georg Brandt | Sweden | 1735–39 | Silvery-blue metal: magnets, ceramics, paints |
| Copper | Cu | 29 | Unknown | Unknown | c.5000 BC | Reddish metal: electrical wires, pipes, coins |
| Curium | Cm | 96 | Glen Seaborg & team | USA | 1944 | Silvery radioactive metal: no common uses |
| Dubnium | Db | 105 | Russian/US teams | Russia/USA | 1970 | Radioactive metal: no common uses |
| Dysprosium | Dy | 66 | Paul de Boisbaudran | France | 1886 | Silvery metal: alloys and magnets |
| Einsteinium | Es | 99 | Albert Ghiorso & team | USA | 1952 | Radioactive metal: no practical uses |
| Erbium | Er | 68 | Carl Mosander | Sweden | 1842 | Silvery metal: glass and alloys |
| Europium | Eu | 63 | Eugène Demarcay | France | 1901 | Soft silvery metal: minor uses in alloys |
| Fermium | Fm | 100 | Albert Ghiorso & team | USA | 1953 | Radioactive metal: no practical uses |
| Fluorine | F | 9 | Henri Moissan | France | 1886 | Pale yellow gas: metal-making, drugs |
| Francium | Fr | 87 | Marguerite Perey | France | 1939 | Radioactive metal: no common uses |
| Gadolinium | Gd | 64 | Jean de Marignac | Switzerland | 1880 | Soft silvery metal: alloys used in electronics |
| Gallium | Ga | 31 | Paul de Boisbaudran | France | 1875 | Soft silvery metal: electronics |
| Germanium | Ge | 32 | Clemens Winkler | Germany | 1886 | Silvery metal: electronics and glass |
| Gold | Au | 79 | Unknown | Unknown | c.3000 BC | Shiny yellow metal: jewellery |
| Hafnium | Hf | 72 | Dirk Coster & team | Denmark | 1923 | Silvery metal: nuclear industry, alloys, ceramics |
| Hassium | Hs | 108 | Peter Armbruster & team | Germany | 1984 | Radioactive metal: no practical uses |
| Helium | He | 2 | W. Ramsay & team | UK | 1895 | Light colourless gas: balloons and diving |
| Holmium | Ho | 67 | Per Cleve & team | Sweden | 1878 | Silvery metal: magnetic equipment |
| Hydrogen | H | 1 | Henry Cavendish | UK | 1766 | Lightest gas: was used in balloons, now chemicals |
| Indium | In | 49 | F. Reich/H. Richter | Germany | 1863 | Silvery metal: electronics |
| Iodine | I | 53 | Bernard Courtois | France | 1811 | Black solid: medicines, dyes, photography |
| Iridium | Ir | 77 | Smithson Tennant | UK | 1804 | Hard silvery metal: alloys, spark plugs |
| Iron | Fe | 26 | Unknown | Unknown | c.2500 BC | Silvery metal: has many uses, as steel |
| Krypton | Kr | 36 | W. Ramsay/M. Travers | UK | 1898 | Colourless gas: no practical uses |
| Lanthanum | La | 57 | Carl Mosander | Sweden | 1839 | Soft silvery-white metal: optical glass, flints |
| Lawrencium | Lr | 103 | Albert Ghiorso & team | USA | 1961 | Radioactive metal: no practical uses |
| Lead | Pb | 82 | Unknown | Unknown | c.1000 BC | Soft grey metal: batteries, solder, glass |
| Lithium | Li | 3 | Johann Arfvedson | Sweden | 1817 | Light metal: alloys, greases, batteries |
| Lutetium | Lu | 71 | Georges Urbain | France | 1907 | Hard metal: used only in chemical research |
| Magnesium | Mg | 12 | Sir Humphry Davy | UK | 1808 | Silvery-white metal: alloys, fireworks, electrical uses |
| Manganese | Mn | 25 | Johan Gahn | Sweden | 1774 | Brittle silvery metal: steel, ceramics, fertilizers |
| Meiterium | Mt | 109 | Peter Armbruster & team | Germany | 1982 | Radioactive metal: no practical uses |

# THE RAREST METAL IS RHODIUM – JUST 3 TONNES (2.9 TONS) ARE PRODUCED EACH YEAR

| ELEMENT | SYMBOL | ATOMIC NUMBER | DISCOVERER | COUNTRY | DATE | DESCRIPTION AND USES |
|---|---|---|---|---|---|---|
| Mendelevium | Md | 101 | Glen Seaborg & team | USA | 1955 | Radioactive metal: no practical uses |
| Mercury | Hg | 80 | Unknown | Unknown | c.1500 BC | Liquid silvery metal: thermometers, street lights |
| Molybdenum | Mo | 42 | Carl Scheele | Sweden | 1778 | Silvery metal: alloys and electrical uses |
| Neodymium | Nd | 60 | Carl Auer | Austria | 1885 | Silvery-white metal: lasers, magnets, glass |
| Neon | Ne | 10 | W. Ramsay/M. Travers | UK | 1898 | Colourless gas: neon lighting |
| Neptunium | Np | 93 | E. McMillan/P. Abelson | USA | 1940 | Silvery radioactive metal: nuclear research |
| Nickel | Ni | 28 | Axel Cronstedt | Sweden | 1751 | Silvery-white metal: alloys, coins, metal-plating |
| Niobium | Nb | 41 | Charles Hatchett | UK | 1801 | Silvery metal: stainless steel |
| Nitrogen | N | 7 | Daniel Rutherford | UK | 1772 | Colourless gas: fertilizers, explosives, plastics |
| Nobelium | No | 102 | Albert Ghiorso & team | USA | 1958 | Radioactive metal: no practical uses |
| Osmium | Os | 76 | Smithson Tennant | UK | 1804 | Heavy silvery metal: alloys and catalysts |
| Oxygen | O | 8 | J. Priestley/C. Scheele | UK/Sweden | 1774 | Colourless gas: medicine, chemicals, steel-making |
| Palladium | Pd | 46 | William Wollaston | UK | 1803 | Silvery-white metal: catalysts |
| Phosphorus | P | 15 | Hennig Brand | Germany | 1669 | White and red versions: fertilizers, foods, detergents |
| Platinum | Pt | 78 | Julius Caesar Scalgier | Italy | 1557 | Silvery-white metal: jewellery, cancer drugs, catalysts |
| Plutonium | Pu | 94 | Glen Seaborg & team | USA | 1940 | Silvery radioactive metal: nuclear weapons and fuel |
| Polonium | Po | 84 | Pierre & Marie Curie | France | 1898 | Silvery radioactive metal: nuclear research, satellites |
| Potassium | K | 19 | Sir Humphry Davy | UK | 1807 | Soft white metal: fertilizers, chemicals, glass |
| Praseodymium | Pr | 59 | Carl Auer | Austria | 1885 | Soft silvery metal: magnets, protective glass |
| Promethium | Pm | 61 | J. A. Marinsky & team | USA | 1945 | Radioactive metal: miniature batteries |
| Protactinium | Pa | 91 | O. Hahn/F. Soddy & team | Germany/UK | 1917 | Silvery radioactive metal: no practical uses |
| Radium | Ra | 88 | Pierre & Marie Curie | France | 1898 | Soft silvery radioactive metal: once used for cancer |
| Radon | Rn | 86 | Friedrich Dorn | Germany | 1900 | Colourless radioactive gas: sometimes used for cancer |
| Rhenium | Re | 75 | Walter Noddack & team | Germany | 1925 | Silvery metal: aero engines, lightbulbs, catalysts |
| Rhodium | Rh | 45 | William Wollaston | UK | 1803 | Hard silvery metal: catalysts |
| Rubidium | Rb | 37 | R. Bunsen/G. Kirschoff | Germany | 1861 | Soft white metal: no practical uses |
| Ruthenium | Ru | 44 | Karl Klaus | Russia | 1844 | Silvery metal: alloys, catalysts |
| Rutherfordium | Rf | 104 | Russian/US teams | Russia/USA | 1969 | Radioactive metal: no practical uses |
| Samarium | Sm | 62 | Paul de Boisbaudran | France | 1879 | Silvery-white metal: glass, catalysts, electronics |
| Scandium | Sc | 21 | Lars Nilson | Sweden | 1879 | Soft silvery-white metal: powerful lights |
| Seaborgium | Sg | 106 | Albert Ghiorso & team | USA | 1974 | Radioactive metal: no practical uses |
| Selenium | Se | 34 | Jöns Berzelius | Sweden | 1817 | Silvery metal/red powder: photocopiers |
| Silicon | Si | 14 | Jöns Berzelius | Sweden | 1823 | Blue-grey crystals: semiconductors, alloys |
| Silver | Ag | 47 | Unknown | Unknown | c.3000 BC | Soft metal: silverware, jewellery, photography |
| Sodium | Na | 11 | Sir Humphry Davy | UK | 1807 | Soft silvery-white metal: industrial/nuclear processes |
| Strontium | Sr | 38 | A. Crawford | UK | 1790 | Silvery-white metal: glass for computer screens |
| Sulphur | S | 16 | Unknown | Unknown | Ancient | Yellow powder (and other forms): chemicals |
| Tantalum | Ta | 73 | Anders Ekberg | Sweden | 1802 | Shiny silver metal: electronics, cutting tools |
| Technetium | Tc | 43 | C. Perrier/E. Segrè | Italy | 1937 | Radioactive metal: no practical uses |
| Tellurium | Te | 52 | Franz Müller | Romania | 1782 | Silvery-white semi-metal: alloys, electronics |
| Terbium | Tb | 65 | Carl Mosander | Sweden | 1843 | Silvery metal: electronics, lasers |
| Thallium | Tl | 81 | Sir William Crookes | UK | 1861 | Soft silvery-white metal: glass-making |
| Thorium | Th | 90 | Jöns Berzelius | Sweden | 1828 | Silvery radioactive metal: nuclear industry, gas mantles |
| Thulium | Tm | 69 | Per Cleve | Sweden | 1879 | Silvery metal: X-ray machines |
| Tin | Sn | 50 | Unknown | Unknown | c.2100 BC | Soft silvery-white metal: tinplate, alloys |
| Titanium | Ti | 22 | William Gregor | UK | 1791 | Hard silvery metal: alloys, hip replacement joints |
| Tungsten | W | 74 | Fausto & Juan de Elhuyar | Spain | 1783 | Silvery-white metal: alloys, cutting tools, light bulbs |
| Ununbium | Uub | 112 | Peter Armbruster & team | Germany | 1996 | Radioactive metal: no practical uses |
| Ununnilium | Uun | 110 | Peter Armbruster & team | Germany | 1994 | Radioactive metal: no practical uses |
| Unununium | Uuu | 111 | Peter Armbruster & team | Germany | 1994 | Radioactive metal: no practical uses |
| Uranium | U | 92 | Martin Klaproth | Germany | 1789 | Silvery radioactive metal: nuclear fuel and weapons |
| Vanadium | V | 23 | Nils Selfström | Sweden | 1830 | Silvery metal: alloys |
| Xenon | Xe | 54 | W. Ramsay/M. Travers | UK | 1898 | Colourless gas: few practical uses |
| Ytterbium | Yb | 70 | Jean de Marignac | Switzerland | 1878 | Soft silvery-white metal: stress gauges, few other uses |
| Yttrium | Y | 39 | Johan Gadolin | Finland | 1794 | Soft silvery-white metal: TV screens, X-rays, alloys |
| Zinc | Zn | 30 | Andreas Marggraf | Germany | 1746 | Bluish-white metal: galvanizing, batteries, in brass |
| Zirconium | Zr | 40 | Martin Klaproth | Germany | 1789 | Hard silvery metal: alloys, nuclear reactors |

**DID YOU KNOW?** Besides the 112 elements listed here, there are another six unnamed elements – numbers 113–118 – that exist theoretically, but have not yet been synthesized.

**DID YOU KNOW?** The elements are often arranged as a Periodic Table. The first person to set them out in this way was Russian chemist Dmitri Mendeleyev (1834–1907).

# MATHEMATICS

## MATHEMATICAL SYMBOLS

| SYMBOL | MEANING | SYMBOL | MEANING |
|--------|---------|--------|---------|
| + | Plus or positive | < | Less than |
| - | Minus or negative | ≤ | Equal or less than |
| ± | Plus or minus, positive or negative | ≥ | Equal or greater than |
| x | Multiplied by | ~ | Of the order of, similar to |
| ÷ or / | Divided by | √ | Square root |
| % | Per cent | Σ | Sum of |
| = | Equal to | π | Pi |
| ≠ | Not equal to | ° | Degree |
| > | Greater than | ∞ | Infinity |

## FAMOUS MATHEMATICIANS

**PYTHAGORAS** The Greek mathematician, Pythagoras (c.580–500 BC) is remembered for his theories on trigonometry. His most-used theorem is named after him.

**EUCLID** One of the founders of geometry, the Greek theorist Euclid (c.300 BC) wrote a 13-volume book, *The Elements*, in which he detailed the main geometric shapes.

**NAPIER** Scotsman John Napier (1550–1617) is best-known for inventing logarithms. Many mathematicians have used logarithms to devise new theories.

**NEWTON** Famous for his laws of motion and gravitation, Isaac Newton (1642–1727) made discoveries in maths and physics.

## REGULAR SOLIDS

**POLYHEDRON** Solid shape that has polygons as faces.

**TETRAHEDRON** Solid shape that has four equal triangles as faces.

**CUBE** Cubes have six equal square faces. Every angle is a right angle.

**OCTAHEDRON** Polyhedron with eight triangles as faces.

**DODECAHEDRON** Solid with 12 regular faces.

## ALL THE PRIME NUMBERS UNDER 1,000

| 2 | 3 | 5 | 7 | 11 | 13 | 17 | 19 |
|---|---|---|---|----|----|----|----|
| 23 | 29 | 31 | 37 | 41 | 43 | 47 | 53 |
| 59 | 61 | 67 | 71 | 73 | 79 | 83 | 89 |
| 97 | 101 | 103 | 107 | 109 | 113 | 127 | 131 |
| 37 | 139 | 149 | 151 | 157 | 163 | 167 | 173 |
| 179 | 181 | 191 | 193 | 197 | 199 | 211 | 223 |
| 227 | 229 | 233 | 239 | 241 | 251 | 257 | 263 |
| 269 | 271 | 277 | 281 | 283 | 293 | 307 | 311 |
| 313 | 317 | 331 | 337 | 347 | 349 | 353 | 359 |
| 367 | 373 | 379 | 383 | 389 | 397 | 401 | 409 |
| 419 | 421 | 431 | 433 | 439 | 443 | 449 | 457 |
| 461 | 463 | 467 | 479 | 487 | 491 | 499 | 503 |
| 509 | 521 | 523 | 541 | 547 | 557 | 563 | 569 |
| 571 | 577 | 587 | 593 | 599 | 601 | 607 | 613 |
| 617 | 619 | 631 | 641 | 643 | 647 | 653 | 659 |
| 661 | 673 | 677 | 683 | 691 | 701 | 709 | 719 |
| 727 | 733 | 739 | 743 | 751 | 757 | 761 | 769 |
| 773 | 787 | 797 | 809 | 811 | 821 | 823 | 827 |
| 829 | 839 | 853 | 857 | 859 | 863 | 877 | 881 |
| 883 | 887 | 907 | 911 | 919 | 929 | 937 | 941 |
| 947 | 953 | 967 | 971 | 977 | 983 | 991 | 997 |

**TRY THIS YOURSELF!** Prime numbers can only be divided by themselves and 1. All, except the number 2, are odd numbers. Try dividing a few of these by other numbers and see for yourself!

## TYPES OF NUMBER

**FRACTION** Amounts expressed as one number divided by another are called fractions. If a cake is halved, each piece is equivalent to the whole, or 1, divided by two. This is written as ½, one-half.

**POWER** Useful when dealing with very large or small numbers, powers show how many times a number is multiplied or divided by itself to give a larger or smaller number. For example, 10 multiplied by itself 5 times is 10 to the power of 5, or $10^5$.

**LOGARITHMS** Invented in 1616, logarithms, or logs, are used to simplify complicated maths problems. They show the number of times to multiply a number to get another larger number. For example, the log of raising 10 to 1,000 is 3, because 10 x 10 x 10 = 1,000.

**PERCENTAGES** Literally meaning "for each hundred", per cent can be used to write down fractions. As a percentage, ½ becomes 50 per cent (50%), or $^{50}/_{100}$.

**SCIENTIFIC NOTATION** When writing out very large or small numbers, scientific notation is helpful. It uses powers of 10, for example, 0.75 is $7.5 \times 10^{-1}$.

## NUMBERS ONE TO TEN IN SIX LANGUAGES

| ENGLISH | CHINESE | SPANISH | GERMAN | ITALIAN | FRENCH |
|---------|---------|---------|--------|---------|--------|
| one | 一 | uno | ein | uno | un |
| two | 二 | dos | zwei | due | deux |
| three | 三 | tres | drei | tre | trois |
| four | 四 | cuatro | vier | quattro | quatre |
| five | 五 | cinco | fünf | cinque | cinq |
| six | 六 | seis | sechs | sei | six |
| seven | 七 | siete | sieben | sette | sept |
| eight | 八 | ocho | acht | otto | huit |
| nine | 九 | nueve | neun | nove | neuf |
| ten | 十 | diez | zehn | dieci | dix |

## TIMES TABLES

| x | 1 | 2 | 3 | 4 | 5 | 6 | 7 | 8 | 9 | 10 |
|---|---|---|---|---|---|---|---|---|---|----|
| 1 | 1 | 2 | 3 | 4 | 5 | 6 | 7 | 8 | 9 | 10 |
| 2 | 2 | 4 | 6 | 8 | 10 | 12 | 14 | 16 | 18 | 20 |
| 3 | 3 | 6 | 9 | 12 | 15 | 18 | 21 | 24 | 27 | 30 |
| 4 | 4 | 8 | 12 | 16 | 20 | 24 | 28 | 32 | 36 | 40 |
| 5 | 5 | 10 | 15 | 20 | 25 | 30 | 35 | 40 | 45 | 50 |
| 6 | 6 | 12 | 18 | 24 | 30 | 36 | 42 | 48 | 54 | 60 |
| 7 | 7 | 14 | 21 | 28 | 35 | 42 | 49 | 56 | 63 | 70 |
| 8 | 8 | 16 | 24 | 32 | 40 | 48 | 56 | 64 | 72 | 80 |
| 9 | 9 | 18 | 27 | 36 | 45 | 54 | 63 | 72 | 81 | 90 |
| 10 | 10 | 20 | 30 | 40 | 50 | 60 | 70 | 80 | 90 | 100 |

## CIRCLE TERMS

**ARC** Part of a curve.

**CIRCUMFERENCE** The total distance around the edge of a circle.

**CHORD** A straight line joining any two points on the circumference.

**DIAMETER** A line from one side of circle to another, through the centre.

**PI** The ratio of the circumference of a circle to its diameter. It is approximately equal to 3.14159 and is the same for all circles.

**RADIUS** (*pl.* radii) The distance from centre of a circle to the edge.

**SECTOR** A slice of a circle between two radii.

## BIG AND LITTLE NUMBERS

| PREFIX | SYMBOL | POWER | NAME | VALUE |
|--------|--------|-------|------|-------|
| peta- | P | $10^{15}$ | quadrillion | 1,000,000,000,000,000 |
| tera- | T | $10^{12}$ | trillion | 1,000,000,000,000 |
| giga- | G | $10^{9}$ | billion | 1,000,000,000 |
| mega- | M | $10^{6}$ | million | 1,000,000 |
| kilo- | k | $10^{3}$ | thousand | 1,000 |
| hecto- | h | $10^{2}$ | hundred | 100 |
| deca- | da | $10^{1}$ | ten | 10 |
| — | — | $10^{0}$ | one | 1 |
| deci- | d | $10^{-1}$ | tenth | 0.1 |
| centi- | c | $10^{-2}$ | hundredth | 0.01 |
| milli- | m | $10^{-3}$ | thousandth | 0.001 |
| micro- | µ | $10^{-6}$ | millionth | 0.000,001 |
| nano- | n | $10^{-9}$ | billionth | 0.000,000,001 |
| pico- | p | $10^{-12}$ | trillionth | 0.000,000,000,001 |
| femto- | f | $10^{-15}$ | quadrillionth | 0.000,000,000,000,001 |

This chart shows short ways of writing very large or small numbers, using powers. Prefixes are the names of amounts, but are not always exact. For example, in computers, one "megabyte" is 1,048,576 bytes!

## FAMOUS EQUATIONS

$e=mc^2$ Einstein's theory of relativity explains that the energy something uses can be calculated by multiplying its mass (m) by the speed of light (c) squared.

$a=\pi r^2$ The area of a circle can be found by multiplying pi by the circle's radius squared.

$a^2=b^2+c^2$ Pythagoras' Theorem states that in a right-angled triangle, the squares of the two sides adjacent to the right angle add up to the square of the longest side (hypotenuse).

## REGULAR POLYGONS

| POLYGON | NUMBER OF SIDES |
|---------|-----------------|
| Triangle | 3 |
| Square | 4 |
| Pentagon | 5 |
| Hexagon | 6 |
| Heptagon | 7 |
| Octagon | 8 |
| Nonagon | 9 |
| Decagon | 10 |
| Undecagon | 11 |
| Duodecagon (or dodecagon) | 12 |

A figure enclosed by straight lines is a polygon. In a regular polygon, all sides are of equal lengths and its internal angles are the same. They will fit within a circle, all their points touching the edge.

## ROMAN NUMERALS

| ROMAN | ARABIC |
|-------|--------|
| I | 1 |
| II | 2 |
| III | 3 |
| IV | 4 |
| V | 5 |
| VI | 6 |
| VII | 7 |
| VIII | 8 |
| IX | 9 |
| X | 10 |
| XX | 20 |
| XXX | 30 |
| XL | 40 |
| L | 50 |
| LX | 60 |
| LXX | 70 |
| LXXX | 80 |
| XC | 90 |
| C | 100 |
| CC | 200 |
| CCC | 300 |
| CCCC | 400 |
| D | 500 |
| DC | 600 |
| DCC | 700 |
| DCCC | 800 |
| CM | 900 |
| M | 1,000 |
| MCMXCIX | 1,999 |
| MM | 2,000 |

Roman numerals are "constructed" from seven letters (I, V, X, L, C, D, M). Small digits appearing before larger ones are subtracted from them. 90, XC, is made from X (10) subtracted from C (100). Small digits appearing after them are added. This can lead to very long strings of numbers!

# WEIGHTS <u>and</u> MEASURES

## ANCIENT MEASUREMENTS

**CUBIT** In ancient Egypt, the cubit was measured as the distance from the tip of the forefinger to the elbow.

**FOOT** A foot is the average length of an adult foot. In ancient times it was equal to 11½ inches (29 cm), but today it is always 12 inches (30 cm).

**HAND** A hand was approximately equal to 5 inches (12.5 cm) and was officially the width of the hand, with all five digits together. A modern hand, used for measuring horses, is 4 inches (10.2 cm) and is the width of only four digits.

**SPAN** A span was the distance between the tip of the little finger and thumb with the hand stretched out – approximately 9 inches (23 cm).

**YARD** The yard, equal to 3 feet (91 cm) is the length of a man's belt. In the 1100s King Henry I of England standardized the yard as the distance from the thumb of his outstretched arm to his nose.

**MILE** The Roman *mille*, a thousand, was based on 1,000 paces of a marching army, and was shorter than a modern mile. A pace was equal to two steps – about 1.5 m (5 ft).

**POUND** The modern imperial pound comes from the Roman weight *libra pondo*. This is why the abbreviation for pound is "lb".

## MEASURING INSTRUMENTS

| INSTRUMENT | WHAT IT MEASURES |
| --- | --- |
| Anemometer | Wind |
| Barometer | Air pressure |
| Calendar | Days and months |
| Clock | Hours, minutes, seconds |
| Hygrometer | Specific gravity |
| Protractor | Angles |
| Ruler | Length |
| Scales | Weight |
| Seismometer | Earthquakes |
| Speedometer | Vehicle speed |
| Thermometer | Temperature |
| Voltmeter | Electricity |

**❗ DID YOU KNOW?**
The division of hours into 60 minutes, and minutes into 60 seconds is based on the ancient Babylonian sexagesimal measurement system, which divides everything into 60.

## STANDARD MEASUREMENTS

In order to ensure that everyone means the same thing when stating measurements, certain basic units have very precisely defined standards, as these examples illustrate.

**KILOGRAM** The worldwide standard kilogram measure is a cylinder made of the metals iridium and platinum, which is kept under carefully controlled conditions at the International Bureau of Weights and Measures at Sèvres, France.

**METRE** One metre was originally calculated as one 10-millionth of a quarter of the circumference of the Earth. Today, a metre is calculated as the distance light travels in a vacuum in 1/299792458th of a second.

**SECOND** One second is defined as "the duration of 9,192,631,770 periods of the radiation corresponding to the transition between the two hyperfine levels of the ground state of the caesium–133 atom"!

**❗ DID YOU KNOW?**
The first standard system of weights arose when traders needed to measure their goods.

ASSYRIAN LION WEIGHT

**❗ DID YOU KNOW?**
The origins of some imperial units can be found in early civilizations of the Near and Middle East. In ancient Assyria, weights were made for the King Shalmaneser.

## THE SEVEN BASE SI UNITS

The seven base units SI (Système Internationale d'Unites, or International System of Units) is the standard system of units for scientists throughout the world.

| QUANTITY | UNIT | SYMBOL |
|---|---|---|
| Mass | Kilogram | kg |
| Length | Metre | m |
| Time | Second | s |
| Electric current | Ampere | A |
| Temperature | Kelvin | K |
| Luminous intensity | Candela | cd |
| Amount of substance | Mole | mole |

## UNITS OF VOLUME

| | |
|---|---|
| 1 cubic mm (mm³) | |
| 1 cubic centimetre (cc³) | 1.000 mm³ |
| 1 cubic metre (m³) | 1,000,000 cm³ |
| 1 cubic kilometre (km³) | 1,000,000,000 m³ |
| 1 litre (l) | 1,000 cm³ |
| 1 cubic inch (in³) | |
| 1 cubic foot (ft³) | 1,728 in³ |
| 1 cubic yard (yd³) | 27 ft³ |
| 1 fluid oz (fl oz) | |
| 1 pint (pt) | 20 fl oz |
| 1 gallon (gal) | 8 pt |

## UNITS OF AREA

| | |
|---|---|
| 1 square millimetre (mm²) | |
| 1 square centimetre (cm²) | 100 mm² |
| 1 square metre (m²) | 10,000 cm² |
| 1 hectare | 10,000 m² |
| 1 square kilometre (km²) | 1,000,000 m² |
| 1 square inch (in²) | |
| 1 square foot (ft²) | 144 in² |
| 1 square yard (yd²) | 9 ft² |
| 1 acre | 4,480 yd² |
| 1 square mile (mile²) | 640 acres |

## SPECIAL MEASUREMENTS

**CARAT** Gems, such as diamonds, are weighed in carats. The word comes from the tiny carob bean, which is remarkable for its consistent weight of 0.2 g (0.007 oz).

**CHAIN** The chain was once a 100-link chain measuring 20.12 m (66 ft) long. To this day, a cricket pitch is one chain long.

**FATHOM** A measure of depth used at sea, a fathom is the distance a man's arms stretch when paying out a rope – 1.83 m (6 ft).

**KNOT** Speed at sea is measured in knots – once the time a ship took to travel along a piece of knotted rope. A knot is now 1 nautical mph. A nautical mile is 6,082.66 ft in the UK, and 6,076.11549 ft in the USA.

**POINT** Used by printers, the point size is the height of a letter such as an x: one point is equal to 0.3528 mm (0.013889 in). The point size of this text is 9.25.

## MEASUREMENT SYSTEMS

People have been dividing things into units for thousands of years. Here are four basic systems that have been used. You may recognize some of them…

**BINARY** Hindus in India divide things into two, such as halves, quarters, eighths, and sixteenths.

**DECIMAL** China was the first country to use a decimal system, which divides things into tenths.

**DUODECIMAL** The Romans used units of 12 – which is why there are 12 months in a year, 12 in a dozen, and 12 inches in a foot.

**SEXAGESIMAL** The Babylonians used units of 60, still used to measure time.

## UNITS OF WEIGHT

| | |
|---|---|
| 1 gram (g) | |
| 1 kilogram (kg) | 1,000 g |
| 1 tonne | 1,000 kg |
| 1 ounce (oz) | |
| 1 pound (lb) | 16 oz |
| 1 stone | 14 lb |
| 1 hundredweight | 112 lb |
| 1 ton (long) | 2,240 lb |
| 1 US short ton | 2,000 lb |

## UNITS OF LENGTH

| | |
|---|---|
| 1 millimetre (mm) | |
| 1 centimetre (cm) | 10 mm |
| 1 metre (m) | 100 cm |
| 1 kilometre (km) | 1,000 m |
| 1 inch (in) | |
| 1 foot (ft) | 12 in |
| 1 yard (yd) | 3 ft |
| 1 mile | 1,760 yd |

## MEASUREMENTS NAMED AFTER PEOPLE

| MEASUREMENT | USED TO MEASURE | NAMED AFTER |
|---|---|---|
| Ampere | Electrical current | André-Marie Ampère (French, 1775–1836) |
| Angstrom | Light | Anders Jonas Ångstrom (Swedish, 1814–1874) |
| Celsius | Temperature | Anders Celsius (Swedish, 1701–1744) |
| Fahrenheit | Temperature | Gabriel Fahrenheit (German, 1686–1736) |
| Hertz | Frequency | Heinrich Rudolf Hertz (German, 1857–1894) |
| Joule | Energy | James Prescott Joule (British, 1818–1889) |
| Kelvin | Temperature | Lord Kelvin (British, 1824–1907) |
| Mach number | Speed of sound | Ernst Mach (Austrian, 1838–1916) |
| Ohm | Electrical resistance | Georg Simon Ohm (German, 1787–1854) |
| Volt | Electrical current | Alessandro Volta (Italian, 1745–1827) |
| Watt | Power | James Watt (British, 1736–1819) |

## ❗ TRICK QUESTION!

Which is heavier – a pound of feathers or a pound of gold? Most people think they weigh the same, but gold is measured in troy pounds, which contain only 12 ounces (373 g), whereas a pound of feathers contains 16 ounces (454 g). So, strange as it may seem, the feathers are in fact heavier!

# MEASUREMENT CONVERSIONS

## LENGTH CONVERSION

| FROM | TO | MULTIPLY BY |
|---|---|---|
| Centimetres (cm) | Inches (in) | 0.3937 |
| Metres (m) | Feet (ft) | 3.2808 |
| Metres (m) | Yards | 1.0936 |
| Kilometres (km) | Miles | 0.6214 |
| Inches (in) | Centimetres (cm) | 2.5400 |
| Feet (ft) | Metres (m) | 0.3048 |
| Yards (yd) | Metres (m) | 0.9144 |
| Miles (mi) | Kilometres (km) | 1.6093 |

## TEMPERATURE

| FROM | TO | MULTIPLY BY |
|---|---|---|
| Celsius (°C) | Fahrenheit (°F) | x 9 ÷ 5 + 32 |
| Fahrenheit (°F) | Celsius (°C) | −32 x 5 ÷ 9 |

## VOLUME CONVERSION

| FROM | TO | MULTIPLY BY |
|---|---|---|
| Cubic centimetres (cc) | Cubic inches (in³) | 0.0610 |
| Cubic metres (m³) | Cubic feet (ft³) | 35.3147 |
| Cubic metres (m³) | Cubic yard (yd³) | 0.7646 |
| Cubic kilometres (km³) | Cubic miles (ml³) | 0.2399 |
| Litres (l) | Pints | 1.7598 |
| Litres (l) | US gallons (gal) | 0.2642 |
| Litres (l) | Gallons (gal) | 0.2200 |
| Cubic inches (in³) | Cubic centimetres (cc) | 16.3871 |
| Cubic feet (ft³) | Cubic metres (m³) | 0.0283 |
| Cubic yards (yd³) | Cubic metres (m³) | 1.3080 |
| Cubic miles (mi³) | Cubic kilometres (km³) | 4.1682 |
| Pints | Litres (l) | 0.5683 |
| US gallons (gal) | Litres (l) | 3.7853 |
| UK gallons (gal) | Litres (l) | 4.5461 |

## SPEED CONVERSION

| FROM | TO | MULTIPLY BY |
|---|---|---|
| Metres per second (m/s) | Feet per second (ft/s) | 3.2808 |
| Kilometres per hour (km/h) | Miles per hour (mph) | 0.6214 |
| Feet per second (ft/s) | Metres per second (m/s) | 0.3048 |
| Miles per hour (mph) | Kilometres per hour (km/h) | 1.609 |

## MASS AND WEIGHT CONVERSION

| FROM | TO | MULTIPLY BY |
|---|---|---|
| Grams (g) | Ounces (oz) | 0.0353 |
| Ounces (oz) | Grams (g) | 28.3495 |
| Kilograms (kg) | Pounds (lb) | 2.2046 |
| Pounds (lb) | Kilograms (kg) | 0.4536 |
| Stones | Kilograms (kg) | 6.3503 |
| Kilograms (kg) | Stones | 0.1575 |
| Hundredweight (cwt) | Kilograms (kg) | 50.8024 |
| Kilograms (kg) | Hundredweight (cwt) | 0.0197 |
| Tonnes | Tons (long) | 0.9842 |
| Tons (long) | Tonnes | 1.0160 |
| Tonnes | US short tons | 1.1023 |
| US short tons | Tonnes | 0.9072 |

## AREA CONVERSION

| FROM | TO | MULTIPLY BY |
|---|---|---|
| Square centimetres (cm²) | Square inches (in²) | 0.1550 |
| Square metres (m²) | Square feet (ft²) | 10.7639 |
| Square metres (m²) | Square yards (yd²) | 1.1960 |
| Square kilometres (km²) | Square miles (mi²) | 0.3861 |
| Hectares | Acres | 2.4711 |
| Square inches (in²) | Square centimetres (cm²) | 6.4516 |
| Square feet (ft²) | Square metres (m²) | 0.0929 |
| Square yards (yd²) | Square metres (m²) | 0.8361 |
| Square miles (mi²) | Square kilometres (km²) | 2.5900 |
| Acres | Hectares | 0.4047 |

## FRACTIONS, DECIMALS, AND PERCENTAGES

TO CONVERT A FRACTION INTO A DECIMAL Divide 1 by the lower number of the fraction then multiply the answer by the top number, e.g. ⅜ = 1 ÷ 8 x 3 = 0.375

TO CONVERT A DECIMAL NUMBER INTO A PERCENTAGE Multiply the decimal number by 100, e.g. 0.375 x 100 = 37.5%

TO CONVERT A PERCENTAGE INTO A FRACTION Make a fraction by putting the percentage over 100, then see if there is a number that will divide exactly into both the top and bottom numbers of the fraction, e.g. 37.5% = 37.5/100. If you divide 37.5 and 100 by 2.5, you get 15/40. Then divide 15 and 40 by 5 to get ⅜. Sometimes, it will be impossible to simplify a fraction, e.g. 41/100. as there is no number that will divide exactly into both 41 and 100.

## COOKING MEASURES AND CONVERSIONS

| OBJECT | METRIC | IMPERIAL |
|---|---|---|
| 1 thimble | 2.5 ml | 30 drops |
| 60 drops/1 teaspoon | 5 ml | 1 teaspoon/1 dram |
| 1 dessertspoon | 10 ml | 2 drams |
| 1 tablespoon | 20 ml | 4 drams |
| 1 wine glass | 100 ml | 2 fl oz |
| 1 tea cup | 200 ml | 5 fl oz (1 gill) |
| 1 mug | 400 ml | 10 fl oz (½ pint) |
| 1 US cup | 227 ml | 8 fl oz |
| 1 US pint | 504 ml | 16 fl oz |

## QUICK CHECK HEIGHT CHART

| M | FT | IN |
|---|---|---|
| 1.12 | 3 | 8 |
| 1.14 | 3 | 9 |
| 1.17 | 3 | 10 |
| 1.19 | 3 | 11 |
| 1.22 | 4 | - |
| 1.24 | 4 | 1 |
| 1.27 | 4 | 2 |
| 1.30 | 4 | 3 |
| 1.32 | 4 | 4 |
| 1.35 | 4 | 5 |
| 1.37 | 4 | 6 |
| 1.40 | 4 | 7 |
| 1.42 | 4 | 8 |
| 1.45 | 4 | 9 |
| 1.47 | 4 | 10 |
| 1.50 | 4 | 11 |
| 1.52 | 5 | - |
| 1.55 | 5 | 1 |
| 1.57 | 5 | 2 |
| 1.60 | 5 | 3 |
| 1.62 | 5 | 4 |
| 1.65 | 5 | 5 |
| 1.68 | 5 | 6 |
| 1.70 | 5 | 7 |
| 1.73 | 5 | 8 |
| 1.75 | 5 | 9 |
| 1.77 | 5 | 10 |
| 1.80 | 5 | 11 |
| 1.83 | 6 | - |

## QUICK CHECK WEIGHT CHART

| KG | STONES | LB | LB |
|---|---|---|---|
| 26 | 4 | 1 | 57 |
| 28 | 4 | 6 | 62 |
| 30 | 4 | 10 | 66 |
| 32 | 5 | 1 | 71 |
| 34 | 5 | 5 | 75 |
| 36 | 5 | 9 | 79 |
| 38 | 6 | - | 84 |
| 40 | 6 | 4 | 88 |
| 42 | 6 | 9 | 93 |
| 44 | 6 | 13 | 97 |
| 46 | 7 | 3 | 101 |
| 48 | 7 | 8 | 106 |
| 50 | 7 | 12 | 110 |
| 52 | 8 | 3 | 115 |
| 54 | 8 | 7 | 119 |
| 56 | 8 | 11 | 1234 |
| 58 | 9 | 2 | 128 |
| 60 | 9 | 6 | 132 |
| 62 | 9 | 11 | 137 |
| 64 | 10 | 1 | 141 |
| 66 | 10 | 6 | 146 |
| 68 | 10 | 10 | 150 |
| 70 | 11 | - | 154 |
| 72 | 11 | 5 | 159 |
| 74 | 11 | 9 | 163 |
| 76 | 12 | - | 168 |
| 78 | 12 | 4 | 172 |
| 80 | 12 | 8 | 176 |
| 82 | 12 | 13 | 181 |

## QUICK TEMPERATURE CONVERSIONS

| CELSIUS | FAHRENHEIT | KELVIN |
|---|---|---|
| 160 | 320 | 433 |
| 150 | 302 | 423 |
| 140 | 284 | 413 |
| 130 | 266 | 403 |
| 120 | 248 | 393 |
| 110 | 230 | 383 |
| 100 | 211 | 373 |
| 90 | 194 | 363 |
| 80 | 176 | 353 |
| 70 | 158 | 343 |
| 60 | 140 | 333 |
| 50 | 122 | 323 |
| 40 | 104 | 313 |
| 30 | 86 | 303 |
| 20 | 68 | 293 |
| 10 | 50 | 283 |
| 0 | 32 | 273 |
| -10 | 14 | 263 |
| -20 | -4 | 253 |
| -30 | -22 | 243 |
| -40 | -40 | 233 |
| -50 | -58 | 223 |

**DID YOU KNOW?** The Kelvin scale is also known as the absolute temperature scale, and is often used in science. To convert Celsius into Kelvin add 273.16.

## OVEN TEMPERATURES

| GAS MARK | ELECTRICITY °C | °F | RATING |
|---|---|---|---|
| 1/2 | 120 | 250 | Slow |
| 1 | 140 | 275 | – |
| 2 | 150 | 300 | – |
| 3 | 170 | 325 | – |
| 4 | 180 | 350 | Moderate |
| 5 | 190 | 375 | – |
| 6 | 200 | 400 | Hot |
| 7 | 220 | 425 | – |
| 8 | 230 | 450 | Very hot |
| 9 | 260 | 500 | – |

## KIDS' SHOE SIZES

| WORLD | UK | US AND CANADA |
|---|---|---|
| 15 | 00 | 0 |
| 16 | ½ | 1 |
| 17 | 1 | 1½ |
| 18 | 2 | 2½ |
| 19 | 3 | 3½ |
| 20 | 3½ | 4 |
| 21 | 4½ | 4 |
| 22 | 5 | 5½ |
| 23 | 6 | 6½ |
| 24 | 7 | 7½ |
| 25 | 7½ | 8 |
| 26 | 8½ | 9 |
| 27 | 9 | 9½ |
| 28 | 10 | 10½ |
| 29 | 11 | 11½ |
| 30 | 11½ | 12 |
| 31 | 12 | 13 |
| 32 | 13 | 13½ |
| 33 | 13½ | 1½ |

## ADULT SHOE SIZES

| EUROPE | UK | US AND CANADA |
|---|---|---|
| 34 | 1½ | 2 |
| 35 | 2½ | 4 |
| 36 | 3 | 4½ |
| 37 | 4 | 5½ |
| 38 | 5 | 6½ / 5½★ |
| 39 | 5½ | 7 / 6★ |
| 40 | 6½ | 8 / 7★ |
| 41 | 7 | 8½ / 7½★ |
| 42 | 8 | 9½ / 8½★ |
| 43 | 9 | 10½ / 9½★ |
| 44 | 9½ | 10★ |
| 45 | 10 | 10½★ |
| 46 | 11 | 11½★ |
| 47 | 11½ | 12★ |

US men's and women's sizes differ. Men's sizes are marked by an asterisk.

53

# MEASURING TIME

## A TIME CAPSULE BENEATH CLEOPATRA'S NEEDLE, LONDON

Cleopatra's needle in London is an ancient Egyptian obelisk, but it has nothing to do with Queen Cleopatra of Egypt (69–30 BC), as it was made 1,400 years before she was born. It was transported to Britain and set up by the river Thames in 1878. Before it was put in place, a "time capsule" was placed beneath it – a sealed urn containing the following items :

- A box of hairpins
- Bibles in various languages
- *Bradshaw's Railway Guide*
- A box of cigars
- A one-shilling razor
- Iron ropes and submarine cables
- Copies of *Engineering* magazine which describes the achievement of bringing the needle to England

- A selection of daily and weekly newspapers
- A baby feeding bottle
- A bronze scale model of the obelisk and a piece of granite chipped from it
- A complete set of British currency and one Indian rupee (Queen Victoria had been proclaimed Empress of India two years earlier)

- Various toys
- A portrait of Queen Victoria
- A parchment copy of Samuel Birch's translation of the Needle's hieroglyphics
- A 2-ft (60-cm) ruler
- A map of London
- A hydraulic jack, used to erect the needle
- Portraits of 12 of Britain's prettiest women

## NAMES OF THE MONTHS

The names of the months in English, and many other languages, come from the Latin language.

**JANUARY** The first month is named after Janus, Roman god of beginnings.

**FEBRUARY** *Februa* was a purification festival that took place in late winter.

**MARCH** Named after Mars, god of war.

**APRIL** The month when plants open – from *aperire* meaning "to open".

**MAY** Probably named after Maia, the goddess of growth and fertility.

**JUNE** Named either after a Roman family name *Junius*, meaning young, or after the goddess Juno.

**JULY** Named in 44 BC by Mark Antony in honour of Julius Caesar.

**AUGUST** Named in honour of Emperor Augustus in 8 BC.

**SEPTEMBER** From *septem*, "seven", the Roman calendar's seventh month.

**OCTOBER** The eighth month in the Roman calendar, from *octo*, "eight".

**NOVEMBER** The ninth month in the Roman calendar, from *novem*, "nine".

**DECEMBER** The tenth month in the Roman calendar, from *decem*, "ten".

## WORLD CALENDARS

### GREGORIAN

The Gregorian calendar, named after Pope Gregory XIII who introduced it in 1582, is the most widely used today. It is based on the time it takes for the Earth to circle the Sun (365.2425 days). The calendar has 365 days – the extra 0.2425 days are made up every four years by adding an extra day to make a leap year. The Gregorian calendar is just one day out in every 3,300 years.

| Month | Days |
|---|---|
| January | 31 |
| February | 28/29 |
| March | 31 |
| April | 30 |
| May | 31 |
| June | 30 |
| July | 31 |
| August | 31 |
| September | 30 |
| October | 31 |
| November | 30 |
| December | 31 |

### JEWISH

The Jewish calendar is based on the Moon's cycle. A "common", non-leap year has 353, 354, or 355 days divided into 12 months. A leap year has 383, 384, or 385 days and 13 months. In a leap year, which falls in years 3, 6, 8, 11, 14, 17, and 19 of a 19-year cycle, Adar has 30 days; it is followed by Adar II with 29 or 30 days. The three year lengths are called "minimal", "regular", and "full".

| Month | Days |
|---|---|
| Tishri | 30 |
| Heshvan | 29/30 |
| Kislev | 30/29 |
| Tevet | 29 |
| Shevat | 30 |
| Adar | 29 |
| Nisan | 30 |
| Iyar | 29 |
| Sivan | 30 |
| Tammuz | 29 |
| Av | 30 |
| Elul | 29 |

### ISLAMIC

The Islamic calendar is based on the Moon's cycle beginning with the year of the *Hejirah* (AD 622) when Muhammad travelled from Mecca to Medina. It runs in cycles of 30 years, of which years 2, 5, 7, 10, 13, 16, 21, 24, 26, and 29 are leap years. A year consists of 12 months of 29 or 30 days. Common years have 354 days, leap years 355. In a leap year the extra day is added at the end of the 12th month.

| Month | Days |
|---|---|
| Muharram | 30 |
| Safar | 29 |
| Rabi'a I | 30 |
| Rabi'a II | 29 |
| Jumada I | 30 |
| Jumada II | 29 |
| Rajab | 30 |
| Sha'ban | 29 |
| Ramadan | 30 |
| Shawwal | 29 |
| Dhu al-Q'adah | 30 |
| Dhu al-Hijjah | 29/30 |

## TIMELINE OF MEASURING TIME

**c.1500 BC** Egyptians use sundials. The Sun's shadow moves round a dial marked with hours.

**c.AD 890** Clock candles appear in England.

**1335** First mechanical clock is erected in Milan, Italy. Their popularity spreads through Europe.

**1364** First domestic clocks made by Italian Giovanni Dondi (1318–1389).

**1657** Dutch physicist Christiaan Huygens (1629–1695) builds the first pendulum clock.

**1800s** American Eli Tery (1772–1852) develops cheaper clocks in the USA.

**c.1900** First wristwatches introduced.

**1929** American Warren Morrison invents the quartz clock.

**1948** The atomic clock is developed in the USA.

**1970s–1990s** Digital watches become popular.

## HOW LONG DOES IT TAKE?

| EXAMPLE | SECONDS |
|---|---|
| Light to travel 30 cm (12 in) in air | 0.000,000,001 |
| A flash of lightning | 0.000,001 |
| Sound to travel 30 cm (12 in) in air | 0.001 |
| Olympic sprinter to run 1 m (3ft 3 in) | 0.1 |
| Quartz in a watch to vibrate 32,768 times | 1 |
| A snail to move 10 m (33 ft) | 1,000 |
| 11.5 days to pass | 1,000,000 |
| Saturn to orbit the Sun | 1,000,000,000 |

**MEMORY TIP!** Remember how many days in each month with this rhyme: "30 days has September, April, June, and November. All the rest have 31, excepting February alone, which has 28 days clear, with 29 in each leap year."

# WORLD CALENDARS

## INDIAN

India has several principal calendars. In 1957 the calendar known as the Saka era was declared the national calendar, to run concurrently with the Gregorian calendar. The Saka era dates from 3 March AD 78 in the Gregorian calendar. It is based on the solar year, which is the time taken for the Earth to orbit the Sun, and begins with the spring equinox. The 365 days (366 in a leap year) are divided into 12 months. In a leap year, the extra day is always added to the first month, Caitra.

| MONTH | DAYS | EQUIVALENT GREGORIAN DATE |
|---|---|---|
| Caitra | 30/31 | 22 March |
| Vaisakha | 31 | 21 April |
| Jyaistha | 31 | 22 May |
| Asadha | 31 | 22 June |
| Sravana | 31 | 23 July |
| Bhadra | 31 | 23 August |
| Asvina | 30 | 23 September |
| Kartika | 30 | 23 October |
| Agrahayana | 30 | 22 November |
| Pausa | 30 | 22 December |
| Magha | 30 | 21 January |
| Phalguna | 30 | 20 February |

## CHINESE

The ancient Chinese calendar is based on a lunar year of 12 months of alternately 29 and 30 days. To keep the calendar in step with the Gregorian calendar, extra months are inserted. The months of the Chinese calendar are numbered and given one of the 12 animal names that are usually attached to years and hours in the Chinese calendar. The Chinese New Year always falls on the first new Moon to occur between 21 January and 19 February. Chinese years are grouped in cycles of 60. Each year is also named after one of 12 animals.

| NUMBER | NAME | ANIMAL | DAYS |
|---|---|---|---|
| 1 | Zzi | Rat | 29 |
| 2 | Chou | Ox | 30 |
| 3 | Yin | Tiger | 29 |
| 4 | Mao | Hare | 30 |
| 5 | Chen | Dragon | 29 |
| 6 | Si | Snake | 30 |
| 7 | Wu | Horse | 29 |
| 8 | Wei | Sheep | 30 |
| 9 | Shen | Monkey | 29 |
| 10 | You | Fowl | 30 |
| 11 | Xu | Dog | 29 |
| 12 | Hai | Pig | 30 |

## TIME PERIODS

| PERIOD | DURATION |
|---|---|
| Nanosecond | 0.000,000,1 second |
| Millisecond | 0.001 second |
| Second | 1/60 minute |
| Minute | 60 seconds |
| Hour | 60 minutes |
| Day | 24 hours |
| Week | 7 days |
| Fortnight | 2 weeks |
| Month | 28, 29, 30, or 31 days, depending on calendar month and year |
| Trimester | 3 months |
| Lunar month | 29.53059 days |
| Year | 12 months, 52 weeks, or 365 days |
| Leap year | 366 days |
| Biennium | 2 years |
| Triennium | 3 years |
| Quadrennium, Olympiad | 4 years |
| Lustrum, half-decade | 5 years |
| Decade | 10 years |
| Half-century | 50 years |
| Century | 100 years |
| Half-millennium | 500 years |
| Millennium | 1,000 years |

# INVENTIONS

**DID YOU KNOW?** Otto Sundback of Sweden invented the first practical zip, or "hookless fastener"

## INVENTIONS BEFORE THEIR TIME

**1662 BUS** French mathematician Blaise Pascal (1623–1662) adapted a horse-drawn coach to help transport the poor in and out of Paris. The first real omnibuses were not invented until 1847.

**1760 ROLLER SKATES** Belgian instrument maker Joseph Merlin made a grand entrance to a masquerade in London on roller skates of his own design – playing a violin! Out of control, he crashed, destroying a valuable mirror. Steerable roller skates were not invented until 1863.

**1783 PARACHUTE** Italian artist Leonardo da Vinci sketched the first parachute design, but there is no evidence that he attempted to use a full-sized version. The first ripcord parachute was not used until 1908.

**1880 BABY INCUBATOR** In this year, a Frenchman called Budin invented a crude type of baby incubator, which consisted of a wooden cabinet heated by pans of hot water, for premature or weak babies. A more sophisticated incubator was introduced by Frenchman Dr Alexandre Lion in 1891.

**1925 IN-FLIGHT MOVIES** During an Imperial Airways flight from London to Paris, a silent film was shown. In-flight movies did not become part of the regular service until 1961.

**DID YOU KNOW?** The gramophone was invented in 1888 by German-born American Emile Berliner (1851–1921).

## "SOMEONE HAD TO INVENT IT" – EVERYDAY INVENTIONS AND THEIR INVENTORS

| DATE | INVENTION | INVENTOR | LOCATION |
|------|-----------|----------|----------|
| 1792 | Pencil | Jacques-Nicolas Conté | France |
| 1882 | Electric iron | Henry W. Seely | USA |
| 1888 | Kodak camera | George Eastman | USA |
| 1891 | Swiss army knife | Karl Elsener | Switzerland |
| 1903 | Safety razor | King Camp Gillette | USA |
| 1906 | Electric washing machine | Alva J. Fisher | USA |
| 1924 | Frozen food | Clarence Birdseye | USA |
| 1926 | Aerosol spray | Erik Rotheim | Norway |
| 1927 | Pop-up toaster | Charles Strite | USA |
| 1945 | Microwave oven | Percy LeBaron Spencer | USA |
| 1948 | Velcro | Georges de Mestral | Switzerland |
| 1955 | Transistor radio | Sony | Japan |
| 1979 | Compact disc player | Sony, Philips Co | Japan, Netherlands |

## FIRST US WOMEN PATENTEES

Patents are legal documents that stop anyone from copying an inventor's idea. The first women to apply for patents were:

| PATENTEE | PATENT | DATE |
|----------|--------|------|
| Mary Kies | Straw weaving with silk or thread | 5 May 1809 |
| Mary Brush | Corset | 21 July 1815 |
| Sophia Usher | Carbonated liquid | 11 September 1819 |
| Julia Planton | Foot stove | 4 November 1822 |
| Lucy Burnap | Weaving grass hats | 16 February 1823 |
| Diana H. Tuttle | Accelerating spinning-wheel heads | 17 May 1824 |

## INVENTIONS NAMED AFTER THEIR INVENTORS

| INVENTION | DESCRIPTION | DATE | NAMED AFTER | LIVED | COUNTRY |
|-----------|-------------|------|-------------|-------|---------|
| Biro | Ballpoint pen | 1938 | László Joszef Biró | 1900–1985 | Hungary |
| Braille | Raised dot type for blind people | 1837 | Louis Braille | 1809–1852 | France |
| Bunsen burner | Gas heater used in laboratories | 1855 | Robert Wilhelm Bunsen | 1811–1899 | Germany |
| Dolby stereo | Sound recording noise reducer | 1966 | Ray Milton Dolby | b.1933 | USA |
| Ferris wheel | Fairground attraction | 1893 | George Washington Gale Ferris | 1859–1896 | USA |
| Mackintosh | Waterproof material | 1823 | Charles Macintosh | 1760–1843 | UK |
| Plimsoll line | Line on ship to show load level | 1876 | Samuel Plimsoll | 1824–1898 | UK |

## BIZARRE INVENTIONS

**FIRE ESCAPE PARACHUTE** American Benjamin B. Oppenheimer invented this safety gadget in 1879. If you should find yourself trapped in a blazing building, you attach the parachute to your head, put on the cushioned shoes, and jump out of the window!

**SELF-RAISING HAT** When the wearer of the hat patented by James C. Boyle of the USA in 1896 tilts his or her head forward, a clockwork motor spins it round and replaces it!

**SPECTACLES FOR CHICKENS** Patented in 1903, American Andrew Jackson Jr's spectacles did not aid his chicken's eyesight, but were designed to protect their eyes from the pecks of other chickens.

**CHOCOLATE RECORDS** Invented in 1903 by German company Gebrüder Stollwerck for chocoholics everywhere. Once you have played the record you can just eat it!

**BABY BOTTOM PATTER** Californian Thomas V. Zelenka patented this device in 1971. Attached to the side of the cot, an electric motor operates a rod at the end of which a gloved hand pats the baby's bottom. Getting baby off to sleep has never been so easy!

**COUGHING CIGARETTE PACKET** Designed by Lewis R. Toppel of the USA in 1972, the packet produces a hacking noise when opened – a reminder of the dangers of smoking.

## LEONARDO DA VINCI'S INVENTIONS

Italian genius Leonardo da Vinci (1452–1519) is hailed as one of the world's greatest inventors. He made plans for countless machines, most of which were never built. They include:

Air conditioner • Alarm clock • Ball-bearings • Clock • Compass • Crane Diving suit and bell • Flying machine Gas mask • Gears • Giant catapults Helicopter • Lifebelt • Mechanical musical instruments • Mileometer Multi-barrelled machine gun One-person battleship • Parachute Pedometer • Revolving stage • Screw-making machine • Spectacles • Steam engine • Tank • Telescope • Water turbine

## YOUNG INVENTORS

**HORATIO ADAMS** In 1870, 16-year-old American schoolboy Adams assisted his father in experiments with chicle, the sap of a Mexican tree, and invented chewing gum!

**LOUIS BRAILLE** In 1837, at the age of 15, Braille, from France, invented raised-dot writing that enabled blind people to read for the first time.

**CHESTER GREENWOOD** In 1873, 15 year-old Chester Greenwood, from the USA, invented earmuffs.

**WALTER LINES** British schoolboy Lines invented the scooter when he was 15 in 1897. He later founded Triang Toys, once Britain's leading toy manufacturer.

**CHARLES BABBAGE** Englishman Babbage was 19 when he first thought of the idea of the mechanical computer in 1834.

## INVENTORS OF 20TH-CENTURY TOYS AND GAMES

| YEAR | TOY/GAME | INVENTOR | COUNTRY |
|------|----------|----------|---------|
| 1900 | Plasticine | William Harbutt | UK |
| 1903 | Teddy bear | Margarete Steiff | Germany |
| 1921 | Pogo stick | George B. Hansburg | USA |
| 1913 | Crossword puzzle | Arthur Wynne | USA |
| 1929 | Yo-yo | Donald F. Duncan | USA |
| 1946 | Slinky spring | Richard James | USA |
| 1948 | Frisbee | Fred Morrisson | USA |
| 1958 | Skateboard | Bill & Mark Richards | USA |
| 1980 | Rollerblades | Scott & Brennan Olsen | USA |

## EDISON'S INVENTIONS

American inventor Thomas Alva Edison (1849–1931) started work as a newspaper boy at the age of 12. By the end of his long working life, he had registered 1,093 patents – more than anybody else has ever done to this day.

**1869** Electric vote recorder (his first patent)

**1870** Stock quotation printer (ticker tape machine)

**1874** Duplex telegraphy (transmitting multiple messages)

**1876** Mimeograph (copying machine)

**1878** Phonograph (sound recording)

**1879** Incandescent light bulb

**1879** Carbon-resistance telephone transmitter

**1889** Kinetoscope (motion picture device)

**1890** Talking dolls

**1890** Electric car motor

**DID YOU KNOW?** American inventor Thomas Edison and British inventor Joseph Swan both invented the screw-in light bulb in about 1880.

## IMPOSSIBLE INVENTIONS

Inflatable dartboard • Night-time sundial Waterproof teabag • One-way lift • Non-slip ice-skates • Blank dice • Fish scuba apparatus

# COMMUNICATIONS

## COMMUNICATIONS MILESTONES

**1793** Frenchman Claude Chappe invents semaphore, a way of sending messages using arm movements.

**1845** Samuel Morse (USA) builds the first telegraph line.

**1876** Telephones are invented by Alexander Graham Bell (USA).

**1901** Guglielmo Marconi astounds the world by transmitting a radio signal across the Atlantic Ocean, from the UK to Canada.

**1945** ENIAC, the first automatic computer, is built in the USA.

**1962** First satellite telephone calls.

**1981** First IBM personal computers using MS-DOS become available.

**1985** First CD-ROMs appear.

**1990s** E-mail becomes widely used.

**1994** Introduction of RISC (reduced instruction set computing) allows faster microchips to improve quality of multimedia images.

## POSTAGE PER PERSON PER YEAR

The average daily postage for the tiny population of the Vatican City appears to be 26 letters per person! In fact, the mail is mostly official letters from the headquarters of the Roman Catholic Church.

| COUNTRY | LETTERS POSTED PER PERSON |
|---|---|
| Vatican City | 9,545 |
| USA | 689 |
| Liechtenstein | 573 |
| Norway | 525 |
| Sweden | 503 |
| Netherlands | 420 |
| France | 416 |
| Finland | 379 |
| Canada | 360 |
| Denmark | 335 |
| Belgium | 329 |
| Austria | 322 |

## FIRST PLACES TO ISSUE POSTAGE STAMPS

| PLACE OF ISSUE | YEAR OF ISSUE |
|---|---|
| Great Britain | 1840 |
| New York City, USA | 1842 |
| Zurich, Switzerland | 1843 |
| Brazil | 1843 |
| Geneva, Switzerland | 1843 |
| Basle, Switzerland | 1845 |
| USA | 1847 |
| Mauritius | 1847 |
| Bermuda | 1848 |

The first adhesive postage stamps were the Penny Blacks which went on sale on 1 May 1840 in Great Britain. The first national stamps in the USA were the 5-cent Benjamin Franklin and the 10-cent George Washington, issued in 1847.

## PHONETIC ALPHABET

| | |
|---|---|
| A | Alpha |
| B | Bravo |
| C | Charlie |
| D | Delta |
| E | Echo |
| F | Foxtrot |
| G | Golf |
| H | Hotel |
| I | India |
| J | Juliette |
| K | Kilo |
| L | Lima |
| M | Mike |
| N | November |
| O | Oscar |
| P | Papa |
| Q | Quebec |
| R | Romeo |
| S | Sierra |
| T | Tango |
| U | Uniform |
| V | Victor |
| W | Whisky |
| X | X-ray |
| Y | Yankee |
| Z | Zulu |

**! DID YOU KNOW?** "Mayday" is an international signal used as a distress call. The word is derived from the French phrase *M'aidez*, which means "Help me!".

**! TRY IT YOURSELF!** You don't need to type http:// when you visit a web site – just the part of the URL beginning with "www" is enough!

## COMMUNICATION FACTS

**SPEEDY SORTING** A mail-sorting machine can handle about 36,000 letters an hour!

**GOOD TO TALK** More than 4,000,000,000 messages are sent by e-mail in North America alone every year.

**MOST POST** The US Postal Service handles 170 billion letters every year.

**WALK AND TALK** Mobile telephones were first thought of in the USA in the 1940s, but they did not appear for 30 years.

**FLYING HIGH** Airmail was first used in 1919, to transport letters quickly between the UK and France.

**BEAMING DOWN** High in the sky, communications satellites receive signals and beam them down to a receiver elsewhere in the world. In 1962, *Telstar 1* re-broadcast the first TV image.

## WHO'S ON THE TELEPHONE?

| COUNTRY | NUMBER OF LINES |
|---|---|
| USA | 169,100,000 |
| Japan | 62,680,000 |
| China | 54,100,000 |
| Germany | 45,800,000 |
| France | 32,580,000 |
| UK | 30,630,000 |
| Russia | 25,900,000 |
| Italy | 25,210,000 |
| South Korea | 19,650,000 |
| Canada | 16,500,000 |

**! DID YOU KNOW?** The telephone network in China has grown rapidly from 6,596,000 lines in 1987 to eight times as many within just ten years!

## COUNTRIES WITH THE MOST INTERNET USERS

| COUNTRY | PERCENTAGE OF POPULATION | INTERNET USERS |
|---|---|---|
| USA | 23.00 | 62,000,000 |
| Japan | 7.00 | 8,840,000 |
| Canada | 27.00 | 8,000,000 |
| UK | 10.00 | 6,000,000 |
| Germany | 7.00 | 5,800,000 |
| Sweden | 22.00 | 1,900,000 |
| India | 0.16 | 1,500,000 |
| Norway | 32.00 | 1,400,000 |
| Taiwan | 6.00 | 1,260,000 |
| Australia | 7.00 | 1,210,000 |

## CHILDREN'S INTERNET SITES

**BERIT'S BEST SITES FOR CHILDREN**
http://db.cochran.com/li_toc:theoPage.db

**CHILDREN SEARCH ENGINES**
http://www.internets.com/children.htm

**GREAT SITES!**
http://www.ala.org/parentspage/greatsites/

**INTERESTING PLACES FOR KIDS**
http://www.starport.com/places/forKids

**KIDS' CORNER**
http://kids.ot.com/

### DID YOU KNOW?

Telephones have not always come in neat, rectangular shapes. This candlestick model from the 1930s was one of the first to allow the caller to dial without using the operator.

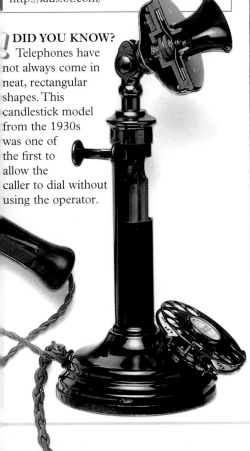

## INTERNET ABBREVIATIONS

| ABBREVIATION | WHAT IT STANDS FOR | WHAT IT MEANS |
|---|---|---|
| ASCII | American Standard Code for Information Interchange | Basic or "plain" text. E-mail messages are sent in ASCII |
| BBS | Bulletin Board System | A system where people leave messages on electronic bulletin boards to be read by other users. |
| bps | Bits Per Second | The speed a modem can send and receive data. |
| DNS | Domain Name Service | The system by which a name (such as an e-mail address or a URL) is converted into a series of numbers. |
| e-mail | Electronic-mail | The way in which messages can be sent and received by computer. |
| FAQ | Frequently Asked Questions | The questions most asked – reading them will save time and help you navigate the site. |
| FTP | File Transfer Protocol | A way of moving files between two Internet sites, used less now than in the early years of the Internet. |
| HTML | HyperText Markup Language | A way of coding text so that words that appear on Internet sites in bold or underlined can be clicked on to take you to another site. |
| http | HyperText Transfer Protocol | Most web page locations begin with "http://", which tells the computers how to connect with each other. |
| IMO | In My Opinion | One of many abbreviations used by people to save time when they send messages, especially to newsgroups. |
| IRC | Internet Relay Chat | A system for many users to have discussions over the Internet via IRC channels. |
| ISDN | Integrated Services Digital Network | A fast way of transferring data over telephone lines. |
| ISP | Internet Service Provider | Allows you to access the Internet. You connect to it every time you log on to the Internet. |
| JPEG | Joint Photographic Experts Group | A type of illustration file. |
| LAN | Local Area Network | Computers connected over a limited area, such as within a university or a business. |
| MIME | Multipurpose Internet Mail Extensions | A coding method by which non-text files can be sent with Internet mail messages. |
| Modem | MOdulator, DEModulator | The device that enables you to connect your computer to another computer, via a phone or cable line. |
| TCP/IP | Transmission Control Protocol/Internet Protocol | The software that lets your computer use the Internet. |
| URL | Uniform Resource Locator | The Internet "address" of a site. |
| www | World Wide Web | Often used to describe the Internet itself, it is the system by which all Internet sites can be accessed from anywhere in the world. |

# BUILDINGS

## TALLEST APARTMENT BUILDINGS

| BUILDING | LOCATION | YEAR | NO OF STOREYS | HEIGHT M | FT |
|---|---|---|---|---|---|
| Lake Point Tower | Chicago | 1968 | 70 | 197 | 645 |
| Central Park Place | New York City | 1988 | 56 | 191 | 628 |
| Olympic Tower | New York City | 1976 | 51 | 189 | 620 |
| May Road Apartments | Hong Kong | 1993 | 58 | 180 | 590 |
| Marina City Apartments | Chicago | 1968 | 61 | 179 | 588 |

## LONG FLIGHTS OF STAIRS

| LOCATION | COUNTRY | STEPS |
|---|---|---|
| Niesenbahn funicular railway, Spiez | Switzerland | 11,674 |
| T'ai Chan Temple | China | 6,600 |
| Mår Power Station | Norway | 3,875 |
| Aura Power Station | Norway | 3,715 |
| CN Tower, Toronto | Canada | 3,642 |
| Ostankino Tower, Moscow | Russia | 3,544 |
| World Trade Centre, New York | USA | 3,140 |
| Empire State Building, New York | USA | 2,908 |

## TALLEST CHIMNEYS

| CHIMNEY | HEIGHT M | FT |
|---|---|---|
| Ekibastuz power station, Kazakhstan | 420 | 1,377 |
| International Nickel Company, Canada | 381 | 1,250 |
| Pennsylvania Electric Company, USA | 371 | 1,216 |
| Kennecott Copper Corporation, USA | 370 | 1,215 |
| Ohio Power Company, USA | 368 | 1,206 |
| Zasavje power station, Yugoslavia | 360 | 1,181 |
| Empresa Nacional de Electricidad SA, Spain | 356 | 1,169 |
| Appalachian Power Company, USA | 336 | 1,103 |
| Indiana & Michigan Electric Company, USA | 316 | 1,037 |

## LARGEST SPORTS STADIUMS

| STADIUM | LOCATION | CAPACITY |
|---|---|---|
| Strahov Stadium | Prague, Czech Republic | 240,000 |
| Maracaña Municipal Stadium | Rio de Janeiro, Brazil | 205,000 |
| Rungnado Stadium | Pyongyang, South Korea | 150,000 |
| Estadio Maghalaes Pinto | Belo Horizonte, Brazil | 125,000 |
| Estadio Morumbi | São Paulo, Brazil | 120,000 |
| Stadio da Luz | Lisbon, Portugal | 120,000 |
| Senayan Main Stadium | Jakarta, Indonesia | 120,000 |
| Yuba Bharati Krirangan | Calcutta, India | 120,000 |
| Estadio Castelão | Fortaleza, Brazil | 119,000 |
| Estadio Arrudão | Recife, Brazil | 115,000 |
| Estadio Azteca | Mexico City, Mexico | 115,000 |
| Nou Camp | Barcelona, Spain | 115,000 |

**DID YOU KNOW?** The New Orleans Superdome, USA, is the largest indoor stadium, with a capacity of 97,365 – only just smaller than the Stadium for the 2000 Olympic Games in Sydney, Australia, which can seat 110,000 people.

## HIGH BUILDINGS YOU CAN VISIT

The chance to go up and look out over vast distances is a feature of buildings the world over. The Eiffel Tower in Paris, France is 274 m (900 ft) high. It was built between 1887 and 1889 and remained the highest viewing platform for 42 years, until the Empire State Building opened. From the 1930s onward, US observatories dominated the world, but have steadily lost ground to Asian buildings, with the KL Tower, Kuala Lumpur, recently joining the list.

| BUILDING | OBSERVATORY | LOCATION | YEAR | HEIGHT M | FT |
|---|---|---|---|---|---|
| CN Tower | Space deck | Toronto, Canada | 1975 | 447 | 1,465 |
| World Trade Center | Roof top Tower B | New York, USA | 1973 | 415 | 1,360 |
| Sears Tower | 103rd floor | Chicago, USA | 1974 | 412 | 1,353 |
| Empire State Building | 102nd floor / Outdoor observatory | New York, USA | 1931 | 381 / 320 | 1,250 / 1,050 |
| Ostankino Tower | 5th floor turret | Moscow, Russia | 1967 | 360 | 1,181 |
| Oriental Pearl | VIP Observation level | Shanghai, China | 1995 | 350 | 1,148 |
| Jin Mao Building | 88th floor | Shanghai, China | 1997 | 340 | 1,115 |
| John Hancock Center | 94th floor | Chicago, USA | 1968 | 314 | 1,030 |
| Sky Central Plaza | 90th floor | Guanghshou, China | 1996 | 310 | 1,016 |
| KL Tower | Revolving restaurant | Kuala Lumpur, Malaysia | 1995 | 282 | 925 |

## LARGEST BUILDINGS

**LARGEST AQUARIUM** The Living Seas Aquarium, EPCOT Center, Florida, USA, is filled with 23,660,000 litres (50,000,000 pints) of water – enough to fill nearly 300,000 baths!

**LARGEST FACTORY** The Boeing aircraft main assembly plant, in Everett, Washington, USA, measured 5,564,200 m³ (196,476,000 ft³) when it was built in 1968. It has since expanded to 13,400,000 m³ (472,000,000 ft³).

**LARGEST CINEMA** The Radio City Music Hall in New York City, USA, can hold 5,874 people.

**LARGEST OPERA HOUSE** New York's Metropolitan Opera House has a total seating capacity of 4,065.

**LARGEST ROMAN STADIUM** The Circus Maximus, in Rome, built in the first century BC, had a track measuring 610 m (2,000 ft) long and 183 m (600 ft) wide. It is said to have drawn crowds of 250,000 spectators!

**LARGEST MONUMENT** The pyramid Quetzalcóatl at Cholula de Rivadabia, Mexico, was built by the Aztecs, who held power in Mexico between the 14th and 16th centuries. The pyramid has an estimated volume of 3,300,000 m³ (4,300,000 yd³) – bigger than Egypt's Great Pyramid, which has a volume of 2,400,000 m³ (9,300,000 ft³).

**LARGEST SHOPPING CENTRE** West Edmonton Mall, in Alberta, Canada, has 11 department stores and 800 shops that cover an areas as large as 90 American football fields!

**LARGEST CASTLE** Built in about AD 850, Prague Castle, in the Czech Republic, covers an area of 8 hectares (20 acres).

## A CENTURY OF TALL BUILDINGS

| BUILDING | LOCATION | YEAR | STOREYS | HEIGHT M | FT |
|---|---|---|---|---|---|
| Auditorium Building | Chicago, USA | 1889 | 15 | 82 | 270 |
| Masonic Temple Building demolished 1939 | Chicago, USA | 1891 | 20 | 84 | 274 |
| American Surety Building (now Bank of Tokyo) | New York, USA | 1895 | 21 | 90 | 306 |
| Saint Paul Building | New York, USA | 1899 | 16 | 94 | 310 |
| Park Row Building | New York, USA | 1899 | 29 | 118 | 386 |
| City Hall | Philadelphia, USA | 1901 | 7 | 155 | 511 |
| Singer Building (demolished 1970) | New York, USA | 1908 | 41 | 200 | 656 |
| Metropolitan Life | New York, USA | 1909 | 50 | 212 | 700 |
| Woolworth Building | New York, USA | 1913 | 57 | 241 | 792 |
| 40 Wall Street | New York, USA | 1929 | 71 | 282 | 927 |
| Chrysler Building | New York, USA | 1930 | 77 | 319 | 1,046 |
| Empire State Building | New York, USA | 1931 | 102 | 381 | 1,250 |
| World Trade Center, New York Tower A | New York, USA | 1972 | 110 | 417 | 1,368 |
| Sears Tower | Chicago, USA | 1974 | 110 | 443 | 1,454 |
| Petronas Towers | Kuala Lumpur, Malaysia | 1996 | 96 | 452 | 1,482 |
| Shanghai World Finance Centre | Shanghai, China | Expected 2001 | 95 | 460 | 1,508 |

## TALL PLACES OF WORSHIP

| PLACE OF WORSHIP | LOCATION | YEAR BUILT | M | FT |
|---|---|---|---|---|
| Rouen Cathedral I | Rouen, France | 1520 | 156 | 512 |
| St Nicholas Church | Hamburg, Germany | 1847 | 145 | 475 |
| Rouen Cathedral II | Rouen, France | 1876 | 148 | 485 |
| Cologne Cathedral | Cologne, Germany | 1880 | 156.4 | 513 |
| Ulm Cathedral | Ulm, Germany | 1890 | 161 | 528 |
| Chicago Methodist Temple | Chicago, USA | 1924 | 173 | 568 |

## CITIES WITH MOST SKYSCRAPERS

| CITY | SKYSCRAPERS |
|---|---|
| New York City, USA | 140 |
| Chicago, USA | 68 |
| Hong Kong, China | 36 |
| Houston, USA | 36 |
| Kuala Lumpur, Malaysia | 25 |

The term "skyscraper" technically describes all habitable buildings with a height of more than 152 m (500 ft).

## SEVEN WONDERS OF THE ANCIENT WORLD

| STRUCTURE | LOCATION | DATE | BUILDERS |
|---|---|---|---|
| Pyramids of Egypt | Egypt | 2575–2465 BC | Ancient Egyptians |
| Hanging Gardens of Babylon | Iraq | 605–562 BC | Ancient Babylonians |
| Temple of Diana at Ephesus | Turkey | 550 BC | Ancient Turks |
| Statue of Zeus by Phidias at Olympia | Greece | c.447 BC | Ancient Greeks |
| Mausoleum at Halicarnassus | Turkey | 350 BC | Ancient Greeks |
| Pharos of Alexandria | Greece | 297 BC | Ancient Greeks |
| Colossus of Rhodes | Greece | c.280 BC | Ancient Greeks |

# BRIDGES, TUNNELS, and DAMS

**DID YOU KNOW?** Built in 1964, the Glen Canyon Dam on the Colorado River, Arizona, USA, is 216 m (710 ft) high and 475 m (1,558 ft) long. It holds back 33 km³ (8 miles³) of water!

## WORLD'S HIGHEST DAMS

| DAM | RIVER | COUNTRY | BUILT | HEIGHT | |
|-----|-------|---------|-------|--------|--|
| | | | | M | FT |
| Rogun | Vakhsh | Russia | Unfinished | 335 | 1,099 |
| Nurek | Vakhsh | Tajikstan | 1980 | 300 | 984 |
| Grand Dixence | Dixence | Switzerland | 1961 | 285 | 935 |
| Inguri | Inguri | Georgia | 1980 | 272 | 892 |
| Vaiont | Piave | Italy | 1961 | 265 | 869 |
| Chicoasén | Grijalva | Mexico | Unfinished | 261 | 856 |
| Tehri | Bhagirathi | India | Unfinished | 261 | 856 |
| Kishau | Tons | India | Unfinished | 253 | 830 |
| Ertan | Yangtze | China | Unfinished | 245 | 804 |

## DEADLY DAMS

**INDIA** The Machu Dam, India, burst on 9 August 1979, flooding the town of Morvi. The death toll was officially 1,000, but may have been as high as 5,000.

**USA** On 31 May 1889 a large earth dam burst at Johnstown, Pennsylvania. It released nearly 20.3 million tonnes (20 million tons) of water that engulfed the town, causing about 2,200 deaths. Incredibly, a 5-month-old baby was rescued alive after floating 121 km (75 miles) downstream on the floor of its wrecked home.

**ITALY** On 9 October 1963, a landslide into the reservoir resulted in the overflowing of the Vaiont Dam, causing a flood that killed more than 2,000 people.

**FRANCE** The Malpasset Dam, Fréjus, collapsed on 3 December 1959, and a 4.5-m (15-ft) wave poured into the town, drowning 419.

**CHINA** During July 1981, the Yangtze River, China, overflowed. Blocked by the Gezhou Dam, vast areas flooded, leaving 753 dead.

## DAM FACTS

**WHAT IS A DAM?** A dam is built to divert or store water.

**OLDEST KNOWN DAM** The Sadd-el-Kafara dam in Egypt was built from rock and earth in about 3000 BC.

**LARGEST DAM** Canada's Syncrude Tailings dam has a capacity of 540,000,000 m³ (706,000,000 ft³).

**LONGEST SEA DAM** Afsluitdijk, Netherlands, is 62.5 km (38.8 miles) long and is built in two sections.

## TUNNEL FACTS

**UNDERWATER TUNNEL** Connecting the Japanese islands of Honshu and Hokkaido, the Seikan tunnel is 53.85 km (33.46 miles) long, of which 23.3 km (14.4 miles) lie 100 m (328 ft) below the sea bed.

**ROAD TUNNEL** Switzerland's St Gotthard tunnel runs for 16 km (10 miles) in the Alps.

**WATER TUNNEL** New York's West Delaware tunnel, which supplies the city with water, is 169 km (105 miles) long.

## LONGEST RAIL TUNNELS

| TUNNEL | COUNTRY | BUILT | KM | MILES |
|--------|---------|-------|-----|-------|
| Alp Transit Link | Switzerland | Unfinished | 57.00 | 35.42 |
| Seikan | Japan | 1988 | 53.85 | 33.46 |
| Channel Tunnel | France, UK | 1994 | 49.94 | 31.03 |
| Moscow Metro (Medvedkovo–Belyaevo) | Russia | 1979 | 30.70 | 19.08 |
| London Underground (Northern Line) | UK | 1939 | 27.84 | 17.30 |
| Daishimizu | Japan | 1982 | 22.23 | 13.81 |
| Simplon II | Italy, Switzerland | 1922 | 19.82 | 12.32 |

## LONGEST ROAD TUNNELS

| TUNNEL | BUILT | KM | MILES |
|--------|-------|-----|-------|
| St Gotthard, Switzerland | 1980 | 16.3 | 10.1 |
| Arlberg, Austria | 1978 | 14.0 | 8.7 |
| Fréjus, France/Italy | 1980 | 12.9 | 8.0 |
| Pinglin Highway, Taiwan | Unfinished | 12.9 | 8.0 |
| Mont-Blanc, France/Italy | 1965 | 11.6 | 7.2 |
| Gudvangen, Norway | 1992 | 11.4 | 7.1 |
| Leirfjord, Norway | Unfinished | 11.1 | 6.9 |
| Kan-Etsu, Japan | 1991 | 11.0 | 6.8 |
| Kan-Etsu, Japan | 1985 | 10.9 | 6.8 |
| Gran Sasso, Italy | 1984 | 10.2 | 6.3 |

## BRIDGE TYPES

**BEAM** The simplest, oldest, and weakest type, a beam bridge is supported at each end and may need to be strengthened underneath.

**ARCH** Built of stone, steel, or concrete, an arch bridge is supported by a keystone in the centre of each arch.

**STEEL ARCH** Similar to an arch bridge, a steel arch is supported by tension on the piers on either shore.

**CANTILEVER** This type has two long arms held in place at the ends by anchors that balance the force. Some swing to let ships through.

**TRESTLE** Supported with diagonal struts or legs, trestle bridges often carry trains across valleys.

**PONTOON** A floating bridge – often temporary – used to replace damaged bridges.

**SUSPENSION** These very long, strong bridges are supported by steel cables from towers on the banks.

**BASCULE** The centre of a bascule bridge opens like a drawbridge to allow tall ships to pass through.

**CABLE-STAYED** Cables from towers support the deck of a cable-stayed bridge.

**GIRDER** A girder bridge is like a beam bridge, but uses strong steel girders.

## FAMOUS BRIDGES

**BRIDGE OF SIGHS, ITALY** Linking Venice's Doge's Palace with the city jail, prisoners sentenced to death travelled over it; its name comes from their sighs of despair.

**LONDON BRIDGE, UK** The replacement for the wooden medieval bridge was dismantled, stone by stone, in 1970 and moved to Arizona, USA.

**SYDNEY HARBOUR BRIDGE, AUSTRALIA** Built in 1932 to carry road and rail, Sydney Harbour Bridge is 49 m (160 ft) wide.

**GOLDEN GATE BRIDGE, USA** San Francisco's Golden Gate was designed for motor vehicles with trains on a deck below – but it has only ever carried road traffic.

## LONGEST CABLE-STAYED BRIDGES

| BRIDGE | LOCATION | BUILT | MAIN SPAN | |
|---|---|---|---|---|
| | | | M | FT |
| Pont de Normandie | Le Havre, France | 1994 | 856 | 2,808 |
| Qunghzhou Minjiang | Fozhou, China | 1996 | 605 | 1,985 |
| Yangpu | Shanghai, China | 1993 | 602 | 1,975 |
| Meiko-Chuo | Nagoya, Japan | 1997 | 590 | 1,936 |
| Xupu | Shanghai, China | 1997 | 590 | 1,936 |
| Skarnsundet | Trondheim Fjord, Norway | 1991 | 530 | 1,739 |
| Ikuchi | Onomichi-Imabari, Japan | 1994 | 490 | 1,608 |
| Higashi-Kobe | Kobe, Japan | 1992 | 485 | 1,591 |
| Ying Kau | Hong Kong, China | 1997 | 475 | 1,558 |
| Seohae Grand | Asan Man, South Korea | 1997 | 470 | 1,542 |

## ENGINEERING EXTREMES

**STRONG SUSPENSION** The Akashi-Kaikyo bridge, Japan, completed in 1998, is the longest suspension bridge, measuring 1,990 m (6,529 ft). It can withstand winds of 290 km/h (180 mph) and earthquakes up to 8.5 on the Richter scale.

**LOST LIVES** Switzerland's St Gotthard Tunnel, completed in 1882, was the costliest in human lives: 310 workers were killed and a further 877 injured.

**TAKING TIME** The concrete used in the Boulder Dam, USA, renamed Hoover in 1947 after the president, is still not fully set after over 60 years!

**DID YOU KNOW?** A novice engineer designed San Francisco's Golden Gate.

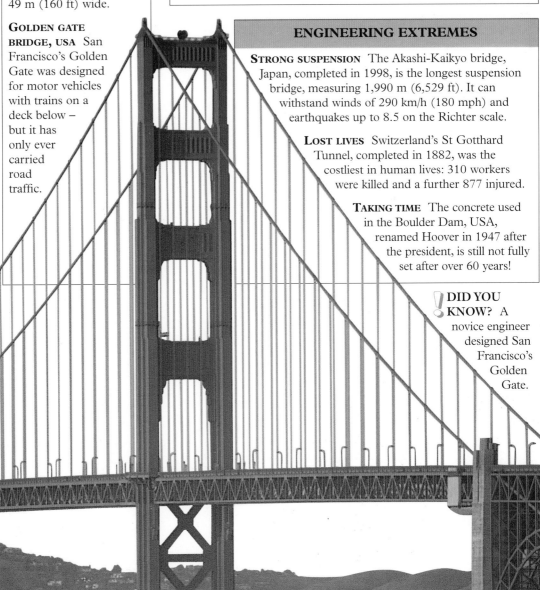

# SHIPS and BOATS

## WATER SPEED RECORD MILESTONES

The first high-speed motor boats were invented in the early years of the 20th century. It was not until Garfield Wood set his 1928 record that speeds were officially measured as the average of two runs (just as with the land speed record).

| PILOT | NATIONALITY | BOAT | YEAR | SPEED | |
|---|---|---|---|---|---|
| | | | | KM/H | MPH |
| Garfield Wood | USA | *Miss America VII* | 1928 | 149.40 | 92.83 |
| Sir Henry Segrave | UK | *Miss England II* | 1930 | 158.94 | 98.76 |
| Sir Malcolm Campbell | UK | *Bluebird K4* | 1939 | 228.10 | 141.74 |
| Stan C. Sayers | USA | *Slo-Mo-Shun IV* | 1952 | 287.26 | 178.50 |
| Donald Campbell | UK | *Bluebird K7* | 1964 | 444.66 | 276.30 |
| Kenneth Warby★ | Australia | *Spirit of Australia* | 1978 | 514.39 | 319.63 |

★ *Current world record-holder*

## WORST OIL TANKER SPILLS OF ALL TIME

In addition to the six major oil spills listed here, it is estimated that an average of 2,000,000 tonnes (1,968,400 tons) of oil are spilled into the world's seas every year. Oil spills cause major environmental damage to sea and bird life and shorelines.

| TANKER | LOCATION | DATE | APPROXIMATE SPILLAGE | |
|---|---|---|---|---|
| | | | TONNES | TONS |
| *Atlantic Empress* and *Aegean Captain* | Trinidad | 1979 | 300,000 | 295,260 |
| *Castillio de Bellver* | Cape Town, South Africa | 1983 | 255,000 | 250,971 |
| *Olympic Bravery* | Ushant, France | 1976 | 250,000 | 246,050 |
| *Showa-Maru* | Malacca, Malaya | 1975 | 237,000 | 233,255 |
| *Amoco Cadiz* | Finistère, France | 1978 | 223,000 | 219,476 |
| *Odyssey* | Atlantic Ocean, off Canada | 1988 | 140,000 | 137,788 |

**DID YOU KNOW?** Although the grounding of the *Exxon Valdez* in Prince William Sound, Alaska, on 24 March 1989, ranks outside the worst oil spills, at about 35,000 tonnes (34,450 tons), it resulted in major environmental damage, with many fish, marine mammals, and birds killed.

## TOP SHIPPING COUNTRIES

| COUNTRY | SHIPS | GROSS TONNAGE |
|---|---|---|
| Panama | 6,188 | 91,128,000,000 |
| Liberia | 1,697 | 60,058,000,000 |
| Bahamas | 1,221 | 25,523,000,000 |
| Greece | 1,641 | 25,288,000,000 |
| Cyprus | 1,650 | 23,653,000,000 |

**WHAT'S TONNAGE?** A ship's gross tonnage is its weight when empty. Its deadweight tonnage is its laden weight including cargo and crew. Tonnage is measured in British tons and never converted into metric tonnes.

## FASTEST SPEEDS ON AND UNDER THE WATER

**ROWING EIGHT** The Oxford and Cambridge Boat Race speed record is 24.28 km/h (15.09 mph), achieved by the Oxford Crew in 1984.

**SAILBOARD** The record is 82.70 km/h (51.39 mph), achieved in France by Frenchman Thierry Bielak in 1993.

**HOVERCRAFT** In 1980, a US Navy Bell SES-1008 experimental vehicle achieved a speed of 170 km/h (105.6 mph).

**YACHT** The Australian trifoil *Yellow Pages Endeavour* reached 86.21 km/h (53.57 mph) in Australia in 1993.

**SUBMARINE (SUBMERGED)** Russian *Alfa* class submarines are believed to attain 83.4 km/h (51.8 mph), and US Navy *Los Angeles* class 74 km/h (46 mph), but the precise figures are military secrets.

## WORLD'S BUSIEST PORTS

| PORT (COUNTRY) | GOODS HANDLED PER YEAR IN MILLIONS OF | |
| --- | --- | --- |
| | TONNES | TONS |
| Rotterdam (Netherlands) | 350 | 345 |
| Singapore (Singapore) | 290 | 285 |
| Chiba (Japan) | 174 | 171 |
| Kobe (Japan) | 171 | 168 |
| Hong Kong (China) | 147 | 145 |

## BIGGEST SHIPS THROUGH HISTORY

| ORIGINAL NAME OF SHIP | LAUNCHED | GROSS TONNAGE |
| --- | --- | --- |
| *Great Western* | 1838 | 1,340 |
| *Himalaya* | 1853 | 4,690 |
| *Lusitania* | 1907 | 31,550 |
| *Mauretania* | 1907 | 31,938 |
| *Titanic* | 1912 | 46,232 |
| *Vaterland* | 1914 | 54,282 |
| *Bismarck* | 1922 | 56,621 |
| *Normandie* | 1935 | 79,301 |
| *Queen Mary* | 1936 | 80,774 |
| *Grand Princess* | 1998 | 104,000 |
| *RCCL Eagle 1* | 1999 | 142,000 |

**DID YOU KNOW?** The *RCCL Eagle 1* is almost 106 times bigger than the *Great Western*!

## FAMOUS SAILORS

**CHRISTOPER COLUMBUS (1451–1506)** Italian sailor, famed for his discovery of America in 1492.

**SIR FRANCIS DRAKE (c.1540–1596)** First Englishman to sail around the globe, in 1588 Drake also defeated the Spanish Armada.

**CAPTAIN JAMES COOK (1728–1779)** British seaman who explored the Australian coast and South Seas.

## FAMOUS SHIPWRECKS

**MARY ROSE** A Tudor galleon, which sank in 1545, was found in 1968, and raised in 1982. It is exhibited in Portsmouth, UK.

**WASA** A Swedish warship that capsized in Stockholm harbour in 1628. The ship and its treasures were recovered from the sea bed in 1961.

**TITANIC** This great liner sank in 1912, with the loss of 1,500 lives. The wreck was discovered and explored in 1986.

**EMPRESS OF IRELAND** The ship sank after a collision in the St Lawrence River, Canada, 1914, killing 1,012. Divers have since visited the wreck.

**ANDREA DORIA** The *Andrea Doria* sank after colliding off the US coast in 1956.

## LARGEST OIL TANKERS

| SHIP | YEAR BUILT | COUNTRY | GROSS TONNAGE | DEADWEIGHT TONNAGE |
| --- | --- | --- | --- | --- |
| *Jahre Viking* | 1979 | Japan | 260,851 | 564,763 |
| *Sea Giant* | 1979 | France | 261,862 | 555,051 |
| *Kapetan Giannis* | 1977 | Japan | 247,160 | 516,895 |
| *Kapetan Michalis* | 1977 | Japan | 247,160 | 516,423 |
| *Sea World* | 1978 | Sweden | 237,768 | 491,120 |
| *Nissei Maru* | 1975 | Japan | 238,517 | 238,517 |

## WORLD'S LONGEST CRUISE SHIPS

| SHIP | YEAR BUILT | COUNTRY | LENGTH | |
| --- | --- | --- | --- | --- |
| | | | M | FT |
| *Norway* | 1961 | France | 315.5 | 1,035.0 |
| *RCCL Eagle 1* | 1999 | Finland | 309.0 | 1,014.0 |
| *RCCL Eagle 2* | 2000 | Finland | 309.0 | 1,014.0 |
| *United States* | 1952 | USA | 301.7 | 990.0 |
| *Disney Magic* | 1998 | Italy | 294.0 | 964.5 |
| *Disney Wonder* | 1998 | Italy | 294.0 | 964.5 |

## FAMOUS MARINE DISASTERS

**WORLD WAR II LINER** Up to 7,800 people were killed in 1945 when the German liner *Wilhelm Gustloff*, laden with refugees, was torpedoed off the Polish coast by a Soviet submarine.

**SPANISH ARMADA** In 1588, a three-month naval conflict off the British coast between Britain and Spain destroyed the Spanish fleet (Armada), killing 4,000.

**FERRY DISASTER** The *Dona Paz* sank in the Philippines in 1987 after being hit by an oil tanker. The official death toll was 3,000 but may be as high as 4,386.

**STEAMBOAT EXPLOSION** In 1865, a boiler explosion destroyed a Mississippi River steamboat, the *Sultana*, killing 1,547. Although the death toll may be an underestimate, it was the USA's worst ever marine accident.

# ROAD TRAVEL

## ON THE BUSES

**FIRST DOUBLE DECKER** Horse-drawn double decker buses were first seen on the streets of London, UK, in 1857. Petrol-engined buses were first used in Germany in 1895, and in Bradford, UK, in 1897.

**LONGEST BUS ROUTE** A bus travels 9,660 km (6,003 miles) from Venezuela to Argentina.

**BIGGEST BUS** The articulated Super City Train Buses used in the Democratic Republic of Congo (formerly Zaire) measure 32.2 m (105 ft 8 in) in length. They can carry 110 seated passengers and 140 standing in the first part, and 60 seated passengers and 40 standing in the second.

## AMAZING CARS

**HEAVIEST** A Lincoln Continental limousine, built in 1968 in the USA, weighed 5.35 tonnes (5.9 tons). More than half of its weight was protective armour plating!

**SMALLEST** The *Peel* is one of the smallest cars ever built, at only 1.34 m (4.4 ft) long. It has no reverse gear.

**MOST LUXURIOUS** A Rolls-Royce Phantom 1 made in 1927 had an interior upholstered in silk tapestry.

**FASTEST SOLAR** In 1988, General Motors' solar-powered *Sunraycer* reached 78.4 km/h (48.71 mph) on sunlight alone. Its special panels convert the sunlight into electrical energy.

!**DID YOU KNOW?** There are about 60,000 taxis in Mexico City, Mexico.

!**DID YOU KNOW?** During its peak production years, over half the new cars in the world were Model T Fords.

## BEST-SELLING CARS

**BEETLEMANIA** Sales of the Volkswagen Beetle, first manufactured in Germany in 1937, now exceed 21,220,000, making it the most-produced model of all time.

**LONG-RUNNER** The British Morgan 4/4 sportscar has been made continuously since 1935.

**MODEL CAR** Production of the Model T Ford began in the USA in 1908 and ended in 1927, by which time 16,536,075 had been built. The Model T was the first to be assembled on a production line.

**BIGGEST MANUFACTURER** The General Motors Corporation, USA, produced a total of 9,297,395 vehicles in 1978, more than any other company before or since that time.

## LAND SPEED RECORD MILESTONES

| DRIVER | COUNTRY | VEHICLE | DATE | LOCATION | RECORD SPEED | |
|--------|---------|---------|------|----------|--------------|--|
| | | | | | KM/H | MPH |
| Barney Oldfield | USA | *Benz Blitzen* | 16 March 1910 | Daytona, USA | 211.27 | 131.28 |
| Tommy Milton | USA | *Duesenberg* | 27 April 1920 | Daytona, USA | 251.11 | 156.03 |
| Henry Segrave | UK | *Golden Arrow* | 11 March 1929 | Daytona, USA | 372.48 | 231.45 |
| John Cobb | UK | *Railton Mobil Special* | 16 September 1947 | Bonneville, USA | 634.396 | 394.196 |
| Donald Campbell | UK | *Bluebird* | 17 July 1964 | Lake Eyre, Australia | 648.730 | 403.100 |
| Art Arfons | USA | *Green Monster* | 7 November 1965 | Bonneville, USA | 927.870 | 576.553 |
| Craig Breedlove | USA | *Spirit of America Sonic 1* | 15 November 1965 | Bonneville, USA | 966.574 | 600.601 |
| Gary Gabelich | USA | *The Blue Flame* | 23 October 1970 | Bonneville, USA | 1,001.667 | 622.407 |
| Richard Noble | UK | *Thrust 2* | 4 October 1983 | Black Rock, USA | 1,019.237 | 633.468 |

## COUNTRIES WITH MOST CAR-OWNERS

| COUNTRY | CARS | COMMERCIAL VEHICLES | TOTAL |
|---|---|---|---|
| USA | 147,171,000 | 48,298,000 | 195,469,000 |
| Japan | 42,678,430 | 22,333,042 | 65,011,472 |
| Germany | 39,917,577 | 2,960,334 | 42,877,911 |
| Italy | 29,800,000 | 2,777,500 | 32,577,500 |
| France | 24,900,000 | 5,140,000 | 30,040,000 |
| UK | 23,831,906 | 3,604,972 | 27,436,878 |
| Russia | 13,549,000 | 9,856,000 | 23,405,000 |

## FIRST ON THE ROAD

**FIRST CAR** In 1886, German engineer Karl Benz exhibited a three-wheeled petrol-driven two-seater called the "Motorwagen". It could go up to 13 km/h (8 mph).

**FIRST ELECTRIC TRAM** Launched in 1901, electric trams took their power from overhead cables, carried no fuel, and did not pollute the streets.

**FIRST TRUCK** Benz produced the first diesel-powered truck in 1923. It became commercially available the following year. Diesel engines are more powerful, run on cheaper fuel, and allow more distance to be covered per tank than petrol engines.

**FIRST FIRE ENGINE** In 1731, in Philadelphia, USA, a hand-operated pump was used to put out fires, instead of a chain of water-filled buckets. Mounted on wheels, it was the first practical fire engine.

**FIRST METERED TAXI** Arguments between taxi drivers and passengers over fares were all too common, so the first metered cabs took to Germany's roads in 1896. The idea spread quickly.

## ROAD RECORDS

**MOST ROADS** Probably not surprisingly, the USA has a network of roads about 6,284,039 km (3,904,721 miles) long. It is followed by India, with roads stretching 2,159,740 km (1,342,000 miles).

**BUSIEST ROAD** In the rush hour, 25,500 vehicles crawl along a 1.5 km (1 mile) stretch of Interstate 405 in California, USA.

**LONGEST ROAD** The Pan-American Highway runs 24,140 km (15,000 miles) through the USA to Brazil.

**HIGHEST ROAD** In places, the road between Tibet and Xinjiang in China lies 5,633 m (18,480 ft) above sea level.

**WIDEST ROAD** The six-lane Monumental Axis in Brasília, Brazil, measures 250 m (820 ft) – the widest road in the world!

**FIRST MOTORWAY** In 1921, the first *Sutobahn* (motorway) was opened in Berlin, Germany.

**DID YOU KNOW?** In the early days of motoring, Italians drove on the left in towns and on the right in the countryside!

## ROAD DISASTERS

**AFGHANISTAN, 3 NOVEMBER 1982** Following a collision with a Soviet army truck, a petrol tanker exploded in the 2.7-km (1.7-mile) Salang Tunnel. Some authorities put the death toll from the explosion, fire, and fumes as high as 3,000.

**COLOMBIA, 7 AUGUST 1956** About 1,200 people were killed when seven army ammunition trucks exploded in Cali, destroying eight city blocks. This included a barracks of 500 sleeping soldiers.

**NEPAL, 23 NOVEMBER 1974** About 148 Hindu pilgrims were killed when a suspension bridge over the River Mahahali collapsed.

## AMAZING VEHICLES

**LONGEST LIMOUSINE** A limousine built by Jay Ohrberg of California measures 30.5 m (100 ft) and has 26 wheels. It is so long that it has to be hinged in the middle to enable it to turn corners!

**BIGGEST FIRE ENGINES** Fire engines made by the Oshkosh Truck Corporation of Wisconsin, USA for use at airports, have eight wheels, 860-horsepower engines, and weigh 60 tonnes (59 tons).

**DID YOU KNOW?** One American limousine is equipped with a swimming pool and helicopter landing pad!

**BIGGEST TYRES** The largest road vehicle tyres are 3.82 m (12 ft 6 in) in diameter, and are made by the Bridgestone Corporation, Japan, for giant dumper trucks.

**LARGEST LAND VEHICLES** The Crawler-Transporters used to move Space Shuttles are 6.1 m (20 ft) high, 34.7 m (114 ft) wide, and 40 m (131 ft) deep. Each weighs 2.7 million kg (6 million lb) unloaded.

**BIGGEST DUMPER TRUCK** The General Motors Terex Titan 33-19 mine truck, first made in 1974, is able to carry 317.5 tonnes (312.5 tons).

**AMAZING FACT!** The first (and last!) "motorized orange" car was made during the 1970s! It had the engine of a mini and a specially built chassis. The bizarre orange vehicle was manufactured by a firm that sold fruit.

# BIKES and MOTORCYCLES

## BICYCLE TIMELINE

**1790 CÉLÉRIFÈRE** This wooden, hobby horse-like machine is built by the French Count de Sivrac.

**1817 HOBBY HORSE** This early ancestor of the bicycle, made by Baron Karl von Drais, has no brakes or pedals.

**1839 PEDAL-POWERED BICYCLE** Built by Scottish blacksmith Kirkpatrick Macmillan, this bicycle is not a success.

**DID YOU KNOW?** Kirkpatrick Macmillan, inventor of the pedal-driven cycle is also the first to be fined for a cycling offence. In 1842, a Scottish police court fines him for riding on the footpath and knocking down a child.

**1861 VÉLOCIPÈDE** Frenchman Ernest Michaux builds a bicycle with pedals at the front.

**1870 ORDINARY, OR PENNY-FARTHING** The big front wheel enables the bicycle to travel farther for each turn of the pedals.

**1885 "ROVER" SAFETY BICYCLE** Produced in England by J. K. Starley, this bicycle is the first to have two equal-sized wheels, the rear one driven by a chain from the pedals.

**1888 PNEUMATIC TYRES** Scotsman John B. Dunlop reinvents air-filled, pneumatic tyres for his son's bicycle.

**1903 FIRST TOUR DE FRANCE CYCLE RACE**

**1961 MOULTON** This small-wheeled bicycle is the first new design for 50 years.

**1981 MOUNTAIN BIKES** The first all-terrain mountain bike is made by Charles Kelly and Gary Fisher of the USA.

**1983 BMX** Bikes designed for rough terrain and tricks.

**1990s RECUMBENT BICYCLES** Propelled from an almost lying position, these unusual bicycles, with the pedals at the front, reach greater speeds than ordinary bicycles.

## BICYCLES MADE FOR TWO – OR MORE

**TANDEM** The first successful tandems (bicycles for two) became popular in 1886. They were first made in the UK.

**TENDEM** This bicycle made for ten riders, first appeared in Massachusetts, USA in 1924. The riders claim to have reached a speed of 96.6 km/h (60 mph).

**QUINDEM** A group of five US soldiers living in the UK in the 1940s built an unusual five-seater "quindem" so that they could all travel together.

**MOTORIZED TANDEM** Built in France, 1939, this vehicle had 5-cm (2-in) balloon tyres and five chains for motor and pedal drives. The exhaust discharged on to the feet of the front driver.

**FIREMAN'S DUAL TANDEM** A rare team of British firefighters in the early 20th century rushed to fires on two tandems secured side by side. A pump in between was operated by pedalling.

## CYCLING SAFETY TIPS

- Always wear a cycle helmet to protect your head.

- Wear brightly coloured or fluorescent clothes so you can be seen on dull days.

- Give way to pedestrians when you are riding on cycle trails and paths.

- Keep to cycle trails and paths and do not damage crops or plants or disturb livestock or wildlife.

- Always attach lights to your bicycle when you cycle in the dark.

- Check to see what other vehicles are doing, then signal your intentions clearly to traffic.

- Cycle past parked cars with caution, and beware of a car door suddenly opening into your path.

- Seek out quiet routes away from heavy, fast-moving traffic.

- Obey all traffic signals and lights, and learn your highway code.

- Try to think ahead! Anticipating the actions of others on the road and pavement could help you to avoid an accident.

## BICYCLES FOR FUN

**AMPHIBIOUS BICYCLE** In 1914, H. G. Belbin invented an amphibious bicycle with a float either side that could be used on land or water without alteration. It was propelled in water by a screw propeller driven by a long cycle chain.

**BICYCLES ON RAILS** In the early 20th century, a special two-seater "rail cycle" was invented for inspecting the track in northern Britain. It was made of two adapted bicycles held parallel with each other by iron rods.

**WATER CYCLE** E. M. Vareed from India developed a home-made water cycle. It consisted of an ordinary bicycle without the tyres, fitted with a steering wheel, saddle, and three floats.

**ICE-CYCLE** Freddie Chapman, Britain's ice-skating champion in 1928, built an ice-cycle with just a rear wheel for propulsion and a blade in front and behind.

**BED-CYCLE** Canadian bicycle expert Charles Steilauf gave his wife the chance to sleep until the last minute on her way to work, by fitting wheels, pedals, gears, and handlebars to her bed.

**MUSICAL BICYCLES** The Belgian army once added elbow rests to the bicycles ridden by their regimental bands, so that they could play their instruments whilst cycling!

**DID YOU KNOW?** The fastest speed on a bicycle is 245.08 km/h (152.3 mph), achieved by American John Howard in 1985.

## MOTORCYCLE TIMELINE

**1867 STEAM-DRIVEN VELOCIPEDE**
Frenchman L. G. Perreaux creates the first motorcycle when he fits a steam engine to Michaux's *velocipède*.

**1885 DAIMLER MOTORCYCLE** Gottlieb Daimler makes a motorcycle by fitting his internal combustion engine to a wooden-wheeled bicycle.

**1901 STANDARD MOTORCYCLE**
The French Werner brothers design a motorcycle with the engine and the pedals in the same place. This design becomes standard.

**1904 HARLEY-DAVIDSON** US motorcycling manufacturer Harley-Davidson goes into production, with the *Silent Gray Fellow*.

**1907 FIRST TT RACE**
The abbreviation TT stands for "Tourist Trophy". The first TT race is held in the Isle of Man, UK.

**1959 BONNEVILLE** This high performance motorcycle is probably Triumph's most famous model.

**1968 HONDA SUPERBIKE** The development of multi-cylindered engines produces fast, smooth-running, reliable bikes, such as Honda's CB750.

**1990s COMPUTERIZED MOTORCYCLE**
The engine of BMW's R1100 is managed by sophisticated electronics.

## WACKY MOTORCYCLE RECORDS

**SMALLEST MOTORBIKE** A tiny motorbike was made with a front wheel diameter of 1.9 cm (0.75 in). It was ridden for 1 m (3 ft 4 in).

**LONGEST RAMP JUMP** In 1991, Doug Danger from the USA jumped 76.5 m (251 ft) on a Honda CR 500.

**LONGEST MOTORBIKE** Designed and built by American Gregg Reid, the longest street-legal motorbike stretched for 4.57 m (15 ft).

**LONGEST WHEELIE** Yauyuki Kudo of Japan rode non-stop on the back wheel for 331 km (205.75 miles) in 1991.

**DID YOU KNOW?**
The Honda CB750, which went on sale in 1968, has a top speed of 190 km/h (120 mph).

HONDA
SUPERBIKE

### FIRST HOLDERS OF THE MOTORCYCLE SPEED RECORD

In 1920, the Fédération Internationale Motorcycliste (International Motorcycling Federation) became the first organization to officially ratify motorcycle speed records.

| RIDER | MOTORCYCLE | LOCATION | YEAR | KM/H | MPH |
|---|---|---|---|---|---|
| Ernest Walker | 994 cc Indian | Daytona Beach, USA | 1920 | 167.67 | 104.19 |
| Claude F. Temple | 996 cc British Azani | Brooklands, UK | 1923 | 174.58 | 108.48 |
| Herbert Le Vack | 867 cc Brough Superior | Arpajon, France | 1924 | 191.59 | 118.05 |
| Claude F. Temple | 996 cc OEC Temple | Arpajon, France | 1926 | 191.58 | 119.05 |
| Oliver M. Baldwin | 996 cc Zenith JAP | Arpajon, France | 1928 | 200.56 | 124.62 |

## FASTEST MOTORCYCLES

| MODEL | SPEED | |
|---|---|---|
| | KM/H | MPH |
| Bimota SB6R | 290 | 180 |
| Honda CBR1100XX *Blackbird* | 285 | 177 |
| Bimota YB11 | 282 | 175 |
| Kawasaki ZZ-R1100 | 280 | 174 |
| Kawasaki Ninja ZX-9RR | 280 | 174 |
| Yamaha YZF-R1 | 278 | 173 |
| Kawasaki Ninja ZX-7RR | 272 | 169 |
| Kawasaki Ninja ZX-6R | 270 | 168 |
| Honda CBR900RR *Fireblade* | 269 | 167 |

### LATEST HOLDERS OF THE MOTORCYCLE SPEED RECORD

All the records listed here were achieved at the Bonneville Salt Flats, USA. To break a Fédération Internationale Motorcycliste record, the motorcycle has to cover a measured distance, making two runs within one hour, and taking the average of the two. US Motorcycling Association records require a turnround within two hours.

| RIDER | MOTORCYCLE | YEAR | KM/H | MPH |
|---|---|---|---|---|
| Calvin Rayborn | 1,480 cc Harley-Davidson | 1970 | 410.37 | 254.99 |
| Calvin Rayborn | 1,480 cc Harley-Davidson | 1970 | 426.40 | 264.96 |
| Donald A. Vesco | 1,496 cc Yamaha Silver Bird | 1975 | 487.50 | 302.93 |
| Donald A. Vesco | Twin 1,016 cc Kawasaki Lightning Bolt | 1978 | 512.73 | 318.60 |
| Dave Campos | Twin 91 cu in/1,491 cc Ruxton Harley-Davidson Easyriders | 1990 | 518.45 | 322.15 |

# RAIL TRAVEL

## FASTEST RAIL JOURNEYS

| JOURNEY | LOCOMOTIVE | DISTANCE | | SPEED | |
|---|---|---|---|---|---|
| | | KM | MILES | KM/H | MPH |
| Hiroshima-Kokura, Japan | *Nozomi* 503/508 | 192.0 | 119.3 | 261.8 | 162.7 |
| Lille-Roissy, France | TGV 538/9 | 203.4 | 126.4 | 254.3 | 158.0 |
| Madrid-Seville, Spain | *AVE* 9616/9617 | 470.5 | 292.4 | 209.1 | 129.9 |
| Würzburg-Fulda, Germany | ICE | 93.2 | 57.9 | 199.7 | 124.0 |
| London-York, UK | *Scottish Pullman* | 303.3 | 188.5 | 180.2 | 112.0 |
| Hässleholm-Alvesta, Sweden | X2000 | 98.0 | 60.9 | 168.0 | 104.4 |
| Rome-Florence, Italy | 10 Pendolini | 261.0 | 162.2 | 164.9 | 102.5 |

## BUSIEST RAIL NETWORKS

| COUNTRY | PASSENGERS PER ANNUM | |
|---|---|---|
| | PER KM | PER MILE |
| Japan | 396,332,000,000 | 246,269,000,000 |
| China | 354,700,000,000 | 219,965,000,000 |
| India | 319,400,000,000 | 198,500,000,000 |
| Russia | 191,900,000,000 | 119,200,000,000 |
| Ukraine | 75,900,000,000 | 47,200,000,000 |
| France | 58,380,000,000 | 36,276,000,000 |
| Germany | 58,003,000,000 | 36,041,000,000 |

## RAIL FIRSTS

**FIRST WORKING STEAM LOCOMOTIVE** In 1804, Richard Trevithick, of Cornwall, built a steam locomotive that could haul coal wagons and 70 men.

**FIRST TO PROVE STEAM WORKED** In 1829, English engineers Henry Booth and Robert Stephenson built *Rocket*, heralding the age of steam trains.

**FIRST TO SERVE MEALS** The Baltimore and Ohio Railroad in the USA began serving food on its trains in 1853.

**FIRST UNDERGROUND TRAINS** The first underground trains ran in 1863, beneath the bustling streets of London.

**FIRST ELECTRIC TRAIN** The first electric trains ran in Germany in 1881.

**FIRST DIESEL LOCOMOTIVE** Dr Rudolph Diesel, a German engineer, demonstrated the first working diesel engine in 1893, and built the first reliable locomotive in 1897.

**FIRST DRIVERLESS TRAIN** A computer-operated train first ran in France in 1983!

## FIRST RAILWAYS

In their early years, some of the railways listed offered only limited services over short distances, but their opening dates mark the generally accepted beginning of each country's railway system.

| COUNTRY | FIRST ESTABLISHED RAILWAY |
|---|---|
| UK | 27 September 1825 |
| France | 7 November 1829 |
| USA | 24 May 1830 |
| Ireland | 17 December 1834 |
| Belgium | 5 May 1835 |
| Germany | 7 December 1835 |
| Canada | 21 July 1836 |

## LONGEST RAIL NETWORKS

| COUNTRY | TOTAL RAIL LENGTH | |
|---|---|---|
| | KM | MILES |
| USA | 240,000 | 149,129 |
| Russia | 154,000 | 95,691 |
| Canada | 70,176 | 43,605 |
| India | 62,462 | 38,812 |
| China | 58,399 | 36,287 |
| Germany | 43,966 | 27,319 |
| Australia | 38,563 | 23,962 |

**AMAZING FACT!** The rail network of the USA could stretch around the Earth almost six times over!

**SHORTEST RAIL NETWORK!** The Vatican City has just 850 m (2,789 ft) of track.

## RAIL DISASTERS

**FIRST FATALITY** At the opening of the Liverpool and Manchester Railway, UK, in 1830, Member of Parliament William Huskisson was knocked down and killed.

**WORST DISASTER** On 6 June 1981, an Indian train plunged off a bridge when the driver braked to avoid hitting a cow. Officially, 268 bodies were recovered, but it is claimed that the train was so overcrowded that the actual figure was in excess of 800.

**WORST UNDERGROUND DISASTER** On 28 October 1995, a tube train in Azerbaijan, Asia, caught fire during the evening rush hour, killing more than 300 people.

**DID YOU KNOW?** Train toilets were first fitted in the 1850s.

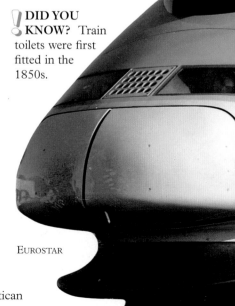

EUROSTAR

## BUSIEST UNDERGROUND RAIL SYSTEMS

| CITY | YEAR OPENED | TOTAL LENGTH KM | TOTAL LENGTH MILES | NUMBER OF STATIONS | PASSENGERS PER YEAR |
|---|---|---|---|---|---|
| Moscow, Russia | 1935 | 244 | 152 | 150 | 3,183,900,000 |
| Tokyo, Japan (TRTA) | 1927 | 169 | 105 | 154 | 2,112,700,000 |
| Mexico City, Mexico | 1969 | 178 | 111 | 154 | 1,422,600,000 |
| Seoul, Korea | 1974 | 133 | 83 | 112 | 1,354,000,000 |
| Paris, France | 1900 | 201 | 125 | 372 | 1,170,000,000 |
| New York, USA | 1904 | 398 | 247 | 469 | 1,100,000,000 |
| Osaka, Japan | 1933 | 106 | 66 | 99 | 988,600,000 |
| St Petersburg, Russia | 1955 | 92 | 57 | 50 | 850,000,000 |
| Hong Kong, China | 1979 | 43 | 269 | 38 | 804,000,000 |

**! AMAZING FACT!** New York's bustling Grand Central Terminal station is the world's largest, with 44 platforms. Half a million people pass through the station every day.

## OLDEST UNDERGROUND RAILWAY SYSTEMS

| CITY | OPENED |
|---|---|
| London, UK | 1863 |
| Budapest, Hungary | 1896 |
| Glasgow, UK | 1896 |
| Boston, USA | 1897 |
| Paris, France | 1900 |
| Wuppertal, Germany | 1901 |
| Athens, Greece | 1901 |
| Berlin, Germany | 1902 |
| New York, USA | 1904 |
| Philadelphia, USA | 1907 |
| Hamburg, Germany | 1912 |

## RAILWAY RECORDS

**HEAVIEST TRAIN** *Challenger*, built in 1942, ran on the Union Pacific Railroad, and weighed 494 tonnes (486 tons).

**MOST POWERFUL DIESEL-ELECTRIC TRAIN** When the Deltic Train was built in 1956, it was the fastest in the world. In 1987, a British Airways High Speed Train achieved 283.9 km/h (176.4 mph).

**FASTEST TRAIN** A record trip of 515 km/h (320 mph) was made by the French TGV in May 1990.

**LONGEST PLATFORM** The Washington-Monroe-Jackson platform in Chicago, USA, stretches 1,067 m (3,500 ft)!

**FASTEST STEAM TRAIN** In 1938, the *Mallard* made its most famous journey when it set the world speed record at 203 km/h (126 mph).

**MOST LUXURIOUS** South Africa's Blue Train has been described as "a five-star hotel on wheels". Introduced in 1939, it runs between Pretoria and Cape Town.

**LONGEST JOURNEY** A train on the Russian Trans-Siberian line runs continuously from Moscow to Vladivostok, a distance of 9,297 km (5,777 miles).

**! DID YOU KNOW?** Eurostar, which runs through the Channel Tunnel can run on different voltages.

## FAMOUS TRAINS

**FLYING SCOTSMAN** Built in 1923, the UK's *Flying Scotsman* took express passenger trains between London, England, and Edinburgh, Scotland. It continued in service until 1963.

**BIG BOYS** Built by the American Locomotive Company for the Union Pacific Railroad these locomotives were in production between 1941 to 1944 and were among the largest ever built.

**ORIENT EXPRESS** This luxurious train was used by so many secret agents that it became known as the "Spies Express". It was introduced in 1883, and ran between London, Paris, Vienna, Budapest, and Constantinople (now Istanbul).

**BULLET TRAIN** Japan's high-speed, bullet-shaped train began running between Tokyo and Osaka in 1965. It is capable of speeds of up to 210 km/h (130 mph)!

**FLYING HAMBURGER** This speedy diesel train was introduced in Germany in 1933. It ran between Berlin and Hamburg at 161 km/h (100 mph).

**HIAWATHA** Introduced in 1935, in the USA, this steam train travelled between Chicago and Minneapolis-St Paul in five hours and five minutes.

# PIONEERS of FLIGHT

## FIRST BALLOON FLIGHTS

**FIRST PASSENGERS** The Montgolfier Brothers, Joseph and Etienne, were invited to demonstrate their balloon to Louis XVI at Versailles, France. On 19 September 1783, it took off with the first-ever air passengers: a sheep, a rooster, and a duck!

**FIRST HUMANS TO FLY** On 21 November 1783, François Laurent, Marquis d'Arlandes, and Jean-François Pilâtre de Rozier took off from the Bois de Boulogne, Paris, France, in a Montgolfier hot-air balloon. This first-ever manned flight covered a distance of about 9 km (5.5 miles) in 23 minutes, before landing near Gentilly.

**FIRST SOLO** On 1 December 1783, Jacques Alexandre César Charles and Nicholas-Louis Robert made the first-ever flight in a hydrogen balloon. They took off from the Tuileries, Paris, France, and travelled 43 km (27 miles) north to Nesle in about two hours. Charles then took off alone, becoming the first solo flier.

**FIRST STOWAWAY** On 19 January 1784, in Lyons, France, a man called Fontaine leaped into *La Flesselle*, a huge 40-m (131-ft high) Montgolfier hot-air balloon, as it was taking off. He shared the journey with pilot Pilâtre de Rozier, and Joseph Montgolfier, Prince Charles de Ligne, and the Comtes de La Porte d'Anglefort, de Dampierre, and de Laurencin.

**FIRST FEMALE TO FLY** On 4 June 1784, Elisabeth Thiblé, a French opera singer, became the first woman to fly in a balloon. She accompanied Monsieur Fleurant in his balloon *Le Gustava* in a flight from Lyons. The Marchioness de Montalembert and other aristocratic ladies had already ascended on 20 May 1784 – but in a tethered balloon.

**FIRST TO CROSS THE CHANNEL, FIRST AMERICAN, AND FIRST AIRMAIL** On 7 January 1785, Jean-Pierre Blanchard and Dr John Jeffries (the first American to fly) achieved the first Channel crossing and carried the first airmail letter. As their balloon lost height, they had to reduce weight, so they threw everything overboard including their clothes!

## EARLY FLYING DEATHS

**FIRST TO DIE** On 15 June 1785, Pilâtre de Rozier and Jules Romain were the first air fatalities near Boulogne, France, when their hydrogen balloon caught fire during an attempted Channel crossing.

**ROBERT COCKING** On 24 July 1837, pioneer parachutist Robert Cocking from Kent, UK, jumped from *Great Nassau Balloon*, but his parachute collapsed.

**HENRI LETUR** Parachutist Letur from France, was injured when he fell from a balloon on 27 June 1854; he died eight days later.

**VINCENT DE GROOF** On 9 July 1874, the Belgian pioneer De Groof was killed when his ornithopter (a type of aircraft) crashed after being dropped from a balloon at Chelsea, UK.

## FIRST ROCKET AND JET-POWERED AIRCRAFT

| AIRCRAFT | COUNTRY | FIRST FLIGHT |
|---|---|---|
| Heinkel He 176★ | Germany | June 1939 |
| Heinkel He 178★ | Germany | August 1939 |

!  **DID YOU KNOW?** Prototypes of the rocket-powered Heinkels 176 and 178 first flew prior to World War II.

| AIRCRAFT | COUNTRY | FIRST FLIGHT |
|---|---|---|
| DFS 194★ | Germany | August 1940 |
| Caproni-Campini N-1 | Italy | August 1940 |
| Heinkel He 280V-1 | Germany | April 1941 |
| Gloster E.28/39 | UK | May 1941 |
| Messerschmitt Me 163 Komet★ | Germany | August 1941 |
| Messerschmitt Me 262V-3 | Germany | July 1942 |
| Bell XP-59A Airacomet | USA | October 1942 |
| Gloster Meteor F Mk 1 | UK | March 1943 |
| Arado Ar234V-1 Blitz | Germany | June 1943 |

*★ Rocket-powered*

## FIRST TO FLY IN HEAVIER-THAN-AIR AIRCRAFT

**ORVILLE WRIGHT (1871–1948)** On 17 December 1903 at Kitty Hawk, North Carolina, American inventor Orville Wright made the first-ever manned flight in his *Wright Flyer I*. It lasted 12 seconds, and covered a distance of 37 m (120 ft).

**ALBERTO SANTOS-DUMONT (1873–1932)** The Brazilian pilot set a European record of 21.2 seconds over 220 m (722 ft) on 12 November 1906. In the USA in 1905, Wilbur Wright had flown over 39 km (24 miles).

**HENRI FARMAN (1874–1958)** On 11 January 1908 at Issy-les-Moulineaux, France, in his *Voisin-Farman I-bis*, Farman became the first European to fly for more than a minute and to cover more than 1 km (0.6 miles). Two days later, he flew the first kilometre circle in Europe. On 28 March 1908, Farman also became the first aircraft passenger when he flew with Delagrange at Issy.

**LÉON DELAGRANGE (1873–1910)** On 5 November 1907 at Issy-les-Moulineaux, France, Frenchman Delagrange flew his *Voisin-Delagrange I* for 40 seconds, covering 500 m (1,640 ft).

## FIRST AND LAST FLIGHT

**SPRUCE GOOSE** This flying boat, was built for $40,000,000 by rich American flying enthusiast Howard Hughes (1905–1976). It had a wingspan of 97.5 m (320 ft) – just under twice that of a Boeing 747 Jumbo jet – making it the widest of all time. Weighing 181 tonnes (179 tons), it flew once, on 2 November 1947, with Hughes at the controls on its test flight off Long Beach Harbour, Los Angeles. The plane skimmed the surface of the water for only 914 m (3,000 ft).

## FIRST TRANSATLANTIC FLIGHTS

**FIRST TO "HOP" ACROSS** Albert Cushing Read and his crew crossed the Atlantic from Newfoundland, Canada, to Lisbon, Portugal, in a series of hops, refuelling at sea, between 6–27 May 1919. On 31 May, their Navy/Curtiss flying boat NC-4 reached Plymouth, UK, having covered 7,591 km (4,717 miles)!

**FIRST SOLO FLIGHT** One of the most famous flights of all is that of Charles Lindbergh. Although he was actually the 92nd person to fly the Atlantic, he was the first to cross entirely alone. Lindbergh's epic journey took place on 20–21 May 1927 from Long Island, New York to Paris, France in the *Spirit of St Louis*, a single-engined Ryan monoplane. Lindbergh covered a total distance of 5,810 km (3,610 miles) in a time of 33 hr 29.5 min.

**FIRST AIRSHIP** The British R-34 airship, flying from East Fortune, Scotland to Roosevelt Field, New York, between 2–6 July 1919, was piloted by George Herbert Scott. It made the first Atlantic east-west crossing, and included the first ever transatlantic air stowaway, William Ballantyne. When it returned to Pulham, England on 13 July, it also became the first to complete a double crossing!

**FIRST NON-STOP** On 15 June 1919, British pilot John Alcock and navigator Arthur Whitten Brown achieved the first Atlantic non-stop flight. They flew from Newfoundland, Canada, to Galway, Ireland, in a twin Rolls-Royce-engined converted Vickers Vimy bomber, ditching in Derrygimla bog after 16 hours and 28 minutes!

**FIRST TO CROSS THE ATLANTIC BY ACCIDENT!** On 11 July 1938, US pilot Douglas Corrigan left New York to fly southwest for California. Instead he ended up in Dublin, Ireland. From then, he was known as "wrong way" Corrigan!

**FIRST WOMAN TO FLY SOLO** When American pilot Amelia Earhart (1898–1937) repeated Lindbergh's brave solo flight in 1932, she became the first woman to fly across the Atlantic Ocean. In 1937, in an attempt to fly around the world, she disappeared somewhere near New Guinea.

AMELIA EARHART

## FLYING FAST

**FIRST SPEED RECORD** On 20 May 1909, Paul Tissander flew at 54.77 km/h (34.03 mph) in *Wright Flyer*.

**FASTEST AIRCRAFT** On 3 October 1967, William J. Knight (USA) flew an X-15A-2 to 7,274 km/h (4,520 mph), or 6.7 times the speed of sound. The aircraft was air-launched, and hence does not hold the official record.

## FLYING HIGH

**FIRST ALTITUDE RECORD** Jean François Pilâtre de Rozier (France) rose 25 m 82 ft in a tethered hot-air balloon in Paris on 15 October 1783.

**HIGHEST AIRCRAFT** The unofficial altitude record was set on 22 August 1963, when Joseph A. Walker (USA) piloted an X-15 to 107,960 m (354,200 ft) – 108 km (67 miles) high.

## ROUND-THE-WORLD FLIGHT MILESTONES

**FIRST TO "HOP" AROUND THE WORLD** American pilot teams Lowell H. Smith and Alva L. Harvey in the aeroplane *Douglas Chicago,* and Erik Nelson and John Harding Jr in *Douglas New Orleans,* were the first to fly around the world in a series of "hops" from one place to the next, refuelling as they went. They made their trips between 6 April and 28 September 1924.

**FIRST IN AN AIRSHIP** Hugo Eckener and his crew circumnavigated the world in their airship *Graf Zeppelin*. They began their record journey from Lakehurst, USA on 8 April 1929, and finished the trip on 29 April that year.

**FIRST SOLO** Wiley Post made history in a Lockheed Vega named *Winnie Mae*, between 15 and 22 July 1933. He began and finished his historic journey in New York, USA.

**FIRST NON-STOP (WITH REFUELLING)** During 26 February to 2 March 1949, James Gallagher and his crew made the first non-stop trip around the world from Fort Worth, USA, in *Lucky Lady II*. They refuelled in mid-air.

**FIRST WOMAN** Between 9 March and 17 April 1964, Geraldine Mock became the first woman to fly solo around the world. She flew in *Spirit of Columbus*, named after the town from which she began her historic flight – Columbus, USA.

**FIRST IN A HELICOPTER** Beginning in Dallas, USA, on 1 September 1982, H. Ross Perot Jr and Jay W. Coburn circled the world in a Bell 206L LongRanger II, *The Spirit of Texas*.

**FIRST NON-STOP (WITHOUT REFUELLING)** American pilots Dick Rutan and Jeana Yeager successfully flew around the world, without stopping, in their aeroplane *Voyager*. Their journey took place between 14 and 23 December 1986.

GRAF ZEPPELIN

D-LZ127

# AIR TRAVEL

## AIRLINES WITH MOST AIRCRAFT

| AIRLINE | COUNTRY | AIRCRAFT IN SERVICE |
|---|---|---|
| American Airlines | USA | 665 |
| Delta Airlines | USA | 566 |
| United Airlines | USA | 564 |
| USAir | USA | 509 |
| Northwest Airlines | USA | 366 |
| Continental Airlines | USA | 307 |
| Lufthansa | Germany | 218 |
| British Airways | UK | 214 |
| TWA | USA | 191 |
| Air France | France | 137 |
| JAL | Japan | 121 |
| Qantas | Australia | 86 |

**DID YOU KNOW?** The official name of the US President's aircraft is *Air Force One*. Two Boeing 747-200B aircraft are used for the President. Both are six storeys high, and are equipped with 57 antennae, several anti-missile devices, 4 computers, and 85 telephones!

## WHICH AIRCRAFT HAVE YOU FLOWN ON?

| AIRCRAFT | APPROXIMATE NUMBER IN SERVICE |
|---|---|
| Boeing B-737 | 2,310 |
| Douglas DC-9/MD-80 | 1,760 |
| Boeing B-727 | 1,440 |
| Boeing B-747 | 910 |
| Airbus A-300/A-310 | 600 |
| Boeing B-757 | 600 |
| Boeing B-767 | 500 |
| Airbus A-320 | 460 |
| Douglas DC-10 | 300 |
| Lockheed L-1011 TriStar | 230 |

The list above includes turbo-jet airliners only. It excludes the airlines of China and the former Soviet territories

## AIRCRAFT RECORDS

**FIRST AIRLINE SERVICE** DELAG, the first airline, was established on 16 October 1909 to carry passengers between German cities by Zeppelin airships. Up to November 1913, more than 34,000 people had used the service.

**FIRST ELECTRICALLY POWERED** The Militky *MB-E1* took flight in Linz, Austria on 21 October 1973.

**HEAVIEST AIRCRAFT** The Anatov An-225 *Mriya* (Dream) weighs 600 tonnes (591 tons)!

**LARGEST PASSENGER AIRLINER** The Boeing 747-400, has a wingspan of 64.9 m (213 ft) and can carry a total of 567 passengers.

**SMALLEST AIRCRAFT** Built in the USA, *Bumble Bee II*, had a wingspan of just 1.9 m (6 ft 3 in).

**GREATEST GLIDE** The world glider distance record is 495 km (308 miles), set by American Larry Tudor, on 1 July 1994.

**HIGHEST HELICOPTER** The altitude record is 12,442 m (40,820 ft). It was set by Frenchman Jean Boulet, on 21 June 1972 in an Aérospatiale SA 315 Lama.

## AIRSHIP RECORDS

**FIRST AIRSHIP** German Count Ferdinand von Zeppelin devised a 128-m (420-ft) airship called *LZ1* in 1900.

**BIGGEST** Germany's *Hindenburg* airship was 245 m (804 ft) long – more than 2.5 soccer pitches laid end to end! It had a capacity of 1,799,893 m³ (2,354,033 yd³) and could carry 75 passengers and 25 crew members. The giant airship had a cruising speed of 126 km/h (78 mph). In 1937, the *Hindenburg* caught fire – a terrible disaster that was captured on film. The accident killed 35 people.

**WORST AIRSHIP DISASTER** On 4 April 1933, in a bad storm, the US Navy airship *Akron* crashed into the sea off the Atlantic coast of the USA. As many as 73 people were killed, leaving only three survivors in the world's worst airship tragedy.

## WORST AIR DISASTERS

**TENERIFE, CANARY ISLANDS** On 27 March 1977, a Pan Am Boeing 747 collided with a KLM Boeing 747 on the runway at Los Rodeos airport, after the KLM pilot took off without permission from the control tower. Both planes caught fire, killing a total of 583 people.

**MOUNT OGURA, JAPAN** On 12 August 1985, a JAL Boeing 747 on an internal flight from Tokyo to Osaka crashed, killing 520. There were four survivors.

**CHARKHI DADRIO, INDIA** On 12 November 1996, a Saudi Airways Boeing 747 collided with a Kazakh Airlines Ilyushin IL-76 cargo aircraft on its descent and exploded, killing all 312 on the Boeing and 37 on the Ilyushin – 349 in total.

**PARIS, FRANCE** On 3 March 1974, a Turkish Airlines DC-10 crashed at Ermenonville, north of Paris, France, just after take-off for London, killing 346.

## BIZARRE FLIGHT STORIES

**FALLING IN LOVE** On 25 August 1940, Arno Rudolphi and Ann Hayward were married in mid air by the Reverend Homer Tomlinson as all three – and a small party of guests – parachuted towards Earth.

**DOWN TO EARTH** On 26 January 1972, following an aircraft explosion, stewardess Vesna Vulovic fell 10,160 m (33,300 ft). She landed in a snowdrift, with only a leg injury. The other 27 passengers and crew were killed.

**BALLOONATIC** In 1982, Larry Walters attached 45 helium-filled balloons to his deckchair and took off from California. He rose 4,877 m (16,000 ft), narrowly avoiding aircraft, then shot ten balloons, and sailed down. He was heavily fined.

## POPULAR AIR SPORTS

**BALLOONING** Ballooning ascents in the 1780s make ballooning the first aerial sport. Gas ballooning is expensive and less common today, but hot-air ballooning has become increasingly popular since the 1960s.

**SKYDIVING** The first parachutists jumped from balloons 200 years ago. Skydiving as a sport began in the 1950s. BASE (Buildings, Antennae, Spans, Earth) jumping began in the USA in the late 1970s. Parachutists leap from tall structures, such as cliffs or buildings. In parascending, parachutists are launched by being towed behind a vehicle, such as a boat.

**GLIDING** The first gliders, unpowered aircraft that need to be towed into the air by another aircraft, date from the 1850s. However, gliding did not become a popular sport until the 1920s.

**HANGLIDING AND PARAGLIDING** Hangliding, with rigid wings made from modern lightweight materials, has been popular with air-sport enthusiasts since the 1970s. In paragliding, a parachute-like canopy is used – the motorized versions of these are called microlights (also spelt microlites and microlytes).

**WING WALKING** Standing on the wings of an aircraft in flight – while securely strapped in place – has attracted enthusiasts since the early years of flying. Not surprisingly, this pastime, known as wing walking, is a minority sport.

**AUTOGYROS** These are usually single-seaters, powered by a "pusher" propeller. Autogyros enable pilots to enjoy flying without the expense of larger aircraft.

## BUSIEST INTERNATIONAL AIRPORTS

| INTERNATIONAL AIRPORT | LOCATION | PASSENGERS PER YEAR |
|---|---|---|
| London Heathrow | London, UK | 44,262,000 |
| Frankfurt | Frankfurt, Germany | 27,546,000 |
| Charles de Gaulle | Paris, France | 25,690,000 |
| Hong Kong | Hong Kong | 25,248,000 |
| Schiphol | Amsterdam, Netherlands | 22,943,000 |
| New Tokyo International (Narita) | Tokyo, Japan | 20,681,000 |
| Singapore International | Singapore | 20,203,000 |
| London Gatwick | Gatwick, UK | 19,417,000 |
| J.F. Kennedy International | New York, USA | 15,898,000 |
| Bangkok | Bangkok, Thailand | 13,747,000 |

**DID YOU KNOW?** The first microlights were flown in the mid 1970s, in the UK. They have a strong, fibreglass "tricycle" to hold the pilot and an average wingspan of 10 m (33 ft).

## CONCORDE MILESTONES

**WHAT IS CONCORDE?** Concorde is a supersonic aircraft that travels at 2,494 km/h (1,550 mph) – twice the speed of sound!

**1955** Concorde's "droop-snoot" nose is patented as early as 1955.

**1963** On 13 January 1963, Concorde is first named in a speech by General de Gaulle; the Anglo-French project is on the drawing board the following year.

**DECEMBER 1967** The first prototype is shown in France at the Toulouse Air Show.

**MARCH 1969** The first French flight takes place.

**APRIL 1969** The first British flight takes place.

**SEPTEMBER 1970** Concorde's first landing at London Heathrow.

**SEPTEMBER 1971** French Concorde flies on test to South America.

**DID YOU KNOW?** Concorde is the fastest passenger plane – it can fly from London to New York in three hours!

**SEPTEMBER 1973** First landing in the USA, at Dallas-Fort Worth.

**JANUARY 1976** First scheduled flight, beginning Concorde's commercial service, from Paris to Rio de Janeiro in Brazil.

**MAY 1976** The first scheduled flight to the USA (Washington, D.C.) involves the simultaneous landing of a British and French Concorde.

**APRIL 1989** During one of Concorde's flights from Christchurch, New Zealand, to Sydney, Australia, part of Concorde's rudder falls off. Even so, the aircraft still manages to fly safely and without mishap at twice the speed of sound!

# COUNTRIES

## COUNTRIES and CONTINENTS

### SMALLEST COUNTRIES

**VATICAN CITY** Situated in central Rome, this micro-state covers an area measuring 0.44 sq km (0.17 sq miles). Although the Vatican had become part of unified Italy in the 19th century, it was recognized as a fully independent state by a treaty of 11 February 1929. Vatican City is the seat of the Catholic Church and holds a neutral stance in world affairs.

**MONACO** With an area of only 1.81 sq km (0.7 sq miles), Monaco is an independent principality that lies on the French and Italian border.

**NAURU** This tiny Pacific island has an area of just 21.2 sq km (8.2 sq miles), and is home to 11,000 people.

**TUVALU** A warm Pacific island, Tuvalu was a British colony until its independence in 1978. It has an area of 26 sq km (10 sq miles).

### LONGEST COASTLINES

| PLACES | LENGTH | |
| --- | --- | --- |
| | KM | MILES |
| Canada | 243,791 | 151,485 |
| Indonesia | 54,716 | 33,999 |
| Greenland | 44,087 | 27,394 |
| Russia | 37,653 | 23,396 |
| Philippines | 36,289 | 22,559 |
| Japan | 29,751 | 18,486 |
| Australia | 25,760 | 16,007 |
| Norway | 21,925 | 13,624 |
| USA | 19,924 | 12,380 |
| New Zealand | 15,134 | 9,404 |
| China | 14,500 | 9,010 |
| Greece | 13,676 | 8,498 |

**DID YOU KNOW?** Monaco's coastline is only 4 km (2 miles) in total.

### HIGHEST ESTIMATED POPULATION IN 2000

World population is constantly growing. The US Bureau of the Census estimates that the total world population will be 6,090,914,000 by the year 2000! Mexico will join the 100-million-plus club in 2000, with a population of 102,912,000!

| COUNTRY | POPULATION |
| --- | --- |
| China | 1,253,438,000 |
| India | 1,012,909,000 |
| USA | 274,943,000 |
| Indonesia | 219,267,000 |
| Brazil | 169,545,000 |
| Russia | 147,938,000 |
| Pakistan | 141,145,000 |
| Bangladesh | 132,081,000 |
| Japan | 126,582,000 |

### LARGEST COUNTRIES

| COUNTRY | AREA | |
| --- | --- | --- |
| | SQ KM | SQ MILES |
| Russia | 17,075,400 | 6,592,812 |
| Canada | 9,970,537 | 3,849,646 |
| China | 9,596,961 | 3,705,408 |
| USA | 9,166,600 | 3,539,224 |
| Brazil | 8,456,510 | 3,265,059 |
| Australia | 7,617,930 | 2,941,283 |
| India | 2,973,190 | 1,147,949 |
| Argentina | 2,736,690 | 1,056,636 |
| Kazakhstan | 2,717,300 | 1,049,156 |

**DID YOU KNOW?** Russia covers two continents – Europe in the west and Asia in the east – and is almost twice the size of the USA!

### CONTINENT FACTS

**WHAT ARE THE CONTINENTS?** The world's total land mass is divided into seven continents: Asia, Africa, North America, South America, Antarctica, Europe, and Australia.

**WHICH IS THE LARGEST?** Asia makes up 30 per cent of the world's land mass and has the biggest population – home to 60 per cent of the world's population.

**WHICH HAS THE MOST COUNTRIES?** Africa has the most countries, 53, and is also the warmest continent.

**WHICH IS THE COLDEST?** Antarctica is the coldest and least inhabited continent.

**DID YOU KNOW?** Australia is both a country and a continent!

### COUNTRIES WITH MOST NEIGHBOURS

**CHINA** Bordered by 15 other countries, China has more neighbours than any other country. They are Afghanistan, Bhutan, India, Kazakhstan, Kyrgyzstan, Laos, Macao, Mongolia, Burma, Nepal, North Korea, Pakistan, Russia, Tajikistan, and Vietnam.

**RUSSIA** The 14 countries of Azerbaijan, Belorussia, China, Estonia, Finland, Georgia, Kazakhstan, Latvia, Lithuania, Mongolia, North Korea, Norway, Poland, and Ukraine are all neighbours of Russia.

**BRAZIL** Nine countries share a border with Brazil: Argentina, Bolivia, Colombia, Guyana, Paraguay, Peru, Surinam, Uruguay, and Venezuela.

## COUNTRY SYMBOLS

| COUNTRY | SYMBOL |
|---|---|
| Canada | Maple leaf |

**DID YOU KNOW?** Canada produces 75 per cent of the world's maple syrup.

| | |
|---|---|
| USA | Bald eagle |
| Colombia | Orchid |
| Spain | Red carnation |
| Russia | Brown bear |
| India | Royal Bengal tiger |
| Japan | Cherry blossom |
| Denmark | Beech tree |
| South Africa | Blue crane |
| Greece | Olive branch |
| China | Dragon |
| Argentina | Ceibo (flower) |
| Bulgaria | Lion |
| England | Rose |
| Wales | Leek, dragon |
| Scotland | Thistle |
| Turkey | Tulip |
| Australia | Golden wattle flower |
| Ireland | Shamrock |

**DID YOU KNOW?** The three leaves of Ireland's national emblem, the clover or shamrock, was used by Christians to represent the Holy Trinity; it was once an Arabian religious symbol too. A four-leaved clover is thought to bring luck!

## COUNTRIES WITH NEW NAMES

| USED TO BE | NOW NAMED | SINCE |
|---|---|---|
| British Honduras | Belize | 1973 |
| Ceylon | Sri Lanka | 1972 |
| Dahomey | Benin | 1975 |
| East Pakistan | Bangladesh | 1971 |
| French Somaliland | Djibouti | 1977 |
| Gold Coast | Ghana | 1957 |
| Mesopotamia | Iraq | 1921 |
| Siam | Thailand | 1939 |
| South West Africa | Namibia | 1990 |
| Southern Rhodesia | Zimbabwe | 1980 |
| Zaïre | Democratic Republic of Congo | 1997 |

## LANDLOCKED COUNTRIES

**WHAT IS A LANDLOCKED COUNTRY?** A landlocked country is one that is surrounded on all sides by land.

**HOW MANY ARE THERE?** There are more than 40 landlocked countries.

**WHICH IS THE LARGEST?** Kazakhstan covers an area of 2,717,300 sq km (1,049,156 sq miles). Mongolia follows in second place, with a total area of 1,565,000 sq km (604,250 sq miles). Hungary is Europe's largest landlocked state, at 93,030 sq km (35,919 sq miles).

**WHICH IS THE SMALLEST?** Europe also contains the world's smallest landlocked states. Andorra, Liechtenstein, the Vatican City, and San Marino all have areas of less than 500 sq km (193 sq miles).

## LONGEST FRONTIERS

This list represents the total length of each country's frontiers, or borders. It was compiled by adding together the lengths of individual land borders.

| COUNTRY | TOTAL FRONTIER KM | MILES |
|---|---|---|
| China | 22,143 | 13,759 |
| Russia | 20,139 | 12,514 |
| Brazil | 14,691 | 9,129 |
| India | 14,103 | 8,763 |
| USA | 12,248 | 7,611 |
| Kazakhstan | 12,012 | 7,464 |
| Congo (Zaïre) | 10,271 | 6,382 |
| Argentina | 9,665 | 6,006 |
| Canada | 8,893 | 5,526 |

**DID YOU KNOW?** The border between Canada and the USA is the world's longest frontier, stretching an incredible 6,416 km (3,987 miles)!

GREAT WALL OF CHINA

## TIME ZONES

The Earth is divided into 24 time zones. Greenwich Mean Time (GMT), is the time in Greenwich, England, set at 0° longitude. Time advances by one hour for each 15° of longitude east of Greenwich.

| TIME GMT | REGIONS |
|---|---|
| 1200 | UK, Iceland, Portugal |
| 1300 | Western Europe, W. Africa |
| 1400 | Southern and northern Europe, Africa |
| 1500 | Russia., Middle East |
| 1600 | Central Russia |
| 1700 | Russia, India, E. Europe |
| 1800 | Bangladesh, Burma, Bhutan |
| 1900 | Russia, Indonesia |
| 2000 | Russia, China, Australia |
| 2100 | Russia, Japan, Australia |
| 2200 | Russia, eastern Australia |
| 2300 | Micronesia |
| 0000 | South Pacific islands |
| 0100 | South Pacific islands |
| 0200 | None |
| 0300 | Alaska, western Canada |
| 0400 | Western Canada, western USA |
| 0500 | Peru, Cuba, Panama |
| 0600 | Mexico, central USA |
| 0700 | Eastern Canada, USA |
| 0800 | Caribbean, Brazil, Chile |
| 0900 | Argentina, Greenland |
| 1000 | Atlantic islands |
| 1100 | Eastern Greenland |

## NATURAL BORDERS

**RIVERS** More than one-sixth of the borders between countries are formed by rivers. The River Danube borders many southeastern European countries including Romania, Hungary, Croatia, Slovakia, Austria, Germany, and Bulgaria.

**MOUNTAINS** Ranges such as the Alps, Pyrenees, and Himalayas form natural country borders. The Andes, for example, divide Chile and Argentina.

**LAKES** The borders of countries that lie next to lakes are often fixed in the centre of the lake. Lake Nyasa is shared between Malawi, Tanzania, and Mozambique.

# INDEPENDENT COUNTRIES

| COUNTRY | CAPITAL | AREA SQ KM (SQ MILES) | POPULATION 2000 (EST.) | GOVERNMENT | MAIN LANGUAGE(S) | MAJOR RELIGION(S) | CURRENCY |
|---|---|---|---|---|---|---|---|
| Afghanistan | Kabul | 652,090 (251,772) | 26,668,000 | *Mujahideen* coalition | Dari, Pashtu | Muslim | Afghani |
| Albania | Tirana | 27,400 (10,579) | 3,427,000 | Multiparty republic | Albanian | Muslim | Lek |
| Algeria | Algiers | 2,381,740 (919,590) | 31,788,000 | Military regime | Arabic | Muslim | Dinar |
| Andorra | Andorra | 468 (181) | 73,000 | Parliamentary democracy | Catalan | Christian | Fr. Franc Sp. peseta |
| Angola | Luanda | 1,124,670 (434,235) | 11,440,000 | Multiparty rep. | Portuguese | Christian | Kwanza |
| Antigua & Barbuda | St John's | 440 (170) | 68,000 | Parliamentary democracy | English | Christian | E. Caribbean dollar |
| Argentina | Buenos Aires | 2,736,690 (1,156,636) | 36,202,000 | Multiparty rep. | Spanish | Christian | Peso |
| Armenia | Yerevan | 29,800 (11,506) | 3,481,000 | Multiparty rep. | Armenian | Christian | Dram |
| Australia | Canberra | 7,617,930 (2,941,283) | 18,950,000 | Parliamentary democracy | English | Christian | Dollar |
| Austria | Vienna | 82,730 (31,942) | 8,108,000 | Multiparty rep. | German | Christian | Schilling |
| Azerbaijan | Baku | 86,600 (33,436) | 7,902,000 | Multiparty rep. | Azeri | Muslim | Manat |
| Bahamas | Nassau | 10,010 (3,864) | 269,000 | Parliamentary democracy | English | Christian | Dollar |
| Bahrain | Manama | 680 (263) | 642,000 | Absolute monarchy | Arabic | Muslim | Dinar |
| Bangladesh | Dhaka | 133,910 (51,703) | 132,081,000 | Multiparty rep. | Bengali | Muslim | Taka |
| Barbados | Bridgetown | 430 (166) | 260,000 | Parliamentary democracy | English | Christian | Dollar |
| Belgium | Brussels | 32,820 (12,672) | 10,144,000 | Constitutional monarchy | Flemish, French | Christian | Franc |
| Belize | Belmopan | 22,800 (8,803) | 242,000 | Parliamentary democracy | English | Christian | Franc |
| Belorussia | Minsk | 207,600 (80,154) | 10,545,000 | Multiparty rep. | Belorussian | Christian | Rouble |
| Benin | Porto-Novo | 110,620 (42,710) | 6,517,000 | Multiparty rep. | French | Traditional | Franc |
| Bhutan | Thimphu | 47,000 (18,147) | 1,996,000 | Constitutional monarchy | Dzongkha | Buddhist | Ngultrum |
| Bolivia | La Paz; Sucre | 1,084,390 (418,683) | 7,680,000 | Multiparty rep. | Spanish, Aymará, Quechua | Christian | Boliviano |
| Bosnia & Herzegovina | Sarajevo | 51,130 (19,741) | 2,618,000 | Multiparty rep. | Serbo-Croat | Muslim, Christian | Dinar |
| Botswana | Gaborone | 566,730 (218,814) | 1,557,000 | Multiparty rep. | English, Setswana | Trad., Christian | Pul |
| Brazil | Brasilia | 8,456,510 (3,265,059) | 169,545,000 | Multiparty rep. | Portuguese | Christian | Real |
| Brunei | Bandar Seri Begawan | 5,270 (2,055) | 331,000 | Absolute monarchy | Malay, English | Muslim | Dollar |
| Bulgaria | Sofia | 110,550 (42,683) | 8,769,000 | Multiparty rep. | Bulgarian | Christian | Lev |
| Burkina | Ouaga-dougou | 273,800 (105,714) | 11,684,000 | Multiparty rep. | French | Muslim | Franc |
| Burma | Rangoon | 657,540 (253,876) | 49,388,000 | Military regime | Burmese | Buddhist, Christian | Kyat |

**DID YOU KNOW?** The majority of the countires in the world are governed by a democracy. In most cases, it is a multi-party democracy in which citizens are given a choice between several parties to elect into office. Some countries have difficulties with this system; while they claim to be democratic, real power is held by the president.

| COUNTRY | CAPITAL | AREA SQ KM (SQ MILES) | POPULATION 2000 (EST.) | GOVERNMENT | MAIN LANGUAGE(S) | MAJOR RELIGION(S) | CURRENCY |
|---|---|---|---|---|---|---|---|
| Burundi | Bujumbura | 25,650 (9,903) | 6,493,000 | Multiparty rep. | French, Rundi | Christian | Franc |
| Cambodia | Phnom Penh | 176,520 (68,154) | 12,098,000 | Constitutional monarchy | Khmer | Buddhist | Riel |
| Cameroon | Yaoundé | 465,400 (179,691) | 15,966,000 | Multiparty rep. | English, French | Trad., Christian | Franc |
| Canada | Ottawa | 9,220,970 (3,560,217) | 29,989,000 | Multiparty rep. | English, French | Christian | Dollar |
| Cape Verde | Praia | 4,050 (1,556) | 503,000 | Multiparty rep. | Portuguese | Christian | Escudo |
| Central African Rep. | Bangui | 622,980 (240,530) | 3,539,000 | Multiparty rep. | French | Christian | Franc |
| Chad | N'Djamena | 1,259,200 (486,177) | 7,760,000 | Transitional | Arabic, French | Muslim | Franc |
| Chile | Santiago | 748,800 (289,112) | 14,996,000 | Multiparty rep. | Spanish | Christian | Peso |
| China | Beijing | 9,326,410 (3,600,927) | 1,253,438,000 | Single-party rep. | Mandarin Chinese | Trad., Buddhist | Yuan |
| Colombia | Bogota | 1,038,700 (401,042) | 39,172,000 | Multiparty rep. | Spanish | Christian | Peso |
| Comoros | Moroni | 2,230 (861) | 656,000 | Islamic rep. | Arabic, French | Muslim | Franc |
| Congo | Brazzaville | 341,500 (131,855) | 2,750,000 | Multiparty rep. | French | Trad., Christian | Franc |
| Costa Rica | San Jose | 51,060 (19,714) | 3,744,000 | Multiparty rep. | Spanish | Christian | Colón |
| Croatia | Zagreb | 56,538 (21,829) | 5,044,000 | Multiparty rep. | Serbo-Croat | Christian | Kuna |
| Cuba | Havana | 110,860 (42,803) | 11,272,000 | Socialist rep. | Spanish | Christian | Peso |
| Cyprus | Nicosia | 9,251 (3,572) | 777,000 | Multiparty rep. | Greek, Turkish | Christian | Pound |
| Czech Rep. | Prague | 78,864 (30,449) | 10,358,000 | Multiparty rep. | Czech | Christian | Koruna |
| Dem. Rep. of Congo | Kinshasa | 2,267,600 (875,520) | 51,374,000 | Constitutional monarchy | French | Christian | Zaïre |
| Denmark | Copenhagen | 43,070 (16,629) | 5,255,000 | Constitutional monarchy | Danish | Christian | Krone |
| Djibouti | Djibouti | 23,180 (8,950) | 454,000 | Single-party rep. | Arabic, French | Muslim | Franc |
| Dominica | Roseau | 750 (290) | 84,000 | Multiparty rep. | English | Christian | Dollar |
| Dominican Republic | Santo Domingo | 48,730 (18,815) | 8,635,000 | Multiparty rep. | Spanish | Christian | Peso |
| Ecuador | Quito | 276,840 (106,888) | 12,360,000 | Multiparty rep. | Spanish | Christian | Sucre |
| Egypt | Cairo | 995,450 (384,343) | 68,437,000 | Multiparty rep. | Arabic | Muslim | Pound |
| El Salvador | San Salvador | 20,720 (8,000) | 6,252,000 | Multiparty rep. | Spanish | Christian | Cólon |
| Equatorial Guinea | Malabo | 28,050 (10,830) | 478,000 | Multiparty rep. | Spanish | Christian | Franc |
| Eritrea | Asmara | 93,680 (36,170) | 4,537,000 | Provisional military govt. | Arabic, English | Christian, Muslim | Ethiopian birr |
| Estonia | Tallinn | 45,125 (17,423) | 1,422,000 | Multiparty rep. | Estonian | Christian | Kroon |
| Ethiopia | Addis Ababa | 1,101,000 (425,096) | 63,514,000 | Multiparty rep. | Amharic | Christian, Muslim | Birr |
| Fiji | Suva | 18,270 (7,054) | 823,000 | Multiparty rep. | English | Christian | Dollar |
| Finland | Helsinki | 304,610 (117,610) | 5,153,000 | Multiparty rep. | Finnish, Swedish | Christian | Markka |
| France | Paris | 551,100 (212,394) | 59,239,000 | Multiparty rep. | French | Christian | Franc |
| Gabon | Libreville | 257,670 (99,486) | 1,244,000 | Multiparty rep. | French | Christian | Franc |

| COUNTRY | CAPITAL | AREA SQ KM (SQ MILES) | POPULATION 2000 (EST.) | GOVERNMENT | MAIN LANGUAGE(S) | MAJOR RELIGION(S) | CURRENCY |
|---|---|---|---|---|---|---|---|
| Gambia, The | Banjul | 10,000 (3,861) | 1,154,000 | Military regime | English | Muslim | Dalasi |
| Georgia | Tbilisi | 69,700 (26,911) | 5,132,000 | Republic | Georgian | Christian | Lari |
| Germany | Bonn | 349,520 (134,910) | 85,684,000 | Multiparty rep. | German | Christian | Deutsche Mark |
| Ghana | Accra | 238,540 (92,100) | 19,272,000 | Multiparty rep. | English | Christian | Cedi |
| Greece | Athens | 130,850 (50,521) | 10,878,000 | Multiparty rep. | Greek | Christian | Drachma |
| Grenada | St. George's | 340 (131) | 98,000 | Parliamentary democracy | English | Christian | Dollar |
| Guatemala | Guatemala City | 108,430 (41,865) | 12,408,000 | Multiparty rep. | Spanish | Christian | Quetzal |
| Guinea | Conakry | 245,860 (94,926) | 7,640,000 | Multiparty rep. | French | Muslim | Franc |
| Guinea-Bissau | Bissau | 28,120 (10,857) | 1,263,000 | Multiparty rep. | Portuguese | Traditional | Franc |
| Guyana | Georgetown | 196,850 (76,004) | 693,000 | Multiparty rep. | English | Hindu, Christian | Dollar |
| Haiti | Port-au-Prince | 27,560 (10,641) | 7,223,000 | Multiparty rep. | French | Christian | Gourde |
| Honduras | Tegucigalpa | 111,890 (43,201) | 6,192,000 | Multiparty rep. | Spanish | Christian | Lempira |
| Hungary | Budapest | 93,040 (35,652) | 9,795,000 | Multiparty rep. | Magyar | Christian | Forint |
| Iceland | Reykjavik | 100,250 (38,707) | 277,000 | Constitutional republic | Icelandic | Christian | Króna |
| India | New Delhi | 2,973,190 (1,147,949) | 1,012,909,000 | Multiparty rep. | Hindi, English | Hindu, Muslim, Christian | Rupee |
| Indonesia | Jakarta | 1,811,570 (699,447) | 219,267,000 | Multiparty rep. | Indonesian Malay | Muslim, Christian | Rupiah |
| Iran | Teheran | 1,636,000 (631,660) | 71,879,000 | Islamic republic | Farsi | Muslim | Rial |
| Iraq | Baghdad | 437,370 (168,869) | 24,731,000 | Single-party rep. | Arabic | Muslim | Dinar |
| Ireland | Dublin | 68,890 (26,598) | 3,627,000 | Multiparty rep. | Irish, English | Christian | Punt |
| Israel | Jerusalem | 20,330 (7,849) | 5,507,000 | Multiparty rep. | Hebrew, Arabic | Jewish | Shekel |
| Italy | Rome | 294,060 (113,536) | 57,807,000 | Multiparty rep. | Italian | Christian | Lira |
| Ivory Coast | Abidjan | 318,000 (122,780) | 16,172,000 | Multiparty rep. | French | Muslim, Christian, trad. | Franc |
| Jamaica | Kingston | 10,830 (4,181) | 2,664,000 | Parliamentary democracy | English | Christian | Dollar |
| Japan | Tokyo | 376,520 (145,374) | 126,582,000 | Constitutional monarchy | Japanese | Shinto, Buddhist | Yen |
| Jordan | Amman | 88,930 (34,336) | 4,704,000 | Constitutional monarchy | Arabic | Muslim | Dinar |
| Kazakhstan | Astana | 2,717,300 (1,049,150) | 16,943,000 | Multiparty rep. | Kazakh | Muslim, Christian | Tenge |
| Kenya | Nairobi | 566,970 (218,907) | 30,490,000 | Multiparty rep. | Swahili, English | Christian, trad. | Shilling |
| Kiribati | Tarawa | 710 (274) | 87,000 | Multiparty rep. | English, Gilbertese | Christian | Dollar |
| Korea, North | Pyongyang | 120,410 (46,490) | 25,491,000 | Single-party rep. | Korean | Traditional | Won |
| Korea, South | Seoul | 98,730 (38,120) | 47,351,000 | Multiparty rep. | Korean | Buddhist, Christian | Won |
| Kuwait | Kuwait | 17,820 (6,880) | 2,420,000 | Constitutional monarchy | Arabic | Muslim | Dinar |
| Kyrgyzstan | Bishkek | 198,500 (76,640) | 4,664,000 | Multiparty rep. | Kyrgyz | Muslim | Som |
| Laos | Vientiane | 230,800 (89,112) | 5,557,000 | Single-party rep. | Lao | Buddhist | Kip |

| COUNTRY | CAPITAL | AREA SQ KM (SQ MILES) | POPULATION 2000 (EST.) | GOVERNMENT | MAIN LANGUAGE(S) | MAJOR RELIGION(S) | CURRENCY |
|---|---|---|---|---|---|---|---|
| Latvia | Riga | 64,589 (24,938) | 2,380,000 | Multiparty rep. | Latvian | Christian | Lats |
| Lebanon | Beirut | 10,230 (3,950) | 4,115,000 | Multiparty rep. | Arabic | Muslim | Pound |
| Lesotho | Maseru | 30,350 (11,718) | 2,114,000 | Constitutional monarchy | English, Sesotho | Christian | Loti |
| Liberia | Monrovia | 96,320 (37,189) | 3,048,000 | Transitional | English | Christian | Dollar |
| Libya | Tripoli | 1,759,540 (679,358) | 6,294,000 | Socialist state | Arabic | Muslim | Dinar |
| Liechtenstein | Vaduz | 160 (62) | 32,000 | Constitutional monarchy | German | Christian | Franc |
| Lithuania | Vilnius | 65,200 (25,174) | 3,629,000 | Multiparty rep. | Lithuanian | Christian | Litas |
| Luxembourg | Luxembourg | 2,585 (998) | 415,000 | Parliamentary democracy | Luxemburgian | Christian | Franc |
| Macedonia | Skopje | 25,715 (9,929) | 2,152,000 | Multiparty rep. | Macedonian | Christian | Dinar |
| Madagascar | Antananarivo | 581,540 (224,533) | 15,295,000 | Multiparty rep. | Malagasy, French | Traditional, Christian | Franc |
| Malawi | Lilongwe | 118,480 (45,745) | 10,011,000 | Multiparty rep. | English, Chewa | Christian | Kwacha |
| Malaysia | Kuala Lumpur | 328,550 (126,853) | 21,610,000 | Fed. constitutional monarchy | Malay | Muslim, trad., Buddhist | Dollar |
| Maldives | Male | 300 (116) | 310,000 | Republic | Dhivehi | Muslim | Rufiyaa |
| Mali | Bamako | 1,220,190 (471,115) | 10,911,000 | Multiparty rep. | French | Muslim | Franc |
| Malta | Valletta | 320 (124) | 382,000 | Multiparty rep. | English, Maltese | Christian | Lira |
| Marshall Islands | Majuro | 181 (70) | 68,000 | Republic | Marshallese | Christian | Dollar |
| Mauritania | Nouakchott | 1,025,520 (395,955) | 2,653,000 | Multiparty rep. | Arabic | Muslim | Ouguiya |
| Mauritius | Port Louis | 1,860 (718) | 1,194,000 | Multiparty rep. | English | Hindu, Christian | Rupee |
| Mexico | Mexico City | 1,908,690 (736,945) | 102,912,000 | Multiparty rep. | Spanish | Christian | Peso |
| Micronesia | Palikir | 702 (271) | 133,000 | Republic | English | Christian | Dollar |
| Moldavia | Chisinau | 33,700 (13,000) | 4,543,000 | Multiparty rep. | Moldavian | Christian | Leu |
| Monaco | Monaco | 1.95 (0.75) | 32,000 | Constitutional monarchy | French | Christian | Franc |
| Mongolia | Ulan Bator | 1,565,000 (604,247) | 2,655,000 | Multiparty rep. | Khalkha | Buddhist | Tugrik |
| Morocco | Rabat | 446,300 (172,316) | 32,229,000 | Constitutional monarchy | Arabic | Muslim | Dirham |
| Mozambique | Maputo | 784,090 (302,737) | 19,829,000 | Multiparty rep. | Portuguese | Trad., Christian | Metical |
| Namibia | Windhoek | 824,290 (318,260) | 1,886,000 | Multiparty rep. | Afrikaans, English | Christian | Dollar |
| Nauru | — | 21.2 (8.2) | 11,000 | Parliamentary democracy | Nauruan, English | Christian | Dollar |
| Nepal | Kathmandu | 136,800 (52,818) | 24,364,000 | Constitutional monarchy | Nepali | Hindu, Buddhist | Rupee |
| Netherlands | Amsterdam | 33,920 (13,097) | 15,801,000 | Constitutional monarchy | Dutch | Christian | Guilder |
| New Zealand | Wellington | 268,670 (103,733) | 3,698,000 | Constitutional monarchy | English, Maori | Christian | Dollar |
| Nicaragua | Managua | 118,759 (45,849) | 4,729,000 | Multiparty rep. | Spanish | Christian | Córdoba |
| Niger | Niamey | 1,266,700 (489,073) | 10,260,000 | Multiparty rep. | French | Muslim | Franc |
| Nigeria | Abuja | 910,770 (351,648) | 117,328,000 | Military regime | English, Hausa | Muslim, trad., Christian | Naira |
| Norway | Oslo | 306,830 (118,467) | 4,387,000 | Constitutional monarchy | Norwegian | Christian | Krone |

| COUNTRY | CAPITAL | AREA SQ KM (SQ MILES) | POPULATION 2000 (EST.) | GOVERNMENT | MAIN LANGUAGE(S) | MAJOR RELIGION(S) | CURRENCY |
|---|---|---|---|---|---|---|---|
| Oman | Muscat | 212,460 (82,030) | 2,512,000 | Monarchy with council | Arabic | Muslim | Omani |
| Pakistan | Muslimabad | 770,880 (297,637) | 141,145,000 | Multiparty rep. | Urdu | Muslim | Rupee |
| Palau | Koror | 508 (196) | 18,000 | Multiparty rep. | English, Palauan | Christian | Dollar |
| Panama | Panama City | 75,990 (29,340) | 2,828,000 | Multiparty rep. | Spanish | Christian | Balboa |
| Papua New Guinea | Port Moresby | 452,860 (178,849) | 4,812,000 | Parliamentary democracy | English, Tok Pisin | Christian | Kina |
| Paraguay | Asuncion | 397,300 (153,398) | 6,104,000 | Multiparty rep. | Spanish | Christian | Guarani |
| Peru | Lima | 1,280,000 (494,208) | 26,198,000 | Multiparty rep. | Spanish, Quechua | Christian | Sol |
| Philippines | Manila | 298,170 (115,123) | 80,961,000 | Multiparty rep. | English, Pilipino | Christian | Peso |
| Poland | Warsaw | 304,460 (117,552) | 39,010,000 | Multiparty rep. | Polish | Christian | Zloty |
| Portugal | Lisbon | 91,950 (35,502) | 9,906,000 | Multiparty rep. | Portuguese | Christian | Escudo |
| Qatar | Doha | 11,000 (4,247) | 587,000 | Absolute monarchy | Arabic | Muslim | Riyal |
| Romania | Bucharest | 230,340 (88,934) | 20,996,000 | Multiparty rep. | Romanian | Christian | Leu |
| Russia | Moscow | 17,075,400 (6,592,812) | 147,950,000 | Multiparty rep. | Russian | Christian | Rouble |
| Rwanda | Kigali | 24,940 (9,633) | 8,900,000 | Multiparty rep. | Rwanda, French | Christian | Franc |
| St Kitts & Nevis | Basseterre | 360 (139) | 43,000 | Parliamentary democracy | English | Christian | Dollar |
| St Lucia | Castries | 620 (239) | 165,000 | Parliamentary democracy | English | Christian | Dollar |
| St Vincent & Grenadines | Kingstown | 340 (131) | 121,000 | Parliamentary democracy | English | Christian | Dollar |
| Samoa | Apia | 2,842 (1,097) | 235,000 | Parliamentary state | English, Samoan | Christian | Tala |
| San Marino | San Marino | 61 (24) | 25,000 | Multiparty rep. | Italian | Christian | Italian lira |
| Sao Tome & Principe | Sao Tome | 960 (371) | 159,000 | Multiparty rep. | Portuguese | Christian | Dobra |
| Saudi Arabia | Riyadh | 2,149,690 (829,995) | 22,246,000 | Absolute monarchy | Arabic | Muslim | Riyal |
| Senegal | Dakar | 192,530 (74,336) | 10,390,000 | Multiparty rep. | French | Muslim | Franc |
| Seychelles | Victoria | 270 (104) | 80,000 | Multiparty rep. | Seselwa | Christian | Rupee |
| Sierra Leone | Freetown | 71,620 (27,652) | 5,580,000 | Military regime | English | Muslim, trad., | Leone |
| Singapore | Singapore | 610 (236) | 3,620,000 | Multiparty rep. | Chinese, English, Malay, Tamil | Buddhist | Dollar |
| Slovakia | Bratislava | 49,036 (18,933) | 5,472,000 | Multiparty rep. | Slovak, Czech, Hungarian | Christian | Koruna |
| Slovenia | Ljubljana | 20,250 (7,820) | 1,937,000 | Multiparty rep. | Slovene, Serbo-Croat | Christian | Tolar |
| Solomon Islands | Honiara | 28,900 (11,158) | 470,000 | Parliamentary democracy | English | Christian | Dollar |
| Somalia | Mogadishu | 627,340 (242,216) | 10,880,000 | Transitional | Somali | Muslim | Shilling |
| South Africa | Cape Town, Pretoria, Bloemfontein | 1,221,040 (471,443) | 44,462,000 | Multiparty rep. | Afrikaans, English, Zulu, | Christian | Rand |
| Spain | Madrid | 499,440 (192,834) | 38,658,000 | Constitutional monarchy | Spanish | Christian | Peseta |
| Sri Lanka | Colombo | 64,740 (24,996) | 19,377,000 | Multiparty rep. | Sinhala, Tamil, English | Buddhist, Hindu | Rupee |

| COUNTRY | CAPITAL | AREA SQ KM (SQ MILES) | POPULATION 2000 (EST.) | GOVERNMENT | MAIN LANGUAGE(S) | MAJOR RELIGION(S) | CURRENCY |
|---|---|---|---|---|---|---|---|
| Sudan | Khartoum | 2,376,000 (917,374) | 35,454,000 | Military regime | Arabic | Muslim, trad. | Dinar |
| Surinam | Paramaribo | 161,470 (62,344) | 465,000 | Multiparty rep. | Dutch | Hindu, Christian Christian | Guilder |
| Swaziland | Mbabane | 17,200 (6,641) | 1,137,000 | Executive monarchy | English, Swazi | Christian | Lilangeni |
| Sweden | Stockholm | 411,620 (158,926) | 8,994,000 | Constitutional monarchy | Swedish | Christian | Krona |
| Switzerland | Bern | 39,770 (15,355) | 7,268,000 | Federal rep. | French, German, Italian | Christian | Franc |
| Syria | Damascus | 184,060 (71,066) | 17,759,000 | Single-party rep. | Arabic | Muslim | Pound |
| Taiwan | Taipei | 32,260 (12,456) | 22,214,000 | Multiparty rep. | Mandarin Chinese | Traditional, Buddhist | Dollar |
| Tajikistan | Dushanbe | 143,100 (55,251) | 6,384,000 | Single-party rep. | Tajik | Muslim | Rouble |
| Tanzania | Dar es Salaam | 886,040 (342,100) | 31,045,000 | Single-party rep. | Swahili, English | Muslim, traditional | Shilling |
| Thailand | Bangkok | 510,890 (197,255) | 61,164,000 | Constitutional monarchy | Thai | Buddhist | Baht |
| Togo | Lome | 54,390 (21,000) | 5,253,000 | Multiparty rep. | French | Traditional | Franc |
| Tonga | Nukualofa | 720 (278) | 110,000 | Constitutional monarchy | English, Tongan | Christian | Pa'anga |
| Trinidad & Tobago | Port-of-Spain | 5,130 (1,981) | 1,273,000 | Multiparty rep. | English | Christian | Dollar |
| Tunisia | Tunis | 155,360 (59,984) | 9,671,000 | Multiparty rep. | Arabic | Muslim | Dinar |
| Turkey | Ankara | 769,630 (297,154) | 66,618,000 | Multiparty rep. | Turkish | Muslim | Lira |
| Turkmenistan | Ashgabat | 488,100 (188,455) | 4,466,000 | Single-party rep. | Turkmenian | Muslim | Manat |
| Tuvalu | Funafuti | 26 (10) | 11,000 | Constitutional monarchy | English | Christian | Dollar |
| Uganda | Kampala | 199,550 (77,046) | 21,891,000 | Multiparty rep. | English | Christian | Shilling |
| Ukraine | Kiev | 603,700 (233,090) | 50,380,000 | Multiparty rep. | Ukrainian | Christian | Hryvna |
| United Arab Emirates | Abu Dhabi | 83,600 (32,278) | 3,582,000 | Federation of monarchs | Arabic | Muslim | Dirham |
| United Kingdom | London | 244,600 (93,282) | 58,894,000 | Constitutional monarchy | English | Christian | Pound |
| United States | Washington, D.C. | 9,166,600 (3,539,224) | 276,621,000 | Multiparty rep. | English | Christian | Dollar |
| Uruguay | Montevideo | 124,810 (67,494) | 3,333,000 | Multiparty rep. | Spanish | Christian | Peso |
| Uzbekistan | Tashkent | 447,400 (172,741) | 25,245,000 | Single-party rep. | Uzbek | Muslim | Sum |
| Vanuatu | Port-Vila | 12,190 (4,707) | 193,000 | Multiparty rep. | Bislama, English, French | Christian | Vatu |
| Vatican City | — | 0.44 (0.17) | 750 | Papal commission | Italian | Christian | Lira |
| Venezuela | Caracas | 882,050 (340,560) | 23,596,000 | Multiparty rep. | Spanish | Christian | Bolívar |
| Vietnam | Hanoi | 325,360 (125.621) | 78,350,000 | Single-party rep. | Vietnamese | Buddhist | Dông |
| Yemen | Sana | 527,970 (203,849) | 15,547,000 | Multiparty rep. | Arabic | Muslim | Riyal |
| Yugoslavia | Belgrade | 102,173 (39,449) | 10,787,000 | Multiparty rep. | Serbo-Croat | Christian | Dinar |
| Zambia | Lusaka | 740,720 (285,992) | 9,899,000 | Multiparty rep. | English | Christian | Kwacha |
| Zimbabwe | Harare | 390,580 (149,293) | 11,777,000 | Multiparty rep. | English | Christian | Dollar |

**DID YOU KNOW?** About ten million people live in "dependent territories", ruled by either the UK, the USA, France, Denmark, Norway, Portugal, New Zealand, or Australia.

**DID YOU KNOW?** The United Nations (UN) was established in 1945 to promote world peace and understanding. Nearly every country is now a member of the UN.

# WORLD CITIES

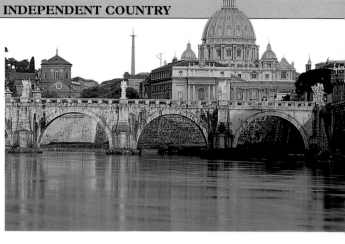

## WHAT IS A CITY?

**CITY** A large town: in some countries, a city has a special status – in the UK it may have been given a royal charter, in the US it is an urban area with its own government.

**TOWN** A densely populated area with a defined boundary and its own government.

**VILLAGE** A small group of houses and other buildings in a rural area.

**HAMLET** A small village or a cluster of houses in a country area. In the UK, a village is considered a hamlet if it does not have a church.

**SETTLEMENT** A small group of inhabited buildings.

**DID YOU KNOW?**
Rome, the capital city of Italy, is built on seven hills: Aventine, Caelian, Capitoline, Esquiline, Palatine, Quirinal, and Viminal.

## HIGHEST TOWNS AND CITIES

| CITY | COUNTRY | MOUNTAIN RANGE | HEIGHT | |
|------|---------|----------------|--------|----|
| | | | M | FT |
| Wenchuan | China | Nyenchen Tangla | 5,099 | 16,730 |
| Potosí | Bolivia | Andes | 3,976 | 13,045 |
| Oruro | Bolivia | Andes | 3,702 | 12,146 |
| Lhasa | Tibet | Himalaya | 3,684 | 12,087 |
| La Paz | Bolivia | Andes | 3,632 | 11,916 |
| Cuzco | Peru | Andes | 3,399 | 11,152 |

**DID YOU KNOW?**
Although Sucre is Bolivia's official capital city, the country is governed from La Paz, which also has capital status.

## FASTEST-GROWING CITIES

| CITY | COUNTRY | ANNUAL GROWTH RATE (%) |
|------|---------|------------------------|
| Tanjung Karang | Indonesia | 6.52 |
| Maputo | Mozambique | 6.07 |
| Esfahan | Iran | 5.66 |
| Kabul | Afghanistan | 5.56 |
| Conakry | Guinea | 5.17 |
| Nairobi | Kenya | 5.16 |
| Lagos | Nigeria | 5.05 |
| Dacca | Bangladesh | 5.03 |
| Luanda | Angola | 4.99 |
| Yaounde | Cameroon | 4.94 |
| Kampala | Uganda | 4.87 |
| Lusaka | Zambia | 4.80 |
| Peshawar | Pakistan | 4.72 |
| Bogor | Indonesia | 4.65 |
| Douala | Cameroon | 4.65 |
| Abidjan | Cote d'Ivoire | 4.56 |

**AMAZING FACT!** A city of one million people that grows by five per cent in a year will have an extra 50,000 mouths to feed at the end of it!

## MOST POPULATED CITIES IN YEAR 2000

These figures are based on an international system that calculates city populations based on "urban agglomerations". This means that certain cities connect, and totals will differ from those based on actual city boundaries.

| CITY | COUNTRY | POPULATION IN 2000 |
|------|---------|--------------------|
| Tokyo-Yokohama | Japan | 29,971,000 |
| Mexico City | Mexico | 27,872,000 |
| São Paulo | Brazil | 25,354,000 |
| Seoul | South Korea | 21,976,000 |
| Bombay | India | 15,357,000 |
| New York | USA | 14,648,000 |

## LOST CITIES

**ANGKOR, CAMBODIA** Once the world's largest city, it covered 78 sq km (30 sq miles). Surrounded by a moat, it had a population of over 1,000,000. About AD 1100, it was abandoned and was not discovered by westerners until 1861, when French naturalist Henri Mouhot stumbled upon it.

**ATLANTIS** Some people believe that the city and island of Atlantis, perhaps in the Mediterranean, was destroyed by an earthquake and flooded almost 12,000 years ago. Its story remains a mystery.

**CHICHÉN ITZÁ, MEXICO** Once the centre of the Mayan empire, the city, built in AD c.400, was abandoned in AD 1200.

**CLIFF PALACE, USA** This Native American Indian city in Colorado was built on a cliff side, but was abandoned during drought conditions in the 13th century. It remained unknown until 1888.

**MACHU PICCHU, PERU** The fortified Inca city built in the 15th century on top of a mountain was abandoned for centuries, but was rediscovered in 1911.

**POMPEII, ITALY** The Roman city was buried by volcanic ash when Mount Vesuvius erupted in AD 79. Excavations began in 1748, and many treasures have been found.

**TROY, TURKEY** Believed to exist only in Greek legend, the site of Troy was discovered in the 1870s.

**UR, IRAQ** Once a great city, Ur was abandoned in c.300 BC. It was excavated between 1922 and 1934.

## ANCIENT CITIES

**CAIRO, EGYPT** Egypt's capital and Africa's largest city, Cairo has a population of 6,000,000. It has at least 1,000 mosques, and bustling bazaars (markets) sit alongside modern bars.

**BEIJING, CHINA** China's capital for 2,000 years, Beijing is built symmetrically in three rectangles, with the Forbidden City at its heart. It has many ancient temples.

**SAMARKAND, UZBEKISTAN** This ancient city includes buildings from the 14th century, and was once the centre of the silk trade from China. Cotton and textiles are still the city's main industry.

**TBILISI** The city of Tbilisi, on the banks of the River Kura, has been Georgia's capital since the fifth century.

## OLDEST CITIES

The following are the oldest cities on each continent that remain inhabited. Many equally old, or even older settlements on each continent have been abandoned.

| CITY | COUNTRY | FIRST SETTLED |
|---|---|---|
| Gaziantep | Turkey, Asia | c.3650 BC |
| Zurich | Switzerland, Europe | c.3000 BC |
| Giza and Minya | Egypt, Africa | pre-2568 BC |
| Quito | Ecuador, South America | c.AD 1000 |
| St Augustine | USA, North America | 1565 |
| Sydney | Australia | 1788 |

The oldest inhabited settlements in what is now the USA are the subject of much debate. Some sources give Tallahassee, Florida as having been originally settled in 1539. This date relates only to the winter camp of the Spanish explorer Hernando de Soto (c.1500–1542) and his 600 companions.

## ONE AND ONLY CITIES

**CITY IN TWO CONTINENTS** Istanbul, Turkey's largest city and main port, is the only city in the world to lie in two continents. It is split between Europe and Asia by a narrow channel of water called the Bosphorus.

**CITY WITH NO CARS** The ancient city of Venice, Italy is built on water. The only way to get around is on foot or by boat.

**NON-US CAPITAL CITY NAMED AFTER A US PRESIDENT** Monrovia, the capital of Liberia, in Africa, was named after James Monroe, the fifth US president.

## FIRST CITIES WITH MORE THAN ONE MILLION PEOPLE

| CITY | COUNTRY | ONE MILLION BY THE YEAR |
|---|---|---|
| Rome | Italy | 133 BC |
| Angkor | Cambodia | AD 900 |
| Hangchow | China | 1279 |
| London | UK | 1810 |
| Paris | France | 1850 |
| Beijing | China | 1860 |
| Canton | China | 1870 |
| Berlin | Prussia | 1875 |
| New York | USA | 1875 |
| Vienna | Austria | 1880 |
| Tokyo | Japan | 1880 |
| St Petersburg | Russia | 1880 |
| Nanking | China | 1885 |
| Chicago | USA | 1887 |
| Philadelphia | USA | 1888 |
| Birmingham | UK | 1900 |
| Calcutta | India | 1900 |
| Boston | USA | 1900 |

**DID YOU KNOW?** Today, there are at least 300 cities in the world that have a population of one million or more inhabitants.

# UNITED STATES of AMERICA

| STATE | STATE NICKNAME | CAPITAL CITY | AREA SQ KM (SQ MILES) | POPULATION |
|---|---|---|---|---|
| Alabama | Cotton state, heart of Dixie | Montgomery | 135,293 (52,237) | 4,319,154 |
| Alaska | America's last frontier | Juneau | 1,593,438 (615,230) | 609,311 |
| Arizona | Grand Canyon state | Phoenix | 295,274 (114,006) | 4,554,966 |
| Arkansas | Land of opportunity | Little Rock | 137,741 (53,182) | 2,522,819 |
| California | Golden state | Sacramento | 411,469 (158,869) | 32,268,301 |
| Colorado | Switzerland of America | Denver | 269,618 (104,100) | 3,892,644 |
| Connecticut | Land of steady habitats | Hartford | 4,359 (5,544) | 3,269,858 |
| Delaware | First state, peach state | Dover | 6,206 (2,396) | 731,581 |
| Florida | Sunshine state, alligator state | Tallahassee | 155,213 (59,928) | 14,653,945 |
| Georgia | Goober state, cracker state | Atlanta | 152,750 (58,977) | 7,486,242 |
| Hawaii | Aloha state, pineapple state | Honolulu | 16,729 (6,459) | 1,186,602 |
| Idaho | Gem state | Boise | 216,456 (83,574) | 1,210,232 |
| Illinois | Prairie state, Land of Lincoln | Springfield | 150,007 (57,918) | 11,895,849 |
| Indiana | Hoosier state | Indianapolis | 94,327 (36,420) | 5,864,108 |
| Iowa | Hawkeye state, corn state | Des Moines | 145,754 (56,276) | 2,852,423 |
| Kansas | Sunflower state, cyclone state | Topeka | 213,109 (82,282) | 2,594,840 |
| Kentucky | Bluegrass state, tobacco state | Frankfort | 104,664 (40,411) | 3,908,124 |
| Louisiana | Pelican state, sugar state | Baton Rouge | 128,595 (49,651) | 4,351,769 |
| Maine | Pine tree state | Augusta | 87,389 (33,741) | 1,242,051 |
| Maryland | Free state, old line state | Annapolis | 31,849 (12,297) | 5,094,289 |
| Massachusetts | Bay state, baked bean state | Boston | 23,934 (9,241) | 6,117,520 |
| Michigan | Wolverine state, auto state | Lansing | 151,585 (58,527) | 9,773,892 |
| Minnesota | North star state, land of 10,000 lakes | St Paul | 225,181 (86,943) | 4,685,549 |
| Mississippi | Magnolia state, eagle state | Jackson | 125,060 (48,286) | 2,730,501 |
| Missouri | Show me state, bullion state | Jefferson City | 180,545 (69,709) | 5,402,058 |
| Montana | Treasure state, stub toe state | Helena | 380,847 (147,046) | 878,810 |
| Nebraska | Tree-planters state, antelope state | Lincoln | 200,356 (77,358) | 1,656,870 |
| Nevada | Sagebrush state, battle-born state | Carson City | 286,367 (110,567) | 1,676,809 |
| New Hampshire | Granite state | Concord | 24,043 (9,283) | 1,172,709 |
| New Jersey | Garden state, clam state | Trenton | 21,277 (8,215) | 8,052,849 |
| New Mexico | Cactus state, land of enchantment | Santa Fe | 314,937 (121,598) | 1,729,751 |
| New York | Empire state | Albany | 139,831 (53,989) | 18,137,226 |
| North Carolina | Tarheel state, old north state | Raleigh | 136,420 (52,672) | 7,425,183 |
| North Dakota | Flickertail state, peace garden state | Bismarck | 183,123 (70,704) | 640,883 |
| Ohio | Buckeye state | Columbus | 116,104 (44,828) | 11,186,331 |
| Oklahoma | Sooner state, Boomer's paradise | Oklahoma City | 181,048 (69,903) | 3,317,091 |
| Oregon | Beaver state, sunset state | Salem | 251,571 (97,132) | 3,243,487 |
| Pennsylvania | Keystone state, Quaker state | Harrisburg | 119,290 (46,058) | 12,019,661 |
| Rhode Island | Little Rhody, ocean state | Providence | 3,188 (1,231) | 987,429 |
| South Carolina | Rice state, swamp state | Columbia | 80,779 (31,189) | 3,760,181 |
| South Dakota | Coyote state, sunshine state | Pierre | 199,742 (77,121) | 737,973 |
| Tennessee | Volunteer state, big bend state | Nashville | 109,158 (42,146) | 5,368,198 |
| Texas | Lone star state, beef state | Austin | 692,244 (267,277) | 19,439,337 |
| Utah | Beehive state, Mormon state | Salt Lake City | 219,900 (84,904) | 2,059,148 |
| Vermont | Green mountain state | Montpelier | 24,903 (9,615) | 588,978 |
| Virginia | Mother of presidents | Richmond | 109,624 (42,326) | 6,733,996 |
| Washington | Evergreen state, Chinook state | Olympia | 182,949 (70,637) | 5,610,362 |
| West Virginia | Mountain state, panhandle state | Charleston | 62,758 (24,231) | 1,815,787 |
| Wisconsin | Badger state, copper state | Madison | 169,642 (65,499) | 5,169,677 |
| Wyoming | Equality state, cowboy state | Cheyenne | 253,347 (97,818) | 479,743 |

**DID YOU KNOW?** Washington, District of Columbia, or D.C., is not a state, but is the capital city of the USA, from where the government rules. It has its own tree, the scarlet oak, a district flower, the American Beauty rose, and its own bird, the woodthrush. Washington, D.C. is home to 528,964 people, and covers an area of 176 sq km (68 sq miles).

| ENTERED UNION | MAIL CODE | STATE TREE | STATE FLOWER | STATE BIRD |
|---|---|---|---|---|
| 14 December 1819 | AL | Longleaf yellow pine | Camellia | Yellowhammer |
| 3 January 1959 | AK | Sitka spruce | Forget-me-not | Willow ptarmigan |
| 14 February 1912 | AZ | Paloverde (green-barked acacia) | Saguaro cactus blossom | Cactus wren |
| 15 June 1836 | AR | Pine | Apple blossom | Northern mockingbird |
| 9 September 1850 | CA | California redwood | Golden poppy | California valley quail |
| 1 August 1876 | CO | Colorado blue spruce | Rocky Mountain columbine | Lark bunting |
| 9 January 1788 | CT | White oak | Mountain laurel | American robin |
| 7 December 1787 | DE | American holly | Peach blossom | Blue hen (chicken) |
| 3 March 1845 | FL | Cabbage palm | Orange blossom | Mockingbird |
| 2 January 1788 | GE | Live oak | Cherokee rose | Brown thrasher |
| 21 August 1959 | HI | Kukui (candlenut) | Yellow hibiscus | Nene (Hawaiian goose) |
| 3 July 1890 | ID | Western white pine | Mock orange | Mountain bluebird |
| 3 December 1818 | IL | White oak | Native violet | Northern cardinal |
| 11 December 1816 | IN | Tulip poplar | Peony | Northern cardinal |
| 28 December 1846 | IA | Oak | Wild rose | Eastern goldfinch |
| 29 January 1861 | KS | Cottonwood | Native sunflower | Western meadowlark |
| 1 June 1792 | KY | Coffee tree | Golden rod | Kentucky cardinal |
| 30 April 1812 | LA | Bald cypress | Southern magnolia | Eastern brown pelican |
| 15 March 1820 | ME | Eastern white pine | White pine cone | Black-capped chickadee |
| 28 April 1788 | MD | White oak | Black-eyed Susan | Baltimore oriole |
| 6 February 1788 | MA | American elm | Mayflower | Chickadee |
| 26 January 1837 | MI | White pine | Apple blossom | American robin |
| 11 May 1858 | MN | Red (Norway) pine | Showy lady's slipper | Loon |
| 10 December 1817 | MS | Evergreen magnolia | Magnolia | Northern mockingbird |
| 10 August 1821 | MO | Dogwood | Hawthorn | Bluebird |
| 8 November 1889 | MT | Ponderosa pine | Bitterroot | Western meadowlark |
| 1 March 1867 | NE | Cottonwood | Golden rod | Western meadowlark |
| 31 October 1864 | NV | Single-leaf pinyon | Sagebrush | Mountain bluebird |
| 21 June 1788 | NH | White birch | Lilac | Purple finch |
| 18 December 1787 | NJ | Northern red oak | Purple violet | Eastern goldfinch |
| 6 January 1912 | NM | Pinon (nut pine) | Yucca | Greater roadrunner |
| 26 July 1788 | NY | Sugar maple | Rose | Bluebird |
| 21 November 1789 | NC | Longleaf pine | Dogwood | Northern cardinal |
| 2 November 1889 | ND | American elm | Wild prairie rose | Western meadowlark |
| 1 March 1803 | OH | Buckeye | Scarlet carnation | Northern cardinal |
| 16 November 1907 | OK | Redbud | Mistletoe | Scissor-tailed flycatcher |
| 14 February 1859 | OR | Douglas fir | Oregon grape | Western meadowlark |
| 12 December 1787 | PA | Hemlock | Mountain laurel | Ruffed grouse |
| 29 May 1790 | RI | Red maple | Violet | Rhode Island red (chicken) |
| 23 May 1788 | SC | Cabbage palm | Yellow jessamine | Carolina red |
| 2 November 1889 | SD | Black Hills spruce | American pasque flower | Ring-necked pheasant |
| 1 June 1796 | TN | Tulip poplar | Iris | Mockingbird |
| 29 December 1845 | TX | Pecan | Bluebonnet | Mockingbird |
| 4 January 1896 | UT | Blue spruce | Sego lily | Seagull |
| 4 March 1791 | VT | Sugar maple | Red clover | Hermit thrush |
| 25 June 1788 | VA | Flowering dogwood | Flowering dogwood | Northern cardinal |
| 11 November 1889 | WA | Western hemlock | Coast rhododendron | Willow goldfinch |
| 20 June 1863 | WV | Sugar maple | Rhododendron | Northern cardinal |
| 29 May 1848 | WI | Sugar maple | Wood violet | American robin |
| 10 July 1890 | WY | Cottonwood | Indian paintbrush | Meadowlark |

# PLACE NAMES

## LONGEST ⬥ PLACE NAMES

**KRUNG THEP MAHANAKHON BOVORN RATANAKOSIN MAHINTHARAYUTTHAYA MAHADILOK POP NOPARATRATCHATHANI BURIROM UDOMRATCHANIVETMAHASATHAN AMORNPIMAN AVATARNSATHIT SAKKATHATTIYAVISNUKARMPRASIT** The 167-letter full name of Bangkok, the capital of Thailand, is rarely used, but it is sometimes abbreviated to "Krung Thep", meaning "City of Angels".

**TAUMATAWHAKATANGIHANGAKOAUAUOTAMATEAT URIPUKAKAPIKI-MAUNGAHORONUKUPOKAI WHEN UAKITANATAHU** This is the 85-letter version of the Maori name of a hill in New Zealand. It translates as "The place where Tamatea, the man with the big knees, who slid, climbed, and swallowed mountains, known as land-eater, played on the flute to his loved one".

**GORSAFAWDDACHA'IDRAIGODANHEDDOGLEDDOL LÔNPENRHYN-AREURDRAETHCEREDIGION** A 67-letter name, which was invented by the Fairbourne Steam Railway, Gwynedd, North Wales, in order to gain publicity for the railway. It means "The Mawddach station and its dragon teeth at the Northern Penrhyn Road on the golden beach of Cardigan Bay".

## CITY NICKNAMES

**ATHENS OF THE NORTH** Edinburgh, Scotland has been so-called since the 18th century, when, like Athens, Greece, the city became famous for its culture and architecture.

**BRIDE OF THE SEA** Traditionally, the ruler of Venice sailed into the Adriatic on Ascension Day, dropping a wedding ring into the sea as a symbol of Venice's status as a sea power.

**CITY OF DAVID** The city of Jerusalem, in Israel, is called the City of David in the Bible, after King David.

**CITY OF LIGHT** Paris, the capital of France, is notable for its colourful nightlife.

**ETERNAL CITY** This nickname describes the enduring quality of Rome's architecture.

**BIG APPLE** New York, USA, is so-called after a translation of "*manzana principal*", Spanish for the main apple orchard, or most important place.

**SMOKE** In the 19th century, the chimneys of thousands of homes and factories belched out so much soot and smoke that London was often shrouded in fog, hence its nickname.

## THINGS NAMED AFTER PLACES

**JEANS** The word "jeans" comes from the name given to material once made in Genoa, *Gênes* in old French. The blue denim from which jeans are most often made was once a product of the city of Nîmes, or *de Nîmes*, in French.

**BADMINTON** The game of badminton, played with rackets and shuttlecocks, was invented in about 1870 at Badminton House, the home of the English Duke of Beaufort. It spread throughout the world, and in 1992 became an Olympic sport.

**BAYONET** A bayonet is a dagger-like steel weapon, which is attached to the muzzle of a gun, and used for attacking an opponent in hand-to-hand combat. The weapon is named after Bayonne in France, where it was first made or used.

**MARATHON** In 490 BC, the news that the Athenians had defeated the Persians at the Battle of Marathon was carried by Pheidippides, a messenger, who ran non-stop to Athens. He died from exhaustion. At the first modern Olympics, held in Athens in 1896, runners covered the same 42-km (26-mile) route, and the marathon was born.

## CITIES WITH NEW NAMES

| USED TO BE CALLED | IS NOW CALLED |
| --- | --- |
| Batavia, Indonesia | Jakarta |
| Christiania/Kristiania, Norway | Oslo |
| Ciudad Trujillo, Dominican Republic | Santo Domingo |
| Constantinople, Turkey | Istanbul |
| Danzig, Poland | Gdansk |
| Kecho, Vietnam | Hanoi |
| Leningrad, USSR | St. Petersburg, Russia |
| Peiping, China | Beijing |
| Rangoon, Burma | Yangon |
| Saigon, Vietnam | Ho Chi Minh City |
| Salisbury, Rhodesia | Harare, Zimbabwe |
| Stalingrad, USSR | Volgograd, Russia |

## PLACES NAMED AFTER REAL PEOPLE

**COLOMBIA** Italian explorer Christopher Columbus (1451–1506) named the country of Colombia, one of the many places he visited during his four voyages to South America.

**COOK ISLANDS** These Pacific Ocean islands are named after British explorer Captain James Cook (1728–1779).

**SAUDI ARABIA** Abdul Aziz ibn-Saud (1882–1953), named the country that he ruled after himself.

**UNITED STATES OF AMERICA** The maps of famous Italian explorer Amerigo Vespucci (1451–1512), were so good that people referred to the area he charted as "Amerigo's Land", or "America".

## WHAT DO YOU CALL A PERSON FROM…?

| CITY | INHABITANT |
| --- | --- |
| Aberdeen, Scotland | Aberdonian |
| Brussels, Belgium | Bruxellois |
| Buffalo, USA | Buffalonian |
| Calcutta, India | Calcuttan |
| Cambridge, UK | Cantabrigian |
| Chicago, USA | Chicagoan |
| Dublin, Ireland | Dubliner |
| Dundee, Scotland | Dundonian |
| Glasgow, Scotland | Glaswegian |
| The Hague, Netherlands | Hagenaar |
| Hamburg, Germany | Hamburger |
| Los Angeles, USA | Angeleno |
| Manchester, UK | Mancunian |
| Mosow, Russia | Muscovite |
| Oslo, Norway | Osloer |
| Paris, France | Parisian (m), Parisienne (f) |
| Tangier, Morocco | Tangerine |
| Troy, USA | Trojan |
| Yucatan, Mexico | Yucatec |
| Zurich, Switzerland | Zurcher |

## DUPLICATE TOWNS

**BIRMINGHAM** There are places called Birmingham in Canada, the UK, and in three of the US states: Alabama, Iowa, and Michigan!

**EGYPT** The most famous place of this name is the African country, but there are also Egypts in Georgia, Mississippi, Texas, and Pennyslvania, USA, and a village near Slough, UK.

**HALIFAX** The first Halifax is in Yorkshire, UK, but there is also a Halifax in Canada, at least three in the USA, and two in Queensland, Australia.

**KINGSTON** Probably best-known for being Jamaica's capital, this is one of the most travelled names. There are three Australian Kingstons, and a Kingston Beach. Canada and New Zealand have also used the name, and there are five Kingstons in the UK including a Kingston-upon-Thames and a Kingston-upon-Hull. There are at least 11 Kingstons in the USA.

## COUNTRIES WITH LONG OFFICIAL NAMES

| OFFICIAL NAME | ENGLISH NAME | LETTERS |
| --- | --- | --- |
| Al-Jamahiriyah al 'Arabiyah al Libiyah ash Sha'biyah al Ishtirakiyah | Libya | 56 |
| Al-Jumhuriyah al Jaza'iriyah ad Dimuqratiyah ash Sha'biyah | Algeria | 49 |
| United Kingdom of Great Britain and Northern Ireland | United Kingdom | 45 |
| Sri Lanka Prajathanthrika Samajavadi Janarajaya | Sri Lanka | 43 |
| Jumhuriyat al-Qumur al-Ittihadiyah al-Islamiyah | Comoros | 41 |

## SHORTEST NAMES

| | |
| --- | --- |
| **A** | Danish village |
| **E** | Scottish river |
| **L** | American lake |
| **O** | English brook |
| **Y** | French village |
| **AE** | Scottish town |
| **EA** | Irish inlet |
| **OA** | Scottish town |
| **TA** | Irish town |
| **UZ** | American town |

## MISLEADING PLACE NAMES

**BUENOS AIRES** The name of the capital of Argentina means "good winds" – but not because the city has them. Part of the original full name included "Our Lady the Virgin Mary of Good Winds" – because sailors prayed that she grant favourable winds for their sailing ships.

**SINGAPORE** The name means "City of Lions", but none has ever been seen there.

**CAPE OF GOOD HOPE** The sea off south-west Africa was called Cabo Tormentoso, or "Cape of Storms", by sailor Bartolomeu Dias, who first sailed round it in 1488. The Portuguese king, John II, thought it would deter future explorers, so he renamed it Cabo da Bõa Esperança, or "Cape of Good Hope".

**GREENLAND** Some 85 per cent of Greenland is not green, but icy white. It was named in 982 AD by Norse sailor Erik the Red, who wanted to encourage his countrymen to settle there.

**NOME** The Alaskan port was marked by a British mapmaker as "Name?", but his writing was bad, and his question is what it became!

**PACIFIC** When explorer Ferdinand Magellan crossed the Pacific (1520–1521), he named it "Mar Pacifico", meaning "calm sea". He was lucky – what we now call the Pacific Ocean can experience some of the world's stormiest weather.

**PAGO PAGO** Allegedly, the correct name of the Samoan port is "Pango Pango", but missionaries who were printing a newspaper there did not have not enough Ns when they printed the heading, so it became Pago Pago.

**YUCATAN** According to one account, the Spanish explorer Hernando Cortez asked a local man what he called the Mexican peninsula. He replied "Yukatan", meaning "I don't understand you".

# TRAVEL and TOURISM

## NATIONAL PARKS

National parks are set up by governments to preserve areas of land, and the plants and wildlife it contains. Yellowstone National Park in the USA, established in 1870, was the first.

**GREAT BARRIER REEF, AUSTRALIA** Situated off the Queensland coast, this reef extends across 34,380,000 hectares (84,956,418 acres). Founded as a national park in 1979, the reef supports many rare marine animals and plants.

**GALÁPAGOS ISLANDS, ECUADOR** These volcanic islands are home to a variety of birds, seals, and unique creatures, including giant turtles and iguanas. Founded in 1986, the park measures 7,990,000 hectares (19,744,089 acres).

**WOOD BUFFALO, CANADA** Founded in 1922, this 4,480,700-hectare (11,072,257-acre) area of forests, plains, and lakes has the largest herd of wild buffalo in the world. It preserves rare animals and birds, such as the whooping crane.

**WRANGELL-ST ELIAS, USA** The largest US national park, founded in 1978, this Alaskan wilderness covers 3,382,014 hectares (8,357,294 acres). It contains many glaciers and peaks of more than 4,880 m (16,000 ft), as well as wild animals.

**SERENGETI, TANZANIA** Founded in 1951, this 1,476,300-hectare (3,648,084-acre) park is home to many wild animals.

## FAMOUS GRAVES

**KARL MARX** The originator of communism, Karl Marx died in London, England, in 1883, and is buried in the city's Highgate Cemetery.

**JOHN F. KENNEDY** The popular US President, shot in the head as he was driven in an open-toppped car through Dallas, Texas, USA, in 1963, is buried at Arlington National Cemetery, USA.

**ELVIS PRESLEY** Rock singer Presley died in 1977, and was buried at his home, Graceland, Memphis, Tennessee, USA. His grave is visited by thousands.

**PRINCESS DIANA** Killed in a car crash in Paris, France, in 1997, Diana's grave is on an island at Althorp House, Northamptonshire, England – her family home. It is not accessible to the public.

## TOP AMUSEMENT AND THEME PARKS

| PARK | LOCATION | ATTENDANCE (1997) |
|---|---|---|
| Tokyo Disneyland | Tokyo, Japan | 17,368,000 |
| Disneyland, Anaheim | California, USA | 17,000,000 |
| Magic Kingdom at Walt Disney World | Lake Buena Vista, Florida, USA | 17,000,000 |
| Disneyland Paris | Marne-la-Vallée, France | 14,250,000 |
| EPCOT at Walt Disney World | Lake Buena Vista, Florida, USA | 11,796,750 |
| Disney-MGM Studios | Lake Buena Vista, Florida, USA | 10,473,750 |

## TRAVELLING TALES

Since ancient times, people have had to travel to survive – to graze their livestock, to trade, or to escape persecution. However, not all travel was a matter of life and death and many people travelled for pleasure and enlightenment.

**TAKING THE WATERS** The Romans placed great value on bathing, and settled in many places close to natural springs, developing cities as spas (the name comes from Spa in Belgium). It became fashionable to visit spas to "take the waters" – drinking and bathing as cures for various illnesses.

**THE GRAND TOUR** From the 18th century onwards, taking the "Grand Tour" of the great European cities was regarded as part of a gentleman's or lady's education. The idea of sightseeing holidays – visiting buildings and art treasures – has grown from this.

**COASTAL TOURISM** The health benefits of sea bathing were first promoted in the mid-18th century, when seaside holidays were taken by the wealthy. This marked the start of the development of coastal resorts as tourist attractions.

**EXHIBITIONS** In the 19th and 20th centuries, major exhibitions in Europe and the USA attracted millions of people to the major cities of the world. Many people had never previously travelled beyond their own homes.

**PILGRIMAGE** The religion of Islam requires its followers to visit Mecca, in the west of Saudi Arabia – the birthplace of the prophet Muhammad. Millions of pilgrims a year flock to Mecca to visit the sacred Ka'ba shrine.

**ANNUAL EVENTS** Festivals such as the Lent carnival held in Rio De Janeiro, Brazil, are attended by vast numbers of people every year. In Rio, there are all-night street parties, live music, and a contest for the best costume and float.

**THE PACKAGE TOUR** In 1841, 570 people were taken by train from Leicester, England, to a park in Loughborough, for a day trip. This ten-mile journey, organized by Thomas Cook (1808–1892), was the first ever package tour. From this small beginning, Cook opened up travel for the masses, and developed one of the world's best-known travel companies.

## THINGS TO SEE IN...

### USA

**STATUE OF LIBERTY**
A gift from the French to the American people in 1884, this statue stands on an island in New York harbour.

**MOUNT RUSHMORE**
It took more than 14 years to carve the faces of four US presidents in the granite cliffs in South Dakota. Finished in 1941, the heads are 18 m (60 ft) tall.

**SEARS TOWER**
The Sears Tower, Chicago, is the tallest skyscraper in the USA, at 443 m (1,453 ft). It has 110 storeys, 100 lifts, and 16,000 windows!

### UK

**NELSON'S COLUMN**
This 50-m (165-ft) statue commemorates Admiral Lord Nelson, who beat Napoleon at the Battle of Trafalgar. It stands in Trafalgar Square, London.

**CAERPHILLY CASTLE**
This castle was built in Wales in the 13th century by an English nobleman. Concentric walls (one wall inside another) and complex waterways make this one of the best-defended of all castles.

**LOCH NESS** This lake, near Inverness, Scotland, is home to the elusive Loch Ness monster, whose existence has been speculated for many years.

### FRANCE

**LASCAUX II** Lascaux, southwest France, is the site of ancient caves, notable for their prehistoric paintings. Due to deterioration, they are closed to the public, but a reconstruction, Lascaux II, has been created close to the original site.

**MUSÉE DU LOUVRE**
This museum in Paris, contains important art collections, including Leonardo da Vinci's *Mona Lisa*.

**NOTRE-DAME**
Standing on the site of a Roman temple, this cathedral in Paris was completed in about 1330.

### CHINA

**GREAT WALL**
Built over 2,000 years ago to protect China from invaders, this wall, found in the northeast, is 5,400 km (3,375 miles) long.

**IMPERIAL PALACE**
This palace, in Bejing, dates from the 15th century, and houses a priceless collection of relics from various dynasties.

**MAGAO CAVES**
These are hand-crafted Buddhist shrines, which date back to the second century AD. A national treasure, they are situated in Dunhuang, northwest China.

### ITALY

**COLOSSEUM** This ancient open theatre in Rome held fights, in which gladiators and wild beasts fought to the death.

**LEANING TOWER OF PISA** This 56.2-m (184.5-ft) marble bell tower was built about 700 years ago. It began to lean during its construction!

**SANTA CROCE**
This Gothic church in Florence was built in the late 13th century. The tombs of many famous Florentines, including the sculptor Michelangelo, are found there.

---

## TOP TOURIST COUNTRIES

In 1997, it was reckoned that about 613,488,000 people – almost one in ten of the world's population – travelled as tourists to another country. Of these, more than half visited the destinations listed here. Certain trends are emerging, such as the increasing popularity of countries like Poland, which was ranked 27th in the world in 1990, but is now the seventh most popular country to visit.

| COUNTRY | % OF WORLD TRAVELLERS | VISITORS PER YEAR |
|---|---|---|
| France | 10.9 | 66,800,000 |
| USA | 8.0 | 49,038,000 |
| Spain | 7.1 | 43,403,000 |
| Italy | 5.6 | 34,087,000 |
| UK | 4.2 | 25,960,000 |
| China | 3.9 | 23,770,000 |
| Poland | 3.2 | 19,514,000 |
| Mexico | 3.2 | 19,351,000 |
| Canada | 2.9 | 17,610,000 |
| Czech Republic | 2.8 | 17,400,000 |

**AMAZING FACT!** France's Eiffel Tower, a popular tourist attraction, has 1,652 steps up to the third level!

## FAMOUS BEACHES

**BONDI** Situated in Sydney, Australia, Bondi is one of the best and most popular surfing beaches in the world.

**TAHITI** Surfing originated in the waves breaking on the beaches of this South Pacific island.

**MALIBU** A fashionable Californian surfing beach, Malibu is a popular place to live for many celebrities.

**SKELETON COAST** In Namibia, the Namib Desert joins the sea, creating one of the world's longest beaches – 1,900 km (1,200 miles) in length.

**BLACKPOOL** One of the world's most-visited beaches, Blackpool, UK attracts some 7,500,000 people a year to attend tourist attractions on the sea front.

**CONEY ISLAND** Situated close to New York, Coney Island's beach and amusements once attracted up to 50,000,000 visitors a year.

**COPACABANA** Found in Rio de Janeiro, Brazil, Copacabana is one of the world's most popular beach resorts.

**VIRGINIA BEACH** The world's largest pleasure beach at 45 km (28 miles) long, Virginia Beach is found in Virginia, USA.

## NATURAL WONDERS OF THE WORLD

**ULURU** This huge red sandstone boulder rises 348 m (1,143 ft) above the Australian desert, and is 2.4 km (1.5 miles) long. Its colours change from pink at dawn, to orange at midday, red at sunset, and lavender at night.

**GRAND CANYON** The Grand Canyon, USA, was gouged out of rock by the Colorado River. It is 349 km (217 miles) long, up to 30 km (19 miles) wide, and 1.6 km (1 mile) deep. Its deepest point cuts through 2,000-million-year-old rock.

**ANGEL FALLS** The Angel Falls in Venezuela are the tallest in the world, with a total drop of 979 m (3,212 ft), almost three times as high as the Empire State Building, New York, USA.

**DEAD SEA** This inland sea situated between Israel and Jordan lies 400 m (1,300 ft) below sea level, and is the lowest point on Earth. Its water is so salty that it allows people to float easily.

**NORTHERN LIGHTS** In the Arctic, on dark nights, coloured lights known as Aurora can be seen in the sky. They are caused by electricity in the upper atmosphere, and are brightest in mid winter, when the sun never rises.

# PEOPLE

## HUMAN BODY

### BODY SYSTEMS

**RESPIRATORY SYSTEM** The body needs a regular supply of oxygen. Air is filtered through the nose and mouth, and then passes into the lungs, where oxygen is absorbed into the blood through tiny air sacs called alveoli. Carbon dioxide is breathed out.

**DIGESTIVE SYSTEM** Food is broken down and processed in the digestive system. Nutrients are absorbed, and undigested waste is expelled.

**SKELETAL SYSTEM** The internal framework of the body, the skeleton has 206 bones. It keeps the body rigid and protects the delicate internal organs.

**CARDIOVASCULAR SYSTEM** The heart and blood vessels keep blood circulating around every part of the body and supply chemicals that regulate body processes.

**NERVOUS SYSTEM** The brain and the spinal cord make up the central nervous system (CNS), which carries messages to and from the brain, and co-ordinates the body's actions.

**ENDOCRINE SYSTEM** These glands release hormones that stimulate and co-ordinate processes within the body. For example, the pancreas produces insulin to regulate blood sugar levels.

! **DID YOU KNOW?** The spinal column is made up of 33 bones called vertebrae. A human neck has the same number of vertebrae as a giraffe!

### BRAIN FACTS

**HEAVY HEAD** An average brain weighs 1.3 kg (3 lb).

**GREY MATTER** The grey matter, or cortex, of the brain is made up of nerve cell bodies. If the cortex was spread out flat, it would cover an office desk!

**CELL MATES** One brain cell connects to up to 25,000 others.

**LEFT AND RIGHT** The brain is made up of two halves: the right controls logic and speech, while the left nurtures creativity.

### LARGEST ORGANS

| ORGAN | | AVERAGE WEIGHT | |
|---|---|---|---|
| | | G | OZ |
| Skin | | 10,886 | 384.0 |
| Liver | | 1,560 | 55.0 |
| Brain | male | 1,408 | 49.7 |
| | female | 1,263 | 44.6 |
| Lungs | both | 1,090 | 38.5 |
| Heart | male | 315 | 11.1 |
| | female | 265 | 9.3 |
| Kidneys | both | 290 | 10.2 |
| Spleen | | 170 | 6.0 |
| Pancreas | | 98 | 3.5 |

### BODY NUMBERS

**MUSCLES** The body has 650 muscles to pull bones and enable movement. It takes 17 muscles to smile, and 42 to frown!

**WATER** Your body is 70 per cent water.

**NERVES** Messages are sent to the brain, via nerves, at 360 km/h (224 mph). Neurons, which carry these messages, are the longest cells in the human body, and can measure 1.2 m (4 ft) long.

**BLOOD** Your body contains 5 litres (9 pints) of blood that travels along 100,000 km (62,000 miles) of blood vessels – equivalent to 2.5 times round the Equator.

**TEMPERATURE** The human body's normal temperature is 37°C (98.6°F).

### THE FIVE SENSES

**TOUCH** The skin contains nerve endings that send messages to the brain and detect degrees of pressure, cold, warmth, and pain.

**TASTE** The tongue contains more than 10,000 taste buds that detect chemicals in food and drink. A baby is born with taste buds all over its mouth, but they slowly disappear. Taste buds are renewed weekly.

**SMELL** The nose detects smells by sensing chemicals in the air. You can identify 2,000–4,000 different smells. Smells are processed by the same part of the brain that deals with emotions and memories.

**HEARING** Sound vibrations trigger off a chain of movements in the skull. Our ears can detect 1,500 different tones, 350 degrees of loudness, and gauge the direction of a sound within three degrees.

**SIGHT** Light is detected by the eye and focused to form an image. Humans can detect a lighted candle 1.6 km (1 mile) away.

## BODY NAMES AND THEIR MEANINGS

| PART | MEANING |
| --- | --- |
| Appendix | To append, or add to |
| Auricle | Latin *auricula*, or external ear |
| Biceps (forearm muscle) | Latin *biceps*, meaning two heads |
| Canine (tooth) | Latin *canis*, meaning a dog |
| Clavicle (shoulder blade) | Latin *clavis*, meaning a key |
| Coccyx (tail bone) | Cuckoo – its triangular shape resembles a cuckoo's beak! |
| Cranium | Greek *kranion*, meaning skull |
| Fibula (calf bone) | Latin *figere*, to fasten |
| Follicle | Latin *folicula*, small bag |
| Incisor | Latin *incidere*, to cut |
| Liver | Greek *liparos*, fat |
| Mandible (lower jawbone) | Latin *mandibula*, jaw |
| Orbit (eye socket) | Latin *orbis*, a circle or orb |
| Pancreas | Greek *pan* (all) and *kreas* (flesh) |
| Pelvis (hip etc) | Basin (its shape) |
| Phalanges (finger bones) | Greek *phalaggion*, spider's web |
| Sacrum (base of spine) | Latin *os sacrum*, holy bone (used in sacrifices) |
| Triceps (forearm muscles) | Latin *triceps*, meaning three heads |

## LITTLE-USED NAMES FOR PARTS OF THE BODY

| NAME | BODY PART |
| --- | --- |
| Axilla | The armpit |
| Canthus | Either corner of the eye |
| Cilia | The eyelashes |
| Columella | The part of the nose between the nostrils |
| Darwinian tubercule | A small lump found on the edges of some people's ears |
| Dorsum | The back of the tongue |
| Fossette | A dimple on the chin |
| Frenum | The muscle beneath the tongue |
| Gelasin | A dimple in the cheek |
| Hallux | The big toe |
| Lunula | The white half-moon shapes on the nails |
| Popliteal space | The area behind the knee |
| Sclera | The white of the eye |

## YOUR AMAZING BODY

**BREATHING** You take between 13 and 17 breaths per minute at rest, and up to 80 during exercise. If you take an average of 20 breaths a minute, you breathe 28,800 times a day!

**ELEMENTS** The human body contains many elements, including gold! In one human, there is enough carbon to fill 900 pencils and enough iron to make a 7.6-cm (3-in) nail. To make a 3-g (0.1-oz) 18 carat gold wedding ring, you would need the gold from 316 people, or to make a thermometer, you would need the mercury from the bodies of 40 people.

**CELLS** There are 50 trillion cells in your body, of which 3 billion die per minute. Most of them are replaced.

**DIGESTION** Your stomach produces up to 2 litres (3.5 pints) of hydrochloric acid daily and 500,000 cells are replaced every minute so acid cannot damage the stomach walls.

**SNEEZES** Your sneezes, a result of an irritation in the nasal passages, can travel at 160 km/h (99 mph)!

**BRAIN** Your brain contains about 15 billion cells. You can retain about seven facts at any one time in your short-term memory, but over the long-term your brain has to forget things to make room for new memories.

**TASTE** With 10,000 tastebuds on your tongue, you can identify 500 different tastes.

**VISION** Some 10,000 colours can be detected by the human eye. Colour blindness can affect 1 in 30 people, but as many as 1 in 12 men.

**DID YOU KNOW?** You are 1 cm (0.4 in) taller in the morning than the evening, because the cartilage in the spine compresses during the day.

## LONGEST BONES IN THE BODY

| BONE | AVERAGE LENGTH | |
| --- | --- | --- |
| | CM | IN |
| Femur (thighbone – upper leg) | 50.50 | 19.88 |
| Tibia (shinbone – inner lower leg) | 43.03 | 16.94 |
| Fibula (outer lower leg) | 40.50 | 15.94 |
| Humerus (upper arm) | 36.46 | 14.35 |
| Ulna (inner lower arm) | 28.20 | 11.10 |
| Radius (outer lower arm) | 26.42 | 10.40 |
| Seventh rib | 24.00 | 9.45 |
| Eighth rib | 23.00 | 9.06 |
| Innominate bone (hipbone – half pelvis) | 18.00 | 7.28 |
| Sternum (breastbone) | 17.00 | 6.69 |

**DID YOU KNOW?** The bones in the female skeleton are usually 6 to 13 per cent smaller than in that of the male, with the exception of the sternum which is virtually identical. However, in childhood, girls grow much faster than boys!

# AMAZING PEOPLE

## WORLD'S TALLEST PEOPLE

| NAME | DATES | COUNTRY | HEIGHT | | |
|------|-------|---------|--------|----|----|
| | | | CM | FT | IN |
| Robert Pershing Wadlow | 1918–1940 | USA | 272 | 8 | 11.1 |
| John William Rogan | 1871–1905 | USA | 264 | 8 | 8.0 |
| John F. Carroll | 1932–1969 | USA | 263.5 | 8 | 7.75 |
| Väinö Myllyrinne | 1909–1963 | Finland | 251.4 | 8 | 3.0 |
| Bernard Coyne | 1897–1921 | USA | 248.9 | 8 | 2.0 |
| Don Koehler | 1925–1981 | USA | 248.9 | 8 | 2.0 |

## WORLD'S OLDEST PEOPLE

This list includes only those for whom there are accurate records.

| NAME | DATES | COUNTRY | AGE | |
|------|-------|---------|-------|------|
| | | | YEARS | DAYS |
| Jeanne Calment | 1875–1997 | France | 122 | 164 |
| Shigechiyo Izumi | 1865–1986 | Japan | 120 | 237 |
| Carrie White | 1874–1991 | USA | 116 | 88 |
| Christian Mortensen | 1882–1998 | Denmark/USA | 115 | 252 |
| Charlotte Hughes | 1877–1993 | UK | 115 | 229 |

## WORLD'S HEAVIEST PEOPLE

Precise weights of certain people have never been verified, but these are the main contenders for the list of "world's heaviest", based on records of peak weights (some later dieted and reduced their weights):

| NAME | DATES | COUNTRY | MAXIMUM WEIGHT | |
|------|-------|---------|------|-------|
| | | | KG | LB |
| Jon Minnoch | 1941–83 | USA | 635 | 1,400 |
| Walter Hudson | 1944–91 | USA | 545 | 1,201 |
| Rosalie Bradford | b.1943 | USA | 544 | 1,199 |
| Michael Walker | b.1934 | USA | 538 | 1,186 |

## FAMOUS LEFT-HANDED PEOPLE

Ludwig van Beethoven, composer • Julius Caesar, Roman emperor
Fidel Castro, Cuban president • Bill Clinton, US president
Leonardo da Vinci, artist • Albert Einstein, scientist • Elizabeth II,
British queen • Jimi Hendrix, guitarist • Michelangelo, painter
Wolfgang Amadeus Mozart, composer • Pablo Picasso, painter

**DID YOU KNOW?** People called Kerr are more likely to be left-handed, because they descend from a Scottish clan which had so many left-handers that they built spiral staircases in their castles anti-clockwise!

**DID YOU KNOW?** Your largest bone, the thighbone, or femur, is 150 times as long as your smallest bone, the stirrup bone, inside your ear.

## HIGHEST MALE LIFE EXPECTANCY

Half a century ago, the vast majority of the population died before the age of 50. Today, most survive well beyond that age. Global average life expectancy is now 64 years for men.

| LIFE EXPECTANCY | |
|---------|------|
| COUNTRY | YEARS |
| Iceland | 76.8 |
| Japan | 76.4 |
| Sweden | 75.4 |
| Greece | 75.0 |
| Cyprus | 74.8 |
| Australia | 74.7 |
| Switzerland | 74.7 |
| Israel | 74.6 |
| Spain | 74.6 |
| Netherlands | 74.4 |
| Canada | 74.2 |

## HIGHEST FEMALE LIFE EXPECTANCY

On average, women around the world live longer than men. The average life expectancy for women is now 67 years.

| LIFE EXPECTANCY | |
|---------|------|
| COUNTRY | YEARS |
| Japan | 82.5 |
| Switzerland | 81.2 |
| Sweden | 81.1 |
| France | 80.8 |
| Iceland | 80.8 |
| Canada | 80.7 |
| Australia | 80.6 |
| Italy | 80.6 |
| Spain | 80.5 |
| Netherlands | 80.4 |
| Norway | 80.3 |
| Greece | 80.1 |

## IN ONE DAY...

Your body sheds 36 million skin cells.

A man produces 300 million sperm cells.

173 billion red blood cells are created and destroyed.

Your heart beats 100,800 times.

You take 30,000 breaths a day.

10 billion white blood cells are made.

You blink 9,365 times.

Your kidneys filter 3,600 litres (792 gallons) of blood – equivalent to 45 baths!

100 hairs are lost and replaced.

Enough body heat is produced to power a light bulb for 1.5 days.

Your toenails grow 0.1 mm (0.004 in).

About 1.7 litres (3 pints) of urine is made.

Your mouth produces 1 litre (1.8 pints) of saliva.

Your stomach produces 2 litres (3.5 pints) of hydrochloric acid.

Your body expels an average of 2 litres (3.5 pints) of gas.

One teaspoonful of tears spill from your eyes – though crying empties out more.

## AMAZING PEOPLE

**LONGEST NAILS** Shridar Chillal of Pune, India (b.1937) has not cut the nails on his left hand since 1952. By 1996, his nails measured 587 cm (231 in) in total.

**LONGEST BEARD** The 5.33-m (17 ft 6-in) beard of Norwegian-born US immigrant Hans Langseth (1846–1927) has been in the Smithsonian Institution, Washington D.C., USA, since 1967.

**LONGEST MOUSTACHE** The moustache of Kalyan Ramji Sain of Sundargath, India, spans 3.29 m (11 ft 11.5 in)!

**LONGEST HAIR** Swami Pandarasannadhi, the religious leader of a monastery in Madras, India, had hair that was measured in 1949 at 7.9 m (26 ft).

**MOST SNEEZES** Donna Griffiths of Pershore, UK, sneezed for 978 days, starting on 13 January 1981.

**MOST HICCUPS** Charles Osbourne from Anthon, Iowa, USA, hiccuped from 1922 to 1990.

**! DID YOU KNOW?** You have 100 billion brain cells, of which 100,000 are irretrievably lost each day!

## AMAZING BRAINS

**MATHS GENIUS** In seconds, Zerah Colburn (1804–1840) from the USA, correctly calculated how many seconds had elapsed since the birth of Christ!

**INFANT PRODIGY** By the age of four, Kim Ung-Yong of Korea (b.1963) could speak fluent Korean, English, Japanese, and German.

**PHONE NUMBERS** Gon Yang-ling of Harbin, China, has memorized more than 15,000 telephone numbers.

## FAMOUS SHORT PEOPLE

| NAME | OCCUPATION | HEIGHT | | |
|------|-----------|------|----|----|
| | | CM | FT | IN |
| Alexander Pope | English writer | 137 | 4 | 6 |
| Queen Victoria | British monarch | 152 | 5 | 0 |
| Dolly Parton | Country singer | 152 | 5 | 0 |
| Danny DeVito | US actor | 152 | 5 | 0 |
| Paul Simon | US singer | 157 | 5 | 2 |
| Yuri Gagarin | Soviet cosmonaut | 160 | 5 | 3 |
| Nikita Kruschev | Soviet leader | 160 | 5 | 3 |
| Michael J. Fox | US actor | 162 | 5 | 4 |
| Pablo Picasso | Spanish painter | 162 | 5 | 4 |

## DWARFS OF THE PAST

**"COUNT" JOSEPH BORUWLASKI (1739–1837)** Known as the Polish Dwarf, Boruwlaski was 1 m (3 ft 3 in) at his tallest. In 1782, he met English giant Patrick Cotter, whose knee was level with the top of the Count's head!

**JEFFREY HUDSON (1619–1682)** A court dwarf who once leaped out of a pie at a banquet for Charles I, Hudson was said to have grown to 1.07 m (3 ft 6 in).

**"TOM THUMB" (1838–1883)** US showman Phineas T. Barnum persuaded the parents of 4-year-old, 0.6-m (2-ft) tall Charles Stratton to exhibit him in a show. He was advertised as "General Tom Thumb, a dwarf eleven years of age, just arrived from England".

## FEATS OF GREAT STRENGTH

**STONE THE CROWS** Basque strongman Mielxto Saralegi holds the world record for lifting a block of stone onto his shoulder – 327 kg (721 lb) – the weight of five adults!

**TAKING THE PLANE** At Sydney Airport, Australia, on 2 April 1996, David Huxley pulled a Boeing 747-400 weighing 187 tonnes (184 tons), for 54.7 ft (179.5 ft).

**PULLING TEETH** Robert Galstyan of Armenia dragged two Russian railway wagons weighing 219 tonnes (215 tons) a distance of 7 m (23 ft) using his teeth.

**AHEAD OF TRAFFIC** In 1972, Walter Cornelius pushed a bus 0.8 km (0.5 mile) with his head, at Peterborough, UK.

**PRESS UPS** On 12 January 1985, British strongman Mick Gooch did 16 press-ups using one finger balanced on a coconut!

# HEALTH <u>and</u> MEDICINE

## ALTERNATIVE MEDICINE

Alternative therapies often aim to restore the body's state of balance, using natural methods or ingredients.

**AROMATHERAPY** A natural therapy where oils extracted from plants are used in massage or bathing, or are inhaled.

**YOGA** A course of exercises designed to promote physical and mental health.

**ALEXANDER TECHNIQUE** This therapy aims to treat and prevent a range of disorders by improving posture.

## NUTRIENTS

Nutrients are the essential elements for healthy eating. They include:

**VITAMINS** Aid the release of energy from glucose, and assist the body's growth and repair.

**MINERALS** Help growth and repair processes, the release of energy from nutrients, and help to form new tissues.

**CARBOHYDRATES** Compounds of carbon, hydrogen, and oxygen, such as starch and sugar, that provide the body with energy.

**PROTEIN** A substance needed by the body for growth and repair.

## MEDICAL MYTHS

**COLDS** Colds are caused by cold temperatures.

**HICCUPS** Being given a fright cures hiccups.

**HAIR** Hair can turn white in a night.

**STRENGTH** Spinach makes you strong.

**RIBS** Men have one rib less than women.

**BONES** The "funny bone" on the elbow is a bone.

**TAPEWORMS** Tapeworms ingest food in the human intestine, which causes hunger.

**VITAMIN C** Large amounts of Vitamin C do not help to ward off colds.

**EYESIGHT** Carrots give you good eyesight, and help you see in the dark.

**DID YOU KNOW?** The medical myth that eating fish is good for your brain probably originated in the Middle Ages, when monks, who were noted for their literacy and intelligence, always ate fish on a Friday. The association of intelligence with the consumption of fish has persisted!

## MOST COMMON CAUSES OF DEATH WORLDWIDE

| CAUSE | APPROXIMATE DEATHS PER YEAR |
|---|---|
| Ischaemic heart disease | 7,200,000 |
| Cancers | 6,346,000 |
| Cerebrovascular disease | 4,600,000 |
| Acute lower respiratory infection | 3,905,000 |
| Tuberculosis | 3,000,000 |
| Chronic obstructive pulmonary disease | 2,888,000 |
| Diarrhoea, including dysentery | 2,473,000 |

## MOST EFFECTIVE KEEP-FIT ACTIVITIES

These are the sports and activities recommended by keep-fit experts as the best means of acquiring all-round fitness, building stamina and strength, and increasing suppleness.

| | |
|---|---|
| Swimming | Dancing |
| Cycling | Football |
| Rowing | Jogging |
| Gymnastics | Walking (briskly!) |
| Judo | |

## MEDICAL MILESTONES

**c.460 BC** First medical studies are made by Greek physician Hippocrates.

**1543** Accurate medical drawings are done by Flemish doctor Andreas Vesalius.

**1796** A vaccination against the deadly smallpox virus is pioneered by English doctor Edward Jenner.

**1805** German Friedrich Sertürner discovers the painkiller morphine.

**1816** First stethoscope is invented by French doctor René Laënnec.

**1818** First blood transfusion is carried out by Thomas Blundell, in England.

**1864** The Red Cross is founded by Swiss businessman Henri Dunant.

**1895** German physicist William von Röntgen discovers the X-ray.

**1928** Penicillin is discovered by Scottish bacteriologist Alexander Fleming.

**1954** First internal heart pacemaker is fitted in Stockholm, Sweden.

**1967** First heart transplant is performed by South African surgeon Christiaan Barnard.

**1978** The first test-tube baby, Louise Brown, is born in Britain.

**1980s-1990s** Laser surgery is used in eye operations and to remove cancer cells.

## STRANGE PHOBIAS

| FEAR OF | PHOBIA NAME |
|---|---|
| Ants | Myrmecophobia |
| Bathing | Ablutophobia |
| Beards | Pogonophobia |
| Chickens | Alektorophobia |
| Chins | Geniophobia |
| Dolls | Pediophobia |
| Flutes | Aulophobia |
| Frogs | Batrachophobia |
| Going to bed | Clinophobia |
| Knees | Genuphobia |
| Mirrors | Eisoptrophobia |
| Paper | Papyrophobia |
| Slime | Blennophobia |
| Teeth | Odontophobia |

## DISEASES NAMED AFTER REAL PEOPLE

| DISEASE | NAMED AFTER/DATES | NATIONALITY | AFFECTS |
|---|---|---|---|
| Alzheimer's Disease | Alois Alzheimer (1864–1915) | German | brain |
| Bell's Palsy | Sir Charles Bell (1774–1842) | Scottish | face muscles |
| Crohn's Disease | Burrill Bernard Crohn (1884–1983) | American | digestion |
| Graves' Disease | Robert James Graves (1796–1853) | Irish | thyroid gland |
| Lou Gehrig's Disease | Henry Louis Gehrig (1903–1941) | American | nervous system |
| Hodgkin's Disease | Thomas Hodgkin (1798–1866) | British | lymph system |
| Ménière's Disease | Prosper Ménière (1799–1862) | French | ears |
| Parkinson's Disease | James Parkinson (1755–1824) | British | nervous system |
| Raynaud's Disease | A. G. Maurice Raynaud (1834–1881) | French | fingers and toes |

**DID YOU KNOW?** The first stethoscope, invented in 1816, was made from a roll of paper!

## HOME SAFETY TIPS

- Do not use electrical equipment in the bathroom or near water.

- Store dangerous items, such as household products containing chemicals, in a high cupboard, away from young children.

- Keep saucepan handles turned inward so they do not hang over the work surface, and use the back rings of the hob first.

- Run cold water into the bath first, and keep testing the temperature as you add the hot water.

- Do not put an iron on the floor to cool; put it in a place where it cannot be easily touched.

- Every home and car should have a first-aid kit, containing items needed for emergency treatment.

## MOST COMMON ALLERGENS

| FOOD | ENVIRONMENTAL |
|---|---|
| Nuts | House dust mite |
| Shellfish and seafood | Grass pollens |
| Milk | Tree pollens |
| Wheat | Cats |
| Eggs | Dogs |
| Fresh fruit | Horses |
| Fresh vegetables | Moulds |
| Cheese | Birch pollen |
| Yeast | Weed pollen |

## MOST COMMON PHOBIAS

| OBJECT OF PHOBIA | MEDICAL TERM |
|---|---|
| Spiders | Arachnephobia or arachnophobia |
| People and social situations | Anthropophobia or sociophobia |
| Flying | Aerophobia or aviatophobia |
| Open spaces | Agoraphobia, cenophobia, or kenophobia |
| Confined spaces | Claustrophobia, cleisiophobia, cleithrophobia, or clithrophobia |
| Vomiting | Emetophobia or emitophobia |
| Heights | Acrophobia, altophobia, hypsophobia, or hypsiphobia |
| Thunderstorms | Brontophobia or keraunophobia |
| Death | Necrophobia or thanatophobia |
| Cancer | Carcinomaphobia, carcinophobia, carcinomatophobia, or cancerophobia |

## ODD ACCIDENTS

**PLAY ACTING** While watching a production of Hamlet in Pittsburgh, USA, Patricia Spahic received head wounds when Hamlet's dagger slipped out of his hand and flew into the audience.

**WEIGHTY PROBLEM** In 1836, a paddle steamer carrying a circus menagerie was shipwrecked off the US coast. Some of the sailors launched a raft, but were drowned when an elephant leaped onto it.

**ANGLING FOR TROUBLE** An angler on the Amazon accidentally struck a tree with his fishing rod, dislodging a nest of bees. To escape the bees, he jumped into the river – and was eaten by piranhas.

**TOOTH TROUBLE** In 1918, magician William Ellsworth Robinson, was shot dead on stage in London, England, when a trick in which he appeared to catch bullets in his teeth went wrong.

**STICKY END** In 1919, 21 people were killed in Boston, USA, when a tank containing 9 million litres (2 million gallons) of sticky molasses burst and flooded the city.

# PEOPLE'S NAMES

**DID YOU KNOW?** By the mid 1990s, Madonna was the biggest-selling female recording artist in the world.

## FAMOUS PEOPLE KNOWN BY ONE NAME

| NAME | REAL NAME |
|---|---|
| Cher | American singer Cherilyn Sarkasian, b.1946 |
| Dion | American singer Dion DiMucci, b.1939 |
| Donovan | British singer Donovan P. Leitch, b.1943 |
| Fabian | American singer Fabian Forte, b.1943 |
| Giles | British cartoonist Carl Giles, 1916–1995 |
| Houdini | American escapologist Erich Weiss, 1874–1926 |
| Liberace | American pianist Wladziu Valentino Liberace, 1919–1987 |
| Lulu | British singer Marie McDonald McLaughlin, b.1948 |
| Madonna | American singer Madonna Louise Ciccone, b.1958 |
| Michelangelo | Italian painter Michelangelo Buonarroti, 1475–1564 |
| Sade | Nigerian singer Helen Folasade Adu, b.1960 |
| Sting | British singer Gordon Matthew Sumner, b.1951 |
| Topol | Israeli actor Chaim Topol, b.1935 |
| Vangelis | Greek composer Evangelos Papathanassious, b.1943 |

## SANTA CLAUS NAMES

**FATHER CHRISTMAS**
England

**BABBO NATALE**
Italy

**JUL EMANDED**
Denmark

**JULTOMTEN**
Sweden

**KRISS KRINGLE**
Hungary

**LE PERE NOEL**
France

**PAPA NOEL**
Brazil

**ST NICHOLAS**
Germany

**SHEN TAN LAO JEN**
China

**UKKO**
Finland

**SINTER KLAUS**
Holland

## FAMOUS STAGE NAMES

**MARILYN MONROE** American film actress, who died in 1962. Her real name was Norma Jean Baker.

**JOHN WAYNE** American film actor, who died in 1979. His real name was Marion Morrison.

**CLIFF RICHARD** British singer and actor, whose real name is Harry Clive Webb.

**ELTON JOHN** British singer. His real name is Reginald Dwight.

**WOODY ALLEN** American film actor and director, whose real name is Allen Konigsberg.

**MICHAEL CAINE** British film actor. His real name is Maurice Micklewhite.

**CARY GRANT** American film actor, whose real name was Archibald Leach.

**CILLA BLACK** British television presenter. Her real name is Priscilla White!

## WORLD'S MOST COMMON SURNAMES

| COUNTRY | SURNAME |
|---|---|
| France | Martin |
| UK/USA | Smith |
| Germany | Müller |
| Spain | Garcia |
| Netherlands | De Vries |
| Sweden | Johansson |
| Russia | Ivanov |
| Italy | Rossi |
| China | Li |

**DID YOU KNOW?**
One of the longest surnames ever recorded is that of Major Tollemache-Tollemache de Orellana-Plantagenet-Tollemache-Tollemache (1858–1917), a British soldier.

## ROYAL NICKNAMES

| NICKNAME | REAL NAME |
|---|---|
| Alfonso the Fat (reigned 1212–1223) | Alfonso II, king of Portugal |
| Charles the Bald (reigned 840–877) | Charles I, king of France |
| Christian the Cruel (reigned 1513–1523) | Christian II of Denmark and Norway |
| Fulk the Surly (reigned 1068–1109) | Fulk IV, count of Anjou |
| Ivan the Terrible (reigned 1533–1584) | Ivan IV, tsar of Russia |
| Louis the Sluggard (reigned 986–987) | Louis V, king of France |
| Sebastian the Madman (reigned 1557–1578) | Sebastian of Portugal |
| Selim the Grim (reigned 1512–1520) | Selim I, Turkish sultan |
| William the Bad (reigned 1154–1166) | William I of Sicily |

## LONGEST NAMES

**USA** Rhoshandiatellyneshiaunneveshenk Koyaanfsquatsiuty Williams was born in Texas, USA in 1984.

**FRANCE** Louis George Maurice Adolph Roch Albert Abel Antonio Alexandre Noé Jean Lucien Daniel Eugène Joseph-le-Brun Josephe-Barême Thomas Thomas-Thc Pierre-Cerbon Pierre-Maurel Barthelemi Artus Alphonse Bertrand Dieudonne Emanuel Josue Vincent Luc Michel Jules-de-la-Plane Jules-Bazin Julio-César Jullien, was a French composer (1812–1860).

**HAWAII** Dawn Lee of Honolulu, Hawaii, was born in 1967, and given a 94-letter middle name: Napaumahalaonaonekawehiwehionakuahiweanenawawakehoonkakehoaalekeeaonanainananiakeao'Hawaiikawao.

**SAUDI ARABIA** The full name of the Sultan of Brunei is Kebawah Duli Yang Maha Hulia Paduka Seri Baginda Sultan Dan Yang Dipertuan Sir Muda Hassanal Bolkiah Muizzaddin Waddaulah Ibni Duli Yang Teramat Mulia Paduka Seri Begawan Sultan Sir Muda Omar Ali Saifuddin Sa'adul Khairi Waddin.

**ENGLAND** Ann Pepper, born in Derby, England, in 1882, was given 25 first names: Ann Bertha Cecilia Diana Emily Fanny Gertrude Hypatia Inez Jane Kate Louisa Maud Nora Orphelia Quince Rebecca Starkey Teresa Ulysis Venus Winifred Xenophen Yetty Zeus Pepper.

**DID YOU KNOW?** You can legally change your name to be as long or strange as you like!

## UNUSUAL NAMES FOR CELEBRITY CHILDREN

**DANDELION** Daughter of Keith Richard, a member of the group the Rolling Stones.

**DWEEZIL AND MOON UNIT** Children of Frank Zappa, singer.

**FIFI TRIXIBELLE, PIXIE, AND PEACHES** Children of Paula Yates, UK television presenter, and Bob Geldof, British musician.

**LARK SONG** Daughter of Mia Farrow, actress, and André Previn, conductor.

**ZOWIE** Child of David Bowie, singer.

**BETTY KITTEN** Daughter of Jonathon Ross, UK television presenter, and his wife Jane Goldman.

## NAMES FOR COLLECTORS

| NAME | COLLECTS |
|---|---|
| Philographist | Autographs |
| Plangonologist | Dolls |
| Bibliosphilist | Books |
| Conchologist | Shells |
| Numismatist | Coins |
| Philatelist | Stamps |
| Deltiologist | Postcards |
| Copoclephilist | Keyrings |
| Archtophilist | Teddy bears |

**DID YOU KNOW?** Teddy bears get their name from US President Theodore "Teddy" Roosevelt, who, on a hunting trip, refused to shoot a bear cub.

## POP GROUP NAME ORIGINS

**ABBA** The group members' first names are Agnetha, Benny, Björn, and Annifried. The initials form the name Abba.

**BEE GEES** The Brothers Gibb.

**DURAN DURAN** The name of a mad scientist in the film *Barbarella*.

**R.E.M** R.E.M stands for Rapid Eye Movement, a psychological term describing the dream state during sleep.

**SIMPLY RED** The group's singer Mick Hucknall has red hair.

## ONCE UPON A TIME... FAIRYTALE NAMES

**ALADDIN** A young boy who rubs a magic lamp, releasing a genie.

**SNOW WHITE** Named for her fair complexion, Snow White is deemed the fairest in the land by a magical mirror.

**SEVEN DWARFS** Dopey, Bashful, Sleepy, Grumpy, Happy, Doc, and Sneezy are Snow White's companions.

**CINDERELLA** Made to do household chores by her cruel step-sisters, Cinderella eventually marries a prince.

**RED RIDING HOOD** Dressed in a red cape, Red Riding Hood goes to visit her grandmother, but meets a wolf on the way.

**RAPUNZEL** Locked in a tower, the princess Rapunzel's hair grew so long that a prince was able to use it as a rope to climb up and rescue her.

**GOLDILOCKS** A golden haired girl who encountered a family of bears after she had eaten their porridge.

**PINOCCHIO** A wooden puppet whose nose grew longer every time he told a lie.

**HANSEL AND GRETEL** A brother and sister who find a house made of sweets and gingerbread.

**DID YOU KNOW?** One of the main characters in the book *Peter Pan*, by James Barrie, is called Wendy, a name which had never been used prior to the book's publication!

# RULERS and LEADERS

## RULING SYSTEMS

**COMMUNISM** Communists believe that everyone should eventually be equal, but until that time, the government should hold all the wealth of the country and share it fairly among the people. In communist countries, the Communist Party controls the government, the army, the civil service, economy, education, and the media.

**DEMOCRACY** Within a democracy, all persons have the right to play a part in the government of their country. Today, most democracy is representative, which means that the people elect representatives to make decisions on their behalf.

**MONARCHY** In a monarchy, a king or queen rules the country. Today, only a few monarchs, such as the king of Saudi Arabia, have real power, but four centuries ago in Europe, kings and queens made all the laws and collected the taxes.

**PRESIDENCY** In a republic such as the USA, three branches of government share power: the president leads the members of the executive branch in deciding the government's policy; members of the legislature make the laws; and the judges, who are appointed by the executive branch, interpret the law.

## FIRST TEN ROMAN EMPERORS

| EMPEROR | BORN | ACCEDED | DIED | FATE |
|---|---|---|---|---|
| Julius Caesar | 12 July 100 BC | 48 BC | 15 March 44 BC | Assassinated |
| Augustus | 23 September 63 BC | 27 BC | 19 August AD 14 | Died |
| Tiberius | 16 November 42 BC | AD 14 | 16 March AD 37 | Died |
| Caligula | 31 August AD 12 | AD 37 | 24 January AD 41 | Assassinated |
| Claudius | 1 August AD 10 | AD 41 | 13 October AD 54 | Assassinated |
| Nero | 15 December AD 37 | AD 54 | 9 June AD 68 | Suicide |
| Galba | 24 December AD 3 | AD 68 | 15 January AD 69 | Assassinated |
| Otho | 28 April AD 32 | AD 69 | 16 April AD 69 | Suicide |
| Vitellius | 24 September AD 15 | AD 69 | 22 December AD 69 | Assassinated |
| Vespasian | 18 November AD 9 | AD 69 | 23 June AD 79 | Died |

## WORLD'S LONGEST-REIGNING MONARCHS

| MONARCH | COUNTRY | REIGN | AGE AT ACCESSION | REIGN YEARS |
|---|---|---|---|---|
| Louis XIV | France | 1643–1715 | 5 | 72 |
| John II | Liechtenstein | 1858–1929 | 18 | 71 |
| Franz-Josef | Austria–Hungary | 1848–1916 | 18 | 67 |
| Victoria | Great Britain | 1837–1901 | 18 | 63 |
| Hirohito | Japan | 1926–1989 | 25 | 62 |
| Kangxi | China | 1662–1722 | 8 | 61 |
| Qianlong | China | 1736–1796 | 25 | 60 |
| George III | Great Britain | 1760–1820 | 22 | 59 |
| Louis XV | France | 1715–1774 | 5 | 59 |

## REIGNS OF BRITAIN'S MONARCHS

**SAXON KINGS:** Edward the Confessor (1042–1066) • Harold II (1066)

**NORMAN KINGS:** William I (1066–1087) William II (1087–1100) • Henry I (1100–1135)

**BLOIS KING:** Stephen (1135–1154)

**PLANTAGENETS:** Henry II (1154–1189) Richard I (1189–1199) • John (1199–1216) Henry III (1216–1272) • Edward I (1272–1307) Edward II (1307–1327) • Edward III (1327–1377) • Richard II (1377–1399) Henry IV (1399–1413) • Henry V (1413–1422) Henry VI (1422–1461)

**YORK:** Edward IV (1461–1470)

**LANCASTER:** Henry VI (1470–1471)

**YORK:** Edward IV (1471–1483) • Edward V (1483) • Richard III (1483–1485)

**TUDOR:** Henry VII (1485–1509) • Henry VIII (1509–1547) • Edward VI (1547–1553) Jane (1553) • Mary I (1553–1558) Elizabeth I (1558–1603)

**STUART:** James I (1603–1625) • Charles I (1625–1649)

**COMMONWEALTH:** Council of State (1649–1653) • Oliver Cromwell (1653–1658) Richard Cromwell (1658–1659)

**STUART:** Charles II (1660–1685) • James II (1685–1688) • Mary II (1689–1694) • William III and Mary II (1689–1694) • William III (alone) (1694–1702) • Anne (1702–1714)

**HANOVER:** George I (1714–1727) • George II (1727–1760) • George III (1760–1820) George IV (1820–1830) • William IV (1830–1837) Victoria (1837–1901)

**SAXE-COBURG:** Edward VII (1901–1910)

**WINDSOR:** George V (1910–1936) Edward VIII (1936) • George VI (1936–1952) Elizabeth II (1952–)

**DID YOU KNOW?** The Crown Jewels of the British royal family have been housed under tight security in the Jewel House of the Tower of London, London, UK, since the early 14th century. They include the regalia used in the coronations of British monarchs since that of Charles II in 1660.

## ROYAL TITLES

**KING/QUEEN** The ruler of a monarchy: that is, the chief authority over a country and people. Kings and queens were once thought to receive their power directly from God.

**RAJAH** A king or prince in India.

**EMPEROR/EMPRESS** The sovereign or supreme ruler of an entire empire, such as the Roman Empire.

**PHARAOH** An Egyptian king was referred to as the pharaoh. This name derives from the word *per-ao*, meaning "great house", and referred to the palace where the king lived.

**SULTAN** The ruler or sovereign of an Islamic country, such as Turkey.

**TSAR** An emperor or king. A former emperor of Russia.

**! DID YOU KNOW?** After his release from prison in 1990, Nelson Mandela began the long task of modernizing and stabilizing South Africa.

## FAMOUS WORLD LEADERS

**CHAIRMAN MAO** Born Mao Zedong (1893–1976), he set up the Chinese Communist Party in 1921, which took power in China in 1949. He founded the People's Republic of China in the same year, and was its first leader.

**LENIN** Vladimir Lenin (1870–1924) was the leader of the Social Democratic Party. In 1917, he led a revolution that overthrew the tyrannical tsarist rulers of Russia. He then set up the world's first communist regime in the country.

**CASTRO** In 1959, Fidel Castro (b.1927), a Cuban lawyer, led a revolution against Cuba's dictator, President Batista. Castro became head of government, and Cuba became a communist state.

**MANDELA** Nelson Mandela (b.1918) was the leader of the African National Congress (ANC), a political party and black rights group, which was banned in 1960. In 1964, he was imprisoned for life, but was finally released in 1990. Mandela became the first black president of South Africa in 1994.

## FIRST WOMEN PRIME MINISTERS AND PRESIDENTS

| NAME | COUNTRY | DATES |
|---|---|---|
| Sirimavo Bandaranaike (PM) | Ceylon (Sri Lanka) | 1960–1965 1970–1977 |
| Indira Gandhi (PM) | India | 1966–1977 1980–1984 |
| Golda Meir (PM) | Israel | 1969–1974 |
| María Estella Peron (President) | Argentina | 1974–1976 |
| Elisabeth Domitien (PM) | Central African Republic | 1975– |
| Margaret Thatcher (PM) | UK | 1979–1990 |
| Dr Maria de Lurdes Pintassilgo (PM) | Portugal | 1979– |
| Vigdís Finnbogadóttir (President) | Iceland | 1980–1996 |

## ALL THE PRESIDENTS OF THE USA

| NO. | NAME | PARTY | OFFICE |
|---|---|---|---|
| 1 | George Washington | Federalist | 1789 |
| 2 | John Adams | Federalist | 1797 |
| 3 | Thomas Jefferson | Dem-Rep | 1801 |
| 4 | James Madison | Dem-Rep | 1809 |
| 5 | James Monroe | Dem-Rep | 1817 |
| 6 | John Quincy Adams | Dem-Rep | 1825 |
| 7 | Andrew Jackson | Democrat | 1829 |
| 8 | Martin Van Buren | Democrat | 1837 |
| 9 | William Henry Harrison | Whig | 1841 |
| 10 | John Tyler | Whig | 1841 |
| 11 | James Knox Polk | Democrat | 1845 |
| 12 | Zachary Taylor | Whig | 1849 |
| 13 | Millard Fillmore | Whig | 1850 |
| 14 | Franklin Pierce | Democrat | 1853 |
| 15 | James Buchanan | Democrat | 1857 |
| 16 | Abraham Lincoln | Republican | 1861 |
| 17 | Andrew Johnson | Democrat | 1865 |
| 18 | Ulysses Simpson Grant | Republican | 1869 |
| 19 | Rutherford Birchard Hayes | Republican | 1877 |
| 20 | James Abram Garfield | Republican | 1881 |
| 21 | Chester Alan Arthur | Republican | 1881 |
| 22 | Grover Cleveland | Democrat | 1885 |
| 23 | Benjamin Harrison | Republican | 1889 |
| 24 | Grover Cleveland | Democrat | 1893 |
| 25 | William McKinley | Republican | 1897 |
| 26 | Theodore Roosevelt | Republican | 1901 |
| 27 | William Howard Taft | Republican | 1909 |
| 28 | Woodrow Wilson | Democrat | 1913 |
| 29 | Warren Gamaliel Harding | Republican | 1921 |
| 30 | Calvin Coolidge | Republican | 1923 |
| 31 | Herbert Clark Hoover | Republican | 1929 |
| 32 | Franklin Delano Roosevelt | Democrat | 1933 |
| 33 | Harry S. Truman | Democrat | 1945 |
| 34 | Dwight David Eisenhower | Republican | 1953 |
| 35 | John Fitzgerald Kennedy | Democrat | 1961 |
| 36 | Lyndon Baines Johnson | Democrat | 1963 |
| 37 | Richard Milhous Nixon | Republican | 1969 |
| 38 | Gerald Rudolph Ford | Republican | 1974 |
| 39 | Jimmy Carter | Democrat | 1977 |
| 40 | Ronald Reagan | Republican | 1981 |
| 41 | George Bush | Republican | 1989 |
| 42 | Bill Clinton | Democrat | 1993 |

# HUMAN ACHIEVEMENTS

## POLE POSITIONS

**THE FIRST TO REACH THE NORTH POLE?**  Dispute continues as to which – if either – of two men was the first to reach the North Pole: American adventurer Frederick Albert Cook (1865–1940) announced that he had attained his goal, accompanied by two Inuit, on 21 April 1908, but his claim appears to have little foundation, as he is known to have committed other fraudulent actions. It is more likely that American Robert Edwin Peary (1856–1920) and his black companion Matthew Alexander Henson (1866–1955), accompanied by four Inuit, were first at the Pole on 6 April 1909. If Peary's claim is valid, Henson also becomes the first black person to reach the Pole.

**THE FIRST TO FLY OVER THE POLES IN AN AEROPLANE**  Two Americans, Lieutenant Commander (later Admiral) Richard Evelyn Byrd (1888–1957), who was team-leader and navigator, and pilot Floyd Bennett (1890–1928) traversed the North Pole on 9 May 1926. Their aircraft was a three-engined Fokker F.VIII-3m, named *Josephine Ford* after the granddaughter of motor magnate Henry Ford, who sponsored the exploit with John D. Rockefeller. On 29 November 1929, Byrd also became the first to fly over the South Pole.

**THE FIRST TO FLY OVER THE NORTH POLE IN AN AIRSHIP**
A team of 16 led by Roald Amundsen (1872–1928), the Norwegian explorer who first reached the South Pole in 1911, flew across the North Pole on 12 May 1926 in the Italian-built airship *Norge*. Amundsen and his companion Oscar Wisting, who was with him at the South Pole, became the first people to see both Poles.

**THE FIRST TO LAND AT THE NORTH POLE IN AN AIRCRAFT**
A Soviet team comprising Pavel Afanaseyevich Geordiyenko, Mikhail Yemel'yenovich Ostrekin, Pavel Kononovich Sen'ko, and Mikhail Mikhaylovich Somov arrived at and departed from the Pole by air on 23 April 1948. The first US landing at the Pole was that of Lieutenant Colonel William Pershing Benedict, with ten Air Force officials and scientists on 3 May 1952. In the same year, the Scandinavian airline SAS became the first to fly scheduled flights over the Pole.

## FIRST TO GO OVER NIAGARA FALLS AND SURVIVE

| NAME | DATE | VESSEL |
|---|---|---|
| Annie Edison Taylor | 24 October 1901 | Barrel |
| Bobby Leach | 25 July 1911 | Steel barrel |
| Jean Lussier | 4 July 1928 | Rubber ball fitted with oxygen cylinders |
| William Fitzgerald (aka Nathan Boya) | 15 July 1961 | Rubber ball |

## FIRST CROSS-CHANNEL SWIMMERS

| SWIMMER | COUNTRY | TIME HR:MIN | DATE |
|---|---|---|---|
| Matthew Webb | UK | 21:45 | 24–25 August 1875 |
| Thomas Burgess | UK | 22:35 | 5–6 September 1911 |
| Henry Sullivan | USA | 26:50 | 5–6 August 1923 |
| Enrico Tiraboschi | Italy | 16:33 | 12 August 1923 |
| Charles Toth | USA | 16:58 | 8–9 September 1923 |

## FAMOUS HANDICAPPED ACHIEVERS

**SARAH BERNHARDT** (1844–1923)  Despite having her leg amputated in 1915 after a fall, this French tragic actress determinedly continued with her acting career.

**DAVID BLUNKETT** (b.1947) The British Minister of Education is blind and attends parliamentary sessions accompanied by his guide dog.

**STEPHEN HAWKING** (b.1942) This celebrated UK physicist, who suffers from motor-neurone disease, is confined to a wheelchair and speaks with the aid of a voice synthesizer.

**HELEN KELLER** (1880–1968) Although she was blind, deaf, and dumb, American author Helen Keller campaigned for rights for the handicapped.

## FIRST EUROPEANS TO LAND IN THE AMERICAS

| EXPLORER | COUNTRY | DISCOVERY/ EXPLORATION | YEAR |
|---|---|---|---|
| Christopher Columbus | Italy | West Indies | 1492 |
| John Cabot | Italy/ England | Nova Scotia/ Newfoundland | 1497 |
| Alonso de Hojeda | Spain | Brazil | 1499 |
| Vicente Yañez Pinzón | Spain | Amazon | 1500 |
| Pedro Alvarez Cabral | Portugal | Brazil | 1500 |
| Gaspar Corte Real | Portugal | Labrador | 1500 |
| Rodrigo de Bastidas | Spain | Central America | 1501 |
| Vasco Nuñez de Balboa | Spain | Panama | 1513 |
| Juan Ponce de León | Spain | Florida | 1513 |
| Juan Díaz de Solís | Spain | Río de la Plata | 1515 |

## YOUNG ACHIEVERS

**YOUNGEST BRITISH MONARCH**
Henry VI was born on 6 December 1421 and became king of England on 1 September 1422, at the age of eight months.

**YOUNGEST PATENT HOLDER ON INVENTIONS** John J. Stone-Parker received a US Patent in 1989 when he was four years old, for an attachment to stop ice slipping out of a glass.

**YOUNGEST ARTIST TO EXHIBIT AT THE ROYAL ACADEMY** Lewis Lyons' painting *Trees and Monkeys* was shown on 29 April 1967, a day before his fifth birthday.

**YOUNGEST PUBLISHED AUTHOR**
Allen Welsh Dulles (1892–1969) had his book *The Boer War: A History* published in 1902, when he was eight. Dulles later became the director of the Central Intelligence Agency (CIA).

**DID YOU KNOW?** A team of 12 husky dogs can pull a loaded sledge weighing 0.5 tonnes (0.49 tons).

## LADIES FIRST

**PARACHUTIST**
Jean Genevieve Garnerin was the first female parachutist. She parachuted from a hot-air balloon in Paris, in 1799.

**NOBEL PRIZE WINNER**
In 1903, Marie Curie of Poland shared the Nobel Prize for physics for her work on radioactivity.

**POLICEWOMAN**
Alice Stebbins Wells became the first ever policewoman, in Los Angeles in 1910.

**CLIMBER** Junko Tabei from Japan was the first woman to reach the top of Everest. She achieved this in 1975.

**SAILOR** In 1969, American Sharon Adams became the first woman to sail across the Pacific single-handed.

**EDITOR** In 1762, Anna Maria Smart became the first female editor in the UK when she edited the *Reading Mercury*. In the USA, Ann Franklin became editor of the *Newport Mercury*, in the same year.

## ROUND-THE-WORLD FIRSTS

**ROUND THE WORLD**
Juan Sebastian de Elcano, and his crew of 17 on board *Vittoria*, sailed round the world from Spain, returning to Italy on 6 September 1522. The expedition was originally led by Ferdinand Magellan, but he was murdered in the Philippines, 27 April 1521.

**ROUND THE WORLD IN LESS THAN 80 DAYS**
US journalist "Nellie Bly" (Elizabeth Cochrane) set out to beat the fictitious "record" established in Jules Verne's novel, *Around the World in 80 Days*. She travelled from New York, and returned on 25 January 1890 – a record circumnavigation of 72 days, 6 hours, 11 minutes and 14 seconds.

**SOLO ROUND THE WORLD** In 1895, US sea captain Joshua Slocum (1844–1910) set out from Boston in 1895 in *Spray*, an oyster boat he had built himself, returning three years later. He financed his trip by giving lectures along the way. Surprisingly, Slocum was unable to swim!

**DID YOU KNOW?** Sun rays shining on Arctic snow can cause temporary blindness.

**DID YOU KNOW?** Deaths on Everest are on the increase. The sheer volume of people now climbing the mountain means that more and more people are coming to untimely ends.

## FIRST MOUNTAINEERS TO CLIMB EVEREST

| MOUNTAINEER | COUNTRY | DATE |
|---|---|---|
| Edmund Hillary | New Zealand | 29 May 1953 |
| Tenzing Norgay | Nepal | 29 May 1953 |
| Jürg Marmet | Switzerland | 23 May 1956 |
| Ernst Schmied | Switzerland | 23 May 1956 |
| Hans-Rudolf von Gunten | Switzerland | 24 May 1956 |
| Adolf Reist | Switzerland | 24 May 1956 |
| Wang Fu-chou | China | 25 May 1960 |
| Chu Ying-hua | China | 25 May 1960 |
| Konbu | Tibet | 25 May 1960 |
| Nawang Gombu | India | 1 May 1963 |
| James Whittaker | USA | 1 May 1963 |

Nawang Gombu and James Whittaker both arrived at Everest's summit at the same time – neither wishing to deny the other the privilege of being first, they ascended the last stretch side by side.

# INDUSTRY

## THE WORLD of WORK

! **DID YOU KNOW?** The first plough was called an ard.

## COUNTRIES WITH THE MOST WORKERS

As defined by the International Labour Organisation, the "labour force" includes people between the ages of 15 and 64 who are currently employed and those who are also unemployed.

| COUNTRY | LABOUR FORCE |
|---|---|
| China | 709,000,000 |
| India | 398,000,000 |
| USA | 133,000,000 |
| Indonesia | 89,000,000 |
| Russia | 77,000,000 |
| Brazil | 71,000,000 |
| Japan | 66,000,000 |
| Bangladesh | 60,000,000 |
| Pakistan | 46,000,000 |
| Nigeria | 44,000,000 |
| Germany | 40,000,000 |

## MOST HOLIDAYS

| COUNTRY | AVERAGE NO. OF DAYS OFF PER YEAR |
|---|---|
| Austria | 30 |
| Belgium | 30 |
| Finland | 25 |
| France | 25 |
| Norway | 25 |

## MOST STRESSFUL JOBS

The following jobs are considered the most stressful. Most of them involve a high level of responsibility.

- Firefighter
- Racing car driver
- Astronaut
- Surgeon
- National Football League player
- Police officer
- Highway patrol officer
- Air traffic controller

## LEAST STRESSFUL JOBS

- Musical instrument repairer
- Industrial machine repairer
- Medical records technician
- Pharmacist
- Software engineer
- Typist, word processor
- Librarian
- Janitor
- Bookkeeper
- Forklift operator

## ANIMALS AT WORK

Many animals work with people, helping with tasks that make use of their special skills.

**DOGS** Often described as "man's best friend", dogs are chosen to work with people in many jobs, ranging from guiding the blind and assisting the police, to pulling sledges, rounding up sheep, and even sniffing for drugs.

**CAMELS** These strong animals are chosen to carry people and goods across the desert because they can go for long periods without rest or water.

**ELEPHANTS** The strength of Asian elephants is put to good use in tropical forests where they haul logs.

## DANGEROUS JOBS

Life assurance companies base their premiums on statistics according to the likelihood of people being involved in an accident at work. These are the most dangerous jobs:

- Formula One Driver
- Bomb disposal officer
- Test pilot
- Special forces soldier
- Circus performer
- Film stuntman
- Commercial diver
- Oil rig worker
- Scaffolder
- Fisherman
- Miner
- Dockworker
- Merchant Navy
- Linesman (electrics)

## 20TH-CENTURY ENTREPRENEURS

| NAME | BUSINESS |
|---|---|
| Sochiro Honda (1906–1991) | Motorcycles and cars |
| William Hewlett (b.1913) and David Packard (1912–1996) | Computers |
| Akio Morita (b.1921) | Sony electronic products |
| Sir Terence Conran (b.1931) | Retail shops, restaurants |
| Sir Clive Sinclair (b.1940) | Electronic products |
| Anita Roddick (b.1942) | Eco-friendly body products |
| Alan Sugar (b.1947) | Amstrad electronic products |
| Richard Branson (b.1950) | *Virgin* records, airline, trains |
| Bill Gates (b.1955) | Computer software |
| Steve Jobs (b.1955) | Apple computers |

**DID YOU KNOW?** The largest food company in the world is Nestlé. Their top-selling product is *Kit Kat* – about 400 are eaten every second!

## COUNTRIES WITH MOST FARMERS

This list is compiled by the United Nations and is based on the number of people that depend on agriculture for their livelihood, even if they do not own land of their own.

| COUNTRY | PER CENT FARMING |
|---|---|
| Bhutan | 93.9 |
| Nepal | 93.3 |
| Burkina | 92.4 |
| Rwanda | 91.2 |
| Burundi | 90.7 |
| Niger | 89.2 |
| Mali | 89.2 |
| Ethiopia | 85.3 |
| Guinea Bissau | 84.1 |
| Uganda | 83.1 |
| Tanzania | 81.6 |

**AMAZING FACT!** Although most people in Bhutan are farmers, only three per cent of its land can actually be cultivated.

**DID YOU KNOW?** When farmers grow only enough food to support themselves and their families, it is called subsistence farming.

## US COMPANIES WITH MOST EMPLOYEES

| COMPANY | EMPLOYEES |
|---|---|
| Wal-Mart Stores | 825,000 |
| General Motors | 608,000 |
| Ford Motor | 363,892 |
| United Parcel Service | 331,000 |
| Sears Roebuck | 296,000 |
| Columbia/HCA Healthcare | 285,000 |
| General Electric | 276,000 |
| IBM | 269,465 |
| J. C. Penney | 260,000 |
| Kmart | 258,000 |
| Boeing | 239,000 |
| McDonalds | 237,000 |
| Kroger | 212,000 |

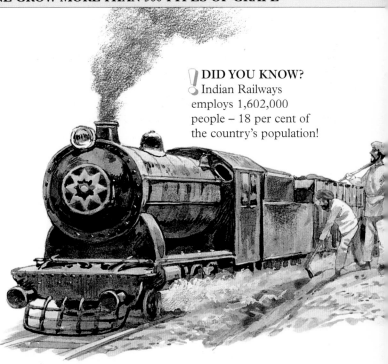

**DID YOU KNOW?** Indian Railways employs 1,602,000 people – 18 per cent of the country's population!

## PROFESSIONS THAT WALK THE MOST

This list is based on a survey conducted in the USA by footwear manufacturer Dr Scholl's, and the American Podiatry Association. These figures are averages, and certain individuals may walk much more or less than these suggest.

| PROFESSION | AVERAGE WALKED PER YEAR | |
|---|---|---|
| | KM | MILES |
| Policeman/woman | 2,626 | 1,632 |
| Postman/woman | 1,699 | 1,056 |
| TV reporter | 1,622 | 1,008 |
| Nurse | 1,516 | 942 |
| Doctor | 1,352 | 840 |
| Shop assistant | 1,294 | 804 |
| Secretary | 1,275 | 792 |
| Actor | 1,249 | 776 |
| Public relations executive | 1,072 | 666 |
| Estate agent | 1,001 | 622 |

## PRESIDENTS' PREVIOUS JOBS

| PRESIDENT | OCCUPATION |
|---|---|
| Ronald Reagan | Actor |
| George Bush | Oilman |
| Jimmy Carter | Peanut farmer |
| Harry Truman | Haberdasher |
| Theodore Roosevelt | Rancher |
| George Washington | Surveyor, planter |

## MOST PHYSICALLY DEMANDING JOBS

Firefighter • Labourer

Farmer • Lumberjack

Cowboy • Construction worker

Ironworker • Refuse collector

Miner • Sportsman/woman

Stuntman • Acrobat

## UK COMPANIES WITH MOST EMPLOYEES

This list includes only companies with shares on the Stock Exchange. Government, and other organizations, are also major employers – the National Health Service, for example, employs about a million people.

| COMPANY | EMPLOYEES |
|---|---|
| British Telecom | 129,600 |
| BTR | 115,805 |
| HSBC Holdings | 109,298 |
| Compass Group | 107,843 |
| Rentokil Initial | 107,767 |
| J. Sainsbury | 102,544 |
| Tesco | 98,440 |
| Lonrho | 93,497 |
| Lloyds TSB Group | 90,383 |
| Barclays | 87,400 |
| Bass | 84,872 |
| Boots | 81,260 |
| BAT Industries | 81,039 |
| GEC | 79,846 |
| National Westminster Bank | 79,100 |
| P & O Steam Navigation | 71,205 |
| Coats Viyella | 69,488 |

# MONEY and WEALTH

## MONEY FIRSTS

**COINS** The first coins were staters, minted in Lydia, (now Turkey) from 680 to 645 BC. Their value depended on their weight.

**BANKNOTES** Paper money was invented by the Chinese in the tenth century.

**CREDIT CARD** The Diners Club card issued in the USA in 1950 was the first credit card. It enabled the first 200 members to eat on credit at 27 New York restaurants.

## RICHEST PEOPLE IN THE WORLD – EXCLUDING RULERS

| NAME | COUNTRY | SOURCE | WORTH (US $) |
|---|---|---|---|
| William H. Gates III | USA | Computer software | 51,000,000,000 |
| Walton Family | USA | Stores | 48,000,000,000 |
| Warren E. Buffett | USA | Investments | 33,000,000,000 |
| Paul Gardner Allen | USA | Computer software | 21,000,000,000 |
| Kenneth Thomson | Canada | Newspapers | 14,400,000,000 |
| Jay A. and Robert Pritzker | USA | Finance | 13,500,000,000 |
| Mars family | USA | Inheritance | 13,500,000,000 |
| Lee Shau Kee | China | Property | 12,700,000,000 |
| Albrecht family | Germany | Stores | 11,700,000,000 |
| Steven A. Ballmer | USA | Computer software | 10,700,000,000 |
| Mulliez family | France | Stores | 10,300,000,000 |
| Michael Dell | USA | Computers | 10,000,000,000 |
| Li Ka-Shing | China | Property | 10,000,000,000 |

## POOREST COUNTRIES

Gross Domestic Product (GDP) is the total value of a country's goods and services, produced annually. Dividing a country's GDP by its population can give an indication of how "rich" it is.

| COUNTRY | GDP PER HEAD (US $) |
|---|---|
| Sudan | 36 |
| Sao Tome & Principe | 49 |
| Mozambique | 77 |

## RICHEST COUNTRIES

| COUNTRY | GDP PER HEAD (US $) |
|---|---|
| Liechtenstein | 42,416 |
| Switzerland | 42,416 |
| Japan | 41,718 |

**! DID YOU KNOW?**
A lack of raw materials in Switzerland led to the development of specialized high-tech industries, bringing the country great wealth.

## COUNTRIES WITH THE MOST GOLD

| COUNTRY | GOLD RESERVES, 1998 | | |
|---|---|---|---|
| | TROY OUNCES | TONNES | TONS |
| USA | 261,710,000 | 8,140 | 8,011 |
| Germany | 95,180,000 | 2,960 | 2,913 |
| Switzerland | 83,280,000 | 2,590 | 2,549 |
| France | 81,890,000 | 2,547 | 2,507 |
| Italy | 66,670,000 | 2,073 | 2,040 |
| Netherlands | 27,070,000 | 841 | 828 |
| Japan | 24,230,000 | 753 | 741 |
| UK | 18,420,000 | 572 | 563 |
| Portugal | 16,070,000 | 499 | 491 |

## WORLD'S HIGHEST-EARNING ACTORS AND ACTRESSES

| ACTOR | COUNTRY | RECENT WORK | INCOME 1996–1997 US $ |
|---|---|---|---|
| Arnold Schwarzenegger | Germany/USA | *Batman and Robin* | 74,000,000 |
| Harrison Ford | USA | *Air Force One* | 72,000,000 |
| Tim Allen | USA | *Home Improvement* (TV) | 66,000,000 |
| John Travolta | USA | *Michael, Face Off* | 61,000,000 |
| Mel Gibson | Australia | *Ransom* | 59,000,000 |
| Roseanne | USA | *Roseanne* (TV) | 55,000,000 |
| Jim Carrey | USA | *Liar, liar* | 53,000,000 |
| Robin Williams | USA | *Flubber, Good Will Hunting* | 50,000,000 |
| Eddie Murphy | USA | *The Nutty Professor, The Metro* | 49,000,000 |
| Kevin Costner | USA | *Tin Cup, The Postman* | 42,000,000 |

## HISTORIC TREASURES MADE OF GOLD

**BUDDHA** The world's largest single gold object is a 15th-century statue of Buddha in Bangkok, Thailand. It is 3 m (10 ft) high and weighs 5.5 tonnes (5.4 tons).

**TUTANKHAMUN'S TOMB** In 1923, British archaeologist Howard Carter discovered the tomb of 14th-century-BC pharaoh Tutankhamun. The treasures included a gold mask inside a solid gold coffin, weighing 110 kg (243 lb).

**SALT CELLAR** An elaborate salt cellar was crafted in gold by Italian Benvenuto Cellini (1500–1571).

## RICHEST RULERS IN THE WORLD

| NAME | COUNTRY | IN POWER SINCE | ESTIMATED WEALTH (US $) |
|---|---|---|---|
| Sultan Hassanal Bolkiah | Brunei | 1967 | 38,000,000,000 |
| King Fahd Bin Abdulaziz Alsaud | Saudi Arabia | 1982 | 20,000,000,000 |
| Sheikh Jaber Al-Ahmed Al-Jaber Al-Sabah | Kuwait | 1977 | 15,000,000,000 |
| Sheikh Zayed Bin Sultan Al Nahyan | United Arab Emirates | 1966 | 10,000,000,000 |
| President Saddam Hussein | Iraq | 1979 | 5,000,000,000 |
| Queen Beatrix | Netherlands | 1980 | 4,700,000,000 |
| Prime Minister Rafik al-Hariri | Lebanon | 1992 | 3,000,000,000 |
| King Bhumibol | Thailand | 1946 | 1,800,000,000 |

## HIGHEST-EARNING CELEBRITIES

| NAME | OCCUPATION | INCOME 1996–1997 US $ |
|---|---|---|
| Steven Spielberg | Film producer/director | 313,000,000 |
| George Lucas | Film producer/director | 241,000,000 |
| Oprah Winfrey | TV host/producer | 201,000,000 |
| Michael Crichton | Novelist/screenwriter | 102,000,000 |
| Jerry Seinfeld | TV performer | 94,000,000 |
| David Copperfield | Illusionist | 85,000,000 |
| Stephen King | Novelist/screenwriter | 84,300,000 |
| Arnold Schwarzenegger | Actor | 74,000,000 |
| John Grisham | Novelist/screenwriter | 66,000,000 |
| Celine Dion | Singer | 65,000,000 |
| Siegfried and Roy | Illusionists | 58,000,000 |
| Michael Jackson | Singer | 55,000,000 |
| Michael Flatley | Dancer | 54,000,000 |
| Spice Girls | Singers | 47,000,000 |
| U2 | Band | 40,000,000 |

## FAMOUS MISERS

**HETTY GREEN (1834–1916)** Hetty Green was the daughter of a US shipping and whaling magnate. Despite her great wealth, she lived in cheap boarding houses, on a diet of porridge.

**J. PAUL GETTY (1892–1976)** One of the 20th century's richest men, US oil magnate Getty made his guests pay for telephone calls by installing coin-operated telephones in the bedrooms of his mansion in Surrey, England.

## MONEY FACTS

**LARGEST COINS** The Swedish ten-daler copper coins of 1644 weighed 19.71 kg (43 lb 7 oz).

**SMALLEST COINS** The Nepal silver quarter-jawa of c.1740 weighed 0.002g (0.00007 oz). You would need 500,000 coins to weigh 1 kg, or 231,700 to make 1 lb.

**LARGEST BANKNOTES** Chinese 14th-century one-guan notes measured 22.8 x 33 cm (9 x 13 in).

**SMALLEST BANK NOTES** The Romanian ten-bani notes of 1917 had a printed area of just 27.5 x 38 mm (1.6 x 1.5 in).

**MOST MINTED** In 1997, a total of 12,194,723,000 coins were minted in the USA.

## MILLIONAIRES THROUGH HISTORY

**CORNELIUS VANDERBILT (1794–1877)** Steamship owner and once richest man in the USA.

**ANDREW CARNEGIE (1835–1918)** Scots-born US steel millionaire.

**JOHN DAVISON ROCKEFELLER (1835–1937)** US oil millionaire.

**HENRY FORD (1863–1947)** A US motor car industry magnate.

**HOWARD HUGHES (1905–1976)** US aviator and airline owner.

## A MILLION DOLLARS

**WEIGHT ON YOUR SHOULDERS** $1 million in $1 bills would weigh exactly 1 tonne (1 ton), and if you put them in a pile, it would be 110 m (361 ft) high – as tall as 60 adults standing on each other's shoulders! If you had $1 million in $100 bills, it would weigh only 10 kg (22 lb), so you'd be able to carry it. However, if you had $1 million in one-cent coins – 100,000,000 of them – it would weigh 250 tonnes (246 tons).

**WHO WANTS TO BE A MILLIONAIRE?** The first reference to "millionaire" appears in British author Benjamin Disraeli's novel *Vivian Grey* (1826): "Were I the son of a millionaire, or a noble, I might have all".

**SAVING A MILLION** If you earned 100 pounds (dollars) a week, it would take 192 years to earn one million pounds (dollars) – and that's before tax!

**DID YOU KNOW?** In 1864, American John Washington Steel inherited more than $1 million. He spent the entire inheritance in one year.

# FOOD PRODUCTION

## TOP FARMING COUNTRIES

| COUNTRY | AGRICULTURAL AREA (HECTARES) | | |
| --- | --- | --- | --- |
| | CROPS | PASTURE | TOTAL |
| China | 96,554,000 | 400,000,000 | 496,554,000 |
| Australia | 46,877,000 | 415,885,000 | 462,762,000 |
| USA | 187,776,000 | 239,172,000 | 426,948,000 |
| Brazil | 61,350,000 | 185,500,000 | 246,850,000 |
| Russia | 133,929,000 | 83,100,000 | 217,029,000 |
| India | 169,700,000 | 11,770,000 | 181,470,000 |
| Argentina | 27,200,000 | 142,100,000 | 169,300,000 |
| Mongolia | 1,396,000 | 124,600,000 | 125,996,000 |
| Mexico | 24,720,000 | 74,499,000 | 99,219,000 |
| South Africa | 1,317,000 | 81,378,000 | 82,695,000 |

**DID YOU KNOW?** The total area of agricultural land used for cultivating crops worldwide is 1,441,573,000 hectares (3,562,271,040 acres). There are 3,357,520, 000 hectares (8,296,767,672 acres) of pasture land.

## FISHY FOOD

**DID YOU KNOW?** Fish and shellfish are rich in protein, minerals, and vitamins.

**SALTWATER FISH** This group includes shark, tuna, and swordfish – more unusual types of fish that are becoming increasingly popular to eat.

**CRUSTACEANS** Crustaceans include crabs, lobsters, prawns and shrimps. They are caught and eaten by people around the world.

**SUSHI** Sushi is a traditional Japanese dish of raw or lightly cooked fish, often marinated, and served with rice.

**SHELLFISH** Shellfish, such as mussels, oysters, and scallops, have hard shells, inside which is a soft, edible body. Most shellfish are eaten cooked – except oysters, which are swallowed raw!

## BIGGEST FOODS EVER MADE

**BIGGEST PIZZA** On 8 December 1990, staff at the Norwood Hypermarket, Norwood, South Africa, produced a pizza that measured 37.4 m (122 ft 8 in) in diameter!

**BIGGEST CHEESE** In his *Natural History*, Roman historian Pliny the Elder (AD 23–79) describes a 454-kg (1,000-lb) cheese that was made in the Italian town of Luni. The current record holder is a monster Cheddar made in 1995 in Quebec, Canada, by Loblaws Supermarkets and Agropur Dairies. It weighed 26,085 kg (57,508 lb)!

**BIGGEST BISCUIT** The world's largest biscuit was a chocolate chip cookie baked by Cookie Time of Christchurch, New Zealand, on 2 April 1996. It contained 2.5 tonnes (2.46 tons) of chocolate, had a diameter of 24.9 m (81.8 ft), and covered an area of 486.95 sq m (5, 241.5 sq ft) – almost twice the size of a tennis court!

## LIVESTOCK POPULATIONS

**BEEF** India has almost 200 million cows, more than any other country.

**PIGS** Denmark has twice as many pigs as humans – more than 11 million, with a human population of just over five million.

**HENS** China has the most chickens of any country – more than three billion. The USA has half this number – equal to six chickens for every human inhabitant.

## FOODS AND DRINKS NAMED AFTER PLACES

| FOOD | FROM |
| --- | --- |
| Stilton cheese | Stilton, UK |
| Cantaloupe melon | Cantaluppi, Italy |
| Champagne | Champagne region of France |
| Currants | Corinth, Greece |
| Frankfurter | Frankfurt, Germany |
| Madeira (wine, cake) | Madeira, Spain |
| Mayonnaise | Mahón, Spain |
| Tangerines | Tangier, Morocco |
| Port | Oporto, Portugal |

## TOP FRUIT CROPS

| CROP | COUNTRIES | WORLD PRODUCTION | |
|---|---|---|---|
| | | TONNES | TONS |
| Oranges | Brazil, USA, Mexico | 63,789,600 | 62,781,724 |
| Bananas | India, Brazil, Ecuador | 59,053,950 | 58,120,898 |
| Grapes | Italy, France, USA | 58,108,880 | 57,190,760 |
| Apples | China, USA, Turkey | 56,021,370 | 55,136,232 |
| Watermelons | China, Turkey, USA | 46,436,510 | 45,702,813 |
| Mangoes | India, China, Mexico | 23,649,620 | 23,275,956 |
| Pears | China, USA, Spain | 13,431,820 | 13,219,597 |
| Pineapples | Thailand, Brazil, Philippines | 13,060,250 | 12,853,898 |
| Peaches | China, USA, Italy | 10,911,030 | 10,738,636 |
| Lemons and limes | Mexico, India, Argentina | 8,783,664 | 8,644,882 |

## TOP VEGETABLE CROPS

| CROP | COUNTRIES | WORLD PRODUCTION | |
|---|---|---|---|
| | | TONNES | TONS |
| Sugar cane | Brazil, India, China | 1,251,352,000 | 1,231,580,638 |
| Wheat | China, India, USA | 608,846,200 | 599,226,430 |
| Maize/corn | USA, China, Brazil | 586,922,700 | 577,649,321 |
| Rice | China, India, Indonesia | 570,906,000 | 561,885,685 |
| Potatoes | China, Russia, USA | 291,401,800 | 286,797,652 |
| Sugar beet | France, Germany, USA | 264,546,500 | 260,366,665 |
| Barley | Russia, Canada, Germany | 156,502,100 | 154,029,367 |
| Tomatoes | China, USA, Turkey | 88,735,600 | 87,333,578 |
| Pulses | India, UK, Kenya | 56,384,500 | 55,493,625 |
| Oats | Russia, Canada, USA | 31,240,150 | 30,746,555 |
| Carrots | China, USA, Russia | 17,873,090 | 17,551,374 |

**DID YOU KNOW?** About 15 million burgers are consumed every day in the USA!

## BANANA FACTS

**WHAT IS A BANANA?**
Botanically, the banana is a herb. The name comes from Portuguese, but is adapted from African words.

**HOW DO THEY GROW?**
Bananas grow upside down on a bush.

**WHICH COUNTRY GROWS MOST?**
India grows more bananas than any other country in the world, producing almost ten million tonnes (9.8 million tons) a year.

**HOW MANY ARE EATEN?**
Worldwide, nearly 60 million tonnes (59.1 million tons) of bananas are eaten every year.

## WHEN WERE THEY INVENTED?

| | |
|---|---|
| Popcorn | 3,000 BC |
| Croissants | 1683 |
| Potato crisps | 1853 |
| Chewing gum | 1875 |
| Coca-Cola | 1885 |
| Corn flakes | 1894 |
| Chop suey | 1896 |
| Pepsi-Cola | 1898 |
| Hamburger | 1902 |
| Ice cream cone | 1904 |
| Instant coffee | 1909 |
| Frozen food | 1923 |
| Fish fingers | 1929 |

## POTATO FACTS

**GOING UNDERGROUND** We eat only the potato tuber, which grows underground. The fruits and leaves of the potato plant, which grow above ground, are poisonous.

**POTATO MYTHS** Through the ages, potatoes have been blamed for causing everything from love to leprosy. At one time, the Scots refused to eat them because they were not mentioned in the Bible! In the Andes, the Incas thought the potato made childbirth easier, and also used it to treat injuries.

**A SNACK IS BORN** Potato crisps were invented by a North American Indian called George Crum, in the mid-19th century.

# FOOD <u>and</u> EATING

PAVLOVA

## CRUISE SHIP SHOPPING LIST

On an average 14-day cruise, the 1,975 passengers and 760 crew of the luxurious ocean liner *Oriana* will eat 116,550 meals. The shopping list for the huge amount of food and drink required on the journey is as follows:

| | |
|---|---|
| Fresh fruit and vegetables | 28,000 kg (61,729 lb) |
| Potatoes | 18,000 kg (39,683 lb) |
| Meat | 14,600 kg (32,187 lb) |
| Flour | 8,500 kg (18,739 lb) |
| Poultry and game | 6,900 kg (15,212 lb) |
| Fats and cheese | 4,600 kg (10,141 lb) |
| Fish | 3,700 kg (8,157 lb) |
| Bacon | 3,500 kg (7,716 lb) |
| Sugar | 1,900 kg (4,189 lb) |
| Shellfish | 1,700 kg (3,748 lb) |
| Coffee | 650 kg (1,433 lb) |
| Milk | 10,500 litres (2,310 gallons) |
| Ice cream | 4,000 litres (880 gallons) |
| Fresh eggs | 5,100 |
| Champagne and white wine | 2,600 bottles |
| Red wine | 1,200 bottles |
| Whisky | 1,600 litres (352 gallons) |
| Spirits | 1,200 litres (264 gallons) |
| Cognac | 400 litres (88 gallons) |
| Beer | 33,000 cans |
| Mixers | 28,000 bottles |

## DID YOU KNOW?

A meringue made with fruits and cream was named in honour of the Russian ballerina Anna Pavlova (1885–1931) during a tour of Australia and New Zealand. In Australia, its name is often shortened to a "pav".

## STRANGE APPETITES

**MAN OF IRON**  An inquest into the death of British farmer Frederick Edwards in 1933 found 1 live revolver bullet, 200 nails, 36 staples, 3 penknives, and 43 gramophone needles in his stomach.

**MONSIEUR MANGETOUT**  Frenchman Michel Lotito (b.1950), whose stage name is "Monsieur Mangetout" (Mr Eat-All), has eaten: 15 supermarket trolleys, 7 TV sets, 1 waterbed, 1 coffin, 1 pair of skis, 18 bicycles ("the chain is the tastiest part"), 1 robot, 1 computer, 1 Cessna light aircraft, and numerous razor blades!

**HUNGRY WRITER**  The French author Honoré de Balzac (1799–1850) frequently scoffed about 100 oysters, 12 lamb cutlets, a duck, and a couple of partridges in one sitting.

## DISHES NAMED AFTER PEOPLE

**APPLE CHARLOTTE**  French master chef Marie Antonin Carême (1784–1833) created this dessert while employed by the English Prince Regent. He named it Charlotte after the Prince's daughter.

**MELBA TOAST AND PÊCHE MELBA**  The Australian opera singer Dame Nellie Melba (1861–1931) had several dishes named after her, including Pêche Melba. Melba Toast was created at London's Savoy Hotel, where she was staying.

**SANDWICH**  The first sandwich was created when John Montagu, fourth Earl of Sandwich (1718–1792), allegedly asked for roast beef between slices of bread so that he could continue a marathon card game uninterrupted.

## TOP SUGAR EATERS

| COUNTRY | CONSUMPTION PER HEAD PER YEAR | | |
|---|---|---|---|
| | KG | LB | OZ |
| Swaziland | 203.5 | 448 | 10 |
| Singapore | 82.5 | 181 | 14 |
| Fiji | 78.8 | 173 | 12 |

**DID YOU KNOW?**  Danish people consume 17 kg (37 lb) of sweets and chocolate per head per year!

## TOP FISH EATERS

| COUNTRY | CONSUMPTION PER HEAD PER YEAR | | |
|---|---|---|---|
| | KG | LB | OZ |
| Denmark | 45.6 | 100 | 8 |
| Portugal | 39.8 | 87 | 12 |
| Japan | 37.2 | 82 | 0 |

**DID YOU KNOW?**  Fish is a good source of protein and is healthier and lower in calories than red meat.

## TOP MEAT EATERS

| COUNTRY | CONSUMPTION PER HEAD PER YEAR | | |
|---|---|---|---|
| | KG | LB | OZ |
| USA | 116.9 | 257 | 11 |
| Australia | 104.0 | 229 | 5 |
| New Zealand | 100.8 | 222 | 3 |

**DID YOU KNOW?**  India has one-fifth of the world's cattle, but many Indians don't eat beef due to religious beliefs.

## EXTRAORDINARY FEASTS

**MUSICAL PIE** The highlight of a four-day French banquet given in 1454 by Philip, Duke of Burgundy, came when a huge pie was brought into the room. The lid of the pie was raised to reveal an orchestra of 28 musicians playing within!

**CRAZY CUSTARD CAPER** During a large banquet held in 1521 at Dover Castle, in the south of England, a court jester amused the guests by leaping into a gigantic bowl of custard!

**DEATHLY DINNER** In about 1820, the eccentric French culinary expert, Grimod de la Reynière, staged one of the most macabre meals of all time – in the Paris mortuary. Coffins were placed behind each diner's seat, and 300 spectators observed the bizarre event from the mortuary gallery.

**DIZZY DINNER** On 23 October 1843, just before the statue of Lord Nelson was hauled to the top of Nelson's Column in Trafalgar Square, London, 14 men ate rump steak on the plinth, 51 m (167 ft) above the ground!

**INSIDE A DINOSAUR** On New Year's Eve 1853, Professor Richard Owen, later head of the Natural History Department of the British Museum, hosted a banquet inside the framework of a model of the dinosaur *Iguanodon*!

**ON HORSEBACK** At Sherry's elegant restaurant in New York on 28 March 1903, 36 formally attired gentlemen sat down to dinner on horseback! Their horses were brought to the ballroom by lift and the floor was laid with turf. Pheasant was served in nosebags, and the champagne in rubber buckets!

## GIANT FROG RECIPES

Dr Albert Broel, who described himself as the "originator of canned frog legs", provides a list of over 50 tasty recipes for giant frogs in his strange book, *Frog Raising for Pleasure and Profit* (1950). Don't try these at home!

Fried Frog Legs

Giant Frog Sandwich Spread

Giant Bullfrog Cream Broth

Devilled Giant Bullfrog Meat

American Giant Bullfrog Cocktail

Giant Bullfrog Mince Meat

Jellied Giant Bullfrogs

Chinese-style Bullfrog and Rice

Bullfrog Chop Suey

Escalloped Bullfrog with Celery

Giant Bullfrog Omelette

Stuffed Egg with Giant Bullfrog

Baked Apples Stuffed with Frog Meat

Stuffed Baked Tomatoes with Bullfrogs

Giant Bullfrog Fondue

French Toasted Giant Bullfrog Special

## THE GREATEST BANQUET

A manuscript said to have been found in the Tower of London, England, is the shopping list for a banquet to end all banquets. Organized in York by the Earl of Warwick to commemorate the installation of his brother George as the Archbishop of York in 1465, it was prepared by 62 cooks, backed up by 515 kitchen helpers, and served to the guests by 1,000 waiters. Imagine going to the supermarket to collect this lot!

| | |
|---|---|
| 5,000 Woodcocks | 300 Pigs |
| 4,000 Pigeons | 300 Hogs |
| 4,000 Rabbits | 300 Capons |
| 4,000 Ducks | 300 Quarters of wheat (1 quarter = 291,000 cm$^3$/ 10.3 ft$^3$) |
| 4,000 Bucks, does, and roebucks | |
| 4,000 Cold custards | 300 Tuns of ale (1 tun = 935.8 litres/210 gallons) |
| 4,000 Cold venison pasties | |
| 3,000 Calves | 200 Rees (a bird) |
| 2,000 Chickens | 200 Cranes |
| 2,000 Hot custards | 200 Kids |
| 1004 Wethers (rams) | 204 Bitterns |
| 1,000 Dishes of jellies | 200 Pheasants |
| 1,000 Eggets (perhaps a small egg) | 155 Hot venison pasties |
| 500 Partridges | 100 Peacocks |
| 400 Plovers | 100 Curlews |
| 400 Hernsies (young herons) | 100 Quails |
| 400 Tarts | 104 Tuns of wine |
| 300 Pikes | 10 Fat oxen |
| 300 Breams | 8 Seals |
| | 6 Wild bulls |
| | 4 Porpoises |
| | 1 Pipe of spiced wine (1 pipe = 477.3 litres/105 gallons) |

**DID YOU KNOW?** A South African bullfrog can be 0 cm (35 in) length – longer than our arm!

# THE EARTH'S RICHES

## MOST-EXTRACTED MINERALS PER YEAR

| MINERAL | MILLIONS OF TONNES | TONS |
|---|---|---|
| Iron ore | 988.8 | 973.1 |
| Salt | 184.9 | 181.9 |
| Aluminium ore (bauxite) | 111 | 109.3 |
| Potash | 20.34 | 20.01 |
| Magnesite | 14.7 | 14.46 |
| Chromium | 9.930 | 9.773 |
| Copper ore | 9.522 | 9.372 |
| Manganese | 7.000 | 6.889 |
| Zinc ore | 6.895 | 6.786 |
| Lead ore | 2.764 | 2.721 |
| Nickel ore | 0.802 | 0.789 |
| Tin ore | 0.169 | 0.167 |
| Molybdenum | 0.113 | 0.111 |
| Uranium | 0.039 | 0.035 |
| Tungsten | 0.032 | 0.031 |
| Cobalt ore | 0.028 | 0.027 |
| Vanadium | 0.023 | 0.023 |
| Silver | 0.014 | 0.013 |
| Mercury | 0.003 | 0.003 |
| Gold | 0.002 | 0.002 |

## TOP GOLD PRODUCERS

| COUNTRY | PRODUCTION TONNES | TONS |
|---|---|---|
| South Africa | 495 | 468.8 |
| USA | 329 | 324 |
| Australia | 289 | 284 |
| Canada | 164 | 161 |
| China | 145 | 142 |
| Russia | 130 | 123 |
| Indonesia | 92 | 91 |
| Uzbekistan | 71 | 70 |
| Peru | 65 | 64 |
| Brazil | 64 | 63 |

## DEEPEST DRILLINGS THROUGH HISTORY

| YEAR | DRILLING | LOCATION | DEPTH M | FT |
|---|---|---|---|---|
| 150 BC | Szechuan | China | 610 | 2,000 |
| 1886 | Schladebach | Germany | 1,748 | 5,735 |
| 1928 | Big Lake | Texas, USA | 2,598 | 8,523 |
| 1949 | Sublette County | Wyoming, USA | 6,255 | 20,521 |
| 1958 | Pecos County | Texas, USA | 7,727 | 25,340 |
| 1972 | Beckham County | Oklahoma, USA | 9,159 | 30,050 |

**DID YOU KNOW?** In the 15th century, amethyst was believed to have many unusual powers, including the ability to cure drunkenness!

## CRUDE OIL PRODUCTS

Detergents • Drugs • Dyes
Fertilizers • Oil • Paints
Petrol • Plastic • Tyres

## DEEPEST MINES THROUGH HISTORY

| YEAR | MINE | DEPTH M | FT |
|---|---|---|---|
| 1835 | Kitzbuhel copper mine, Austria | 842 | 2,764 |
| 1875 | St Vojtech mine, Czechoslovakia | 1,000 | 3,280 |
| 1919 | Ooregum goldmine, Kolar, India | 1,652 | 5,419 |
| 1934 | Robinson Deep goldmine, South Africa | 2,560 | 8,400 |
| 1938 | Crown Mines, South Africa | 2,600 | 8,530 |
| 1939 | Champion Reef Mines, South Africa | 2,622 | 8,604 |
| 1953 | East Rand Proprietary Mine, South Africa | 2,831 | 9,288 |
| 1959 | East Rand Proprietary Mine, South Africa | 3,428 | 11,246 |
| 1977 | Western Deep Levels goldmine, South Africa | 3,581 | 11,749 |

**DID YOU KNOW?** It is believed that the world's deepest mine, the Western Deep Levels goldmine, Carletonville, South Africa, will reach 3,841 m (12,600 ft) by the year 2004. Mining engineers need long lift shafts, and the temperature at such depths is 55°C (131°F), which means people cannot work unless the air is refrigerated.

## TOP TIMBER-PRODUCING COUNTRIES

| COUNTRY | ANNUAL PRODUCTION CUBIC M | CUBIC FT |
|---|---|---|
| USA | 495,305,000 | 17,491,533,000 |
| China | 312,957,000 | 11,051,973,000 |
| India | 304,339,000 | 10,747,631,000 |
| Brazil | 220,363,000 | 7,782,047,000 |
| Indonesia | 200,784,500 | 7,090,638,000 |
| Canada | 188,432,000 | 6,654,414,000 |
| Nigeria | 114,311,000 | 4,036,855,000 |
| Russia | 96,250,000 | 3,399,037,000 |
| Sweden | 56,424,000 | 1,992,595,000 |
| Ethiopia | 49,354,700 | 1,742,945,000 |
| Dem. Rep. of Congo | 48,575,000 | 1,715,410,000 |

## TOP OIL PRODUCERS

Despite its huge output, the USA produces less than half the 2,282,192 tonnes (2,246,133 tons) of oil it consumes per day. This is equivalent to more than 3 tonnes (2.95 tons) per person per year, consumed directly through consumption of heating fuel, motor fuel, or indirectly through consumption of electricity produced by processes such as oil-fired power stations.

| COUNTRY | PRODUCTION 1996 | |
|---|---|---|
| | TONNES | TONS |
| Saudi Arabia | 428,800,000 | 422,024,960 |
| USA | 382,900,000 | 376,850,180 |
| Russia | 301,100,000 | 296,342,620 |
| Iran | 183,800,000 | 180,895,960 |
| Mexico | 163,600,000 | 161,015,120 |

## TOP COAL PRODUCERS

| COUNTRY | ANNUAL PRODUCTION | |
|---|---|---|
| | TONNES | TONS |
| China | 1,350,000,000 | 1,328,670,000 |
| USA | 964,200,000 | 948,965,640 |
| India | 308,000,000 | 303,133,600 |
| Russia | 255,000,000 | 250,971,000 |
| Australia | 250,000,000 | 246,050,000 |
| Germany | 235,100,000 | 231,385,420 |
| South Africa | 207,000,000 | 203,729,400 |
| Poland | 199,000,000 | 195,855,800 |
| Czech Republic | 81,500,000 | 80,212,300 |
| Kazakhstan | 76,600,000 | 75,389,720 |

### DID YOU KNOW?

Apple-green chrysoprase, a form of chalcedony, has been used in jewellery since pre-Roman times.

## DIAMOND FACTS

**WEIGH IT UP** The weight of diamonds is measured in carats. The word derives from the carob bean, which is remarkable for its consistent weight of 0.2 g (0.0007 oz). There are approximately 142 carats to the ounce.

**ROUGH DIAMONDS** Fewer than 1,000 rough diamonds weighing more than 100 carats have ever been recorded.

**BIBLICAL GEM** The first recorded reference to diamonds occurs in the Bible: Exodus 28.18 and 39.11 describe how a diamond is mounted on a priest's breastplate.

**CARBON COPY** In 1796, Smithson Tennant (1761–1815), a British scientist, was the first to show that diamonds are composed of carbon. The diamond is the only gem composed of a single element.

## FAMOUS DIAMONDS

**CULLINAN DIAMOND** The Cullinan diamond measured 2.5 cm (5 in) across and weighs 3,106 carats, almost 0.621 kg (1 lb 6 oz), making it the largest diamond ever. It was found at the Premier Mine in South Africa, probably in 1905, although there is some debate about the circumstances of its discovery. The Cullinan has been cut, resulting in 105 separate diamonds, the most important of which are now among the British Crown Jewels. They include the Star of Africa, a pear shape of 530.20 carats, which is mounted in the Queen's Sceptre. This is the largest cut diamond in the world.

**HOPE DIAMOND** The Hope, a 45.52-carat blue diamond, is America's most famous diamond, which was presented to the Smithsonian Institution, Washington D.C., by Harry Winston in 1947. Its fame rests on the legend that it is an "unlucky" jewel and that it has been responsible for some 20 deaths.

**JUBILEE DIAMOND** The 245.35-carat Jubilee is regarded as the world's most perfectly cut diamond. It can be balanced on the culet point (the flat face at the bottom), which is less than 2 mm (0.07 in) in diameter.

# ENERGY

## COUNTRIES MAKING HYDROELECTRICITY

| COUNTRY | PRODUCTION (% OF WORLD TOTAL) |
|---|---|
| Canada | 13.9 |
| USA | 13.2 |
| Brazil | 10.4 |
| China | 7.3 |
| Russia | 6.1 |
| Norway | 4.1 |
| Japan | 3.4 |
| India | 2.8 |
| France | 2.7 |
| Venezuela | 2.1 |

## NUCLEAR REACTORS

Some 442 nuclear power stations are in operation worldwide.

| COUNTRY | REACTORS |
|---|---|
| USA | 110 |
| France | 57 |
| Japan | 53 |
| UK | 35 |
| Russia | 29 |
| Canada | 21 |
| Germany | 20 |
| Ukraine | 16 |
| Sweden | 12 |
| South Korea | 11 |

## POWER CONSUMPTION OF ELECTRICAL ITEMS

**DID YOU KNOW?** One day's hydroelectricity for the world could power a 100W light bulb for 2.7 million years!

| APPLIANCE | WATTS |
|---|---|
| Heater | 3,000 |
| Electric kettle | 2,000 |
| Photocopier | 1,500 |
| Iron | 1,450 |
| Vacuum cleaner | 1,300 |
| Toaster | 850 |
| Microwave oven | 750 |
| Halogen security light | 500 |
| Hair dryer | 500 |
| Food mixer | 460 |
| Power drill | 250 |
| Computer (CPU without monitor) | 175 |
| Stereo | 150 |
| Light bulb | 100 |
| Television | 100 |
| Freezer | 83 |
| Video | 32 |
| Electric razor | 4.5 |

## ENERGY SOURCES TIMELINE

**c.100 BC**  Romans use coal as fuel.

**c.650 BC**  Persians use windmills to harness wind power.

**1712**  Thomas Newcomen manufactures the first steam engine.

**1799**  Alessandro Volta invents the battery from a stack of copper and zinc plates.

**1818**  First geothermal installation, utilizing jets of natural steam, is set up by Frenchman F. de Larderel.

**1881**  First electricity-generating power plant opens at Surrey, UK.

**1891**  First hydroelectric power station is built near Frankfurt, Germany.

**1951**  First nuclear power station opens in Idaho, USA, producing electricity generated by an experimental breeder reactor.

**1954**  Solar batteries are developed for commercial use by American scientists.

**1960**  First solar thermal power plant is built in Turkmenistan.

**1966**  First tidal power station opens in France.

**DID YOU KNOW?** The world produces 9 million tonnes (8,858 million tons) of oil every day.

## NUCLEAR ENERGY TIMELINE

**1905**  German-American physicist Albert Einstein demonstrates that mass can be converted into energy.

**1919**  New Zealand-English physicist Ernest Rutherford splits the nucleus of a nitrogen atom.

**1939**  German chemists Otto Hahn and Fritz Strassman discover nuclear fission.

**1942**  First nuclear reactor is built by Italian-American physicist Enrico Fermi.

**1951**  First nuclear power station to produce electricity starts in the USA.

**1956**  First commercial nuclear power station begins operation in the UK.

**1991**  First controlled nuclear fusion, at JET (Joint European Torus) in the UK.

## WORLD'S TOP ENERGY CONSUMERS

These figures show millions of tonnes (tons) of oil equivalent.

| COUNTRY | OIL | | GAS | | COAL | | NUCLEAR | | HYDROELECTRIC | | TOTAL | |
| --- | --- | --- | --- | --- | --- | --- | --- | --- | --- | --- | --- | --- |
| | TONNES | TONS | TONNES | TONS | TONNES | TONS | TONNES | TONS | TONNES | TONS | TONNES | TONS |
| USA | 833.0 | 819.8 | 569.2 | 560.2 | 516.0 | 508.0 | 183.3 | 180.4 | 28.8 | 28.3 | 2,130.3 | 2,096.6 |
| China | 172.5 | 169.8 | 15.9 | 15.6 | 666.0 | 655.5 | 3.7 | 3.6 | 15.9 | 15.6 | 874.0 | 860.2 |
| Russia | 128.0 | 126.0 | 317.0 | 312.0 | 119.0 | 117.1 | 28.1 | 27.7 | 13.2 | 13.0 | 605.3 | 595.7 |
| Japan | 269.9 | 265.6 | 59.5 | 58.6 | 88.3 | 86.9 | 76.8 | 75.6 | 7.4 | 7.3 | 501.9 | 494.0 |
| Germany | 137.4 | 135.2 | 75.2 | 74.0 | 88.9 | 87.5 | 41.7 | 41.0 | 1.8 | 1.77 | 345.0 | 340.0 |
| India | 78.7 | 77.5 | 19.5 | 19.2 | 140.3 | 138.1 | 2.1 | 2.06 | 6.0 | 5.9 | 246.6 | 242.7 |
| France | 91.0 | 89.6 | 29.0 | 28.5 | 14.7 | 14.5 | 102.8 | 101.2 | 6.0 | 5.9 | 243.5 | 240.0 |
| UK | 83.7 | 82.4 | 76.7 | 75.5 | 44.9 | 44.2 | 24.5 | 24.1 | 0.3 | 0.295 | 230.1 | 226.5 |

## THE WORLD'S ENERGY SOURCES

Industry, transport, and homes need energy to power everything from furnaces to televisions. Much of this energy is produced by burning fossil fuels like oil, but supplies of these are running out, so renewable energy sources, such as solar power, are becoming increasingly important.

| SOURCE | OBTAINED BY | POWER PRODUCED BY | % |
| --- | --- | --- | --- |
| Oil | Mining | Burning | 39.7 |
| Coal, peat, etc | Mining | Burning | 27.2 |
| Natural gas | Mining | Burning | 23.2 |
| Nuclear | Mining | Chemical reaction | 7.0 |
| Hydroelectric | Water | Turbines | 2.5 |
| Geothermal and wind | Hot gases and wind | Turbines | 0.4 |

## SOURCES OF RENEWABLE ENERGY

**WIND** Wind turbines generate electricity at "wind farms", many of which were established during the 1980s. By the middle of the 21st century, scientists hope that wind power could provide over ten per cent of the world's electricity.

**SUN** Solar energy can be converted into electricity in special cells, which are used to power calculators, amongst other things. Heat from the Sun can also be used for heating water in hot countries.

**WATER** Tidal power is made at barriers built across estuaries. As the tide rises or falls, water is kept at a high or low level inside the barrier. When this level differs by about 3 m (10 ft), water flows through huge turbines, creating power which is in turn used to make electricity.

**HYDROELECTRIC** This type of power is generated at dams and waterfalls. Falling water drives turbines, which create electricity. Around seven per cent of the world's energy is provided by hydroelectricity.

**DID YOU KNOW?** The total amount of sunshine that falls on roads in the USA in one year contains twice as much energy as all the coal and oil used around the world in the same amount of time!

## ENERGY RECORDS

**LARGEST SOLAR PLANT** The Harper Lake Site in the Mohave Desert, California, USA, has two 80 megawatt plants.

**LARGEST WIND GENERATOR** The largest generator is the Boeing Mod-5B at Oahu, Hawaii. It has 97.5-m (320-ft) rotors, and produces 3,200 kilowatts (kW) at a wind speed of 51 km/h (32 mph).

**TIDAL POWER** The first and largest tidal power station is the Usine Marmémotrice de la Rance, Brittany, France, opened in 1966. It can produce 544 million kW a year – enough to supply power to 120,000 households.

**LARGEST OIL PRODUCER** Saudi Arabia produces 8,965,000 barrels of oil every day.

**LARGEST ELECTRICITY GENERATOR** The turbo-generator at Lithuania's Ignalina atomic power station has a capacity of 1,450 megawatts.

# ENVIRONMENT

## BIGGEST PAPER CONSUMERS

The amount of paper consumed in total per year compared with the amount consumed per person depends on different factors, such as how industrialized a country is. For example, Germany has a high total annual paper consumption, but consumption per individual member of the population is lower than in other countries. The United Nations has predicted that by the year 2010, the US's total demand will have reached 389 kg (858 lb) for each member of the 291,290,000 population projected for that year.

| COUNTRY | PER PERSON | | TOTAL CONSUMPTION | |
|---|---|---|---|---|
| | KG | LB | TONNES | TONS |
| USA | 308 | 679 | 77,502,000 | 76,277,468 |
| Sweden | 299 | 659 | 2,574,000 | 2,533,331 |
| Denmark | 259 | 571 | 1,337,000 | 1,315,875 |
| Japan | 235 | 518 | 29,091,000 | 28,631,362 |
| Belgium/ Luxembourg | 227 | 500 | 2,345,000 | 2,307,949 |
| Netherlands | 221 | 487 | 3,322,000 | 3,269,514 |
| Finland | 220 | 485 | 1,103,000 | 1,085,572 |
| Switzerland | 215 | 474 | 1,455,000 | 1,432,011 |
| Germany | 208 | 459 | 16,629,000 | 16,366,262 |
| Canada | 207 | 456 | 5,583,000 | 5,494,788 |

**DID YOU KNOW?** The average US citizen "consumes" five times his or her own weight in paper annually!

## ENVIRONMENTAL DISASTERS

**NUCLEAR DISASTER** In 1986, a reactor at Chernobyl, Ukraine, exploded. It killed 31 people, and sent tonnes of radioactive material into the atmosphere. Thousands of people were affected by radioactive contamination.

**CHEMICAL SPILLS** Waste mercury released into Minamata Bay, Japan, in 1952, caused thousands of people to develop paralysis and mental disease.

**OIL SPILLS** In 1989, the Exxon Valdez tanker ran aground in Alaska, and dispersed 35,000 tonnes (34,450 tons) of oil, which covered the shoreline and killed wildlife.

**RUBBISH MOUNTAIN** At Georgswerder, Germany, 150 million cubic metres (196,200,000 cubic yards) of waste form a landfill site 40 m (131 ft) high.

**WATER CONTAMINATION** Waste from industry, farming, and sewage can increase water contamination to dangerous levels. One of the world's most polluted rivers is the Huang He in China: it contains 2.42 g (0.085 oz) of suspended solids per litre.

**GLOBAL WARMING** High levels of carbon dioxide gas ($CO_2$) in the Earth's atmosphere are causing global temperatures to rise, leading to altered climate zones.

## TOP CARBON DIOXIDE EMITTERS

| COUNTRY | EMISSIONS | |
|---|---|---|
| | TONNES | TONS |
| United Arab Emirates | 30.78 | 30.29 |
| USA | 19.42 | 19.11 |
| Singapore | 19.05 | 18.75 |
| Norway | 16.85 | 16.58 |
| Australia | 16.12 | 15.87 |
| Canada | 14.66 | 14.43 |
| Saudi Arabia | 13.92 | 13.70 |
| Kazakhstan | 13.19 | 12.98 |
| Trinidad and Tobago | 13.19 | 12.98 |
| Russia | 12.09 | 11.90 |

Carbon dioxide ($CO_2$) emissions derive mainly from the burning of fossil fuels, such as oil and coal; cement manufacturing; and gas flaring. In the latter half of the 20th century growing industrialization has resulted in large increases in carbon output, which is seriously affecting world climate. Today, most countries actively monitor $CO_2$ output.

## TOP RUBBISH PRODUCERS

| COUNTRY | DOMESTIC WASTE PER HEAD PA | |
|---|---|---|
| | KG | LB |
| USA | 730 | 1,609 |
| Australia | 690 | 1,521 |
| Canada | 660 | 1,455 |
| Finland | 620 | 1,367 |
| Iceland | 560 | 1,235 |
| Norway | 510 | 1,124 |
| Netherlands | 500 | 1,102 |
| Luxembourg | 490 | 1,080 |
| France | 470 | 1,036 |
| Denmark | 460 | 1,014 |

## DOMESTIC RUBBISH

| ITEM | MINIMUM TIME TO DECOMPOSE |
|---|---|
| Apple core | 20 days |
| Plastic | 100 years |
| Glass | 4,000 years |

**DID YOU KNOW?** Each year, the average family throws away 270 glass bottles and jars, and 50 kg (110 lb) of plastic.

## THE MOST COMMON TYPES OF LITTER

Chewing gum • Cigarette ends Matches • Bits of paper • Sweet wrappers • Glass fragments Plastic fragments • Tin foil Chewing gum wrappers • Tickets

## TOP WATER USERS

This list gives the volume of water used per person per year.

| COUNTRY | LITRES | GALLONS |
|---|---|---|
| USA | 730 | 1,609 |
| Australia | 690 | 1,521 |
| Canada | 660 | 1,455 |

## ENVIRONMENTAL CONCERNS

In 1997, MORI, a British market research organization, carried out a survey of almost 2,000 adults, asking them which conservation and environmental issues concerned them most. Pollution is clearly the primary concern, including air pollution, industrial pollution, and especially pollution caused by traffic. When considering the environment, most people think about issues that affect them directly, such as air quality. World issues such as deforestation, global warming, and destruction are not so important to them.

- Air pollution
- Exhaust fumes from cars and lorries
- Too much traffic
- Pollution of rivers, streams and water
- Pollution of seas; waste disposal at sea
- Litter in streets and countryside
- Pollution of beaches and coastline
- Nuclear waste
- Dumping of toxic and chemical waste
- Destruction of the rainforests; deforestation
- Animal testing
- Increase in asthma rates from pollution
- Loss of the greenbelt; overbuilding
- Destruction of the ozone layer
- Preservation of wildlife; protection of the countryside
- Animal welfare
- Lack of water; sufficient water to meet everyone's needs
- Waste disposal
- Crop spraying; use of insecticides

## HOW TO SAVE WATER

**STOP DRIPS** A dripping tap can waste about 90 litres (19.8 gallons) of water a week. It is worth checking and replacing worn washers.

**QUICK SHOWERS** Take a five-minute shower a day instead of a bath – it uses a third of the water.

**USE WHAT YOU NEED** Fill your kettle with just enough water for your needs, but don't fill it up every time you boil it. This will also reduce fuel bills.

**SWITCH OFF** Turn off the tap when brushing your teeth. Leaving it running wastes almost 9 litres (1.98 gallons) a minute.

## WAYS YOU CAN HELP

- Read or watch television programmes about environmental issues.
- Take bottles, glass, paper, or cans for recycling. You can also recycle clothes and books.
- Volunteer your help to environmental charities.
- Use unleaded petrol.
- Select environmentally friendly products, and use recycled paper and card.
- Request information from an environmental organization, or join one.
- Visit or write a letter to an MP or councillor about an environmental issue.
- Walk or cycle to school instead of being driven.
- Switch off lights and other electrical appliances when not in use.
- Turn down the central heating by one degree: this will save ten per cent of the energy used to heat your home.
- When ordinary light bulbs are spent, replace them with energy-efficient, compact fluorescent light bulbs.

## DEFORESTING COUNTRIES

### AREA LOST 1990–1995

This list shows the area of forest lost in key countries between 1990 and 1995. The total global loss of tropical forest during this period was 563,460 sq km (217,552 sq miles), an area equivalent to twice the size of the UK.

| COUNTRY | AREA LOST | |
| --- | --- | --- |
| | KM | MILE |
| Brazil | 25,540 | 9,861 |
| Indonesia | 10,840 | 4,185 |
| Dem. Rep. of the Congo | 7,400 | 2,857 |
| Bolivia | 5,810 | 2,243 |
| Mexico | 5,080 | 1,961 |
| Venezuela | 5,030 | 1,942 |
| Malaysia | 4,000 | 1,544 |
| Burma | 3,870 | 1,494 |
| Sudan | 3,530 | 1,363 |
| Thailand | 3,290 | 1,270 |
| Paraguay | 3,270 | 1,263 |
| Tanzania | 3,230 | 1,247 |
| Zambia | 2,640 | 1,019 |
| Colombia | 2,620 | 1,012 |
| Philippines | 2,620 | 1,012 |
| Angola | 2,370 | 915 |
| Peru | 2,170 | 838 |
| Ecuador | 1,890 | 730 |
| Cambodia | 1,640 | 633 |

### PERCENTAGE LOST

Whilst Brazil tops the list of countries with the highest area of forest loss, because Brazil has so much rainforest its rate of deforestation is only 0.5 per cent. Other countries are losing a much higher proportion of their total forest cover, as the following list shows:

| COUNTRY | PERCENTAGE LOST PER YEAR |
| --- | --- |
| Lebanon | 7.8 |
| Jamaica | 7.2 |
| Afghanistan | 6.8 |
| Comoros | 5.6 |
| Philippines | 3.5 |
| Haiti | 3.4 |
| El Salvador | 3.3 |
| Costa Rica | 3.0 |
| Sierra Leone | 3.0 |
| Pakistan | 2.9 |
| Bahamas | 2.6 |
| Paraguay | 2.6 |
| Thailand | 2.6 |
| Jordan | 2.5 |
| Nicaragua | 2.5 |
| Malaysia | 2.4 |
| Honduras | 2.3 |
| Syria | 2.2 |
| Panama | 2.1 |

## TOP RECYCLABLE PRODUCTS

**WATER** Water can be recycled by watering plants with dirty washing-up water.

**PAPER** Paper forms half of all rubbish! Recycling reduces the need to fell trees, and decreases pollution caused by bleaching wood pulp.

**GLASS** This forms one-tenth of all household rubbish. It can be recycled easily by crushing and melting.

**ALUMINIUM** This is often used to make drinks cans. Recycling reduces energy usage by 95 per cent and pollution by 97 per cent.

**PLASTIC** The wide range of different kinds of plastics available makes recycling hard. Some plastic products are graded at the time of manufacture to make sorting and recycling easier.

# WORLD BELIEFS

## RELIGIONS of the WORLD

### TOP WORLD RELIGIONS

| RELIGION | FOLLOWERS | MAIN AREAS PRACTISED |
|---|---|---|
| Christianity | 1,965,993,000 | Europe, Americas, Australasia |
| Islam | 1,179,326,000 | Asia, Africa |
| Hinduism | 767,424,000 | India |
| Buddhism | 356,875,000 | Asia |
| Native religions | 244,164,000 | Africa, Australasia, Americas, Southeast Asia |
| New religions | 99,191,000 | Asia |
| Sikhism | 22,874,000 | India |
| Judaism | 15,050,000 | North America, Asia |

**DID YOU KNOW?** There are 146,406,000 atheists in the world. Atheists deny the existence of any kind of god.

### NOBLE TRUTHS OF BUDDHISM

Buddhists believe in the Four Noble Truths, or holy principles, which summarize the Buddha's view of the world and humanity.

**DUKKHA** All forms of existence are subject to suffering.

**SAMUDAYA** The craving, or search, for pleasure is the source of suffering.

**NIRVANA** It is possible to be free from these cravings by achieving a state of peace and contentment called nirvana.

**THE EIGHTFOLD PATH** The way to nirvana is through the Eightfold Path of Buddhism.

### THE FIVE PILLARS OF ISLAM

Islamic life is based on a set of rules called the Five Pillars of Islam. Muslims believe that by following these rules, they will reach heaven.

**SHAHADAH** The affirmation of faith in Islam: "There is no god but God, and Muhammad is the messenger of God".

**SALAT** Prayers five times a day, in the direction of the Ka'ba, the sacred shrine at the centre of the mosque at Mecca.

**SAWM** The daily fast between daylight and dusk that is performed throughout the month of Ramadan.

**ZAKAT** Almsgiving, which entails contributing usually one-fortieth of the annual income for the poor and needy.

**THE HAJJ** The pilgrimage to Mecca in the 12th Islamic month, which all healthy Muslims should try to make at least once in their lifetime.

**DID YOU KNOW?**
All able-bodied Muslims are required to defend Islam, whenever it is threatened in the lesser Jihad, or Holy War.

### JEWISH RULES AND RITUALS

**CIRCUMCISION** Baby boys are circumcised eight days after birth.

**SABBATH** The weekly day of rest – from dusk on Friday until after dark on Saturday – commemorates the way God rested after the creation.

**FOOD** Jews only eat food that is *kosher*, or fit to eat. Animals must have been slaughtered according to specific rules.

**ADULTHOOD** At the age of 13, boys become *Bar-Mitzvah* – adult members of Jewish life. There is a similar ceremony for girls, which is known as *Bat Mitzvah*.

**SYNAGOGUE** Jews visit the synagogue to pray on the Sabbath day (Saturday).

### THE FIVE Ks OF SIKHISM

To prove their deep commitment to Sikhism, the Khalsa, or Pure Ones, must wear or carry five items.

**KESH** Hair must remain uncut and in a turban.

**KANGHA** The comb is a symbol of cleanliness.

**KACHH** An undergarment that is practical in battle and a symbol of chastity.

**KIRPAN** The dagger symbolizes resistance of evil.

**KARA** The steel bangle is a symbol of allegiance to God.

## HINDU GODS AND GODDESSES

Hindus have many gods. Most important is the Triad of Vishnu, Shiva, and Brahma, and the unifying spirit of Brahman.

| GOD | ROLE |
|-----|------|
| Agni | God of fire |
| Brahma | The Creator |
| Durga | Warrior goddess |
| Ganesh | Elephant-headed god of luck |
| Indra | God of rain and thunder |
| Kali | Goddess of destruction |
| Lakshmi | Goddess of wealth and fortune |
| Mahadevi | The Great Goddess |
| Shiva | The Destroyer |
| Skanda | God of armies and battles |
| Sarasvati | Goddess of arts and music |
| Vishnu | The Preserver |

## SIKH GURUS

| NAME | DATES |
|------|-------|
| Nanak | 1469–1539 |
| Angad | 1539–1552 |
| Amar Das | 1552–1574 |
| Ram Das Sodhi | 1574–1581 |
| Arjun Mal | 1581–1606 |
| Hargobind | 1606–1644 |
| Har Rai | 1644–1661 |
| Hari Krishen | 1661–1664 |
| Tegh Bahadur | 1664–1675 |
| Gobind Rai | 1675–1708 |

### ! DID YOU KNOW?

Gobind Rai was a child when he became Guru. He introduced the name Singh ("lion") for his followers, and such rules as not cutting the hair.

## OTHER WORLD FAITH FACTS

**BAHA'I FAITH** Based on the worship of one God, the Baha'i faith was founded in Persia (now Iran) in the 19th century by Baha'u'lla (1817–1892).

**CONFUCIANISM** Based on following the *Tao* (The Way), not a god, Confucianism teaches the wisdom of living a balanced life in harmony with nature.

**JAINISM** Based on non-violence and rebirth, Jainism was founded in India in the sixth century BC by Mahavira (c.540–468 BC). Most Jains live in India.

**TAOISM** Taoism, which began in China in about the fourth century, has many popular gods. Taoists live in China and the Far East. It is symbolized by *yin* and *yang*, the balance of existence.

**SHINTOISM** Based on the worship of gods of nature, Shintoism started in Japan in the eighth century BC. Followers worship alone.

**ZOROASTRIANISM** Founded in Persia (now Iran) c.1000 BC, Zoroastrianism is based on the balance of good and evil. Zoroaster was the major prophet. Most followers live in India and Iran.

## KEY RELIGIOUS LEADERS

**JESUS CHRIST – CHRISTIANITY** Jesus, the son of God, was born in Bethelehem, now in modern Israel, in c.4 BC. From the age of 30, he began to preach and heal the sick. A few years later he was tried and executed by the Roman authorities in Jerusalem.

**MUHAMMAD – ISLAM** The Islamic faith is based on belief in one God, Allah. The most important messenger of Allah is Muhammad, the last and greatest of the 26 Islamic prophets, who was born in Mecca in c.AD 570.

**SIDDHARTHA GAUTAMA – BUDDHISM** The Buddhist religion is based on the teachings of Siddhartha Gautama, who was born in India c.563 BC. Brought up as a prince, he left his home, aged 29, giving up his riches, to lead a life of meditation and preaching. He was named Buddha, which means "the enlightened one".

**GURU NANAK – SIKHISM** The Sikh religion was founded by Guru Nanak, who was born in 1469 in the Punjab region of north India and Pakistan. It has now spread to North America and the UK.

**JUDAISM** Abraham was the first leader of the Hebrews. He was born in Ur, in present-day Iraq, in about 2000 BC.

## HINDU BELIEFS

**CASTE SYSTEM** Hinduism divides people up into four groups, or varnas. These broad divisions are also split into smaller castes, or jatis. Traditionally, people would not mix with castes lower than their own, but today there is more social flexibility.

**REINCARNATION** Hindus believe in a cycle of death and rebirth – when we die, our souls live on in another person, animal, or plant. The Hindu goal is to live such a good life that the soul breaks this cycle and becomes part of Brahman.

**HOLY RIVER** Hindus consider the River Ganges in northern India to be sacred. The waters are believed to wash away sin. The ashes of the dead are often scattered there.

**SACRED COW** Hindus respect all animals, especially cows, as sacred beings. Feeding a cow is considered an act of worship.

**FOOD** Most Hindus are vegetarians.

## SACRED MOUNTAINS

**ARARAT, TURKEY** In Christian tradition, it was on the peak of this mountain that Noah's Ark came to rest after the Flood.

**ATHOS, GREECE** The Holy Mountain of the Greek Orthodox religion is occupied by monasteries, forbidden to women, and even to female animals.

**EVEREST, TIBET** Everest is known to Tibetans as Chomolungma, or "Goddess Mother of the World".

**MOUNT OF OLIVES, JERUSALEM** A holy site for Jews and Christians alike; the Garden of Gethsemane, on the Mount of Olives, is where Christ was buried after the crucifixion.

**OLYMPUS, GREECE** The home of Zeus and other important gods of ancient Greece.

**SINAI, ISRAEL** The place where the Christian and Jewish God gave Moses the Ten Commandments.

## RELIGIOUS BOOKS

| RELIGION | BOOK |
|----------|------|
| Christianity | Bible |
| Islam | Koran |
| Buddhism | Pali Canon (three books) |
| Judaism | Torah |
| Hinduism | Vedas (four books) |
| Sikhism | Guru Granth Sahib |

# WORLD FESTIVALS

## CELEBRATIONS AROUND THE WORLD

**CHINESE NEW YEAR**  One of the world's most colourful celebrations, the Chinese New Year festival starts on the first day of the Chinese calendar, usually in February, and lasts for 15 days. The celebrations are based on bringing luck, health, happiness, and wealth throughout the coming year.

**CARNIVAL**  Originally pagan festivals that celebrated the rebirth of nature in spring, carnivals later became seen as the last chance to feast before Lent, the Christian period of abstinence. Thousands of people line city streets around the world to watch processions of performers in elaborate costumes and majestic floats in a flamboyant spectacle.

**MAY DAY**  This ancient fertility festival marked the first day of spring after the long, harsh months of winter. The traditional May Day celebration of dancing round the maypole still takes place in parts of northern Europe, but May Day is better known now as an international public holiday to honour workers. In Russia, trade union parades take place.

**KODOMONO-HI**  This Japanese festival, meaning Children's Day, takes place on 5 May. Families with young boys fly colourful streamers and enormous kites, in the shape of carp fish, above their homes. Carp fish symbolize courage and persistence, and the festival is designed to teach young boys the importance of strength and determination.

**MOON FESTIVAL**  On the 15th day of the eighth lunar month, some Asian countries take part in a mid-autumn festival to celebrate the beauty of the moon, which is brighter and whiter than at any other time of the year. Moon-viewing parties are held and traditional moon cakes eaten. Prayers are addressed to the moon for protection from storms and for a good harvest.

**DAY OF THE DEAD**  During this festival, Mexicans pray to the souls of their dead relatives so that they will return to the land of the living for just one night. They build altars in their homes and in cemeteries, and decorate them with cooked foods, candles, sugar skulls, and colourful flowers to welcome back the dead.

**THANKSGIVING**  This is one of the most important festivals in the USA. It marks the early settlers' first harvest in 1621 when they gave thanks to God that they survived their first harsh winter. Each year, on the fourth Thursday in November, families gather for a Thanksgiving feast of turkey, cranberry sauce, and pumpkin pie.

**HALLOWE'EN**  This ancient Celtic festival takes place on 31 October, when it was once believed that witches and spirits roamed the world. Children in Europe and North America dress up in disguises and, as night falls, go from door to door, asking "trick or treat?". Glowing pumpkins are made to ward off evil spirits.

## CHRISTIAN FESTIVALS

**ADVENT**  The Christian year begins on Advent Sunday – the fourth Sunday before Christmas. Advent means "coming" and the period is one of preparation for Christmas. Advent calendars and candles count off the days until Christmas Day.

**CHRISTMAS**  Held on 25 December, this is a celebration of the birth of Jesus Christ. The many Christmas customs include giving presents and cards, decorating Christmas trees, singing carols, and eating traditional meals with the family.

**EPIPHANY**  Christmas ends with Epiphany, which commemorates the visit of the Three Wise Men to Bethlehem. In Spain and Italy, presents are exchanged.

**LENT**  Beginning on Ash Wednesday, this is a 40-day period of preparation for Easter, recalling the 40 days Jesus spent fasting in the wilderness. It is a period of spiritual discipline and many Christians abstain from certain foods and luxuries.

**EASTER**  This is the major festival in the Christian year. On Good Friday solemn prayers are held to commemorate the death of Jesus on the cross. Easter Sunday falls three days later, and is a celebration of his resurrection. Easter eggs are given out.

**PENTECOST/WHITSUN**  This celebrates the day when God sent his Holy Spirit to the apostles, ten days after the ascension of Jesus. It marks the beginning of the Christian Church.

## HINDU FESTIVALS

| FESTIVAL | MEANING |
| --- | --- |
| Ramanavami | Birthday of Lord Rama |
| Rathayatra | Pilgrimage of the Chariot at Jaggannath |
| Jhulanayatra | Swinging the Lord Krishna |
| Rakshabandhana | Tying on Lucky Threads |
| Janamashtami | Birthday of Lord Krishna |
| Durga-puja | Homage to Goddess Durga |
| Navaratri | Festival of Nine Nights |
| Lakshmi-puja | Homage to Goddess Lakshmi |
| Diwali, Dipavali | New Year festival of Lights |
| Guru Nanak Janati | Birthday of Guru Nanak |
| Sarasvati-puja | Homage to Goddess Sarasvati |
| Maha-sivaratri | Great Night of Lord Shiva |
| Holi | Festival of Fire |
| Dolayatra | Swing Festival |

**DID YOU KNOW?** Every year, millions of Hindus flock to the River Ganges, India. The waters are believed to wash away sin.

## SIKH HOLY DAYS

The Sikh faith was founded by Guru Nanak in 1469 and is based on the worship of one God. There are three main holy days:

**BAISAKHI** New Year and formation of Khalsa.

**DIWALI** Release from prison of Guru Hargobind, the sixth guru.

**GURU NANAK** Birthday of the founder of Sikhism.

## ISLAMIC FESTIVALS

Most Islamic festivals commemorate events in the life of the religion's founder, the Prophet Muhammad:

**NEW YEAR'S DAY** On this day in AD 622, Muhammad set out from Mecca to Medina. Gifts are exchanged.

**BIRTHDAY OF MUHAMMAD** This day is celebrated with processions and lectures on the life of Muhammad.

**NIGHT OF ASCENT** This is a celebration of the night when Muhammad was taken up to heaven.

**RAMADAN** During the month of Ramadan, Muslims do not eat or drink between sunrise and sunset.

**NIGHT OF POWER** To remember the first revelation of the Koran to Muhammad by angel Gabriel, Muslims pray at night.

**FEAST OF BREAKING OF THE FAST** To mark the end of Ramadan, Muslims give food to the poor, and exchange presents.

**FESTIVAL OF SACRIFICE** Taking place after the Mecca pilgrimage, a sheep is sacrificed and shared with the poor.

## BUDDHIST FESTIVALS

| WHEN CELEBRATED | FESTIVAL |
| --- | --- |
| Sakyamuni (or Wesak) | Birth of Siddhartha Gautama |
| Bodhi Day | Buddha's enlightenment |
| Parinirvana | Buddha's ascent from Earth |
| Phagguna | Origin of life cycle |

**DID YOU KNOW?** In the Esala Perahera festival in Sri Lanka, Buddha's tooth is paraded in a casket on an elephant's back.

## JEWISH FESTIVALS

**ROSH HASHANAH (NEW YEAR)** This is a time of quiet reflection and soul-searching. A ram's horn trumpet, or shofar, is blown as a call to make sinners repent.

**YOM KIPPUR (DAY OF ATONEMENT)** The most solemn event in the Jewish calendar. Jews spend the day praying, fasting, and seeking God's forgiveness.

**SUKKOTH (FEAST OF TABERNACLES)** A seven-day harvest festival during which families eat meals outside under booths called sukkahs. They commemorate the way God looked after the Israelites in the wilderness on their way to the Promised Land.

**SIMCHAT TORAH (REJOICING OF THE LAW)** During this celebration the scrolls of the Law (or Torah) are paraded around the synagogue, followed by children singing and dancing.

**HANUKKAH (FESTIVAL OF LIGHTS)** An eight-day long midwinter festival that is marked by the lighting of eight candles. Each is lit from the central candle on a candlestick called a hannukkiah. This symbolizes a drop of oil that was used to light the reclaimed Temple of Jerusalem in 164 BC. Children receive presents, and games are played.

**PURIM (FEAST OF LOTS)** A thanksgiving celebrating Esther's victory over Haman, which prevented a Jewish massacre. During this festival parties are held in which masks and elaborate costumes are sometimes worn.

**PESACH (PASSOVER)** This week-long spring festival celebrates the Exodus of the Jews from Egypt, when the angel of death "passed over" the Israelites, sparing their lives. In place of ordinary bread, unleavened bread (matzah) is eaten.

**HOLOCAUST REMEMBRANCE DAY** This day commemorates the mass murder of an estimated six million European Jews by the German Nazi regime during World War II.

**ISRAEL INDEPENDENCE DAY** This is a modern celebration, commemorating the creation of the political state of Israel as a homeland for the world's Jews in 1948.

**SHAVUOTH (FEAST OF WEEKS)** This festival celebrates God giving the Ten Commandments to Moses on Mount Sinai, and the offering of the first fruits. Synagogues are decorated with flowers and dairy foods are eaten.

**DID YOU KNOW?** The symbol of Islam is a star and a crescent moon.

**DID YOU KNOW?** The symbol of Judaism is the Star of David.

# THE CHRISTIAN WORLD

## EARLY CHRISTIAN TIMELINE

**c.6–4 BC** Jesus of Nazareth is born in Bethlehem.

**c.27** John the Baptist baptizes Jesus, who begins three years of preaching and healing the sick.

**c.AD 30** Jesus is crucified on a cross. Three days later he is raised from the dead (the Resurrection).

**c.37** Saul of Tarsus is converted from Judaism to Christianity. He is now known as Paul.

**c.41–65** Paul goes on journeys, spreading Christianity in the eastern Mediterranean, until he reaches Rome.

**c.67** Paul is imprisoned and executed in Rome on the orders of Emperor Nero.

**c.40–100** Despite persecution by the Romans, Christianity gradually spreads throughout the Roman Empire.

**c.380** Christianity becomes the official Roman religion.

## MAIN CHRISTIAN BELIEFS

**GOD** For Christians, God is the creator of the universe and life.

**JESUS CHRIST** Christians believe Jesus is the only Son of God, who has existed with God the Father from before time began.

**JESUS'S BIRTH** Jesus was incarnated, or given human form when, by the power of the Holy Spirit, his human mother, the Virgin Mary, gave birth to him.

**WHY JESUS WAS SENT** Christ appeared to reconcile people with God, as human sin had broken the relationship with God.

**CRUCIFIXION** Through the death of Jesus upon the Cross at Calvary, God broke the power of sin and evil.

**RESURRECTION** When Jesus rose from the dead on the third day, God showed the triumph of life over death and gave the promise of everlasting life to people who believe in Jesus.

**THE HOLY TRINITY** Christians believe that God is one but has three co-equal "persons": God, the Father, God the Son (Jesus Christ), and God the Holy Spirit.

## PATRON SAINTS

Christian saints are devout people who have lived – and often died – for the Christian cause. They often oversee a particular profession or circumstance.

| PROFESSION/CIRCUMSTANCE | SAINT |
|---|---|
| Authors and journalists | Francis de Sales |
| Aviators | Joseph of Cupertino |
| Business people | Homobonus |
| Cab drivers | Fiacre |
| Children | Nicholas |
| Communications | Gabriel the Archangel |
| Desperate situations | Jude (and Rita of Cascia) |
| Possessed by devil | Gemma Galgani |
| Disabled | Giles |
| Doctors | Luke (and Cosmas and Damian) |
| Firemen | Florian |
| Homes and families | Joseph |
| Lost articles | Antony of Padua |
| Nature and animals | Francis of Assisi |
| Office workers | Catherine of Siena |
| Race relations | Martin de Porres |
| Schools and universities | Thomas Aquinas |
| Sweethearts | Valentine |

## SYMBOLIC NUMBERS

| NUMBER | MEANING |
|---|---|
| 1 | The one God |
| 3 | The Holy Trinity |
| 7 | God created the world in 7 days; 7 deadly sins |
| 10 | 10 Commandments 10 Plagues of Egypt |
| 12 | 12 days of Christmas 12 disciples 12 tribes of Israel |
| 13 | There were 13 at Jesus's fateful Last Supper |
| 40 | Moses' 40 days in the desert; the Flood lasted 40 days and 40 nights |

## LONGEST-SERVING POPES

The head of the Roman Catholic Church is the Pope, who traditionally lives in the Vatican in Rome. Popes are usually chosen from the ranks of cardinals, who are customarily men of advanced years. As a result, it is unusual for a pope to remain in office for more than 20 years.

| POPE | TIME IN OFFICE | YEARS |
|---|---|---|
| Pius IX | 1846–1878 | 31 |
| Leo XIII | 1878–1903 | 25 |

**AMAZING FACT!** Leo XIII died aged 93, making him the oldest pope in this list.

| POPE | TIME IN OFFICE | YEARS |
|---|---|---|
| Peter | c. 42–67 | c. 25 |
| Pius VI | 1775–1799 | 24 |
| Adrian I | 772–795 | 23 |
| Pius VII | 1800–1823 | 23 |
| Alexander III | 1159–1181 | 21 |
| Sylvester | 314–335 | 21 |
| Leo I | 440–461 | 21 |

**DID YOU KNOW?** The shortest-serving pope was Urban VII (d.1590), who held office for just 12 days before he died of malaria.

## CHRISTIAN POPULATIONS

Christianity is the world's most widespread religion, with 1.6 billion Christians worldwide.

| COUNTRY | POPULATION |
|---|---|
| USA | 224,457,000 |
| Brazil | 139,000,000 |
| Mexico | 86,210,000 |
| Germany | 67,170,000 |
| Philippines | 63,470,000 |
| UK | 51,060,000 |
| Italy | 47,690,000 |

## SEVEN DEADLY SINS

Pride • Rage • Envy • Lust
Greed • Meanness • Laziness

## RELIGIOUS OBJECTS

**ICON** Painting of Christ or Mary.

**CRUCIFIX** Statuette of Christ crucified on the cross.

**ROSARY BEADS** A prayer is recited for each bead.

## CHRISTIAN DENOMINATIONS

The Christian church is split into many denominations but all are united in their belief in the life and teachings of Christ.

| DENOMINATION | ADHERENTS |
|---|---|
| Roman Catholic | 872,104,646 |
| Slavonic Orthodox | 92,523,987 |
| United (including Lutheran/Reformed) | 65,402,685 |
| Pentecostal | 58,999,862 |
| Anglican | 52,499,051 |
| Baptist | 50,321,923 |
| Lutheran (excluding United) | 44,899,837 |
| Reformed (Presbyterian) | 43,445,520 |
| Methodist | 31,718,508 |
| Disciples (Restorationists) | 8,783,192 |

**DID YOU KNOW?** At the Last Supper, Jesus broke bread and poured wine, which he blessed and shared with his disciples, saying that the bread was his body and the wine was his blood. At Eucharist, or mass, Christians partake ritually of the body and blood of Christ.

## MODERN SAINTS AND MARTYRS

**MOTHER TERESA (1910–1997)** Born Agnes Gonxha Bojaxhiu, in Albania, Mother Teresa of Calcutta devoted her whole life to tending poor and dying children in India. She was awarded the Nobel Peace Prize in 1979, and is regarded by some to be a modern-day saint.

**OSCAR ROMERO (1917–1980)** Romero cared for the poor in El Salvador, where he alienated those who exploited them, and was murdered.

**DIETRICH BONHOEFFER (1906–1945)** A Lutheran theologian who opposed Hitler, Bonhoeffer sought to resolve the conflicts of World War II without bloodshed. He was executed for his stand in 1945.

**MARTIN LUTHER KING JR (1929–1968)** Champion of civil rights in the USA, King was assassinated for a commitment born of his Christian faith.

**JOSEPHINE BUTLER (1828–1907)** Butler fought against exploitation of women and is remembered by the Church of England on 30 December.

## THE SEVEN SACRAMENTS

The most important Christian ceremonies are the sacred rites known as sacraments. The Roman Catholic and Orthodox Churches recognize seven sacraments.

**BAPTISM** The rite of entry into the Church; believers are cleansed in water.

**CONFIRMATION** After baptism, believers reaffirm their allegiance to the Church.

**EUCHARIST, OR MASS** Believers receive the bread and wine of the body of Christ.

**PENANCE** Believers turn to God to confess their sins.

**EXTREME UNCTION** Prayers, anointing with oil, or touch, help prepare the sick for death.

**ORDINATION** The ceremony in which the Church appoints people as priests and deacons.

**MARRIAGE** To Christians, marriage symbolizes the relationship of Christ with his Church.

## SOME OF THE BIGGEST RELIGIOUS ORDERS

Monks, nuns, and friars are people who choose to live apart from the world as members of religious orders, some almost as ancient as Christianity.

**JESUITS** Founded in 1540 by St Ignatius Loyola, the Jesuits are the biggest religious order. Today, there are about 33,000 Jesuit monks worldwide.

**BENEDICTINES** Founded in 1530 by St Benedict, Benedictine monks pass their time in prayer, reading, and manual work. Today there are about 9,000 Benedictine monks and more than 24,000 nuns.

**CARMELITES** Founded in 1451 and re-formed in 1562, the Carmelite nuns are a poor order. There are more than 24,000 Carmelite nuns today.

**FRANCISCANS** Founded in 1209 by St Francis of Assisi, Franciscan friars live very frugally. There are still about 20,000 Franciscans worldwide.

# THE BIBLE

## SEVEN DAYS OF CREATION

1   On the first day, God created night and day, separating light from dark.

2   On the second day, God created the sky, which he called Heaven.

3   On the third day, God created land, dividing the waters into seas.

4   On the fourth day, God created the Sun, the Moon, and the stars.

5   On the fifth day, God created living creatures on the land and in the sea.

6   On the sixth day, God created a man and a woman.

7   On the seventh day, creation of the world was complete and God rested.

## TEN PLAGUES OF EGYPT

In Exodus 7–13, Moses asks the pharaoh of Egypt to release the Israelites from slavery. When the king refuses, God strikes the country with a series of ten horrible disasters, which are known as the Ten Plagues of Egypt.

1   The River Nile turns to blood.

2   Frogs cover the land of Egypt.

3   Lice crawl over all men and women.

4   Swarms of flies attack people.

5   Disease strikes all livestock.

6   Boils inflict people and animals.

7   Hail and thunder damage crops.

8   The ground is covered by locusts.

9   Darkness lasts for three days.

10  All the first-born are slain.

## THE TEN COMMANDMENTS

The set of rules or Commandments that God gave to Moses (Exodus 20) showed people how to live together in harmony.

1   You shall have no other gods before me.

2   You shall not make for yourself an idol.

3   You shall not misuse the name of the Lord your God.

4   Remember the Sabbath day by keeping it holy.

5   Honour your father and your mother.

6   You shall not murder.

7   You shall not commit adultery.

8   You shall not steal.

9   You shall not give false testimony against your neighbour.

10  You shall not covet… anything that belongs to your neighbour.

## BIBLICAL SAYINGS

Some of our most familiar sayings and words come from the Bible. Here are a few you are sure to recognize, with their Bible references so you can look them up.

**A MAN AFTER HIS OWN HEART**
1 Samuel 13.14

**ALL THINGS TO ALL MEN**
1 Corinthians 9.22

**APPLE OF YOUR EYE**  Psalms 17.8

**BY THE SKIN OF YOUR TEETH**  Job 19.20

**CRUMBS FROM THE RICH MAN'S TABLE**  Luke 16.21

**PRIDE BEFORE A FALL**  Proverbs 16

**SCAPEGOAT**  Leviticus 16

**SEE EYE TO EYE**  Isaiah 52.8

**SEPARATING THE SHEEP FROM THE GOATS**  Matthew 25.32

**THE FOUR CORNERS OF THE EARTH**
Isaiah 11.12; Revelation 7.1

**THE LEFT HAND DOESN'T KNOW WHAT THE RIGHT IS DOING**  Matthew 6.3

**WOLF IN SHEEP'S CLOTHING**
Matthew 7.15

**WHEELS WITHIN WHEELS**
Ezekiel 1.16, 10.10

## ANIMALS MOST MENTIONED

| ANIMAL | TESTAMENT | | TOTAL |
| | OLD | NEW | |
| --- | --- | --- | --- |
| Sheep | 155 | 45 | 200 |
| Lamb | 153 | 35 | 188 |
| Lion | 167 | 9 | 176 |
| Ox | 156 | 10 | 166 |
| Ram | 165 | 0 | 165 |
| Horse | 137 | 27 | 164 |
| Bullock | 152 | 0 | 152 |
| Ass | 142 | 8 | 150 |
| Goat | 131 | 7 | 138 |
| Camel | 56 | 6 | 62 |
| Serpent | 38 | 15 | 53 |
| Kid | 50 | 1 | 51 |
| Calf | 41 | 7 | 48 |
| Dog | 31 | 9 | 40 |
| Dove | 30 | 10 | 40 |
| Eagle | 30 | 4 | 34 |
| Locust | 24 | 4 | 28 |
| Heifer | 19 | 1 | 20 |
| Owl | 16 | 0 | 16 |

**AMAZING FACT!**  There is no mention of cats or rats in the Bible!

## OLD TESTAMENT LEADERS

| LEADER (FOUND IN) | FAMOUS FOR |
| --- | --- |
| Abraham (Genesis 11–12) | First patriarch of the the Israelite nation |
| Joseph (Genesis 41–46) | Protected Egypt from famine |
| Moses (Exodus 12–14) | Led the Israelites out of slavery |
| David (1 Samuel 17) | Defeated Goliath the giant Philistine |
| Solomon (1 Kings 5–8) | Built a temple for worshipping God |

## GIFTS FROM THE MAGI

| WISE MAN | GIFT |
| --- | --- |
| Melchior | Gold |
| Balthazar | Myrrh |
| Gaspar or Caspar | Frankincense |

**AMAZING FACT?**  In Matthew 2, the Bible says that Magi, or Wise Men, came from the east to Jerusalem, bearing gifts for the infant Jesus. However, contrary to belief, nowhere does it say how many Wise Men there were, nor does it mention their names.

## PARABLES TOLD BY JESUS

A parable is a short story with a hidden message.

**THE GOOD SAMARITAN** (Luke 10) A Jewish man who has been attacked by thieves lay by the wayside. Two passing Jewish holy men ignored him, but a Samaritan helped him, even though Samaritans and Jews were sworn enemies.

**THE SOWER** (Mark 4) When a farmer sowed his seed, some was eaten by birds, and some fell on stones and was wasted. Only the seed that fell on good soil produced a thriving crop. Jesus is like the sower, but sows words rather than seeds.

**THE GOOD SHEPHERD** (Matthew 18) A shepherd had a flock of 100 sheep. When one strayed, he left his flock to find it.

**THE PRODIGAL SON** (Luke 15) The younger of two sons left home and wasted all his money. Poor, hungry, and repentant, the son returned home, and was welcomed by his father who instantly forgave him and welcomed him back with open arms.

## JESUS'S MIRACLES

| MIRACLE | FOUND IN |
| --- | --- |
| Feeding the crowd with five loaves and two fish | Matthew 14 |
| Walking on the waters of the lake | Matthew 14 |
| Raising a child from the dead | Mark 5 |
| Giving sight to a blind beggar | Luke 18 |
| Turning water into wine | John 2 |
| Calming the storm | Mark 4–5 |

**DID YOU KNOW?** The first book ever printed was a Latin version of the Bible in 1455. It was the work of the German inventor of moveable type, Johannes Gutenberg. Before then all Bibles were hand-written by monks.

## THE BOOKS OF THE BIBLE

### OLD TESTAMENT

Genesis • Exodus • Leviticus
Numbers • Deuteronomy
Joshua • Judges • Ruth
1 Samuel • 2 Samuel
1 Kings • 2 Kings
1 Chronicles • 2 Chronicles
Ezra • Nehemiah • Esther
Job • Psalms • Proverbs
Ecclesiastes • Song of
Solomon • Isaiah • Jeremiah
Lamentations • Ezekiel
Daniel • Hosea • Joel
Amos • Obadiah • Jonah
Micah • Nahum • Habakkuk
Zephaniah • Haggai
Zechariah • Malachi

### NEW TESTAMENT

Matthew • Mark • Luke
John • Acts of the Apostles
Romans • 1 Corinthians
2 Corinthians • Galatians
Ephesians • Philippians
Colossians • 1 Thessalonians
2 Thessalonians • 1 Timothy
2 Timothy • Titus • Philemon
Hebrews • James • 1 Peter
2 Peter • 1 John • 2 John
3 John • Jude • Revelation

**DID YOU KNOW?** In the 15th century, when many people were not able to read, Bible stories, such as Noah's Ark (Genesis 6–7) were often depicted in stained glass windows or in frescos on church walls for everyone to see and enjoy.

## TWELVE DISCIPLES OF JESUS

The disciples were the original followers of Jesus, who were chosen to teach people about Christianity. They were later joined by Paul and Matthias and, after the death of Jesus, became known as apostles or messengers of Christ.

**ANDREW**, a fisherman from Galilee, he is said to have died on an x-shaped cross.

**BARTHOLOMEW**, or Nathanael, is thought to have become a missionary in Armenia and India.

**JAMES THE GREATER** was the brother of John and became one of Jesus's closest friends.

**JAMES THE LESSER** was the son of Alphaeus and probably shorter than the other disciple, James.

**JOHN**, known as John the Apostle, wrote one of the gospels in the New Testament.

**JUDAS ISCARIOT** betrayed Jesus to the Romans in return for 30 pieces of silver.

**JUDAS, SON OF JAMES**, was also known by the name of Thaddaeus.

**MATTHEW**, or Levi, was a tax collector before becoming a disciple of Jesus.

**SIMON PETER** was described by Jesus as "the rock" because of his solid faith.

**PHILIP** housed the Christian leader Paul on his visit to Caesarea in Judea.

**SIMON THE ZEALOT** is thought to have been a member of the fanatical Zealots.

**THOMAS**, or Doubting Thomas, refused to believe that Jesus had risen again.

# MYTHS and LEGENDS

## GREEK AND ROMAN GODS AND GODDESSES

| GREEK | ROLE | ROMAN |
|---|---|---|
| Aphrodite | Goddess of love | Venus |
| Apollo | God of the arts and medicine | Apollo |
| Ares | God of war | Mars |
| Artemis | Goddess of hunting | Diana |
| Athene | Goddess of wisdom | Minerva |
| Demeter | Goddess of crops and soil fertility | Ceres |
| Dionysus | God of wine and revelry | Bacchus |
| Hephaestos | God of fire and craftsmanship | Vulcan |
| Hera | Goddess of marriage and childbirth | Juno |
| Hermes | God of travel, roads, trade | Mercury |
| Hestia | Goddess of the hearth and home | Vesta |
| Poseidon | God of the sea | Neptune |
| Zeus | Ruler of the gods | Jupiter |

## THE NINE MUSES

The Muses were daughters of the god Zeus and the Titan Mnemosyne. Originally they were deities associated with mountains and springs, but later they became goddesses of the arts and followers of the god Apollo.

| MUSE | ART |
|---|---|
| Calliope | Poetry and eloquence |
| Clio | History |
| Erato | Love poetry |
| Euterpe | Poetry and flute-playing |
| Melpomene | Tragedy |
| Polyhymnia | Song and mime |
| Terpsichore | Dancing |
| Thalia | Poetry and comedy |
| Urania | Astronomy |

## LITTLE PEOPLE

**ELVES, SPRITES, AND FAIRIES** Often from mountainous areas, these mischievous folk cast spells and play tricks on humans, such as losing things and causing fights.

**DWARFS** Created from the maggots in the flesh of the first giant Ymir, dwarfs were wise. They lived underground and were skilled craftspeople.

**LEPRECHAUN** Irish sprites, often depicted as little old men who will reveal the position of a crock of gold to anyone who can catch them.

## MYTHICAL PLACES

**ASGARD** The fortified home of the Norse gods.

**ATLANTIS** An island, first mentioned by Greek philosopher Plato (427–347 BC), said to have sunk beneath the Atlantic Ocean.

**AVALON** The island where King Arthur is said to have gone at the end of his life.

**EL DORADO** An imaginary land of gold and riches that encouraged the Spanish to conquer South America.

**NIFLHEIM** The Norse realm of the dead.

**SHANGRI-LA** A paradise on earth, after the fictional Tibetan land of eternal youth in the novel *The Lost Horizon* (1933) by James Hilton.

**UTOPIA** A place of perfection as described in Sir Thomas More's *Utopia* (1516).

**VALHALLA** The home, in Asgard, of Norse warriors slain in battle.

## HERAKLES' TWELVE LABOURS

The king of Tiryns set Greek hero Herakles twelve tasks, as penance for killing his own wife and children. Only when he succeeded in all of them would he be granted immortality.

1 Slay the Nemean lion

2 Kill the Lernean Hydra

3 Catch the Arcadian stag

4 Destroy the Erymanthian boar

5 Cleanse the Augean stables

6 Destroy the man-eating birds that lived by Lake Stymphalos

7 Capture the Cretan bull

8 Catch the horses of the Thracian Diomedes

9 Gain the beautiful girdle of Hippolyta, Queen of the Amazons

10 Capture the cattle that belonged to the three-bodied monster Geryon

11 Take the apples of the Hesperides

12 Capture Cerberus from Hades

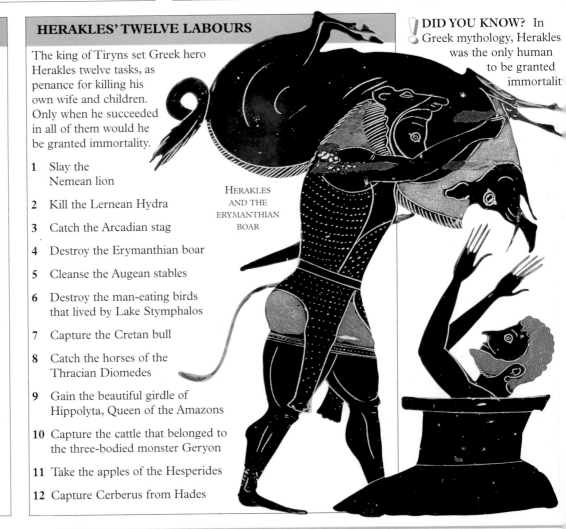

HERAKLES AND THE ERYMANTHIAN BOAR

**DID YOU KNOW?** In Greek mythology, Herakles was the only human to be granted immortalit

## EGYPTIAN GODS AND GODDESSES

| | |
|---|---|
| Anubis | Jackal-headed god of embalming |
| Bastet | Cat goddess |
| Geb | God of the sky |
| Hapy | God of Nile floods |
| Hathor | Cow goddess, guardian of women |
| Horus | Falcon-headed sky god |
| Isis | Divine mother, wife of Osiris |
| Khnum | Ram-headed creator |
| Neith | Mother goddess |
| Nut | Goddess of the sky |
| Osiris | God of underworld |
| Ptah | Creator god |
| Ra-Atum | Sun god |
| Sekhmet | Lion-headed goddess |
| Seth | God of storms |
| Shu | God of air |
| Tefnut | God of moisture |
| Thoth | Ibis-headed god |

## NORSE GODS AND GODDESSES

| | |
|---|---|
| Balder | God of light |
| Bragi | God of poetry |
| Forseti | God of justice, son of Balder |
| Freyr | God of fertility |
| Freyja | Goddess of fertility |
| Frigg | Goddess of fertility |
| Hoder | Blind god |
| Hoenir | Silent god |
| Idun | Spring goddess |
| Loki | Trickster – part god and part giant |
| Njörd | God of the sea |
| Odin | Chief god |
| Skädi | Goddess of mountains |
| Thor | War god, Odin's son |
| Tyr | Sky god, son of Odin and Frigg |
| Vali | Odin's youngest son |

**❗ DID YOU KNOW?**
According to Norse myth the world would end at the battle of Ragnarök.

## MAYA AND AZTEC GODS

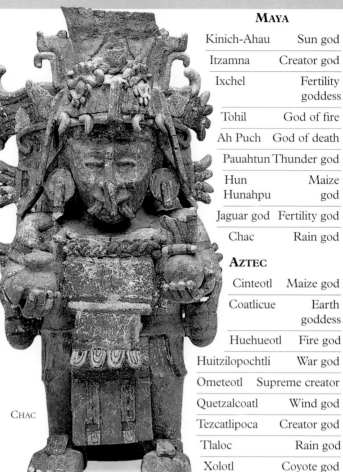

CHAC

### MAYA

| | |
|---|---|
| Kinich-Ahau | Sun god |
| Itzamna | Creator god |
| Ixchel | Fertility goddess |
| Tohil | God of fire |
| Ah Puch | God of death |
| Pauahtun | Thunder god |
| Hun Hunahpu | Maize god |
| Jaguar god | Fertility god |
| Chac | Rain god |

### AZTEC

| | |
|---|---|
| Cinteotl | Maize god |
| Coatlicue | Earth goddess |
| Huehueotl | Fire god |
| Huitzilopochtli | War god |
| Ometeotl | Supreme creator |
| Quetzalcoatl | Wind god |
| Tezcatlipoca | Creator god |
| Tlaloc | Rain god |
| Xolotl | Coyote god |

## MYTHICAL MONSTERS

**CENTAURS** In Greek mythology, a creature with the lower body of a horse and the torso and head of a man.

**VAMPIRE** In Eastern European legend, a dark, undead creature, who wakes at dusk and feeds on human blood.

**DRAGON** A usually evil, fire-breathing, reptilian beast that often appears in European myths. Chinese dragons, however, are benevolent.

**GORGONS** Three monster sisters with wings, claws, and snakes for hair. One, Medusa, was killed by the hero Perseus.

**SPHINX** A mythical creature of ancient Greece and Egypt that had the body of a lion, a woman's head, and bird's wings.

**HARPIES** In Greek mythology the Harpies were birds with women's heads and sharp talons that preyed on people's souls.

MEDUSA

**MINOTAUR** A human-eating monster, part human, part bull, that lived on the Greek island of Crete.

## MYTHICAL GIANTS

**ANTAEUS** A giant in Greek mythology, slain by Herakles. He was said to be 60 cubits – about 27.4 m (90 ft) – tall.

**ATLAS** In Greek mythology, the giant who supports the heavens. Mercator's book of maps (1595) shows him holding the world on his shoulders. Today, a collection of maps is known as an atlas.

**CYCLOPES** A race of giants, each with a single eye. According to Greek myth, they worked in the forge of the god Vulcan.

**ENCELADUS** In Greek legend, the most powerful of the hundred-armed giant sons of Uranus. Legend has it that the flames of the volcano Mount Etna are the breath of Enceladus.

**GARGANTUA** A giant in medieval legend. The word gargantuan, meaning huge, comes from his name.

**GOLIATH** The giant slain by David in the Bible. He was said to be 6 cubits and a span tall, or 2.8 m (9 ft 3 in).

**ORION** In Greek myth, a giant hunter, himself slain by Diana the huntress. The star constellation of Orion is named after him.

**TITANS** In Greek mythology, the race of giants who ruled the universe before Kronos, their leader, was overthrown by Zeus.

**YMIR** In Norse mythology, the first giant from whose body Odin and his brothers create the Universe.

# PREDICTIONS and the UNEXPLAINED

! **DID YOU KNOW?**
The word "zodiac" is from a Greek word meaning "circle of life".

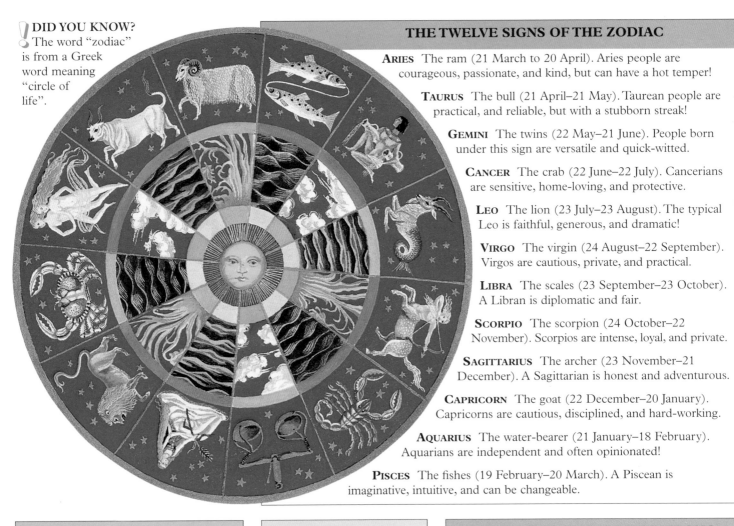

## THE TWELVE SIGNS OF THE ZODIAC

**ARIES** The ram (21 March to 20 April). Aries people are courageous, passionate, and kind, but can have a hot temper!

**TAURUS** The bull (21 April–21 May). Taurean people are practical, and reliable, but with a stubborn streak!

**GEMINI** The twins (22 May–21 June). People born under this sign are versatile and quick-witted.

**CANCER** The crab (22 June–22 July). Cancerians are sensitive, home-loving, and protective.

**LEO** The lion (23 July–23 August). The typical Leo is faithful, generous, and dramatic!

**VIRGO** The virgin (24 August–22 September). Virgos are cautious, private, and practical.

**LIBRA** The scales (23 September–23 October). A Libran is diplomatic and fair.

**SCORPIO** The scorpion (24 October–22 November). Scorpios are intense, loyal, and private.

**SAGITTARIUS** The archer (23 November–21 December). A Sagittarian is honest and adventurous.

**CAPRICORN** The goat (22 December–20 January). Capricorns are cautious, disciplined, and hard-working.

**AQUARIUS** The water-bearer (21 January–18 February). Aquarians are independent and often opinionated!

**PISCES** The fishes (19 February–20 March). A Piscean is imaginative, intuitive, and can be changeable.

## DREAM MEANINGS

**FLYING** Many people dream that they are flying. This can often mean that the dreamer, in waking life, desires freedom and wishes to cast off the problems and ties of the world below.

**SWIMMING** Water symbolizes the emotions, and these dreams could be an indication of your emotional well-being. Are you swimming confidently, or struggling, perhaps even drowning?

**FORGETTING YOUR LINES** Performing in a play and forgetting your lines is a classic anxiety dream that often indicates a lack of self-confidence or problems with communication.

**TREES AND FLOWERS** A tree might represent natural growth, strength, and stability. Dreams about flowers suggest a natural, healthy life, and sexuality.

## GHOST STORIES

**VANISHING HITCHHIKER** A young girl is given a lift, but mysteriously vanishes during the journey. The baffled driver finds out that the girl died years before at the very spot where he picked her up. Different versions of this story exist all over the world.

**ROMAN LEGION** In 1953, an Englishman called Harry Martindale saw a ghostly legion of Roman soldiers marching through the cellar of the Treasurer's House in York, England. Their legs appeared to be chopped off at the knee, which may be because the old Roman road was below the cellar floor.

## PREDICTIONS THAT WERE WRONG

"This telephone has too many shortcomings to be seriously considered as a means of communication." *Western Union internal memo, 1876*

"I think there is a world market for maybe five computers." *Thomas Watson, chairman of IBM, 1943*

"Rail travel at high speed is not possible, because passengers…would die of asphyxia [suffocation]." *Dr Dionysius Lardner, Irish scientist, 1793–1859*

## UNEXPLAINED MONSTERS

**LOCH NESS MONSTER** "Nessie", a huge dinosaur-like sea monster, is reputed to live in Loch Ness, UK.

**YETI** Also known as the Abominable Snowman, the Yeti is a hairy man-beast that is alleged to roam the Himalayas. Giant footprints are cited as proof.

**BIG FOOT** Sometimes called Sasquatch, this hairy, humanlike creature allegedly dwells in North America.

## HOW TO PROTECT YOURSELF AGAINST A VAMPIRE

The legend of the vampire has terrified people across the world for centuries. Lurking in the shadows, waiting for nightfall and their next meal of human blood, they are reputed to possess superhuman strength, and can transform themselves into animals such as bats and wolves. Here are some ways to make sure you never get attacked by one!

**RINGING BELLS**  These are supposed to drive away the undead.

**BLACK DOGS**  Gypsies believe black dogs are the enemies of vampires – but, unfortunately, some experts believe they may act as vampires' assistants.

**FISHNETS AND KNOTS**  Draping fishnets and knotted string around doorways or on graves distracts vampires, because they allegedly feel compelled to untangle them.

**GARLIC**  The classic vampire deterrent is a bulb of garlic worn around the neck or rubbed around doors and windows. Today, eating garlic bread and chicken Kiev may be just as effective.

**HOLY ARTICLES**  Items such as crosses, icons, holy water, and incense usually scare vampires away and may even stop them returning to their graves. Holy water can be thrown at them or sprinkled on their graves. Crosses painted with tar are said to be particularly effective – especially if the vampire gets stuck to them.

**HOLLY OR JUNIPER**  Keeping branches of certain trees in the house will deter vampires; if you leave them on the floor they may even trip over them in the dark.

**MIRRORS**  Vampires are driven mad by mirrors hung on doors because they can't see their own reflections – which must make brushing their hair very difficult.

**STEALING THEIR LEFT SOCK**  Effective only for certain species of vampire – and only if you dare get that close.

**STAKES, KNIVES, AND PINS**  Plunging these weapons into the heart of a sleeping vampire is one way of disposing of him or her – but it must be done in a single blow and is extremely messy…

**SUNLIGHT**  In many horror films, vampires dissolve into dust as soon as a sunbeam hits them. However, in the novel *Dracula*, Count Dracula manages to go out in daylight without any ill effects, so don't rely on this method.

**WATER**  Vampires hate water, so if you have the chance, try to push your vampire into the bath!

## MYSTERIOUS PLACES

**PYRAMIDS**  Recent discoveries have deepened the mystery of the Pyramids of Giza in Egypt. Some people now believe the pyramids were deliberately aligned with the star belt of Orion.

**ULURU**  Also known as Ayers Rock, Uluru has been sacred to the Aboriginal people in Australia for hundreds of years.

**STONEHENGE**  Even today, nobody knows why or how this famous stone circle in southern England was built.

**MACHU PICCHU**  High up in the Andean mountains of Peru, the Inca city of Machu Pichu remained hidden for centuries.

## HOW TO MAKE A WISH

**CANDLES**  A wish is supposed to come true if you make it when you blow out the candles on your birthday cake.

**BONES**  If you pull part a chicken's "wishbone" with another person, and you pull away the longer piece, you can make a wish.

**PUDDINGS**  The person who finds the sixpence (or any small coin wrapped in foil) in a Christmas pudding can make a wish.

## UNEXPLAINED HAPPENINGS

**SPONTANEOUS HUMAN COMBUSTION**  It is popularly believed that people may suddenly burst into flames for no apparent reason. The fire is so hot, that the body is reduced to ashes.

**DISAPPEARANCES**  Vanishing people, and even entire ships and aircraft have been put down to such phenomena as the mysterious "Bermuda Triangle".

**POLTERGEISTS**  One of the most violent of ghostly manifestations, these restless spirits allegedly move or throw furniture and objects around rooms.

## WAYS OF PREDICTING THE FUTURE

Words ending in "-mancy" refer to types of divination, or ways of predicting the future by observing various natural and other phenomena. There are hundreds of methods, of which these are some of the most common – and strangest:

**AILUROMANCY**  By observing the way a cat jumps.

**ALEUROMANCY**  Using flour. The Chinese baked fortunes in dough – the fortune cookie is the well-known modern example.

**ANTHOMANCY**  From flowers – we know this from the practice of removing petals from flowers and reciting, "She loves me, she loves me not!"

**BIBLIOMANCY**  By opening a Bible, using the first passage one sees to predict the future.

**CARTOMANCY**  By the dealing of playing cards.

**CEROMANCY**  Observing the shapes produced by dropping melted wax into water.

**CHEIROMANCY**  This is the art of telling a person's future by reading their palm.

**CRYSTALLOMANCY**  By gazing into a crystal ball, a precious stone, or reflecting metal surface.

**FOLIOMANCY**  By examining the pattern made by loose tealeaves left at the bottom of a cup.

**OOMANCY**  Using eggs, for example, breaking them and observing the shapes produced.

**ORNITHOMANCY**  By observing the flight of birds.

# CRIME and WAR

## LAW and DISORDER

### PLACES WITH THE HIGHEST CRIME RATES

| PLACE | REPORTED CRIMES PER 100,000 POPULATION |
|---|---|
| Surinam | 17,819 |
| St. Kitts and Nevis | 15,468 |
| Gibraltar | 14,970 |
| New Zealand | 14,496 |
| Sweden | 13,750 |
| Canada | 13,297 |
| US Virgin Islands | 10,441 |
| Denmark | 10,399 |
| Netherlands | 10,181 |
| Guam | 10,080 |
| England and Wales | 9,395 |
| Greenland | 9,360 |
| French Guiana | 8,936 |
| Bermuda | 8,871 |
| Botswana | 8,758 |
| Finland | 8,388 |

An appearance in this list does not necessarily confirm these as the most crime-ridden places in the world, since the rate of reporting relates closely to people's confidence in local law enforcement authorities. Hence the rate of reported crimes in the USA is 5,278 – not enough to make it into this list.

**AMAZING FACT!** Togo has the lowest crime rate in the world, with just 11 reported crimes for every 100,000 of the population.

**DID YOU KNOW?** Whilst imprisoned in Spain in 1597, Miguel de Cervantes began writing his classic novel *Don Quixote*.

### TOP CRIME MOVIES

*The Man in the Iron Mask* (1998)

*The Chamber* (1996)

*The Rock* (1996)

*Dead Man Walking* (1995)

*Fortress* (1993)

*Ernest Goes to Jail* (1990)

*Tango & Cash* (1989)

*The Running Man* (1987)

*Kiss of the Spider Woman* (1985)

*Escape from New York* (1981)

*Stir Crazy* (1980)

*Escape from Alcatraz* (1979)

*Midnight Express* (1978)

*Breakout* (1975)

*The Longest Yard* (1974)

*Papillon* (1973)

*Jailhouse Rock* (1957)

### THE LANGUAGE OF CRIMINALS

| SLANG WORD | MEANING |
|---|---|
| Dabs | Fingerprints |
| Dip | Pickpocket |
| Grass | Police informer |
| Peterman | Safecracker |
| Porridge | Imprisonment |
| Slammer | Prison |
| Stretch | Prison sentence of one year |
| Wheelman | Getaway driver |

### WORLD'S CLUMSIEST CRIMINALS

**WRITTEN ALL OVER HIS FACE** Eugene "Butch" Flenough Jr of Texas was tracked down after a robbery at a pizza restaurant. As a disguise, he had worn a helmet printed with with "Butch" and "Eugene Flenough Jr".

**IT'S A HOLDUP** Kevin Thompson, a 26-year-old man from New Jersey, USA, was jailed for bank robbery after police found that his holdup note was written on his payslip.

**WEIGHED DOWN** Two teenagers suspected of burglary were caught in Minnesota, USA, after attempting to swim away from pursuing police. Each was weighed down with about $25-worth of coins in his pocket.

**CAUGHT RED-HANDED** Cecelio Rodriguez and Armando Milian were arrested in Florida, USA, when police caught them breaking into a pawnshop. The burglars failed to hear the deafening burglar alarm over the noise of the power-saw they used to cut through the door.

**SMUG THUG** American John Cotle was imprisoned for burglary. The evidence against him were photographs of himself, posing with the stolen goods within hours of the burglary.

### FICTIONAL DETECTIVES AND THEIR CREATORS

| DETECTIVE | WRITER |
|---|---|
| Father Brown | G. K. Chesterton |
| Mike Hammer | Mickey Spillane |
| Sherlock Holmes | Arthur Conan Doyle |
| Inspector Maigret | Georges Simenon |
| Philip Marlowe | Raymond Chandler |
| Perry Mason | Erle Stanley Gardner |
| Hercule Poirot | Agatha Christie |
| Sam Spade | Dashiell Hammett |
| Lord Peter Wimsey | Dorothy L. Sayers |

## STRANGE LAWS

**NO HANDLING OF THE PELICANS** Under Section 23 of the London Royal and Other Parks and Gardens Regulations of 1977, "touching a pelican" is forbidden, unless written permission is first obtained.

**NO SLURPING** It is against the law to slurp soup in public in New Jersey, USA.

**NO CROAKING** It is illegal for frogs to croak after 11pm in Memphis, USA.

**NO SNOWBALLS** Snowballs must not be thrown at trees in Mount Pulaski, Illinois, USA.

**RED JUMPERS ONLY** On Wimbledon Common, London, UK, "Every person playing golf is required to wear a red outer garment".

**NO ATOM BOMBS** Anyone detonating a nuclear weapon in Chico, California, risks a $500 fine.

**NO SCRUFFINESS** Your licence may be withdrawn if you are unwashed or badly dressed while driving in Athens, Greece.

**NO FOREIGN RICE** Japanese law states that rice grown in other countries can't be eaten.

**NO ILLITERATE MARRIAGES** To get married, Finnish people must be able to read.

## FAMOUS THEFTS

**CROWN JEWELS** In 1671, disguised as a priest, Colonel Thomas Blood stole the jewels. He was pardoned by Charles I, who admired him.

**MONA LISA** Da Vinci's work was stolen in 1911 by Vicenzo Peruggia. He was caught trying to sell it.

**GREAT TRAIN ROBBERY** A gang stopped the Glasgow to London mail train in 1963 and stole £2.6 million.

## PRISONER FACTS

**FORGOTTEN PRISONER** In 1786, Marie-Augustin was arrested for whistling at Queen Marie Antoinette. He remained imprisoned for 46 years.

**LONGEST SENTENCE** In Thailand in 1989, fraudster Chamoy Thipyaso was sentenced to 141,078 years.

**LONGEST IN JAIL** Paul Geidel, a US prisoner, was in prison for 68 years. He was released at the age of 85.

## LITERARY FORGERIES

**SHAKESPEARE'S LOST PLAYS** As a boy, William Ireland (1777–1835) forged old texts which he claimed were by Shakespeare, including letters and the plays *Vortigern and Rowena* and *Henry II*.

**HOWARD HUGHES' AUTOBIOGRAPHY** In 1971, the American author Clifford Irving wrote what he claimed was the autobiography of the reclusive millionaire Howard Hughes and sold it to a US publisher. He received a 30-month jail sentence.

**HITLER'S DIARIES** In 1981, the German magazine *Stern* bought what they and various experts believed were Adolf Hitler's diaries. In 1983, they were exposed as forgeries by Konrad Kujau.

## FAMOUS PRISONS

**NEWGATE** Once London's most notorious prison, Newgate Prison's famed inmates included Jack Sheppard, who escaped from it. Public hangings took place outside its gates, and it features in several Charles Dickens novels. The Central Criminal Court (Old Bailey) was built on the site.

**DARTMOOR** First used for prisoners of war during the Napoleonic Wars, Dartmoor, UK, has served as a high-security long-term prison ever since. Its remote location on a bleak Devon moor hinders any escape attempts by prisoners.

**DEVIL'S ISLAND** Off the coast of French Guiana, France's worst criminals and political prisoners, such as Alfred Dreyfus, were sent here in the period from 1852 to 1938. Henri Charrière, known as Papillon, is one of the few inmates ever to escape. Many prisoners died of disease on the island.

**ALCATRAZ** Known as "The Rock", an island in San Francisco Bay, California, USA, Alcatraz was first used as a military prison. However, for 30 years up to 1963 it housed the country's most dangerous criminals, among them Al Capone. Robert Stroud, a bird expert who became famous as "The Birdman of Alcatraz", spent many years there.

**SING-SING** The New York prison, named after the Sin Sinck Indians who originally lived there, was built between 1825 and 1828. From 1891 onwards, many murderers were electrocuted there.

## THE WORLD'S MOST FAMOUS CRIMINALS

**NED KELLY** Kelly was an Australian outlaw who wore bullet-proof armour in shoot-outs with police. He was caught and hanged on 11 November 1880.

**AL CAPONE** Nicknamed "Scarface", gangland boss Capone controlled Chicago in the 1920s, and in 1929 was responsible for the St Valentine's Day Massacre. He was jailed in 1931 (for tax evasion) and died, insane, in 1947.

**JESSE JAMES** James led a gang that robbed banks and trains and held up stagecoaches. He was shot dead in 1882.

**BUTCH CASSIDY AND THE SUNDANCE KID** Butch (real name Robert LeRoy Parker) and the Sundance Kid (Harry Longbaugh) were train robbers who some believed escaped to Bolivia.

**DR CRIPPEN** American Harold Hawley Crippen (1862–1910), murdered his wife in London and fled to Canada with Ethel Le Neve disguised as a boy. The ship on which they travelled was contacted by radio (its first use in a criminal case), and Crippen was arrested and hanged.

**BONNIE AND CLYDE** Americans Bonnie Parker (1910–1934) and her partner Clyde Barrow (1909–1934) stole from banks, cafes, and filling stations. They were ambushed and shot by rangers.

**LEE HARVEY OSWALD** The assassin of US President John F. Kennedy was himself shot and killed by an assassin, Jack Ruby, on 24 November 1963.

**CHARLES MANSON** In 1969, with his followers, known as "The Family", Manson murdered six people in California, including actress Sharon Tate.

# MURDER and PUNISHMENT

## GRISLY EXECUTION METHODS

**DROWNING** During the Crusades, (1096–1291), King Richard I ordered that any man found guilty of killing another should be tied to the victim's body and thrown into the sea. Later, in the 14th century, traitors were tied to stakes in the River Thames to drown.

**BOILING ALIVE** This punishment was introduced in England by Henry VIII in 1531, but abolished by his son Edward VI in 1547. In 1531, the Bishop of Rochester's cook, Richard Roose, was found guilty of poisoning guests at a banquet, and boiled to death in a large cauldron.

**PRESSING** Victims were chained to the ground and increasingly heavy weights put on their chests until they could not breathe.

**WHEEL** Victims were spreadeagled on a large wheel and repeatedly beaten until they died, "broken on the wheel". Used widely in Europe, it was not abolished in some countries until the early 19th century.

**HAMMER** A large mallet, or *mazzatello*, was used in Italy. Victims were struck until they died.

**ELEPHANT** In India in the 19th century, criminals had their heads placed on wooden blocks, where an elephant stamped on them.

## MOST MURDERS PER YEAR

| COUNTRY | MURDERS PER 100,000 POPULATION |
|---------|-------------------------------|
| Swaziland | 87.8 |
| Bahamas | 52.6 |
| Monaco | 36.0 |
| Philippines | 30.1 |
| Guatemala | 27.4 |
| Jamaica | 20.9 |
| Russia | 19.9 |
| Botswana | 19.5 |

## FAMOUS PEOPLE WHO LOST THEIR HEADS

**JOHN THE BAPTIST** According to legend, John the Baptist was beheaded at the request of Salome, daughter of Herodias, in 30 BC.

**MARY, QUEEN OF SCOTS** The English queen was executed on 8 February 1587, at Fotheringhay Castle, UK. The beheading was bungled, and the executioner dropped the head when her wig fell off.

**SIR WALTER RALEIGH** This English adventurer was beheaded in 1618. His widow carried his embalmed head around for 30 years in a bag.

**NICOLAS JACQUES PELLETIER** A notorious French highwayman, Pelletier was the first to be sent to the guillotine, in Paris, on 25 April 1792.

**LOUIS XVI** The King of France was guillotined on 21 January 1793.

**MARIE ANTOINETTE** Queen of Louis XVI, Marie Antoinette was guillotined in October 1793.

**EUGENE WEIDMANN** The last public guillotine victim in France was executed at Versailles on 17 June 1939.

**KING FAISAL** King Faisal of Saudi Arabia was beheaded in 1975 for murdering his uncle.

**THE CATO STREET CONSPIRATORS** Five plotters were hanged on 1 May 1820 in London, UK. Their heads were then cut off and displayed to the public.

## BURNED AT THE STAKE

**JOAN OF ARC** The famous French patriot Jeanne d'Arc led a battle against the English and turned French fortunes around. The French burned her in 1431 for witchcraft. She was later made a saint.

**THOMAS CRANMER** The Archbishop of Canterbury, and a Protestant martyr, he was burned at the stake in 1556.

**GERMAN WITCHES** Thousands of people, mostly women, were accused of witchcraft and burned in the 16th–18th centuries. As many as 100,000 were burned in Germany alone. In 1589, 133 died in a single day.

**ELIZABETH GAUNT** While Elizabeth Gaunt was burned at the stake for treason, at Tyburn, London, UK, on 28 October 1685, rainfall almost put out the fire. Some saw this as a sign that she was innocent.

**CHRISTIAN MURPHY** In 1789, a female member of a gang of coiners (people who forged coins), was strangled and then burnt in London, UK. She was the last person burned in England – burning was abolished in 1790.

## DID YOU KNOW?

The guillotine was proposed in 1789 by Dr Joseph Guillotin as a humane way of executing people.

## EXECUTION MILESTONES

**1241** Pirate William Marise is the first person in England to be hanged, drawn, and quartered.

**1630** First recorded hanging in the USA.

**1686** Last witch, Alice Molland, hanged in the UK.

**1705** John Smith, hanged at Tyburn, is reprieved and revived 15 minutes later. He becomes known thereafter as "Half-hanged Smith".

**1814** Beheading is abolished in England.

**1831** John Any Bird Bell is executed at Maidstone, UK, aged 14, for murder.

**1868** At the Old Bailey, London, UK, Michael Barrett is the last person to be publicly hanged in the UK.

**1890** First electrocution, at Auburn Prison, New York.

**1916** In Tennessee, USA, Mary, an elephant, is hanged for murder.

**1936** Last public execution takes place in the USA.

**1982** Charles Brooks is the first to be executed by lethal injection, in Texas, USA.

## MOST PROLIFIC PRE-20TH-CENTURY SERIAL KILLERS

**BEHRAM** Behram (or Buhram) was the leader of the Thugee cult in India, believed to be responsible for the deaths of up to 2,000,000 people. At his trial, Behram was found guilty of personally committing 931 murders between 1790 and 1830, mostly by ritual strangulation.

**COUNTESS ERSZÉBET BÁTHORY** Báthory (1560–1614), of Hungary, known as "Countess Dracula", allegedly murdered 300 to 650 girls in the belief that drinking their blood would prevent her from ageing. She was arrested in 1611 and died alone in her castle.

**MARY ANN COTTON** Cotton, a former nurse, was hanged in the UK in 1873. In a 20-year period, she is believed to have killed 14 to 20 people.

**⚠ DID YOU KNOW?** Jack the Ripper, a notorious murderer in 19th-century England, committed his crimes at weekends.

**GILLES DE RAIS** A French aristocrat, Gilles de Laval, Baron de Rais (1404–1440), allegedly dabbled in the occult and committed murders as sacrifices. He was accused of killing up to 200 children. He was strangled, and his body burned, in 1440.

**HERMANN WEBSTER MUDGETT** Also known as "H. H. Holmes", Mudgett, a former doctor, lured women to his Chicago home. Operating as a hotel, it was fully equipped for torturing, murdering, and dissecting victims. Mudgett disposed of the bodies in furnaces or in acid baths. He confessed to killing 27 people, but the remains of 200 victims were discovered in his house. He was hanged in May 1896.

## MURDER COINCIDENCES

**DELIBERATE OR COINCIDENCE?** Sir Edmund Berry Godfrey, an English Member of Parliament, was murdered in 1678. His body was found at Greenberry Hill. Three men – called Green, Berry, and Hill – were executed for the crime.

**BODY DOUBLE** In 1900, King Umberto of Italy was dining in a restaurant when he discovered that the proprietor looked exactly like him. To his amazement, the king found that the restaurateur was also called Umberto, and that they had both been born in Turin on the same day in 1844. They both also married women called Margherita on the same day. Sensing an affinity with his "double", the king invited him to an athletics meeting the following day. As the king took his seat at the meeting, he was told that the other Umberto had been killed that morning in a mysterious shooting accident. As the king expressed his sorrow, an anarchist shot him dead.

**MYSTERY PRESENCE** Robert Todd Lincoln, son of Abraham, was present at Ford's Theatre, Washington, in 1865, when his father was shot. He was at hand when President Garfield was shot in 1881, and in 1901, he was close to President William McKinley when he was shot.

## WORST MASSACRES

**331 BC** Alexander the Great killed 10,000 Tyrians.

**AD 390** Over 3,000 people were killed by Theodosius in Thessalonica, Greece.

**1002** On St Brice's Day, Ethelred II ordered the Danes in the UK to be killed.

**1572** More than 50,000 Huguenots (French Protestants) were killed in the St Bartholomew's Day Massacre.

**1631** 6,400 civilians were slaughtered by the German cavalry in Magdeburg, northern Germany.

**1649** Oliver Cromwell's army massacred 2,000 people in Drogheda, Ireland.

**1890** 300 Sioux men, women, and children were murdered by 500 soldiers at Wounded Knee, South Dakota, USA.

## FAMOUS ASSASSINATION VICTIMS

**JULIUS CAESAR** Roman ruler, stabbed to death by conspirators in Rome, on the Ides of March (15th), in 44 BC.

**SPENCER PERCEVAL** The only British Prime Minister to be murdered, Perceval was killed by John Bellingham on 11 May 1812 in the House of Commons, UK.

**ABRAHAM LINCOLN** The 16th US President was shot by John Wilkes Booth at Ford's Theater, Washington D.C., on 14 April 1865, and died the following day.

**GRIGORY RASPUTIN** The "mad monk" of Russia was poisoned, shot, and drowned in 1916 for fear he would influence government.

**JOHN F. KENNEDY** The 35th President of the USA was shot in the head and killed in Dallas, USA, by Lee Harvey Oswald, on 22 November 1963.

**MARTIN LUTHER KING JR** A civil rights leader, King was shot in Memphis, USA, by James Earl Ray, on 4 April 1968.

**JOHN LENNON** In 1980, the former Beatles musician was shot in New York by religious fanatic Mark Chapman.

**YITZHAK RABIN** The Israeli Prime Minister was shot dead in Jerusalem, Israel, on 4 November 1995.

## FIRST TO ABOLISH CAPITAL PUNISHMENT

Capital punishment is when a criminal is put to death for a serious crime. Some of the countries listed here have since reinstated capital punishment.

| COUNTRY | ABOLISHED |
| --- | --- |
| Russia | 1826 |
| Venezuela | 1863 |
| Portugal | 1867 |
| Brazil | 1882 |
| Costa Rica | 1882 |
| Ecuador | 1897 |

# WAR and BATTLES

## MAJOR WARS

| DATES | WAR |
| --- | --- |
| 431–404 BC | Peloponnesian War |
| 264–146 BC | Punic Wars |
| 1096–1291 | Crusades |
| 1337–1453 | Hundred Years War |
| 1455–1485 | Wars of the Roses |
| 1618–1648 | Thirty Years War |
| 1642–1649 | English Civil War |
| 1701–1714 | War of the Spanish Succession |
| 1740–1748 | War of the Austrian Succession |
| 1756–1763 | Seven Years War |
| 1775–1783 | American War of Independence |
| 1792–1815 | Napoleonic Wars |
| 1812–1814 | War of 1812 |
| 1846–1848 | Mexican-American War |
| 1853–1856 | Crimean War |
| 1861–1865 | American Civil War |
| 1870–1871 | Franco-Prussian War |
| 1894–1895 | Chinese-Japanese War |
| 1898 | Spanish-American War |
| 1880–1902 | Boer Wars |
| 1904–1905 | Russo-Japanese War |
| 1914–1918 | World War I |
| 1931–1933 | Chinese-Japanese War |
| 1936–1939 | Spanish Civil War |
| 1937–1945 | Chinese-Japanese War |
| 1939–1945 | World War II |
| 1950–1953 | Korean War |
| 1954–1975 | Vietnam War |
| 1982 | Falklands War |
| 1991 | Gulf War |
| 1991–1995 | Bosnian War |

**DID YOU KNOW?**  The first records of the use of biological warfare date from the 1300s. Tartars, attacking a Crimean city, catapulted plague-ridden corpses over the walls, infecting inhabitants with the disease.

## WEAPON MILESTONES

**c.100,000 BC**  Neanderthal people use sharpened wooden spear points and simple stone axes.

**c.1000 BC**  The iron sword evolves in southern and central Europe.

**AD 1100**  The mace and the crossbow become popular weapons of war.

**1340–1400**  Cannons are introduced into battles.

**1836**  American gunsmith Samuel Colt (1814–1862) develops the first really effective revolver.

**1890s**  Belt-fed machine guns are introduced, which allowed two people to fire at great speed.

**1916**  The first tank is used in war.

**1945**  The first atomic bomb, dropped on Hiroshima, Japan, changes the nature of warfare.

**1980s**  Attack helicopters, armed with laser-guided missiles and machine guns, prove to be effective in battle.

**DID YOU KNOW?** During battles in past times, officers used to give up their swords as a sign of surrender.

## UNCONVENTIONAL WEAPONS

**CIRCULAR BATTLESHIP**  The brainchild of Vice-Admiral Popov of the Imperial Russian Navy, this bizarre vessel, named *Novgorod*, was launched in the Black Sea in 1873. Designed to spin like a top, and fire its large guns in any direction, it was unstable, and practically impossible to steer. It was taken out of service almost immediately!

**HELMET GUN**  Patented by Albert B. Pratt of Vermont, USA in 1916, the gun and its sights are attached to a helmet and the trigger fired by the wearer's mouth. A powerful strap holds it in place – but may not be sufficient to prevent the recoil from fatally injuring the wearer.

**RIFLE TO SHOOT AROUND CORNERS**  During World War I, Jones Wister of Philadelphia, USA patented a rifle with a curved barrel, so that soldiers could fire over the top of trenches without risking being shot themselves; a periscope took the place of sights.

**HARD CHEESE**  During the 1865 war between Uruguay and Brazil, a Uruguayan ship ran out of cannon balls and fired stale Dutch cheeses – one of which dismasted an enemy vessel and killed two sailors.

**COMBINED GUN AND PLOUGH**  Patented on 17 June 1862, by C. M. French and W. H. Fancher of New York, USA, this unusual weapon was designed to be used by farmers who, if they were attacked while ploughing, could quickly turn their implement into a powerful gun!

**BOOMERANG BULLETS**  Patented in the USA on 4 October 1870 by G. Hope of Kansas, USA, boomerang bullets were designed to fire in a curved line – the only danger being that if they travelled in a complete circle, they could kill the person who fired them.

## 20TH-CENTURY WARS WITH MOST MILITARY FATALITIES

These figures represent military historians' "best guesses", and do not take into account the enormous death tolls among civilian populations during the many wars of the 20th century.

| WAR | YEARS | MILITARY FATALITIES |
|---|---|---|
| World War II | 1939–1945 | 15,843,000 |
| World War I | 1914–1918 | 8,545,800 |
| Korean War | 1950–1953 | 1,893,100 |
| Chinese-Japanese War | 1937–1945 | 1,000,000 |
| Biafra-Nigeria Civil War | 1967–1970 | 1,000,000 |
| Spanish Civil War | 1936–1939 | 611,000 |
| Vietnam War | 1954–1975 | 546,000 |
| India-Pakistan War | 1947 | 200,000 |
| USSR invasion of Afghanistan | 1979–1989 | 200,000 |
| Iran-Iraq War | 1980–1988 | 200,000 |

**! DID YOU KNOW?** War in the 20th century has killed over 100 million people in total; 20 million since 1945.

## GREAT NAVAL BATTLES

**AEGOSOPOTAMI, 405 BC** A flotilla of 80 Athenian triremes battled with 170 Peloponnesian ships. The Athenians were conquered, and the Peloponnesian War ended soon afterwards.

**MYLAE, 260 BC (PUNIC WARS)** The battle at Mylae – the first of three – saw a Roman victory over Carthage, North Africa.

**LEPANTO, 7 OCTOBER 1571 (CYPRUS WAR)** The Turkish fleet was defeated by the Spanish. About 25,000 Turks were lost in 250 galleys.

**SPANISH ARMADA, 29 JULY 1588 (ANGLO-SPANISH WAR)** A fleet of 30 Spanish ships with 2,500 guns and 30,000 men set out to attack England. Although outnumbered, the English fleet inflicted severe damage with their guns, and the rest of the Spanish fleet was destroyed by bad weather.

**TRAFALGAR, 21 OCTOBER 1805** A sea battle between the British fleet under Lord Nelson, and the French. The British won, but Lord Nelson was killed.

**CORAL SEA, 8 MAY 1942 (WORLD WAR II)** The US Navy fought the Japanese in the first major battle using aircraft from carriers.

**LEYTE GULF, 22-27 OCTOBER 1944 (WORLD WAR II)** The US defeated the Japanese, who lost three battleships, four aircraft carriers, ten cruisers, and nine destroyers.

## WORDS OF WAR

These common words all started out as military terms:

Alarm • Ambulance • Bachelor • Caddie/caddy • Canteen • Crusade • Field day
Freelance • Garret • Gauntlet • Gremlin • Jeep • Kamikaze • Loophole
Magazine • Marathon • Picket • Pioneer • Slogan • Snorkel

**! DID YOU KNOW?** During World War II, Japanese *kamikaze* pilots would fly into Allied ships in planes packed with explosives, believing it an honour to die for their country. The word *kamikaze* means "divine wind" in Japanese.

## GREAT MILITARY COMMANDERS

**ALEXANDER THE GREAT (356–323 BC)** Alexander became king of Macedonia when he was 20 years old. He was an ambitious general, and conquered most of the known world. His empire extended from Asia Minor (now Turkey) to India.

**JULIUS CAESAR (100–44 BC)** Caesar became head of the Roman Republic in 49 BC. He conquered Gaul (modern France, Belgium and Switzerland), and also invaded Britain twice.

**HORATIO NELSON (1758–1805)** The daring Commander of the British Royal Navy, Nelson defeated the Spanish and French at the Battle of Trafalgar in 1805, but died of serious wounds.

**NAPOLEON BONAPARTE (1769–1821)** Corsican Bonaparte restored the power of the French government after the French Revolution. A brilliant military commander, he controlled Europe from the English Channel to the Russian border.

## FAMOUS WARRIOR GROUPS

**VIKINGS** In the late eighth century, Vikings from present-day Denmark, Norway, and Sweden began to leave their countries in search of treasure to steal, or new lands to settle in.

**CRUSADERS** Between the 11th and 13th centuries, European Christians, known as Crusaders, organized armed expeditions to regain Jerusalem, which had been seized by the Saracens.

**SAMURAI** The Samurai were an aristocratic class of warriors who first gained power in Japan in the 12th century.

**MONGOLS** In the late 11th century, an army in northeastern Asia, led by a chieftain called Genghis Khan, invaded China and Asia. The Mongols were skilled fighters, and possessed powerful weapons.

**! DID YOU KNOW?** Early machine guns were mounted on carriages and looked like conventional cannons.

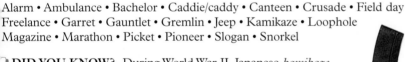

# WORLD WAR I

## KEY EVENTS

**JUNE 1914** The heir to the throne of Austria-Hungary, Archduke Franz Ferdinand, is assassinated. Serbia is blamed for the attack.

**JULY 1914** Austria-Hungary invades Serbia in retaliation for Franz Ferdinand's death. Russia mobilizes troops to help Serbia.

**AUGUST 1914** To help its ally Austria, Germany declares war on Russia and Russia's ally, France. Germany invades Belgium to get to France. Britain, pledged to protect Belgium's neutrality, declares war on Germany. Germany pushes back Britain at Mons, Belgium, and defeats Russia at Tannenberg.

**APRIL 1915** The Germans use poisonous gas at the Battle of Ypres, Belgium. The Allies (Britain, France, and Russia) try to force Turkey out of the war by invading the Gallipoli peninsula.

**MAY 1915** A German U-boat sinks British liner SS *Lusitania* killing 1,200. Italy joins the war to support the Allies.

**FEBRUARY 1916** German forces try to capture the French fortress of Verdun in a ten-month battle.

**JULY 1916** In the four-month battle of the Somme, France, tanks are used for the first time. Both sides suffer enormous losses.

**APRIL 1917** USA enters the war on the side of the Allies.

**JULY 1917** More than 300,000 Allied troops die in the three-month battle of Passchendaele.

**MARCH 1918** Germany and Russia make peace, whilst the German forces make advances on the Western Front.

**AUGUST 1918** With US help, Allied troops succeed in breaking through crucial German lines.

**OCTOBER 1918** Italy defeats Austria-Hungary, and Britain defeats Turkey. The Austria-Hungarians and Turks ask for peace.

**NOVEMBER 1918** Germany and Allies sign an armistice. War ends.

**JUNE 1919** Treaty of Versailles is signed. Germany is forced to pay reparations (damages). These were to become a major cause of World War II.

## NEW WEAPONS

**TANKS** Able to cross rough ground and break through barbed wire defences, tanks were first used in September 1916.

**BOMBERS** Zeppelin airships and multi-engined aircraft capable of carrying heavy bombs were first used during World War I.

**FLECHÉTTES** These were steel darts, designed to be dropped from aircraft on the enemy beneath.

**GASES** Gases such as mustard gas, chlorine, and tear gas, were used to poison the enemy. Gas masks, designed to protect soldiers from gas attacks, quickly followed.

**GIANT MORTARS** "Big Bertha" is the best known of the giant guns built by the German armaments company Krupp.

**MACHINE GUNS** The water-cooled Browning machine gun, named after John Browning, its US inventor, was introduced in 1917. The aircraft machine gun also dates from World War I.

**PERISCOPE RIFLES** In 1915, an Australian soldier invented a rifle with periscopic sights that enabled its user to remain hidden.

## WAR AT SEA

**SUBMARINE WARFARE**
Submarines were used effectively as deadly weapons for the first time in World War I. They fired underwater missiles called torpedoes at enemy ships. In 1917, destroyers were built in the USA. They were smaller and faster than battleships and were used mainly to protect other ships from enemy fire.

**SINKING OF LUSITANIA**
On its journey from the UK to the USA, the British liner SS *Lusitania* was sunk by German torpedoes off the coast of Ireland on 8 May 1915. About 1,200 men, women, and children were drowned, 128 of whom were American. Some were close friends of the US President, Woodrow Wilson.

**JUTLAND BATTLE** In one of the most famous naval battles ever, fleets of British and German Dreadnought battleships fought at Jutland, off the coast of Denmark, on 31 May 1916. Both sides claimed to be victorious, but while the German side was first to retreat, the British Navy suffered greater losses, leaving a stalemate situation.

## MILITARY LOSSES

| COUNTRY | KILLED |
|---|---|
| Germany | 1,773,700 |
| Russia | 1,700,000 |
| France | 1,357,800 |
| Austria-Hungary | 1,200,000 |
| British Empire | 908,371 |
| Italy | 650,000 |
| Romania | 335,706 |
| Turkey | 325,000 |
| USA | 116,516 |
| Bulgaria | 87,500 |
| Serbia | 45,000 |
| Belgium | 13,716 |
| Portugal | 7,222 |
| Greece | 5,000 |
| Montenegro | 3,000 |
| Japan | 320 |

**DID YOU KNOW?** Romania had the highest death rate, losing 45 per cent of its armed forces, while Japan lost just 0.04 per cent of its 800,000-strong force. Only three Japanese were taken prisoner or reported missing.

## FAMOUS AIR ACES

| PILOT | COUNTRY | ENEMY DEATHS |
|---|---|---|
| Rittmeister Manfred von Richthofen ("The Red Baron") | Germany | 80 |
| Capitaine René Paul Fonck | France | 75 |
| Major Edward "Mick" Mannock | UK | 73 |
| Major William Avery Bishop | Canada | 72 |
| Major Raymond Collishaw | Canada | 62 |

**DID YOU KNOW?** The term "air ace" describes a pilot who brought down more than five enemy aircraft.

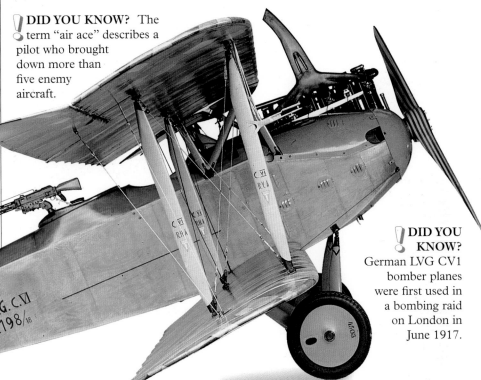

**DID YOU KNOW?** German LVG CV1 bomber planes were first used in a bombing raid on London in June 1917.

**DID YOU KNOW?** The main role of reconnaissance fighter planes was to observe and photograph the enemy.

## MOST TAKEN AS PRISONERS OF WAR

| COUNTRY | CAPTURED |
|---|---|
| Russia | 2,500,000 |
| Austria-Hungary | 2,200,000 |
| Germany | 1,152,800 |
| Italy | 600,000 |
| France | 537,000 |
| British Empire | 191,652 |
| Turkey | 250,000 |
| Serbia | 152,958 |
| Romania | 80,000 |
| Belgium | 34,659 |

## BATTLES WITH MOST CASUALTIES

| BATTLE | DATE | ESTIMATED CASUALTIES |
|---|---|---|
| Somme River I | July–November 1916 | 1,000,000 |
| Verdun | February–December 1915 | 700,000 |
| Gallipoli | April 1915–January 1916 | 500,000 |
| Artois-Loos | September–October 1915 | 428,000 |
| Somme River II | March 1918 | 300,000 |
| Ypres I | October–November 1914 | 250,000 |

**DID YOU KNOW?** More soldiers were killed in the four-month battle of the Somme, northwest France, than in any previous battle in history. Gunfire could be heard as far away as England. More than 650,000 German soldiers, 420,000 British, and 195,000 French lost their lives.

## LARGEST ARMED FORCES

| COUNTRY | COMBATANTS |
|---|---|
| Russia | 12,000,000 |
| Germany | 11,000,000 |
| British Empire | 8,904,467 |
| France | 8,410,000 |
| Austria-Hungary | 7,800,000 |
| Italy | 5,615,000 |
| USA | 4,355,000 |
| Turkey | 2,850,000 |
| Bulgaria | 1,200,000 |
| Japan | 800,000 |
| Romania | 750,000 |
| Serbia | 707,343 |

# WORLD WAR II

## LARGEST ARMED FORCES

| COUNTRY | PERSONNEL |
|---|---|
| USSR | 12,500,000 |
| USA | 12,364,000 |
| Germany | 10,000,000 |
| Japan | 6,095,000 |
| France | 5,700,000 |
| UK | 4,683,000 |
| Italy | 4,500,000 |
| China | 3,800,000 |
| India | 2,150,000 |
| Poland | 1,000,000 |

## KEY EVENTS

**AUGUST 1934** Adolf Hitler becomes Führer (leader) of Germany.

**APRIL 1938** Germany annexes Austria.

**MARCH 1939** Germany occupies the whole of Czechoslovakia.

**SEPTEMBER 1939** Germany invades Poland; Britain, France, Australia, and New Zealand declare war on Germany.

**MAY 1940** Germany invades Belgium, the Netherlands, France, and the Channel Islands. British and French troops leave France via Dunkirk; Winston Churchill becomes Prime Minister of the UK.

**JUNE 1940** Germany occupies Paris; Italy declares war on Britain and France.

**SEPTEMBER 1940** The blitz – air raids on London – begins; Italy invades Egypt.

**APRIL 1941** Germany invades Greece, Yugoslavia, and Russia.

**DECEMBER 1941** Japan attacks Pearl Harbor; the USA enters the war.

**FEBRUARY 1943** Germany is defeated at Stalingrad, Russia.

**JUNE 1944** British troops embark in France in the D-Day landings.

**AUGUST 1944** The Allies liberate Paris.

**APRIL 1945** The Allies liberate the concentration camps; US President Roosevelt dies and Truman takes over.

**APRIL 1945** Mussolini is captured and hanged; the Allies take Venice.

**APRIL 1945** Adolf Hitler commits suicide.

**MAY 1945** The German forces surrender; VE (Victory in Europe) Day.

**AUGUST 1945** Atomic bombs dropped, on Hiroshima and Nagasaki; Japanese surrender; VJ (Victory over Japan) Day.

**SEPTEMBER 1945** United Nations starts.

**NOVEMBER 1945** The Nuremberg war crimes trials begin.

## MILITARY LOSSES

This list covers the number of men who died on the battlefield. Untold millions of civilian war deaths should be added to these figures. Recent estimates have suggested an additional figure of up to 25,000,000 civilian deaths, as a result of Stalinist purges which began just before the outbreak of war.

| COUNTRY | KILLED |
|---|---|
| USSR | 13,600,000 |
| Germany | 3,300,000 |
| China | 1,324,516 |
| Japan | 1,140,429 |
| British Empire | 357,116 |
| Romania | 350,000 |
| Poland | 320,000 |
| Yugoslavia | 305,000 |
| USA | 292,131 |
| Italy | 279,800 |
| Total | 21,268,992 |

**DID YOU KNOW?** The numbers killed in World War II have been the subject of intense argument for more than 50 years. The very high number of military casualties in the USSR in particular is hard to comprehend. Most authorities now reckon that of the 30,000,000 Soviets who bore arms, there were 13,600,000 military deaths. This includes a total of approximately 7,800,000 battlefield deaths, plus up to 2,500,000 who died later of disease and wounds received in battle. Of the 5,800,000 who were taken prisoner, as many as 3,300,000, died in captivity.

**DID YOU KNOW?** Six million Jews are believed to have been killed by the German Nazi regime as part of an attempt by Hitler to rid Europe of all traces of Jewish life and culture.

## WORLD WAR II SLANG

| SLANG TERM | MEANING |
|---|---|
| Bought the Farm (USA) | Dead |
| Doughboy | US soldier |
| Gone for a Burton (UK) | Dead |
| Mae West | Lifejacket |
| Molotov cocktail | Anti-tank fire-bomb |
| Spit | Spitfire fighter plane |
| Write-off | Crashed aircraft |

## SEA BATTLES

**PEARL HARBOR** The Japanese attacked the US naval base of Pearl Harbor, in Hawaii, without warning on 7 December 1941. Five American battleships were sunk and 15 other vessels were also attacked. The USA declared war on Japan immediately.

**BISMARCK** On 27 May 1941, the British sank the German ship *Bismarck* in the Atlantic, killing 1,000 crew.

**PACIFIC BATTLES** The US Navy gained two important successes against the Japanese in the Battle of the Coral Sea and the Battle of Midway, both in 1942. In the Battle of Midway, US torpedo bombers were used to disable and sink Japanese ships.

## DECLARATIONS OF WAR

| DECLARATION | DATE |
|---|---|
| UK on Germany | 3 Sept 1939 |
| Australia on Germany | 3 Sept 1939 |
| New Zealand on Germany | 3 Sept 1939 |
| France on Germany | 3 Sept 1939 |
| South Africa on Germany | 6 Sept 1939 |
| Canada on Germany | 9 Sept 1939 |
| Italy on UK and France | 10 June 1940 |
| France on Italy | 11 June 1940 |
| Japan on USA, UK, Australia, Canada, New Zealand and South Africa | 7 Dec 1941 |
| UK on Finland, Hungary, Romania | 7 Dec 1941 |

## WORLD WAR II BOMBING RAIDS

**BATTLE OF BRITAIN** Hundreds of German bombers attacked the UK during the Summer of 1940. Hermann Goering, commander of the German Luftwaffe, sent 1,000 planes across the channel daily to bomb the UK air bases.

**BRITISH BLITZ** In May 1941, 550 German planes dropped hundreds of explosive bombs over London, killing 1,436 people and starting 2,000 fires.

**DRESDEN DESTRUCTION** In February 1945, Allied troops bombed the German city of Dresden for three nights, resulting in a death toll of nearly 100,000 and casualties numbering 400,000.

**ATOMIC EXPLOSION** In a controversial attack, an American plane dropped an atomic bomb on the Japanese city of Hiroshima in August 1945. About 80,000 Japanese people were killed instantly.

## NEW INVENTIONS

**ATOM BOMBS** Developed by US scientists and used at the end of the War.

**BAILEY BRIDGES** Invented by British engineer Donald Bailey, these were quick replacements for bridges that had been destroyed.

**COMPUTERS** The first programmable computer, *Colossus*, was used in the UK in 1943 to crack codes.

**NYLON** Invented just before the War, it was used for parachute cords.

## TANKS OF WORLD WAR II

| TANK | DATE | COUNTRY | WEIGHT TONNES | TONS | NUMBER PRODUCED |
|---|---|---|---|---|---|
| M4A3 Sherman | 1942 | USA | 31.5 | 31 | 41,530 |

**DID YOU KNOW?** The tank named after US Civil War General William Tecumseh Sherman was used in large numbers by both US and British troops during World War II. It carried a crew of five and could cruise over a distance of 230 km (143 miles) at up to 40 km/h (25 mph).

| TANK | DATE | COUNTRY | WEIGHT TONNES | TONS | NUMBER PRODUCED |
|---|---|---|---|---|---|
| T34 Model 42 | 1940 | USSR | 30.0 | 28.5 | 35,120 |
| T34/85 | 1944 | USSR | 33.0 | 32.0 | 29,430 |
| M3 General Stuart | 1941 | USA | 12.4 | 12.2 | 14,000 |
| Valentine II | 1941 | UK | 17.8 | 17.5 | 8,280 |
| M3A1 Lee/Grant | 1941 | USA | 27.2 | 26.8 | 7,400 |
| Churchill VII | 1942 | UK | 40.5 | 40.0 | 5,640 |

**DID YOU KNOW?** During World War II, ordinary citizens had to make many adjustments to their lives. Scarce foods such as meat, eggs, and sweets were rationed weekly. In Europe, children from the cities were often evacuated to safer homes in rural areas. City families slept in air-raid shelters and tried to blacken out all their windows, so bombers would not see any lights from the sky.

## FAMOUS LEADERS

**WINSTON CHURCHILL, UK (1874–1965)** Considered to be one of the greatest statesman, Churchill became British Prime Minister in 1940, leading the country through the War. Churchill was also a talented painter.

**EMPEROR HIROHITO, JAPAN (1901–1989)** As the ruler of his country during the War, many believed Hirohito should have been tried for crimes committed by Japanese troops.

**BENITO MUSSOLINI, ITALY (1883–1945)** Mussolini led the National Fascist Party, and became Dictator of Italy in 1922. He joined with Germany in 1940, but was defeated and executed in 1945.

**ADOLF HITLER, GERMANY (1889–1945)** The leader of the Nazi party, Hitler became Germany's Chancellor in 1933. He began military action in Europe and a campaign to murder Jews.

**FRANKLIN D. ROOSEVELT, USA (1882–1945)** The 32nd US President, Roosevelt brought the USA into the War in 1941.

**JOSEF STALIN, USSR (1879–1953)** Head of the Soviet Communist Party and Prime Minister during the War, Stalin was a ruthless man who killed many of his own people.

# THE ARTS

# LEARNING

**DID YOU KNOW?** In the 1800s, it was believed that each portion of the brain store a specific kind of knowledge.

## OLDEST UNIVERSITIES

| UNIVERSITY | COUNTRY | FOUNDED |
|---|---|---|
| Quaraouyine, Fez | Morocco | 859 |
| Al-Azhar, Cairo | Egypt | 970 |
| Parma | Italy | 1064 |
| Bologna | Italy | 1088 |
| Modena | Italy | 1175 |
| Paris | France | 1200 |
| Perugia | Italy | 1200 |

## WORLD'S LARGEST UNIVERSITIES

| UNIVERSITY | COUNTRY | STUDENTS |
|---|---|---|
| Paris | France | 308,904 |
| Calcutta | India | 300,000 |
| Bombay | India | 262,350 |
| Mexico City | Mexico | 261,693 |
| Guadalajara | Mexico | 214,986 |
| Buenos Aires | Argentina | 206,658 |
| Rome | Italy | 184,000 |

## MOST STUDENTS

| COUNTRY | UNIVERSITY STUDENTS |
|---|---|
| USA | 8,529,132 |
| India | 4,425,247 |
| China | 3,170,936 |
| Russia | 2,587,510 |
| Japan | 2,311,618 |
| Indonesia | 1,889,408 |

## AMAZING LIBRARIES

**VATICAN LIBRARY** The Vatican library in Vatican City has one of the world's largest and most valuable collections of early manuscripts and books. Founded in the mid-1400s, it is the central library of the Catholic church, and scholars from all over the world are permitted to use it.

**BRITISH LIBRARY** This library, in London, is one of the world's largest. It contains books and manuscripts, newspapers, maps, music, sound recordings, and stamps.

**LIBRARY OF CONGRESS** The largest library in the world is the United States Library of Congress in Washington D.C. Founded in 1800, the library contains over 23,000,000 books and more than 100,000,000 catalogued items. It has 856 km (532 miles) of shelving and approximately 4,600 employees.

**DID YOU KNOW?** The Library of Congress moved to its present building in 1897. It cost $7 million (£4.4 million), making it the world's most expensive library at that time.

## SILLY HOMEWORK EXCUSES

My dog ate my maths book.

We had no paper at home.

It was too difficult.

We had a surprise visit from my gran/cousin/penpal.

My ink ran out.

My sister/brother was sick on it.

My mum thought it was rubbish and threw it in the bin.

## LONGEST SCHOOL YEARS

| COUNTRY | SCHOOL YEAR IN DAYS |
|---|---|
| China | 251 |
| Japan | 243 |
| Korea | 220 |
| Israel | 215 |
| Germany | 210 |
| Russia | 210 |
| Switzerland | 207 |
| Netherlands | 200 |

## COUNTRIES WITH MOST SCHOOL CHILDREN

| COUNTRY | PRIMARY-SCHOOL CHILDREN | SECONDARY-SCHOOL CHILDREN | TOTAL |
|---|---|---|---|
| China | 124,212,400 | 53,837,300 | 178,049.700 |
| India | 108,200,539 | 64,115,978 | 172,316,517 |
| USA | 23,694,000 | 20,578,000 | 44,272,000 |
| Indonesia | 29,876,196 | 11,360,349 | 41,236,545 |
| Pakistan | 15,532,000 | 5,022,416 | 20,554,416 |
| Mexico | 14,574,202 | 7,264,650 | 21,818,852 |
| Russia | 7,849,000 | 13,732,000 | 21,581,000 |

## PEOPLE WHO NEVER FINISHED SCHOOL

**MARK TWAIN (1835–1910)** Classic American novelist and humourist.

**CHARLIE CHAPLIN (1889–1977)** British silent film actor.

**CHARLES DICKENS (1812–1870)** British author.

**THOMAS EDISON (1847–1931)** Prolific American inventor.

**CLAUDE MONET (1840–1926)** French painter, began Impressionism.

## COUNTRIES WITH MOST LIBRARIES

National literary traditions determine the ratio of libraries to population. The people of Japan, for example, do not customarily borrow books, and consequently the country has only 1,950 public libraries.

| COUNTRY | LIBRARIES |
|---|---|
| Russia | 96,177 |
| UK | 24,869 |
| Ukraine | 21,857 |
| Kazakhstan | 15,055 |
| Germany | 13,032 |
| Poland | 9,505 |
| Belorussia | 9,121 |
| USA | 9,101 |
| Czech Republic | 7,986 |
| Mexico | 5,630 |
| Spain | 4,880 |
| Bulgaria | 4,879 |
| Azerbaijan | 4,647 |
| Hungary | 4,468 |
| Georgia | 3,929 |

**DID YOU KNOW?** In the 19th century, working people in the UK who did not have access to a library could borrow books from a horse-drawn mobile library.

**DID YOU KNOW?** Monet's painting of Rouen Cathedral typifies the Impressionist style.

## TIPS FOR DOING WELL IN EXAMS

**KEEP CALM** Try not to panic – you think more clearly when you're calm.

**SLEEP WELL** You won't perform well if you're tired. Have a good night's rest the night before your exam.

**FEED YOUR BRAIN** Make sure you've had something to eat before the exam – your brain needs energy!

**REMEMBER KEY WORDS** When revising, make notes and cut them down to key words – these will trigger your memory when your are in the exam. Some people use colours to aid memory.

**PLAN A CELEBRATION** Plan to do something you enjoy after your exams have finished. You should feel more relaxed if you have something to look forward to!

**TALK TO OTHERS** You're not alone – thousands of people sit exams every year. If you are really worried, talk to friends or family who have been in the same situation. They may offer good advice!

## MOST ILLITERATE COUNTRIES

The United Nations defines an illiterate person as an adult who cannot, with understanding, both read and write a short, simple statement on their daily life.

| COUNTRY | PERCENTAGE OF ILLITERACY |
|---|---|
| Nigeria | 86.4 |
| Burkina | 80.8 |
| Nepal | 72.5 |
| Mali | 69.0 |
| Sierra Leone | 68.6 |
| Afghanistan | 68.5 |
| Senegal | 66.9 |
| Burundi | 64.7 |

# WORDS

## HELLO AROUND THE WORLD

| GREETING | LANGUAGE |
|---|---|
| Ahlan wasahlan | Arabic |
| Dobró útro | Bulgarian |
| Goddag | Danish |
| Hello | English |
| Hyvää päivää | Finnish |
| Bonjour | French |
| Garmardzobat | Georgian |
| Guten Tag | German |
| Kalimera | Greek |
| Namaskar | Hindi |
| Gódan daginn | Icelandic |
| Buongiorno | Italian |
| Konnichiwa | Japanese |
| Nin hao | Mandarin |
| Go dag | Norwegian |
| Dzien dóbry | Polish |
| Bom dia | Portuguese |
| Zdravstvuyitye | Russian |
| Buenos días | Spanish |
| God dag | Swedish |
| Sawatdee | Thai |
| Iya gunler | Turkish |
| Assalm-u-alaikum | Urdu |
| Kunjani | Zulu |

## ONOMATOPOEIC WORDS

Onomatopoeic words are words that sound like the noise they describe. The best place to see these words is in comic strips.

Splash • Crack • Whoosh
Clang • Zoom • Zap
Crunch • Crackle • Pop
Whack • Wham • Boom
Whizz • Bang • Growl
Creak • Roar • Woof • Meow
Oink • Cock-a-doodle-doo
Slam • Snap • Gasp • Tap

## ACRONYMS

Acronyms are sets of initials designed to be said as though they are words – they are thus not the same as abbreviations. The word acronym has itself been used only since 1943.

| ACRONYM | MEANING |
|---|---|
| AIDS | Acquired Immune Deficiency Syndrome |
| ASAP | As Soon As Possible |
| AWOL | Absent Without Leave (from the army, etc) |
| COBOL | Common Business Oriented Language (computers) |
| DAT | Digital Audio Tape |
| FIFA | Fédération Internationale de Football Association |
| GESTAPO | Geheime Staats-Polizei (Secret State-Police in Germany) |
| GULAG | Glavnoye Upravleniye Ispravitelno-Trudovykh Lagerei (Soviet labour camp) |
| LASER | Light Amplification by Simulated Emission of Radiation |
| LEM | Lunar Excursion Module |
| MAD | Mutual Assured Destruction (nuclear war term) |
| MASH | Mobile Army Surgical Hospital |
| NASA | National Aeronautics and Space Administration |
| NATO | North Atlantic Treaty Organization |
| NIMBY | Not In My Back Yard (used by protesters) |
| PLUTO | Pipe Line Under The Ocean |
| POW | Prisoner Of War |
| RADAR | Radio and Ranging |
| SCUBA | Self-contained Underwater Breathing Apparatus |
| SHAPE | Supreme Headquarters Allied Powers in Europe |
| TINA | There Is No Alternative (politics) |
| UFO | Unidentified Flying Object |
| WASP | White Anglo-Saxon Protestant |
| WYSIWYG | What You See Is What You Get (computers) |
| YUPPIE | Young Urban Professional |
| ZIP | Zone Improvement Plan (as in "zip code") |

## LONGEST WORDS AROUND THE WORLD

**GERMAN**  Donaudampfschiffahrtselectrizitätenhauptbetriebs-werkbauunterbeamtengesellschaft – club for subordinate officials of the management of the Danube steamboat company, 80 letters.

**ENGLISH**  Pneumonoultramicroscopicsilicovolcanoconiosis – a lung disease, 45 letters.

**SPANISH**  Superextraordinarisimo – extraordinary, 22 letters.

## TEN COMMONEST ENGLISH WORDS

| SPOKEN | WRITTEN |
|---|---|
| the | the |
| and | of |
| I | to |
| to | in |
| of | and |
| a | a |
| you | for |
| that | was |
| in | is |
| it | that |

**DID YOU KNOW?**
English has about 1 million words – more than any other language.

## MISLEADING WORDS

**PANAMA HATS** come from Ecuador – not Panama.

**KOALA BEARS** are not bears – they are marsupials.

**GUINEA PIGS** do not come from Guinea, and they are not pigs – they come from South America and are rodents.

**LEAD PENCILS** are not made from lead – they contain graphite, a type of carbon.

**TURKEYS** come from North America, not Turkey.

**FIREFLIES** are not flies – they are beetles.

**BLINDWORMS** are not sightless worms – they are legless lizards.

**THE CANARY ISLANDS** are named not after canaries but from *canes*, the Latin word for dogs that Roman invaders found there.

**RICE PAPER** is made not from rice but from the pith of a tree.

**PEANUTS** are a type of bean that grows underground – they are not true nuts at all.

## HOMONYMS

Homonyms are words that sound the same when spoken but have different spellings and meanings.

| WORD | WORD |
|------|------|
| accept (to take) | except (to exclude) |
| access (right of way) | excess (too much) |
| addition (something added) | edition (version of a book etc) |
| aid (help) | aide (assistant) |
| altar (platform in church) | alter (to change) |
| aural (by ear) | oral (by mouth) |
| base (basis, foundation) | bass (a lower part in music) |
| bazaar (marketplace, fair) | bizarre (strange) |
| boy (a male child) | buoy (a floating object) |
| brake (to slow and stop) | break (to fracture, damage) |
| chord (musical tones) | cord (thin rope) |
| cite (to quote) | sight (power of seeing) |
| coarse (rude, rough) | course (series, route) |
| dual (of two, double) | duel (fight between two) |
| idle (inactive) | idol (image of a god) |
| miner (one who mines) | minor (underage person) |
| naval (of the navy) | navel (umbilicus) |
| pedal (foot lever) | peddle (to sell) |
| plane (aeroplane, to level) | plain (ordinary; open land) |
| precede (to go before) | proceed (to continue) |
| principal (chief, head person) | principle (rule) |
| reign (of a monarch) | rein (part of a horse's harness) |
| stationary (fixed) | stationery (paper supplies) |
| stile (steps over a wall or fence) | style (manner of doing things) |
| weather (state of atmosphere) | whether (if) |

## POPULAR SYNONYMS

Synonyms are different words that mean the same.

**POLICE** Fuzz, boys in blue, cops, coppers, bobbies, Old Bill, rozzers, the law

**LAVATORY** Bog, toilet, WC, ladies, gents, cloakroom, powder-room, privy, latrine, loo, lavvie, washroom

**VOMIT** Be sick, spew, throw up, puke, barf, chuck up

**MONEY** Cash, dosh, dough, lolly, wherewithal, bread, brass, loot, readies, tin, dibs, spondulicks, filthy lucre

## PALINDROMES

A palindrome is a word or a phrase that reads the same backwards as well as forwards.

**MADAM I'M ADAM**

**POOR DAN IS IN A DROOP**

**ABLE WAS I ERE I SAW ELBA**

**RATS LIVE ON NO EVIL STAR**

**HANNAH**

**ANNA**

**NOT A TON**

**ROTOR**

## WORDS THAT CHANGED THEIR MEANINGS

The English language is constantly changing to accommodate new words and new meanings of old words. Some of the most surprising changes are those that have altered the original meaning of a word to such an extent that it is now used in a sense quite different from its original one – sometimes even meaning exactly the opposite!

**ACCIDENT** Until the 19th century, an accident was simply anything that happened, good or bad – hence we have such expressions as "by happy accident". Gradually, its meaning changed to mean something unexpected, and ultimately only an unfortunate occurrence.

**COMPANION** This word was once used with contempt to imply an attendant or person of inferior social position – thus English writer William Shakespeare refers to a "scurvy companion". Only gradually did it come to mean "a person who accompanies, irrespective of status".

**GIRL** Amazingly, from the 13th century, a "girl" could mean any young person, whether female or male! To distinguish them, a female was sometimes known as a "gay girl", and a male as a "knave girl".

**IDIOT** An "idiot" was once the word used to describe an ordinary person; it became applied to a layman, as contrasted with a clergyman, and – since few people outside the church were educated – came to mean an uneducated person, and hence an ignorant or foolish one.

**MANUFACTURE** "Manufacture" means literally "hand-made", but once mechanization was introduced into factories, it came to mean the opposite – "machine-made".

**NAUGHTY** In medieval times, "naughty" derived from "naught" and came to mean "having nothing", or "needy". Until the 17th century it meant "inferior", then "morally bad" – but gradually modified to suggest the minor misdemeanours of children, rather than serious criminal activities.

**NICE** The Latin word *nescius* meaning "ignorant" was the root of the English "nice", meaning "foolish". Gradually, in the 15th century it came to mean "coy" and in the 16th century "fastidious" – as in such expressions as "a nice distinction". By the 18th century, nice had come to mean "good" or "agreeable".

**NOON** "Noon" came from "nones", the ninth hour after sunrise, between midday and 3.00 p.m., according to the time of year, a time reserved for praying in medieval monasteries. By the 12th century, prayers were recited earlier, so "noon" became midday.

**QUILT** A "quilt" was once the bedding under a person, from the Latin *culcita*, a mattress; by the 19th century, it had come to mean the covering on the sleeper.

**SKIRT** "Skirt" derives from the Old English word, *scyrte* – which meant a "shirt". How the distinction between the two came about remains something of a mystery.

**VILLAIN** A "villain" was simply a farm labourer, and hence an uneducated person, long before it came to imply a dishonest one.

**WORRY** The original meaning of "worry" survives in the expression used to describe a dog attacking or "worrying" sheep; it formerly meant "to choke".

# LANGUAGE

**DID YOU KNOW?** In silent Aboriginal hunting language, a closed hand slowly opening shows a kangaroo is near.

## EUROPEAN LANGUAGES

Europe has nine official working languages. The percentage indicates the number of mother-tongue speakers:

German (22.1%) • English (17.5%) Italian (16.8%) • French (16.5%) Castilian Spanish (8.5%) • Dutch, including Flemish (5.9%) • Portuguese (3.1%) • Greek (3%) • Danish (1.5%)

**DID YOU KNOW?** Basque, which is spoken in southern France and northern Spain is not related to any other language.

## AMERICAN LANGUAGES

**WHISTLE TALK** The men of the native Mazateco people of Mexico can hold a conversation just by whistling.

**FEWEST CONSONANTS** Mohawk, an American Indian language, has only seven consonants – English has 24!

**NO FUTURE** The Hopi people have no way of expressing the future or past and can only indicate how true a statement is to them. So instead of "he will walk" they say "I expect walking".

## AUSTRALASIAN LANGUAGES

**OFFICIAL PIDGIN** In Papua New Guinea, Pidgin English has become an official national language. Known as Tok Pisin (talk pidgin) it is spoken by more than one million people and even used for road signs and newspapers.

**SHORTEST ALPHABET** Rotokas, from the Solomon Islands, has only 11 letters.

**SPECIALIST WORDS** The people of the Pacific Solomon Islands have nine words for the ripening stages of the coconut.

## ASIAN LANGUAGES

**WRITE IT DOWN!** China has six main languages, and many more dialects making it difficult for people from different regions to talk to each other. However, as all Chinese speakers share the same written language they can communicate in writing.

**MOST VOWEL SOUNDS** English has about 20 vowel sounds, but Sedang, a language spoken in Vietnam, has 50.

**LEAST VOWELS, MOST CONSONANTS** Many of the languages of the Caucasus mountains of southern Russia, such as Abhaz, have only one type of vowel, and more than 70 consonants, compared with the 24 in spoken English.

**MOST COMPLEX SCRIPT** Written Chinese has more than 50,000 signs, but only a few thousand are used.

**LONGEST ALPHABET** The language of Cambodia has 74 letters, compared with only 26 in English.

## MADE-UP LANGUAGES

**ESPERANTO** Devised in 1887 by Lazarus Ludwig Zamenhof of Poland, this phonetic language with 28 letters is written as it sounds and has no irregular grammar rules. More than a million people have learned to speak it.

**IDO** This revised and simplified version of Esperanto was introduced in 1907.

**VOLAPÜK** Devised by German Johann Schleyer in 1879, Volapük was based on German.

**INTERLINGUA** A mix of Latin, English, French, and German, Interlingua was devised by Italian Giuseppe Peano in 1908. Interest was shortlived.

**DID YOU KNOW?** The official language of the people of Mongolia is called Khalka, and is spoken by Mongolia's population of 2.5 million.

## MOST SPOKEN LANGUAGES

| COUNTRY | MILLIONS OF SPEAKERS |
|---|---|
| Chinese (Mandarin) | 1,034 |
| English | 500 |
| Hindustani | 478 |
| Spanish | 413 |
| Russian | 280 |
| Arabic | 230 |

## ENGLISH SPEAKERS

| COUNTRY | NUMBER OF SPEAKERS |
|---|---|
| USA | 228,770,000 |
| UK | 57,190,000 |
| Canada | 18,112,000 |
| Australia | 15,538,000 |
| South Africa | 3,800,000 |
| Ireland | 3,540,000 |
| New Zealand | 3,290,000 |

## AFRICAN LANGUAGES

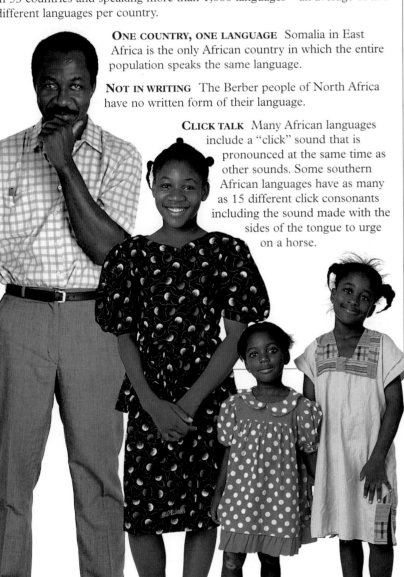

**MANY TONGUES** Africa is home to many hundreds of different peoples living in 53 countries and speaking more than 1,000 languages – an average of five different languages per country.

**ONE COUNTRY, ONE LANGUAGE** Somalia in East Africa is the only African country in which the entire population speaks the same language.

**NOT IN WRITING** The Berber people of North Africa have no written form of their language.

**CLICK TALK** Many African languages include a "click" sound that is pronounced at the same time as other sounds. Some southern African languages have as many as 15 different click consonants including the sound made with the sides of the tongue to urge on a horse.

## SPECIALIST LANGUAGES

**MORSE CODE** In 1844, American Samuel Morse invented a means of communicating over long distances using a transmitter, a receiver, a single wire, and a code of dots and dashes. This is known as Morse code.

**SIGN LANGUAGE** People who cannot hear or speak can communicate through sign language. Signs may stand for whole words as well as individual letters. There are many different sign language systems around the world.

**SEMAPHORE** Until the early 1900s, ships would communicate by means of semaphore flag signals. Today, it remains a quick method of visual signalling and is still occasionally used for passing messages between ships sailing close to each other.

**WAR LANGUAGE** During World War II, the US Marines foxed the Japanese by using Navaho Indians to transmit radio messages in their native language.

**MOTHER-IN-LAW LANGUAGE** Some Australian Aborigines have a special language for speaking to in-laws. In Djirbal, Queensland, the basic language is known as Guwa, but when a man wants to talk to his mother-in-law he speaks a language called Dyalnguy.

**RHYMING SLANG** Cockney rhyming slang probably began in the 19th century as a secret language among thieves in the East End of London. Typical examples are *apples and pears* (stairs), *plates of meat* (feet), *Scapa Flow* (go), *butcher's hook* (look), and *loaf of bread* (head). Often, only the first, non-rhyming half of the phrase is used so strangers cannot understand. Phrases such as "have a butcher's", "use your loaf", and "let's scarper" (from *Scapa Flow*) are now accepted as part of the English language.

**BACK SLANG** Children sometimes develop secret languages. In back slang they say words backwards. The British word "yob" is back slang for "boy".

## BODY LANGUAGE

The way you move your body can mean different things around the world:

**FINGER POINTING** In Hong Kong, to signal to a person, you reach out, palm down, and flutter your fingers. Only animals may be beckoned with a finger.

**FEET** In Pakistan, it is rude to show the soles of your feet or point a foot when you are sitting on the floor.

**HEAD SHAKING** In Sri Lanka, shaking your head means yes, and nodding it up and down means no.

**TEETH** In Japan, it is rude to show your teeth, so when Japanese women laugh they cover their mouth.

**HANDS ON HIPS** In Indonesia, talking with your hands on your hips is a sign of rudeness or anger.

# BOOKS

## KEY AUTHORS

| AUTHOR | DATES | NATIONALITY | FAMOUS WORKS |
|---|---|---|---|
| Geoffrey Chaucer | 1343–1400 | English | *The Canterbury Tales* |
| John Bunyan | 1628–1688 | English | *The Pilgrim's Progress* |
| William Wordsworth | 1770–1850 | English | *Lyrical Ballards* |
| Jane Austen | 1775–1817 | English | *Pride and Prejudice* |
| Victor Hugo | 1802–1885 | French | *Les Misérables* |
| Herman Melville | 1819–1891 | American | *Moby Dick* |
| Feyodor Dostoyevsky | 1821–1881 | Russian | *Crime and Punishment* |
| Leo Tolstoy | 1828–1910 | Russian | *War and Peace* |
| Joseph Conrad | 1857–1924 | English | *Heart of Darkness* |
| Rabindranath Tagore | 1861–1941 | Indian | *Gitanjali* |
| James Joyce | 1882–1941 | Irish | *Ulysses* |
| Franz Kafka | 1883–1924 | Czechoslovakian | *The Trial* |
| D.H. Lawrence | 1885–1930 | English | *Sons and Lovers* |
| F. Scott Fitzgerald | 1896–1940 | American | *The Great Gatsby* |
| Günter Grass | b.1927 | German | *The Tin Drum* |

## GREAT ANIMAL STORIES

| BOOK | AUTHOR |
|---|---|
| *Black Beauty* | Anna Sewell |
| *Animal Farm* | George Orwell |
| *Winnie the Pooh* | A. A. Milne |
| *The Wind in the Willows* | Kenneth Graham |
| *Peter Rabbit* stories | Beatrix Potter |
| *Charlotte's Web* | E. B. White |

## TOP BOOK PRODUCERS

This list gives the total number of new titles, editions, and reprints in 1997.

| COUNTRY | TITLES PUBLISHED |
|---|---|
| UK | 101,504 |
| China | 73,923 |
| Germany | 62,277 |
| USA | 49,276 |

## CHILDREN'S BOOK ILLUSTRATORS

| NAME | COUNTRY | WELL-KNOWN BOOKS |
|---|---|---|
| Alfred Bestall (1892–1986) | UK | Rupert stories |
| Quentin Blake (b.1932) | UK | Illustrations to Roald Dahl |
| Raymond Briggs (b.1934) | UK | *The Snowman* |
| Walter Crane 1845–1915) | UK | *The Baby's Opera* |
| Hergé (Georges Rémi) (1907–1983) | Belgium | *Tintin* books |
| Henriette Willebeek Le Mair (1889-1966) | Netherlands | *Our Old Nursery Rhymes* |
| Beatrix Potter (1866–1943) | UK | *Peter Rabbit* books |
| Ernest Shepard (1879–1976) | UK | *The Wind in the Willows* |
| Albert Uderzo (b.1927) | France | *Astérix* books |

## ALL-TIME BESTSELLERS

**THE BIBLE** No one really knows how many copies of the Bible have been printed, sold, or distributed. In 1992, the Bible Society estimated that six billion had been produced in more than 2,000 languages and dialects – equivalent to one for every person on Earth. Whatever the precise figure, it is the bestselling book of all time.

**QUOTATIONS FROM THE WORKS OF MAO ZEDONG** Chairman Mao's *Little Red Book* has sold 800 million, but could scarcely fail to become a bestseller: between the years 1966 and 1971 it was compulsory for every Chinese adult to own a copy.

**AMERICAN SPELLING BOOK BY NOAH WEBSTER** First published in 1783, this reference book by American wordsmith Noah Webster (1758–1843) – of *Webster's Dictionary* fame – remained a bestseller throughout the 19th century, selling about 100 million copies.

**THE GUINNESS BOOK OF RECORDS** First published in 1955, *The Guinness Book of Records* stands out as the greatest modern publishing achievement. In the UK alone there have been 40 editions, and there have been many foreign language editions. In all, it has sold about 80 million copies.

**THE MCGUFFEY READERS** Published from 1853, these US textbooks were compiled by William Holmes McGuffey (1800–1873), and sold 60 million.

**DID YOU KNOW?** The popular children's story, *Alice in Wonderland*, was translated into European languages soon after its publication in 1865. Today, it has been translated into almost every language in the world, even Esperanto.

## BESTSELLING CHILDREN'S AUTHORS

| AUTHOR (DATES) | COUNTRY | EXAMPLE OF WORK | TOTAL SALES |
|---|---|---|---|
| René Goscinny (1926–1977) Albert Uderzo (b.1927) | France | *Astérix the Gaul* | 250,000,000 |
| Hergé (Georges Rémi) (1907–1983) | Belgium | *Tintin* | 150,000,000 |
| Enid Blyton (1897–1968) | UK | *Noddy* | 100,000,000 |

**DID YOU KNOW?** The total sales of Enid Blyton's works add up to more than 100,000,000 making her the bestselling English-language author of the 20th century.

| | | | |
|---|---|---|---|
| Dr Seuss (Theodor Seuss Geisel) (1904–1991) | USA | *The Cat in the Hat* | 100,000,000 |
| Beatrix Potter (1866–1943) | UK | *The Tale of Peter Rabbit* | 50,000,000 |
| Rev. W. Awdry (1911–1997) | UK | *Thomas the Tank Engine* | 50,000,000 |
| Mark Twain (Samuel Langhorne Clemens) (1835–1910) | USA | *Adventures of Tom Sawyer* | 40,000,000 |

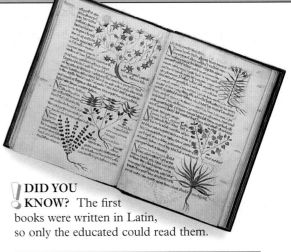

**DID YOU KNOW?** The first books were written in Latin, so only the educated could read them.

## UNUSUAL BOOKS

*Harnessing the Earthworm* by Thomas J. Barrett, 1949

*Wall-Paintings by Snake Charmers in Tanganyika* by Hans Cory, 1953

*Canadian National Egg Laying Contests* by F. C. Elford & A. G. Taylor, 1924

*Cluck! The True Story of Chickens in the Cinema* by Jon-Stephen Fink, 1981

*Scalping in America* by George Frederici, 1906

*Fish Who Answer The Telephone* by Yury Petrovich Frolov, 1937

*The Toothbrush: Its Use and Abuse* by Isador Hirschfeld, 1939

*The Rhinoceros in Art* by T. H. Clark, 1986

*Why Bring That Up? A Guide To and From Seasickness* by Joseph Franklin Montague, 1936

*Frolic and Fun with Egg-Shells* by Meredith Nugent, 1903

*Little-known Sisters of Well-known Men* by Sarah G. Pomeroy, 1912

*The Dentist in Art* by Jens Jorgen Pindborg and L. Marvitz, 1961

## BOOKS BOUND NOT TO PLEASE

**BOUND UP** John Horwood, a murderer, was hanged on 13 April 1821. His skin was used to bind a book describing the dissection of his body by surgeon Richard Smith.

**SKIN DEEP** The Albert Memorial Library, Exeter, UK, possesses a copy of John Milton's *Poetical Works* (1830) bound in the skin of a murderer called George Cudmore.

**ULTIMATE AUTOBIOGRAPHY** The Boston Athenaeum, USA, has a copy of James Allen's book, *Narrative of the Life of James Allen, alias George Walton, alias Jonas Pierce, alias James H. York, alias Burley Grove, the Highwayman, Being His Death-bed Confession to the Warden of the Massachusetts State Prison*, published in Boston, Massachusetts, in 1837, and bound in the author's own skin.

## TYPES OF REFERENCE BOOK

**ALMANAC** An annual calendar of dates and events, originally astronomical data, but now with useful statistical and other information.

**ATLAS** Book of maps. A road atlas is a book of maps used by travellers.

**BILINGUAL DICTIONARY** Dictionary that gives the translation of words and phrases to and from other languages, for example, a French-English, English-French dictionary.

**CHRONOLOGY** A dictionary of dated events.

**DICTIONARY** An alphabetical list of words and their meanings.

**DIRECTORY** An alphabetical list of names and addresses of people or organizations.

**ENCYCLOPEDIA** An information book, often in many volumes, with articles on subjects, usually arranged alphabetically.

**GAZETTEER** A geographical book that lists and describes countries, cities, and towns.

**GLOSSARY** List of words and phrases used in a particular field or subject.

**MANUAL** A subject-specific book that explains in detail how something works or how to do things. Usually includes diagrams.

**PHRASEBOOK** Book for travellers, with translations of words and phrases into and from a foreign language.

**THESAURUS** A book that organizes and groups words that have similar meanings.

**TRAVEL GUIDE** Book of information about a particular country or area.

**YEARBOOK** Annual reference book summarizing information about events of the previous year. Special yearbooks containing statistical information about a country, for example, are often called abstracts.

**DID YOU KNOW?**
Before printing became possible in the 15th century, scribes and artists were appointed to write out every copy of a book by hand. This was a very lengthy process!

# THE PRESS

## TOP-SELLING DAILY NEWSPAPERS

Some newspapers print two daily editions. In these cases, the morning figure has been used.

| NEWSPAPER | COUNTRY | AVERAGE DAILY CIRCULATION |
|---|---|---|
| *Yomiuri Shimbun* | Japan | 10,000,000 |
| *Asahi Shimbun* | Japan | 8,500,000 |
| *Sichuan Ribao* | China | 8,000,000 |
| *Bild-Zeitung* | Germany | 4,892,000 |
| *Mainichi Shimbun* | Japan | 4,500,000 |
| *The Sun* | UK | 3,767,941 |
| *Argumenty y Fakty* | Russia | 3,600,000 |
| *Nihon Keizai Shimbun* | Japan | 3,000,000 |
| *Chunichi Shimbun* | Japan | 2,900,000 |
| *Gongren Ribao* | China | 2,500,000 |
| *The Mirror* | UK | 2,321,608 |
| *The Daily Mail* | UK | 2,247,298 |
| *Renmin Ribao* | China | 2,150,000 |
| *Wall Street Journal* | USA | 1,783,500 |
| *Wenhui Bao* | China | 1,700,000 |
| *USA Today* | USA | 1,591,600 |
| *Trud* | Russia | 1,400,000 |
| *Daily Express* | UK | 1,199,392 |
| *Daily Telegraph* | UK | 1,096,583 |

## NEWSPAPER MILESTONES

**59 BC** First handwritten newspapers are produced in Rome. Called *Acta diurna* (daily acts), they report on events of the day.

**AD 618** Chinese civil servants in Peking circulate newsletter on court affairs.

**1450s** German Johannes Gutenberg (c.1398–1468) develops the first printing press using movable type.

**1513** Newsbooks appear.

**1615** First printed newpapers in Germany.

**1645** The world's oldest continuously published weekly newspaper, the *Postock inrikes tidningar* appears in Sweden.

**1703** Circulation begins of the Austrian *Wiener Zeitung*. It will become the world's oldest surviving daily newspaper.

**1704** *The Boston Newsletter* is the first official newspaper in the USA.

**1815** The British newspaper *The Times* prints 5,000 copies per day.

**1858** German P. J. Reuter (1816–1899) starts a foreign news agency.

**1910–1920s** American publisher Edward Scripps (1854–1926) pioneers ownership of popular working-class newspapers.

**1962** First Sunday colour supplement published in UK by *Sunday Times*.

**1986** *Today* (UK) becomes first national daily printed in colour.

## MOST DAILY NEWSPAPERS

Some countries have a high number of daily newspapers, but as each serves a relatively small area they have only low circulations. In total, the USA has 1,533 daily newspapers, but only four of them have daily sales of more than 1,000,000.

| COUNTRY | NO. OF DAILY NEWSPAPERS |
|---|---|
| India | 1,802 |
| USA | 1,533 |
| Germany | 406 |
| Turkey | 400 |
| Brazil | 320 |
| Mexico | 310 |
| Russia | 292 |
| Pakistan | 223 |
| Argentina | 190 |
| Greece | 168 |
| Japan | 121 |
| Canada | 107 |
| UK | 103 |
| Sweden | 98 |
| Czech Republic | 90 |
| Venezuela | 89 |
| Spain | 85 |
| Norway | 83 |
| France | 80 |
| Switzerland | 79 |

## UNUSUAL NEWSPAPERS

**LARGEST** On 14 June 1993, the Belgian newspaper *Het Volk* had pages measuring 142 × 99.5 cm (55.9 × 39.2 in) – more than six times the area of an ordinary broadsheet.

**HEAVIEST** The Sunday edition of the *New York Times* for 14 September 1987, contained 1,612 pages and weighed 5.4 kg (12 lb).

**SMALLEST** The smallest regular publication is the *Daily Banner*, first published in 1876 in Oregon, USA, which measures 9.5 × 7.6 cm (3.75 × 3 in).

**WORST-SELLING** In 1965, the London publisher of the *Commonwealth Sentinel* forgot to arrange distribution, and sold one copy of 50,000 printed.

**MOST MISTAKES IN ONE STORY** On 22 August 1978, *The Times* contained 97 misprints in one story about the Pope. He was referred to throughout the article as "the Pop".

## COMIC BOOK HEROES AND VILLAINS

| CHARACTER | PUBLICATION | COUNTRY | DATE APPEARED |
|---|---|---|---|
| Tintin | *Le Vingtième Siècle* | Belgium | 1929 |
| Desperate Dan | *Dandy* | UK | 1937 |
| Superman | *Action Comics* No.1 | USA | 1938 |
| Batman | *Detective Comics* No.27 | USA | 1939 |
| The Human Torch | *Marvel Comics* No.1 | USA | 1939 |
| Captain Marvel | *Whiz Comics* No.1 | USA | 1940 |
| The Green Lantern | *All American Comics* No.16 | USA | 1940 |
| The Flash | *Flash Comics* No. 1 | USA | 1940 |
| Catwoman | *Batman* No.1 | USA | 1940 |
| The Joker | *Batman* No.1 | USA | 1940 |
| Robin | *Detective Comics* No. 38 | USA | 1940 |
| The Spectre | *More Fun Comics* No.52 | USA | 1940 |
| Wonder Woman | *All-Star Comics* No.8 | USA | 1941 |
| Captain America | *Captain America Comics* No.1 | USA | 1941 |
| The Penguin | *Detective Comics* No.58 | USA | 1941 |
| Dennis the Menace | *Beano* | UK | 1951 |
| Astérix the Gaul | *Pilote* | France | 1959 |
| Supergirl | *Action Comics* No.25 | USA | 1959 |
| Spiderman | *Amazing Fantasy* No.15 | USA | 1962 |
| Silver Surfer | *Silver Surfer* No.1 | USA | 1968 |

## TYPES OF NEWSPAPER

**BROADSHEET** Newspaper with a large format, usually 61 x 38cm (24 x 15in).

**FEATURE** A non-news article.

**HARD NEWS** Up-to-the minute news.

**HEADLINE** The phrase at the top of an article summarizing its subject.

**LEADER** Article giving opinion of the newspaper.

**OBITUARY** Biography of a famous person who has recently died.

**POPULAR PRESS** Newspapers aiming to provide lively news and entertainment for a mass readership.

**QUALITY PRESS** Newspapers aiming to provide serious news, information, and analysis.

**SOFT NEWS** Background news, or news that is not the latest.

**TABLOID** Newspaper with a smaller format – about half the size of broadsheets.

## MAGAZINE FIRSTS

**FIRST-EVER** *Mercure Galant*, a gossip magazine, was first published in Paris in March 1672.

**BRITISH MAGAZINE** *The Gentleman's Journal*, a monthly magazine, was launched in January 1692, but ceased two years later.

**WOMEN'S MAGAZINE** *The Ladies' Mercury* was first published in London on 27 June 1693.

**AMERICAN MAGAZINE** Published in Philadelphia, USA, *The American Magazine* probably began with the issue of 13 February 1741.

**CHILDREN'S MAGAZINE** *The Lilliputian Magazine* first appeared in June 1751 and ran for just over a year. It was published in London and had a page size of just 10 x 6 cm (4 x 2.5 in). The first in the USA was the *Children's Magazine*, published in Hartford, Connecticut, in January 1789.

**FASHION MAGAZINE** The Paris magazine *Le Cabinet des Modes* was first published in 1785.

**FIRST WITH A FREE RECORD** The November 1955 issue of the US magazine *Pageant* contained a recording of Jaye P. Morgan singing *If You Don't Want My Love*.

## MOST VALUABLE AMERICAN COMICS

**ACTION COMICS NO. 1** Published in June 1938, the first issue of *Action Comics* marked the original appearance of Superman and is now worth $180,000.

**DETECTIVE COMICS NO. 27** Issued in May 1939, the $160,000-*Detective Comics* is prized as the first comic book to feature Batman.

**SUPERMAN NO. 1** The first comic book devoted to Superman, reprinting the original *Action Comics* story, was published in summer 1939 and is worth $125,000.

**MARVEL COMICS NO. 1** The Human Torch and other heroes were first introduced in the $108,000-issue dated October 1939.

**WHIZ COMICS NO. 1** First published in February 1940 – and confusingly numbered "2" – it was the first comic book to feature Captain Marvel. It is now worth $63,000.

**BATMAN NO. 1** Published in Spring 1940, and now worth $62,000, *Batman* was the first comic devoted solely to Batman.

**ALL AMERICAN COMICS NO. 16** The Green Lantern made his debut in the $60,000, July 1940 issue of *All American Comics*.

**CAPTAIN AMERICA COMICS NO. 1** Published in March 1941, this was the original comic book in which Captain America appeared. Its value is estimated at $56,000.

**FLASH COMICS NO. 1** Dated January 1940, and featuring The Flash, this issue is rare because it was produced in small numbers for publicity. It is worth about $55,000. The comic is also unique as the second issue was retitled *Whiz Comics*.

# ART and ARTISTS

## MOST EXPENSIVE AUCTIONED PHOTOGRAPHS

All these photographs were sold in US dollars, except the most expensive, which was sold in France for F. Fr 3,700,000.

**Félix teynard (1817–1892)** The Frenchman's photograph collection *Egypte et Nubie: Sites et monuments les plus intéressants pour l'étude de l'art et de l'histoire*, (1858), was sold in 1990 by Laurin Guilloux Buffetaud Tailleur, in Paris, for the equivalent of $707,000.

**Edward S. curtis (1868–1952)** Curtis's collection *The North American Indian*, (1907–1930), was sold in 1995 by Sotheby's, New York, for $662,500. It had previously been sold by Christie's for $464,500, and in 1992 for $396,000.

**Alfred stieglitz (1864–1946)** The world's most expensive single print, *Georgia O'Keeffe: A Portrait – Hands with Thimble*, (1930), was sold in 1993 by Christie's, New York, USA, for $398,500. A collection by the same artist, *Equivalents (21)*, taken in the 1920s, was sold in 1989 for $396,000.

## FAMOUS ART GALLERIES

| GALLERY | FOUNDED |
| --- | --- |
| Topkapi Palace Museum, Istanbul, Turkey | 1454 |
| Uffizi Gallery, Florence, Italy | 1564 |
| Louvre Museum, Paris, France | 1500s |
| Hermitage Museum, St Petersburg, Russia | 1764 |
| Kunsthistorisches Museum, Vienna, Austria | 1781 |
| Academy Gallery, Florence, Italy | 1784 |
| Prado Museum, Madrid, Spain | 1819 |
| National Gallery, London, UK | 1824 |
| National Gallery, Scotland, UK | 1850 |
| National Gallery, Ottawa, Canada | 1880 |
| Tate Gallery, London, UK | 1897 |

## ART FAKES AND FORGERIES

Fakes are works done in the style of an artist; forgeries are copies of the original.

**Sitting pretty** The world's most valuable painting, Leonardo da Vinci's *Mona Lisa*, was stolen on 21 August 1911 by Vicenzo Peruggia, who strolled out of the Louvre with it under his arm. During the two years it was gone, forger Yves Chaudron painted six replicas, which he sold for $300,000 each.

**What a corker!** In 1929, British writer Evelyn Waugh and a friend, Tom Mitford, invented a painter they called Bruno Hat. They held a successful exhibition of his works, which consisted of bits of cork stuck on canvas.

**Dutch dupe** Han van Meegeren (1889–1947), a Dutch painter, sold numerous fakes which he claimed were by Vermeer and other famous Dutch painters. He made a vast fortune.

*THE THINKER BY AUGUSTE RODIN (1840–1917)*

**DID YOU KNOW?** Painted by Leonardo da Vinci (1452–1519), the *Mona Lisa* was stolen from the Louvre, Paris, in 1911 and took two years to find. Mona Lisa's eyes seem to follow you however you look at her.

## ARTISTS' DEATHS

**Henri gaudier-brzeska** This French sculptor was killed in battle aged 23.

**Vincent van gogh** The tempestuous Dutch painter attempted suicide many times, and finally shot himself aged 37.

**Mark rothko** An American abstract painter, Rothko slashed his elbows in 1970.

**Elizabeth siddal** The talented artist and wife of painter and poet Dante Gabriel Rossetti, died aged 32. Her coffin was dug up by Rossetti to retrieve the poems he had buried with her.

## TALLEST STATUES

**Chief crazy horse** This 172-m (563-ft) high statue on Thunderhead Mountain, USA, was begun in 1948 by Korczak Ziolkowski and is being continued by his children.

**Buddha** The tallest Buddha statue is in Japan and measures 120-m (394-ft) high.

**The indian rope trick** Sculptor Calle Örnemark's statue is 103 m (337 ft) high and was built in Sweden.

## KEY PAINTERS

| ARTIST | DATES | NATIONALITY | FAMOUS WORKS |
| --- | --- | --- | --- |
| Leonardo da Vinci | 1452–1519 | Italian | *Mona Lisa* |
| Michelangelo | 1475–1564 | Italian | Sistine chapel ceiling |
| El Greco | 1541–1614 | Greek | *Burial of Count Orgaz* |
| Rembrandt Van Rijn | 1606–1669 | Dutch | *The Night Watch* |
| Francisco Goya | 1746–1828 | Spanish | *Maja Nude/Clothed* |
| Sir John Millais | 1829–1896 | British | *Ophelia* |
| Edgar Degas | 1834–1917 | French | *The Rehearsal* |
| James Whistler | 1834–1903 | American | *Symphony in White* |
| Paul Cézanne | 1839–1906 | French | *Les Grandes Baigneuses* |
| Claude Monet | 1840–1926 | French | *Waterlilies* |
| Vincent van Gogh | 1853–1890 | Dutch | *Sunflowers* |
| Pablo Picasso | 1881–1973 | Spanish | *Self-portrait* |
| Salvador Dali | 1904–1989 | Spanish | *The Persistence of Memory* |

## WORLD'S LARGEST PAINTINGS

**IL PARADISO** Painted by Iacopo Tintoretto (1518–1594) and his son Domenico (1562–1635) in the Palazzo Ducale, Venice, Italy, this painting measures 7 × 22 m (23 × 72 ft).

**INTERIOR OF WESTMINSTER ABBEY** French painter Jean-Pierre Alaux's painting, *Interior of Westminster Abbey* in the Louvre, Paris, measures 19 × 40 m (62 × 131 ft).

**THE TRIUMPH OF PEACE AND LIBERTY** This painting by Sir James Thornhill (1676–1734) is the largest in the UK. It can be seen on the ceiling of the Royal Naval College, Greenwich, and measures 32 m (106 ft) by 16 m (51 ft) – almost twice the area of a tennis court!

**PANORAMA OF THE MISSISSIPPI** American self-taught artist, John Banvard (1815–1891) painted this from sketches made along the river. Measuring 4 m (12 ft) high and 1,524 m (5,000 ft) long, it was taken to England in 1848 but was later destroyed by fire.

**THE BATTLE OF GETTYSBURG** Completed in 1883 by Paul Dominique Philippoteaux, this painting is 21 m (70 ft) high and 125 m (410 ft) long.

## MOST EXPENSIVE PAINTINGS EVER AUCTIONED

Picasso and van Gogh are notable for their entries in this list.

| ARTIST/WORK/DATE SOLD | PRICE PAID |
| --- | --- |
| Vincent van Gogh, *Portrait of Dr Gachet*, Christie's, New York, 15 May 1990 | $75,000,000 |
| Pierre-Auguste Renoir, *Au Moulin de la Galette*, Sotheby's, New York, 17 May 1990 | $71,000,000 |
| Pablo Picasso, *Les noces de Pierrette*, Binoche et Godeau, Paris, 30 November 1989 | F. Fr 315,000,000 |
| Vincent van Gogh, *Irises* Sotheby's, New York, 11 November 1987 | $49,000,000 |
| Pablo Picasso, *Self Portrait: Yo Picasso*, Sotheby's, New York, 9 May 1989 | $43,500,000 |

## WESTERN ART STYLES

**RENAISSANCE** Means "rebirth" – art of the 15th and 16th centuries that replaced medieval styles and revived the art of the Greek and Roman period.

**BAROQUE** The ornate style first popular in Italy in the 17th and 18th century.

**NEO-CLASSICISM** Style of the 18th century that models itself on Classical (Greek and Roman) art.

**ROMANTICISM** Late 18th- and early 19th-century style that explores emotion.

**REALISM** A 19th-century style that depicted real life.

**PRE-RAPHAELITISM** Invented in 1848, a short-lived but influential style founded in medieval history and mythology.

**IMPRESSIONISM** Developed in France and named in 1874, it has became one of the most appreciated art styles.

**POST-IMPRESSIONISM** A development from Impressionism, including the "Pointillism" (dot painting) of Seurat, and others.

**ART NOUVEAU** The flowing ornamental style of the late 19th and early 20th centuries.

**SYMBOLISM** An attempt by late 19th-century artists to link the real and the spiritual worlds in their work.

**EXPRESSIONISM** Early 20th-century style in which the emotions of the painter are powerfully expressed.

**CUBISM** The main abstract style (art that is not a direct representation of a subject), concerned with shape and colour.

**ART DECO** The angular decorative style popular in the 1930s.

**SURREALISM** A style that emerged between World Wars I and II, in which dreams and fantasy are explored.

**POP ART** A style that began in the 1950s, using images from popular culture (films, comics, advertising, etc).

**PERFORMANCE ART** Dramatic art in which the artists themselves become involved.

**ENVIRONMENTAL ART** Art in which the landscape is decorated or altered.

## ODD ARTYFACTS

**UPSIDE DOWN** In 1961, it was discovered that Henri Matisse's painting, *Le Bateau* (*The Boat*), in the Museum of Modern Art, New York, had been hanging upside-down for two months. None of the 116,000 visitors had noticed.

**SWEET AND SOUR** Spanish surrealist painter Salvador Dali pioneered "futurist" cookery, which included Herrings and Raspberry Jam, Sausage with Nougat, Pineapple with Sardines, and Cooked Salami immersed in Hot Black Coffee.

**PRETTY PAUL** Painter Paul Cézanne taught his parrot to say, "Paul Cézanne is a great painter!"

**SUPER SPAM** At Rhode Island College's first Spam Art Festival, the winning entry was *Spamhenge*, a spam model!

# GREAT COLLECTIONS

## COLLECTABLES

People collect items, small or large, for fun or because they have monetary value.

Animal objects • Antiques Art • Autographs • Beer mats • Cars • Coins • Comics Costumes • Dolls • Erasers Matchboxes • Militaria and weapons • Personalia (items that belonged to famous people) • Pens • Postcards Posters • Rocks and minerals Shells • Sports equipment Stamps • Teapots • Teddy bears • Programmes • Toys

**DID YOU KNOW?** Stamps come in all shapes and sizes. Tonga has produced banana-shaped stamps; Norfolk Island has made them island-shaped; and Sri Lanka has issued triangular stamps!

**DID YOU KNOW?** Your stamp collection would become very sought-after should you acquire an 1856 British Guiana One Cent, because only one was ever made. It was sold in 1980 for $850,000!

## STRANGE MUSEUMS

**BARBIE DOLL HALL OF FAME** Palo Alto, California, USA. A collection devoted to the children's doll Barbie and her accessories from 1959 to the present.

**COCKROACH HALL OF FAME** Plano, Texas, USA. Record-breaking cockroaches, and insects dressed as famous people.

**MUSEUM OF DOG COLLARS** Leeds Castle, Maidstone, Kent, UK. A collection of dog collars, most of them dating from the Middle Ages.

**FISHERMAN'S FRIEND MUSEUM** Fleetwood, Lancashire, England. A museum devoted to the menthol and eucalyptus throat lozenge, invented in 1865.

**MEDIEVAL CRIME MUSEUM** Rothenburg, Germany. Medieval crime, punishment, and torture implements.

**MUSEUM OF THE MOUSETRAP** Bedwas, near Caerphilly, Wales, UK. A collection of more than 150 mousetraps from Ancient Egypt to the present.

**NUT MUSEUM** Old Lyme, Connecticut, USA. Nut carvings, 2.4-m (8-ft) long nutcrackers, and other nut-related exhibits.

**POTTER'S MUSEUM OF CURIOSITY** Jamaica Inn, Cornwall, England. Hundreds of stuffed kittens, rabbits, and other animals are clothed and arranged in various scenes, such as a tea party and a wedding.

**WORLD'S SMALLEST MUSEUM** Weslaco, Texas, USA. A single room containing a collection of antique telephones.

**PLAYING CARD MUSEUM** Antwerp, Belgium. Traces the history of playing cards from the 15th century to the present, and contains some of the earliest cards and printing presses.

**FREIAMT STRAW MUSEUM** Wohlen, Switzerland. Celebrates the straw-plaiting industry, at its height in the 18th and 19th centuries. Crafts produced during that period are on display.

**APPLE AND PEAR MUSEUM** Château Briqebec, France. Exhibits show traditional and modern methods of cider and perry production.

## TIPS FOR PRESERVING YOUR COLLECTION

**STORE IT SAFELY** Keep your collection away from food and drink.

**KEEP IT COOL** Don't store comics, books, cards, or stickers in sunlight – they will fade!

**LAY IT OUT** Arrange your collection in boxes or books to keep it together and clean.

## UNUSUAL THINGS SOLD AT AUCTIONS

**EYE EYE** A box of 300 glass eyes, sold at Christie's, London, on 11 July 1997 for £2,760.

**SWEDISH SKULL** The skull of the Swedish philosopher Emanuel Swedenborg, sold at Sotheby's, London, 6 March 1978 for £1,500. It was bought by the Stockholm Royal Academy of Science, which reunited it with the rest of his body, buried in Uppsala Cathedral.

**FLEMING'S FUNGUS** A dish containing a sample of penicillin mould prepared by Alexander Fleming in 1935, was sold by Christie's, London on 11 July 1997 for £14,950.

**WALKING TALL** The pair of giant Dr Marten boots worn by Elton John in the film *Tommy*, was sold at Sotheby's, London, on 6 September 1988 for £12,100.

**IT'S ELECTRIFYING!** An electric chair, sold by Bristol Auction Rooms, UK, was bought by the Science Museum, London, on 10 September 1997, for £4,800. It came from the Department of Penal Correction, California, and was owned by artist Andy Warhol.

**OLD SOCKS** A pair of socks worn by Emperor Napoleon, sold at Sotheby's, London, 15 May 1996 for £2,990.

**BURNT BREAD** A burnt loaf from the Great Fire of London, 1666, sold at Sotheby's, London, 30 May 1996 for £322.

**ROYAL BRIEFS** Queen Victoria's underpants, sold for £253 at Sotheby's, London, in 1996.

**BUYING A BRIDGE** London Bridge was sold in 1968 for $2,460,000 and taken to Lake Havasu City, Arizona, USA.

# EXHIBITIONS THROUGH HISTORY

**MARQUIS D'AVÉZE, 1798**
A display of the wares made by the leading French porcelain manufacturers.

**GREAT EXHIBITION, LONDON, 1851** A showpiece of the arts and industries of the world, with the Crystal Palace at its centre, seen by more than 6,000,000 visitors.

**PHILADELPHIA CENTENNIAL EXPOSITION, 1876** The first major show in the USA, held in celebration of the 100th anniversary of the Declaration of Independence, was seen by more than 10,000,000 people.

**CENTENNIAL EXPOSITION, PARIS, 1889** Commemorated 100 years since the French Revolution. The Eiffel Tower was built as a temporary exhibit. The exhibition drew a record crowd of 32,000,000.

**WORLD'S COLUMBIAN EXPOSITION, 1893** This celebrated the 400th anniversary of Christopher Columbus' discovery of America. It attracted more than 21,400,000 visitors, many of whom witnessed electricity for the first time.

**PARIS, 1878** The Trocadéro Palace was built for this major show, which was visited by about 16,000,000.

**EXPOSITION INTERNATIONALE DES ARTS DECORATIFS ET INDUSTRIELS MODERNES, PARIS, 1925** This exhibition of art began the "Art Deco" style.

**WORLD'S FAIR, 1939–1940** Held in Flushing Meadow Park, New York, the fair was visited by 34,000,000. It was repeated in 1964–1965.

**FESTIVAL OF BRITAIN, LONDON, 1951** This celebration of post-war life attracted 8,500,000 visitors.

# ANCIENT TREASURES

**TUTANKHAMUN'S MASK** This solid gold headpiece is inlaid with gemstones, and made in the image of the teenage king. It is one of the items discovered in the pharaoh's tomb in 1922.

**NIKE OF SAMOTHRACE** This Greek winged statue, on display at the Louvre, Paris, dates from 200 BC. It is thought to have been created to commemorate a naval victory.

**VENUS DE MILO** The figure depicted in this armless statue of the second century BC is the Greek goddess Aphrodite. The sculpture reflects the ideal classic face.

**ROSETTA STONE** The fragment of a monument, it is inscribed in three languages and helped translation of Egyptian hieroglyphics.

# FAMOUS COLLECTIONS

**QUEEN ELIZABETH II'S ROYAL COLLECTION** The British monarch owns the largest private collection in the world, which contains more than 250,000 works, including 7,000 paintings.

**MUSÉE NATIONAL PICASSO** This French museum contains 251 paintings, 160 sculptures, 29 collages, 16 papiers collés, and more than 3,000 works on paper by the Spanish artist Picasso.

**HERMITAGE MUSEUM** Situated in St Petersburg, Russia, it holds a vast collection, including 12,000 sculptures, 16,000 paintings, 600,000 drawings, and 266,000 examples of applied arts.

# PRICELESS JEWELS ON SHOW

**KOH-I-NOOR** Meaning "mountain of light", this huge diamond is believed to bring bad luck to any male owner. Owned by Indian royalty for centuries, it was presented to Queen Victoria in 1850 and it is now part of the British Crown Jewels.

**STAR OF AFRICA** This jewel was split from the Cullinan diamond – the largest ever discovered. It is pear-shaped, weighs 530.2 carats, and fits into the head of the British monarch's sceptre.

**HOPE DIAMOND** This deep-blue diamond weighs 44.5 carats and is believed to bring misfortune to its owners. It is part of the gem collection at the Smithsonian Institution, Washington D.C., USA.

# PECULIAR EXHIBITS

**ROCK-CRYSTAL SKULL** Experts debate whether the large, translucent skull on show at the British Museum, UK, is the work of Mexican Aztec craftsmen or of more recent origin.

**THE QUEEN'S DOLLS' HOUSE** A scale model of a miniature 1920s' royal residence is on display at Windsor Castle, UK. The dolls' house contains intricate furniture and ornaments and was built by a special team of skilled craftsmen.

**MEGA MODEL** The largest dinosaur ever displayed is the Brachiosaurus in Humboldt University Museum, Berlin, Germany. The specimen on show may have weighed 78.8 tonnes (80 tons) when alive.

**ODD KING** Found in Tutankhamun's tomb, no-one knows who this statue is of.

# MUSIC and INSTRUMENTS

## NOTE VALUES

| NOTE | VALUE |
| --- | --- |
| Breve | musical note equal to 8 beats |
| Semibreve | musical note equal to 4 beats |
| Minim | musical note equal to 2 beats |
| Crochet | musical note equal to 1 beat |
| Quaver | musical note equal to ½ beat |
| Semiquaver | musical note equal to ¼ beat |
| Demisemiquaver | musical note equal to ⅛ beat |
| Hemidemisemiquaver | musical note equal to ¹⁄₁₆ beat |

## MUSICAL TERMS

Written music traditionally uses Italian words to tell the musician how loud, soft, fast, or slow to play the piece.

| TERM | ABBREVIATION | MEANING |
| --- | --- | --- |
| adagio | – | slow and leisurely |
| allegro | – | fast and brisk |
| andante | – | moderately slow |
| crescendo | *cresc.* | gradual increase in volume |
| diminuendo | *dim.* | getting softer |
| forte | *f* | loud or strong |
| fortissimo | *ff* | very loud |
| leggero | – | lightly |
| mezzo-forte | *mf* | moderately loud |
| mezzo-piano | *mp* | moderately soft |
| pianissimo | *pp* | very soft |
| piano | *p* | soft |
| rallentando | *rall.* | slowing down |
| sforzando | *sf* | stress note or chord |
| staccato | – | short, separated notes |

## STRANGE MUSICAL INSTRUMENTS

**ARPEGGIONE** Briefly popular in the 1820s, the arpeggione resembled a guitar, and had six strings, but was as big as a cello and, like a cello, was played with a bow.

**GLASS HARMONICA** Glass bowls suspended in water were rotated by a treadle while the player rubbed the edges. Mozart composed several works for it. American statesman and inventor Benjamin Franklin devised a version called an "armonica".

**KALLIOPE** Invented in 1859 by an American called Arthur Dennis, the kalliope was a steam-powered organ. It was so powerful that its sound could be heard 20 km (12 miles) away!

**LUSTRE CHANTANT** This 19th-century instrument was invented by Frederick Kastner. Its name translates as "singing lamp", and it consisted of a keyboard connected to gas lamps, which made sounds while the brightness of the lights varied according to the notes played.

**OLIPHANT** A curved horn made from an elephant tusk.

**PANOMONICO** Invented by Karl Waezel of Vienna, Austria, the panomonico was a sort of mechanical one-man-band that played 379 instruments: 150 flutes, 150 flageolets, 50 oboes, 18 trumpets, five fanfares, two timbals, one triangle, and three large drums.

**PANTALEON** Invented by George Noel in 1767, the pantaleon had 270 strings, making it one of the largest and most complicated stringed instruments ever devised.

**ROCK HARMONICON** Joseph Richardson (1790–1855), a British mason, discovered that striking certain types of rock produced different notes, and invented an instrument called a "rock harmonicon". His sons played it on tours throughout Britain.

**SERPENT** Still occasionally seen in ancient music ensembles, the serpent is a twisting woodwind instrument, resembling a snake.

## MUSICAL MEMORY TIPS

The five horizontal lines on which music is written are called the stave. The pitch of the stave – either treble (above middle C) or bass (below middle C) – is introduced by the treble or bass clef. Each line or space of the stave represents a different note. Here are some quick ways of remembering what each line and space means, always reading from bottom to top:

**LINES ON THE TREBLE STAVE** Remember **E**very **G**ood **B**oy **D**eserves **F**un, and you will never forget that these lines indicate the notes **E**, **G**, **B**, **D**, and **F**.

**SPACES ON THE TREBLE STAVE** This is simple, the spaces make the word **FACE** – the notes **F**, **A**, **C**, and **E**.

**LINES ON THE BASS STAVE** Remember **G**ood **B**oys **D**eserve **F**un **A**lways for the notes **G**, **B**, **D**, **F**, and **A**.

**SPACES ON THE BASS STAVE** Remember **A**ll **C**ows **E**at **G**rass for the notes **A**, **C**, **E**, and **G**.

## INSTRUMENTS OF THE ORCHESTRA

| STRINGS | WOODWIND | BRASS | PERCUSSION |
|---|---|---|---|

**STRINGS**

Stringed instruments produce their sound through the vibration of strings. They are normally played with a bow, but can be plucked. A harp is occasionally included in the strings section.

**VIOLIN** A violin has four strings tuned to G, D, A, and E. It is the highest pitched of the strings and usually carries the tune.

**VIOLA** Larger and deeper than a violin, the viola is tuned a fifth lower – C, G, D, and A.

**CELLO** The cello or violoncello evolved in the 16th century from an instrument called the violone. Its strings are tuned to C, G, D, and A, an octave lower than the viola. It is played resting on the ground between the performer's knees.

**DOUBLE BASS** The largest and deepest stringed instrument in the orchestra, tuned to E, A, D, and G, it also dates from the 16th century.

**WOODWIND**

Woodwind instruments are either blown through a mouth hole, or played by means of a vibrating reed. The bigger the instrument, the lower its pitch.

**FLUTE** The side-blown flute, dating from the 12th century and improved in the early 19th, is the most familiar type of flute in the orchestra. A piccolo is a small flute dating from the early 18th century.

**OBOE** The oboe is a double-reeded woodwind developed from an old instrument called a shawn. It came into use in the orchestra in the 18th century.

**CLARINET** Developed from the chalumeau, the clarinet was introduced in the early 18th century.

**BASSOON** The bassoon, which dates from the 16th century but was introduced in the 18th century, produces the lowest woodwind notes.

**BRASS**

Brass instruments are played by the action of valves and the position of the player's lips on the mouthpiece.

**FRENCH HORN** The French horn is so-called because it is said to have developed from the French hunting horn. It was introduced to the orchestra in the late 17th century.

**TRUMPET** The descendant of an ancient instrument, the trumpet acquired valves in the early 19th century. Its relative the cornet is also sometimes included in the orchestra.

**TROMBONE** Derived from a medieval instrument called a sackbut, the trombone was first used in the orchestra in 1808, for a performance of Beethoven's *Fifth Symphony* in Vienna.

**TUBA** Most orchestras have just one tuba – a large valved 19th-century instrument that produces a deep sound.

**PERCUSSION**

Percussion instruments are played by being struck, rubbed, or shaken. They provide the rhythmic beat in an orchestra.

**DRUMS** The largest of the drum family is the bass drum, which can be operated by foot. Kettle-drums are usually made of copper with a parchment skin. Strings on the underside of the smaller snare drum create a rattling sound.

**TRIANGLE** A small wire triangle that gives a tinkling sound.

**CYMBALS** Cymbals vary in size, but are clashed together, to make a clanging sound.

**GLOCKENSPIEL** A set of graduated steel bars set in a frame and hit with a hammer.

**GONG** Struck in the centre, a gong makes an impressive noise.

**TAMBOURINE** Small cymbals set in a round frame make a sound when shaken.

## WORLD'S LARGEST INSTRUMENTS

**DOUBLE BASS** Built by American Arthur K. Ferrisin, in 1924 this giant instrument was 4.26 m (14 ft) long and weighed 590 kg (1,301 lb).

**DRUMS** The University of Texas Longhorn Band has a 7.6-m (25-ft) circumference drum that has to be towed by a tractor. A drum with a circumference of 12.5 m (40 ft) was made by the Supreme Drum Co. of London in 1987.

**LARGEST GUITAR** In 1991, students in Jasonville, Indiana, USA, made a scaled-up version of a Gibson guitar measuring 11.63 m (38 ft 2 in) long and weighing 446 kg (1,865 lb).

**LARGEST ORGANS** The 33,112-pipe Auditorium Organ in Atlantic City, USA, was built in 1930. It is powered by a 365-horsepower blower and makes as much noise as 25 brass bands – making it also the world's loudest instrument. It is, however, only partly working. The largest operational organ is the 30,067-pipe organ in the Wanamaker Department Store, Philadelphia, USA. Passau Cathedral, Germany, houses the largest church organ built in 1928 with 16,000 pipes.

**PIANO** The largest is believed to be one weighing 1.25 tonnes (tons) and measuring 3.55 m (11 ft 8 in) long, built by Charles H. Challen of London in 1935.

**TUBA** John Philip Sousa, the American inventor of the Sousaphone, commissioned a 2.3-m (7-ft 6-in) tuba in 1896.

## OUTSIZE ORCHESTRAS

Orchestras usually have about 90 musicians – but there is no limit!

**1872** On 17 June in Boston, USA, an orchestra of 987 players (including 400 first violinists) performed music by Johann Strauss accompanied by a 20,000-strong choir.

**1958** The Norwegian National Meeting of School Bands assembled 12,600 players at Trondheim, Norway.

**1958** An orchestra of 2,023 musicians played on 14 July at Wolverhampton, UK.

## RECORDING TIMELINE

**1876** Alexander Graham Bell invents the microphone.

**1877** Thomas Edison's makes the first recording of a human voice – "Mary had a little lamb" on tin foil.

**1887** Berliner invents the gramophone.

**1898** Danish inventor Valdemar Poulson makes magnetic recordings of sound on to steel piano wire.

**1904** First mass-produced double-sided discs sold in Germany.

**1927** First coin-operated jukebox.

**1930** Magnetic tape is used to record sound.

**1931** Stereo recording introduced.

**1948** First vinyl discs produced.

**1964** Cassette tape becomes available.

**1979** First Sony Walkman portable audio cassette players sold.

**1982** First CDs sold.

# CLASSICAL MUSIC

!DID YOU KNOW? The first concertos were published in Italy about 1600.

## CLASSICAL MUSIC TERMS

**SYMPHONY** Symphonies are pieces of music wirtten for a full range of orchestral instruments. There is no dominant soloist.

**CONCERTO** In a concerto, a soloist is accompanied by an orchestra. A concerto orchestra usually has fewer brass and percussion instruments, which allows the soloist to be heard more clearly.

**SONATA** A musical composition in several movements.

**FUGUE** A musical composition with recurring themes.

**MARCH** A steady rhythmical piece composed to accompany a march.

**WALTZ** A piece of music in triple time, composed to accompany dancing couples.

**MAZURKA** Music to accompany a lively Polish dance. In moderately quick triple time.

**POLKA** Lively dance music, of Bohemian origin, in duple time, or two beats per measure.

## MUSICAL ENSEMBLES

Groups range from duos, with two performers, to symphony orchestras which contain up to 120.

**DUO** In a duo, one musician plays a brass, string, or wind instrument and the other a piano. Pieces for two players are called duets.

**TRIO** A group of three players is called a trio. A string trio uses a violin, viola, and cello. Piano trios are written for violin, cello, and piano.

**QUARTET** Four players together form a quartet. String quartets consist of two violins, a viola, and a cello.

**QUINTET** Five players make a quintet. Most quintets contain wind or brass instruments or instruments from different families.

**CHOIR** A group of singers. A mixed voice choir contains men and women, who sing four parts of the score.

!DID YOU KNOW? A soloist is a musical artist who performs on his or her own. The word soloist was first used in 1864.

## POPULAR OPERAS

An opera is a musical drama in which singers act out a story, accompanied by an orchestra. Most operas include passages of sung dialogue, known as recitative, solo songs called arias, and chorus scenes.

| TITLE | COMPOSER |
|---|---|
| *Aïda* | Giuseppe Verdi |
| *Ariadne auf Naxos* | Richard Strauss |
| *Barber of Seville* | Gioacchino Rossini |
| *La Bohème* | Giacomo Puccini |
| *Carmen* | Georges Bizet |
| *Cosi Fan Tutte* | Wolfgang Mozart |
| *Dido and Aeneas* | Henry Purcell |
| *Don Giovanni* | Wolfgang Mozart |
| *Eugene Onegin* | Peter Ilyich Tchaikovsky |
| *Faust* | Charles Gounod |
| *Fidelio* | Ludwig van Beethoven |
| *Die Fledermaus* | Johann Strauss |
| *Götterdämmerung* | Richard Wagner |
| *Madama Butterfly* | Giacomo Puccini |
| *The Magic Flute* | Wolfgang Mozart |
| *Pagliacci* | Ruggero Leoncavallo |
| *Peter Grimes* | Benjamin Britten |
| *Porgy and Bess* | George Gershwin |
| *Rigoletto* | Giuseppe Verdi |
| *Der Rosenkavalier* | Richard Strauss |
| *Tosca* | Giacomo Puccini |
| *La Traviata* | Giuseppe Verdi |

## MOST PROLIFIC CLASSICAL COMPOSERS

| COMPOSER | DATES | NATIONALITY | HOURS COMPOSED |
|---|---|---|---|
| Franz Joseph Haydn | 1732–1809 | Austrian | 340 |
| George Frederick Handel | 1685–1759 | German | 303 |
| Wolfgang Amadeus Mozart | 1756–1791 | Austrian | 202 |
| Johann Sebastian Bach | 1685–1750 | German | 175 |
| Franz Schubert | 1797–1828 | German | 134 |

!DID YOU KNOW? If the length of the composer's working life were to be included in the calculation of who is the most prolific, Schubert would be the overall winner: his 134 hours were composed in a comparatively short career of 18 years, which means he composed an average of 7 hours 27 minutes per annum.

| | | | |
|---|---|---|---|
| Ludwig van Beethoven | 1770–1827 | German | 120 |
| Henry Purcell | 1659–1695 | English | 116 |
| Giuseppe Verdi | 1813–1901 | Italian | 87 |
| Anton Dvorák | 1841–1904 | Czech | 79 |
| Franz Liszt | 1811–1886 | Hungarian | 76 |
| Peter Ilyich Tchaikovsky | 1840–1893 | Russian | 76 |

## KEY CLASSICAL COMPOSERS

| NAME | NATIONALITY | DATES | FAMOUS WORK |
|---|---|---|---|
| Antonio Vivaldi | Italian | 1678–1741 | *The Four Seasons* |
| Johann Sebastian Bach | German | 1685–1750 | *Brandenburg Concertos* |
| George Frederick Handel | German | 1685–1759 | *Messiah* |
| Franz Joseph Haydn | Austrian | 1732–1809 | *London Symphonies* |
| Wolfgang Amadeus Mozart | Austrian | 1756–1791 | *The Magic Flute* |
| Ludwig van Beethoven | German | 1770–1827 | *Pastoral Symphony* |
| Franz Schubert | Austrian | 1797–1828 | *Die Winterreise* |
| Hector Berlioz | French | 1803–1869 | *Symphonie Fantastique* |
| Felix Mendelssohn | German | 1809–1847 | *A Midsummer Night's Dream* |
| Frédéric Chopin | Polish | 1810–1849 | Piano works |
| Franz Liszt | Hungarian | 1811–1886 | *Les Préludes* |
| Richard Wagner | German | 1813–1883 | *The Flying Dutchman* |
| Giuseppe Verdi | Italian | 1813–1901 | *La Traviata* |
| Johann Strauss | Austrian | 1825–1899 | *Die Fledermaus* |
| Peter Ilyich Tchaikovsky | Russian | 1840–1893 | *Swan Lake* |
| Anton Dvorák | Czech | 1841–1904 | *Slavonic Dances* |
| Edward Elgar | English | 1857–1934 | *Enigma Variations* |
| Giacomo Puccini | Italian | 1858–1924 | *La Bohème* |
| Gustav Mahler | Austrian | 1860–1911 | *Resurrection Symphony* |
| Claude Debussy | French | 1862–1918 | *La Mer* |
| Richard Strauss | German | 1864–1949 | *Der Rosenkavalier* |
| Sergei Rachmaninov | Russian | 1873–1943 | Piano works |
| Gustav Holst | English | 1874–1934 | *The Planets* |
| Maurice Ravel | French | 1875–1937 | *Boléro* |
| Benjamin Britten | English | 1913–1976 | *Billy Budd* |
| Philip Glass | American | b.1937 | *Einstein on the Beach* |

## FAMOUS OPERA HOUSES

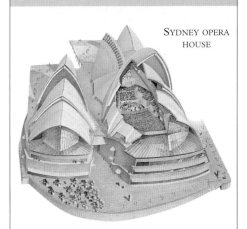

SYDNEY OPERA HOUSE

**SYDNEY OPERA HOUSE, AUSTRALIA** Officially opened by Queen Elizabeth in 1973, Sydney's opera house is on the harbour and has distinctive sail-like roofs.

**ROYAL OPERA HOUSE, LONDON, UK** The present building was designed by E. M. Barry in 1858.

**LA SCALA, MILAN, ITALY** Home of Teatro alla Scala opera company and a major feature of the city.

**METROPOLITAN OPERA, NEW YORK, USA** The world's largest opera house, "The Met" seats 4,065 people and is the focal point of Lincoln Center's Plaza.

**BAYREUTH FESTIVAL THEATRE, GERMANY** This opera house was built for performances of Wagner's operas.

**VIENNA STATE OPERA, AUSTRIA** Opened in 1869, this was bombed in 1945. The new auditorium was opened in 1955.

## GREAT OPERA SINGERS

| NAME | DATES | COUNTRY | VOICE |
|---|---|---|---|
| Jenny Lind | 1820–1887 | Swedish | Soprano |
| Dame Nellie Melba | 1861–1931 | Australia | Soprano |
| Kathleen Ferrier | 1912–1953 | UK | Contralto |
| Tito Gobbi | 1915–1984 | Italy | Baritone |
| Maria Callas | 1923–1977 | Greece | Soprano |
| Luciano Pavarotti | b.1935 | Italy | Tenor |
| Placido Domingo | b.1941 | Spain | Tenor |
| Kiri Te Kanawa | b.1944 | New Zealand | Soprano |
| Frederica von Stade | b.1945 | USA | Mezzo-soprano |
| José Carreras | b.1946 | Spain | Tenor |

## VOICE RANGES

**SOPRANO** Highest female voice.

**MEZZO SOPRANO** Between soprano and contralto.

**CONTRALTO** Lowest female voice.

**ALTO** Highest male voice, traditionally sung by choirboys.

**TENOR** High male voice – counter tenor is very high.

**BARITONE** Male voice, higher than bass, but lower than tenor.

**BASS** Lowest male voice.

## OPERA FACTS

**LONGEST OPERA** *Die Meistersinger von Nurnberg* lasts 5 hours.

**SHORTEST OPERA** *The Sands of Time*, by Rees and Reynolds, lasts just 4 minutes.

**OPERA TEXT** The text of an opera is called the libretto.

**DID YOU KNOW?** Many believe that an opera singer's voice improves with increased body weight, but there is no evidence of this.

# POPULAR MUSIC ARTISTS

## TOP SINGLES OF ALL TIME WORLDWIDE

Global sales are hard to calculate, since for many decades, a large part of the world carried out very little statistical research on record sales. "Worldwide" is thus usually taken to mean the known minimum sales in the "western world".

| ARTIST/TITLE | SALES EXCEED |
|---|---|
| Elton John, *Candle In The Wind* 1997 | 35,000,000 |
| Bing Crosby, *White Christmas* | 30,000,000 |
| Bill Haley and The Comets, *Rock Around The Clock* | 17,000,000 |
| The Beatles, *I Want To Hold Your Hand* | 12,000,000 |
| Elvis Presley, *It's Now Or Never* | 10,000,000 |

## TOP JOHN LENNON & PAUL McCARTNEY HITS

John Lennon and Paul McCartney were two members of the famous and influential group, The Beatles. Their songs dominated the sixties, and still influence many musicians today.

| TITLE | CHARTING ARTIST(S) |
|---|---|
| *She Loves You* | The Beatles |
| *I Want To Hold Your Hand* | The Beatles |
| *Can't Buy Me Love* | The Beatles, Ella Fitzgerald |
| *I Feel Fine* | The Beatles |
| *We Can Work It Out* | The Beatles, Stevie Wonder |
| *Help!* | Bananarama & La La Nee Nee Noo Noo, The Beatles, Tina Turner |
| *Day Tripper* | The Beatles, Otis Redding |
| *Hey Jude* | The Beatles, Wilson Pickett |
| *Let It Be* | The Beatles, Ferry Aid |
| *A Hard Day's Night* | The Beatles, Peter Sellers |

**DID YOU KNOW?** Items such as the barber's shop in the song *Penny Lane* have been put up for sale as Beatles' memorabilia!

## TOP ALBUMS OF ALL TIME

Total worldwide sales of albums have traditionally been hard to gauge, but even with the huge expansion of the album market during the 1980s, and multiple million sales of many major releases, this Top 11 is still elite territory.

| ARTIST/ALBUM | ESTIMATED SALES |
|---|---|
| Michael Jackson, *Thriller* | 40,000,000 |
| Pink Floyd, *Dark Side Of The Moon* | 28,000,000 |
| Meat Loaf, *Bat Out Of Hell* | 27,000,000 |
| Soundtrack, *The Bodyguard* | 26,000,000 |
| Soundtrack, *Saturday Night Fever* | 25,000,000 |
| The Beatles, *Sgt Pepper's Lonely Hearts Club Band* | 24,000,000 |
| Eagles, *Their Greatest Hits 1971–1975* | 24,000,000 |
| Mariah Carey, *Music Box* | 23,000,000 |
| Carole King, *Tapestry* | 22,000,000 |
| Simon and Garfunkel, *Bridge over Troubled Water* | 22,000,000 |
| Soundtrack, *Grease* | 22,000,000 |

## TOP JUKEBOX SINGLES

This list was compiled by the Amusement & Music Operators Association, whose members service and operate more than 250,000 jukeboxes in the USA. It is based on jukebox singles from 1950 to the present.

| ARTIST/GROUP | SINGLE |
|---|---|
| Patsy Cline | *Crazy* (1962) |
| Bob Seger | *Old Time Rock 'n' Roll* (1979) |
| Elvis Presley | *Hound Dog/Don't be Cruel* (1956) |
| Bobby Darin | *Mack the Knife* (1959) |
| Steppenwolf | *Born to be Wild* (1968) |
| Frank Sinatra | *New York, New York* (1980) |
| Bill Haley and The Comets | *Rock around the Clock* (1955) |
| Marvin Gaye | *I heard it through the Grapevine* (1968) |
| Otis Redding | *(Sittin' on) The Dock of the Bay* (1968) |

**DID YOU KNOW?** Conductor Sir Georg Solti has won the most Grammy Awards ever – a total of 31.

## DID YOU KNOW?
An Edison phonograph jukebox, invented by Louis Glass, was set up in 1889 in San Francisco, USA. The first jukebox based on disc recordings was made in Chicago in 1906.

## MOST BRIT AWARDS

The Brit Awards, which started in 1982, are sponsored by Brittania Music, Europe's largest music club. They are presented to UK and international pop musicians in various categories.

| ARTIST | AWARDS |
| --- | --- |
| Annie Lennox | 7 |
| Phil Collins | 6 |
| The artist formerly known as Prince | 6 |
| Michael Jackson | 5 |
| George Michael | 5 |
| Blur | 4 |
| Oasis | 4 |
| Take That | 4 |
| U2 | 4 |

## MOST GRAMMY AWARDS

The Grammy Awards have been presented since 1959 by the US National Academy of Recording Arts and Sciences. These are the leading non-classical winners.

| ARTIST | AWARDS |
| --- | --- |
| Quincy Jones | 26 |
| Henry Mancini | 20 |
| Stevie Wonder | 19 |
| Paul Simon | 16 |
| John Williams | 16 |
| Aretha Franklin | 15 |
| Chet Atkins | 14 |
| David Foster | 14 |
| Ella Fitzgerald | 13 |
| Michael Jackson | 13 |

## DID YOU KNOW?
Buddy Holly's spectacles were sold in 1990 for $45,100 (£30,000).

## POPULAR MUSIC STYLES/TRENDS

**BLUES** A slow type of US folk music that developed from the black spiritual music and work songs of the 19th century.

**ROCK 'N' ROLL** The first of the modern popular music styles, it started in the mid-1950s as a fast blues that could be danced to.

**RHYTHM AND BLUES (R & B)** A style that merged traditional blues and popular music.

**REGGAE** West Indian rock jazz, with a simple two-beat rhythm.

**HEAVY METAL** A highly amplified type of rock music that appeared in the 1970s.

**PUNK ROCK** A style that emerged in the 1970s from groups that rebelled against authority, as their music and wild appearance showed.

**DISCO** Recorded music designed to be danced to. Various dance music styles have also developed in recent years, including garage and electronic styles such as techno and house music.

## MOST EXPENSIVE POP MEMORABILIA

Pioneered particularly by Sotheby's in London, pop memorabilia has become big business. In some instances, the same items have been re-auctioned by a sequence of celebrity owners to raise money for charities.

| ITEM/SALE | PRICE (£) |
| --- | --- |
| John Lennon's 1965 Rolls-Royce Phantom V touring limousine, Sotheby's, New York, 29 June 1985 | 1,768,462 |
| Acoustic guitar owned by David Bowie, Paul McCartney, and George Michael, Christie's, London, 18 May 1994 | 220,000 |
| Jimi Hendrix's Fender Stratocaster electric guitar, Sotheby's, London, 25 April 1990 | 198,000 |
| Paul McCartney's handwritten lyrics for *Getting Better*, 1967, Sotheby's, London, 14 September 1995 | 161,000 |

## FIRST MEMBERS OF THE ROCK AND ROLL HALL OF FAME

These seminal artists were all inducted at the first ceremony which took place on 23 January 1986 at the Waldorf-Astoria Hotel, New York. The Rock and Roll Hall of Fame and Museum is a futuristic building in Cleveland, Ohio, USA, which opened in 1995 at a cost of $90 million (£56 million):

Chuck Berry (b.1926) • James Brown (b.1934) • Ray Charles (b.1930) • Sam Cooke (1935–1964) • Fats Domino (b.1928) Everly Brothers (Don, b.1937; Phil, b.1939) • Buddy Holly (1936–1959) • Jerry Lee Lewis (b.1935) • Elvis Presley (1935–1977) • Little Richard (b.1935)

# DANCE

**DID YOU KNOW?** Italian ballerina Marie Taglioni (1804–1884) became the first to go *en pointe*, on points, in 1832.

## BALLET TERMS

**BARRE** The bar used by dancers to help balance when they are practising.

**CHOREOGRAPHY** The composition, movement, and steps in a ballet.

**CORPS DE BALLET** Chorus of dancers (not those dancing solo).

**PAS DE DEUX** A dance for two (usually the principal male and female dancers in the company).

**PAS SEULE** A solo dance.

**PRIMA BALLERINA** The leading ballerina in a company.

## BALLET POSITIONS

**ARABESQUE** Position in which the dancer stands on one leg, with extended arms and body bent forward, with the other leg stretched back.

**ENTRECHAT** Rapid crossing and uncrossing of the feet during a jump.

**GLISSADE** Gliding move.

**JETÉ** A jump from one foot to the other.

**PIROUETTE** A complete turn on one leg.

**PLIÉ** A knee-bending movement.

**POINTES** Dancing on the tips of the toes.

## MILESTONES OF DANCE

**c.15,000 BC** Stone-Age rock paintings show dance formations.

**3000–1000 BC** Egyptians use dance in the worship of gods and goddesses.

**1300s** Ballroom dances are held in royal palaces.

**1400s** Ballo, an Italian story-based dance, is the earliest form of ballet.

**1681** Women are allowed to dance in ballets. By the 1840s, ballerinas are the most important of ballet dancers.

**1870s** The French high-kicking dance, cancan, becomes popular.

**c.1900** Isadora Duncan (1878–1927), USA, is the first modern dancer.

**1920s** Tap, Charleston, jazz, and many other dance forms of African-American influence become increasingly popular.

**1930s** Dancing pair Fred Astaire (1899–1987) and Ginger Rogers (1911–1995) appear in musical films.

**1950s** Rock 'n' Roll established.

**1970s** Disco dancing evolves.

**1980s** Robotic break dancing is born.

## DEBUTS OF POPULAR BALLETS

| BALLET | FIRST DANCED |
| --- | --- |
| *La Sylphide* | 1832 |
| *Giselle* | 1841 |
| *Coppélia* | 1870 |
| *Sleeping Beauty* | 1890 |
| *The Nutcracker* | 1892 |
| *Swan Lake* | 1895 |
| *The Rite of Spring* | 1913 |
| *Manon* | 1974 |
| *Fait Accompli* | 1984 |
| *Still Life at the Penguin Cafe* | 1988 |

## DANCERS

**ISADORA DUNCAN (1878–1927)** The American contemporary dancer developed free forms of dance.

**MARIE RAMBERT (1888–1982)** A Polish teacher and dancer, Rambert founded the Ballet Rambert (now the Rambert Dance Company).

**DAME MARGOT FONTEYN (1918–1991)** Fonteyn and her celebrated dancing partner Rudolf Nureyev (1938–1993), become one of the most famous dancing pairs ballet has ever seen.

**GENE KELLY (1912–1996)** This American dancer used his athletic dance style in film musicals, including *Singin' in the Rain* (1952).

**ANNA PAVLOVA (1885–1931)** The famous Russian ballerina formed her own ballet company.

**WAYNE SLEEP (b.1948)** The British dancer set a record for achieving 12 *entrechats* in a single jump!

**ARTHUR MITCHELL (b.1934)** Founded the first black dance company, the Dance Theater of Harlem, USA.

## TOP DANCE FILMS

*All That Jazz* (1979) • *Fame* (1980) • *Flashdance* (1983) *Lambada* (1990) • *Oklahoma!* (1955) • *The Red Shoes* (1948) *Saturday Night Fever* (1977) *Seven Brides for Seven Brothers* (1954) • *Singin' in the Rain* (1952) • *Staying Alive* (1983) *Strictly Ballroom* (1992) • *The Tales of Beatrix Potter* (1971)

## UNUSUAL DANCES

**PYRRHIC DANCE** A dance performed in ancient Greece, by soldiers wearing full armour.

**TARANTELLA** A wild dance originating in Naples, Italy. Its gyrations were said to resemble those of a person who had been bitten by a tarantula spider.

**FURRY DANCE** This dance, held annually in Helston in Cornwall, UK, is believed to have its origin in ancient times. It involves large groups of people, with men in top hats, leading their partners in and out of the town's houses.

**DANCE MARATHONS** Starting in 1923, endurance dances were held in the USA, and gained in popularity during the Depression, when people tried to win prize money by dancing until they dropped exhausted. The craze was eventually made illegal in many states.

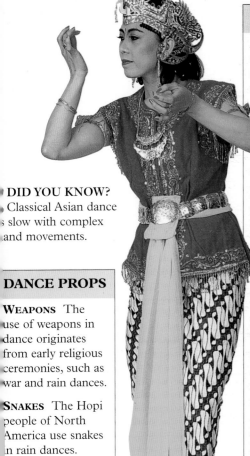

**DID YOU KNOW?** Classical Asian dance is slow with complex hand movements.

## DANCE PROPS

**WEAPONS** The use of weapons in dance originates from early religious ceremonies, such as war and rain dances.

**SNAKES** The Hopi people of North America use snakes in rain dances.

**INSTRUMENTS** Instruments, such as castanets, are often used to help accentuate rhythm.

## DANCE RECORDS

**LONGEST CONGA LINE** The Miami Super Conga, held on 13 March 1988 consisted of 119,986 people.

**LOWEST LIMBO** Dennis Walston (known as "King Limbo") of the USA, limboed under a bar 15.25 cm (6 in) high on 2 March 1991.

**FASTEST TAP DANCER** Stephen Gare, UK, achieved 32 taps per second in March 1990.

**MOST CURTAIN CALLS FOR A BALLET PERFORMANCE** Margot Fonteyn and Rudolf Nureyev received 89 for their performance in *Swan Lake* in Vienna, Austria, in October 1964.

**FASTEST FLAMENCO** Solero de Jerez tapped his heels at a record speed of 16 taps per second in Brisbane, Australia, in September 1967.

**MOST EXPENSIVE COSTUME** Designed by Pablo Picasso in 1917, the costume of the Chinese conjurer in *Parade* fetched £28,000 in 1984.

## WORLD DANCE STYLES

**AFRICAN DANCE** In Africa, important events such as births and deaths are observed by dancing. Usually, African dance is accompanied by rhythmic drumbeats.

**ASIAN DANCE** Many Asian dances make use of stylized hand movements. Thai dancers, for example, use slow, controlled movements, with graceful arm and hand gestures.

**EUROPEAN FOLK DANCING** Folk dances are often performed in traditional costumes, and many involve people forming simple patterns such as lines or circles. Irish jigs are usually performed by pairs or individuals.

**FLAMENCO** This dance is a mixture of both Spanish and Arab cultures. Men use complicated footwork, while women weave patterns with their arms. The dancers are accompanied by fast, dramatic guitar music.

**SOUTH AMERICAN** The dances of Central and South America reflect the cultures of the native peoples, the European colonists, and their African slaves.

**BALLROOM** Developed in the courts of Europe, ballroom dances, such as the waltz, were adapted from folk dances. They were danced on flat, polished floors, which allowed for elegant gliding movements.

**TAP DANCE** In 19th-century America, black slaves combined African rhythms with the jigs of English and Irish settlers.

## DANCE MARATHONS

**LONGEST DANCE** Ritof and Edith Boudreaux danced the marathon of their lives in the USA from 29 August 1930 to 1 April 1931. Their final total of 5,148 hours 28.5 minutes won them a prize of $2,000.

**DISCO MARATHON** Peter Stewart disco danced for a record-breaking 408 hours in Birmingham, UK, from 6 to 21 August 1983.

**MARATHON TWIST** Super dancer Ra Denny twisted the night away for 100 hours at Christchurch, New Zealand, in March 1962.

**BELLY DANCING MARATHON** Supple dancer Eileen Foucher belly danced for a total of 106 hours at Romford, Essex, UK, from 30 July to 10 August 1984.

**MARATHON CHARLESTON** John Giola did the Charleston dance for 22.5 hours at the Roseland Ballroom, New York, USA in 1926.

**DID YOU KNOW?** Judges at Irish jigging contests sit under the stage to assess the dancer's steps in detail.

# THEATRE

## FAMOUS THEATRES

**EPIDAURUS, GREECE** Built around 400 BC, this open-air theatre can seat 14,000 spectators. Fifty-five tiers of stone seats are arranged in a semi-circle around the orchestra and the stage.

**GLOBE, LONDON** This famous theatre was first built in 1599. Many of Shakespeare's plays were performed on its stage. Spectators stood on the open-air courtyard in front of the stage or sat in covered galleries.

**TEATRO OLIMPICO, VICENZA, ITALY** Completed in 1583, it is the world's oldest indoor theatre. It was designed in the Roman style by Palladio.

**DID YOU KNOW?** The English playwright William Shakespeare worked as an actor and also joined a company called the Lord Chamberlain's Men in 1592.

## SHAKESPEARE'S MOST DEMANDING ROLES

| ROLE | PLAY | NUMBER OF LINES |
|---|---|---|
| Hamlet | *Hamlet* | 1,422 |

**DID YOU KNOW?** Hamlet's role comprises 11,610 words – over 36 per cent of the total number of lines spoken in the play.

| | | |
|---|---|---|
| Falstaff | *Henry IV*, Parts I and II | 1,178 |

**DID YOU KNOW?** Falstaff also appears in *The Merry Wives of Windsor* where he has 436 lines. His total of 1,614 lines would thus make him the most talkative of all Shakespeare's characters.

| | | |
|---|---|---|
| Richard III | *Richard III* | 1,124 |
| Iago | *Othello* | 1,097 |
| Henry V | *Henry V* | 1,025 |

## LONGEST-RUNNING PLAYS

| SHOW | VENUE | DATES | PERFORMANCES |
|---|---|---|---|
| *The Golden Horseshoe Revue* | Disneyland, California | 1955–1986 | 47,250 |
| *The Mousetrap* | London | 1952– | 18,872 |
| *La Cantatrice Chauve* | Paris | 1957– | 12,772 |
| *The Drunkard* | Los Angeles | 1933–1959 | 9,477 |
| *No Sex, Please – We're British* | London | 1971–1987 | 6,761 |

**AMAZING FACT!** Samuel Beckett's play *Breath* is the shortest recorded play ever written, consisting of 35 seconds of human cries and breaths.

## SHAKESPEARE'S LONGEST PLAYS

Acclaimed English playwright William Shakespeare (1564–1616) wrote 37 plays and 154 14-line poems called sonnets.

| PLAY | LINES |
|---|---|
| *Hamlet* | 3,901 |
| *Richard III* | 3,886 |
| *Coriolanus* | 3,820 |
| *Cymbeline* | 3,813 |
| *Othello* | 3,672 |

## THEATRE LORE

**GREEN FOR CALM** Before going on stage, actors wait in a green room, as this colour is believed to calm nerves.

**GOOD LUCK** The phrase "break a leg" is often used instead of "good luck".

**UNLUCKY NAME** Some actors consider it unlucky to call *Macbeth* by its title, so they call it "the Scottish play" or use another name.

## ONE-NIGHT STANDS

**PLAY WITHOUT AN A** The one and only performance of J. R. Ronden's play took place at the Paris Théâtre des Variétés on 18 December, 1816. The total absence of words containing the letter "a" was trying for the actors and the audience, who rioted and did not allow it to finish.

**LADY OF LYONS** In 1888, at London's Shaftesbury Theatre this play failed to make its own first night when the safety curtain jammed.

**THE INTIMATE REVUE** A disaster from start to finish, this play opened and closed in London, on 11 March 1930. Scenery changes took so long that seven scenes were left out to allow the audience to go home.

**MUSICAL EXTRAVAGANZA** In 1982, *i*, combining opera, ballet, and circus by Arturo Brachetti, was closed before it opened – the dress rehearsal overran by two hours!

## FAMOUS PUPPETS

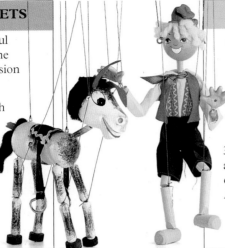

**THE MUPPETS** Colourful puppets who rose to fame through children's television programmes and films.

**PUNCH AND JUDY** Punch quarrels with his wife, Judy in a popular street show.

**PINOCCHIO** This storybook wooden puppet has a nose that grows longer every time he tells a lie.

## PUPPET THEATRE

**ANIMATRONICS** Realistic animal puppets are moved by electric motors mounted within them. Operators use remote control to activate pre-recorded movements.

**JAPANESE BUNRAKU** Four 30.5-cm (12-in) tall puppets are carried on stage by operators dressed in black. A narrator chants the story, while a samisen player provides music.

**INDONESIAN SHADOW PUPPETRY** Intricately cut leather puppets appear as black shadows on a screen. Performances are accompanied by an orchestra of gongs and cymbals called a gamelan.

**VIETNAMESE WATER PUPPETRY** Very large puppets perform on a covered stage set up on a floating raft. The audience watches the show from the water's edge.

## KEY PLAYWRIGHTS

| Name | Nationality | Dates | Famous play |
|---|---|---|---|
| William Shakespeare | English | 1564–1616 | *Hamlet* |
| Pierre Corneille | French | 1607–1684 | *Le Cid* |
| Molière | French | 1622–1673 | *Tartuffe* |
| Jean Racine | French | 1639–1699 | *Phèdre* |
| Johann Goethe | German | 1749–1832 | *Faust* |
| Richard Sheridan | Irish | 1751–1816 | *The Rivals* |
| Henrik Ibsen | Norwegian | 1828–1906 | *A Doll's House* |
| George Bernard Shaw | Irish | 1856–1950 | *Pygmalion* |
| Anton Chekov | Russian | 1860–1904 | *Uncle Vanya* |
| Luigi Pirandello | Italian | 1867–1936 | *Six Characters in Search of an Author* |
| Susan Glaspell | American | 1882–1948 | *Alison's House* |
| Eugene O'Neill | American | 1888–1953 | *Strange Interlude* |
| Bertolt Brecht | German | 1898–1956 | *The Threepenny Opera* |
| Samuel Beckett | Irish | 1906–1989 | *Waiting for Godot* |
| Tennessee Williams | American | 1911–1983 | *The Glass Menagerie* |
| Eugène Ionesco | French | 1912–1994 | *The Bald Prima Donna* |
| Arthur Miller | American | b.1915 | *Death of a Salesman* |
| John Osborne | English | 1929–1994 | *Look Back in Anger* |
| Harold Pinter | English | b.1930 | *The Caretaker* |

## LONGEST-RUNNING MUSICALS

| Show, venue | Date | Performances |
|---|---|---|
| *The Fantasticks*, New York | 1960– | 15,653 |
| *Cats*, London | 1981– | 7,242 |
| *Cats*, New York | 1982– | 6,463 |
| *A Chorus Line*, New York | 1975–1990 | 6,137 |
| *Starlight Express*, London | 1984– | 5,846 |
| *Les Misérables*, London | 1985– | 5,109 |

## TYPES OF THEATRE

**MIME** Emotions or tales are expressed through body and face movement. Medieval court jesters and wandering minstrels used mime to entertain.

**CABARET** Comprised of a mix of songs, dances and theatrical sketches. The earliest shows were given in Paris, in front of dining audiences.

**PANTOMIME** Amusing drama that combines music, dancing and acrobatics. Harlequin the clown is a traditional character.

**MYSTERY PLAYS** These link Biblical scenes with current events. A group of plays is called a cycle and is traditionally performed in summer.

**COMMEDIA DELL'ARTE** Stock characters are played by leather-masked actors. Basic plots are improvised with acrobatics and farcical routines.

**GREEK TRAGEDY** Three principal characters and a chorus were part of each drama. Lead actors wore masks that indicated the character's emotion.

**NOH AND KABUKI** Traditional Japanese theatre, which features a mixture of acting, miming, and dancing. Noh actors wear masks and ornate costumes. Kabuki actors have dramatically painted faces and perform on a revolving stage.

**MUSICALS** Plots are told through a mixture of music, lyrics and dance.

## LARGEST INDOOR THEATRES

| Theatre | Country | Date Opened | No of Seats |
|---|---|---|---|
| National People's Congress Building Theatre | Beijing, China | 1959 | 10,000 |
| Perth Entertainment Centre | Australia | 1976 | 8,003 |
| Chaplin (originally Blanquetta) | Havana, Cuba | 1949 | 6,500 |
| Radio City Music Hall | New York, USA | 1932 | 6,200+ |

# FILMS

## MOST EXPENSIVE FILMS EVER MADE

| FILM | COUNTRY | YEAR | ESTIMATED COST ($) |
|------|---------|------|--------------------|
| *Titanic* | USA | 1997 | 200,000,000 |
| *Waterworld* | USA | 1995 | 175,000,000 |
| *Armageddon* | USA | 1998 | 140,000,000 |
| *Dante's Peak* | USA | 1997 | 116,000,000 |
| *Batman and Robin* | USA | 1997 | 110,000,000 |
| *Tomorrow Never Dies* | USA | 1997 | 110,000,000 |
| *True Lies* | USA | 1994 | 110,000,000 |
| *Speed 2: Cruise Control* | USA | 1997 | 110,000,000 |
| *Inchon* | USA, Korea | 1981 | 102,000,000 |

## LONGEST FILMS EVER SCREENED

The list includes commercially screened films, but not "stunt" films created solely to break endurance records. *The Longest and Most Meaningless Movie in the World* was cut to a more manageable 1 hr 30 min, but remained just as meaningless.

| TITLE | COUNTRY | YEAR | DURATION HR:MIN |
|-------|---------|------|-----------------|
| *The Longest and Most Meaningless Movie in the World* | UK | 1970 | 48:00 |
| *The Burning of the Red Lotus Temple* | China | 1928–1931 | 27:00 |
| **** | USA | 1967 | 25:00 |
| *Heimat* | Germany | 1984 | 15:40 |
| *Berlin Alexanderplatz* | Germany/ Italy | 1980 | 15:21 |

## TOP CINEMA-GOING COUNTRIES

| COUNTRY | ANNUAL VISITS PER PERSON |
|---------|--------------------------|
| Lebanon | 35.3 |
| China | 12.3 |
| Georgia | 5.6 |
| India | 5.0 |
| Iceland | 4.5 |
| Australia | 3.9 |
| New Zealand | 3.9 |
| USA | 3.9 |
| Monaco | 3.7 |

## COUNTRIES WITH THE MOST CINEMAS

| COUNTRY | NUMBER OF CINEMAS |
|---------|-------------------|
| USA | 23,662 |
| Ukraine | 14,960 |
| India | 8,975 |
| China | 4,639 |
| France | 4,365 |
| Italy | 3,816 |
| Germany | 3,814 |
| Belorussia | 3,780 |
| Uzbekistan | 2,365 |

## FILM EQUIPMENT

**PROPS** All the items that are needed to make the costumes and setting authentic.

**BOOM** A long pole on which a microphone is mounted.

**DOLLY** A wheeled stand for the camera and tripod, to help smooth movement.

**GEL** A coloured piece of film that can filter light to create a different atmosphere.

**SPECIAL FX** "Special effects" – everything from creating the weather to exploding buildings!

## MOST PROLIFIC FILM PRODUCERS

| COUNTRY | ANNUAL PRODUCTION |
|---------|-------------------|
| India | 851 |
| USA | 569 |
| Japan | 252 |
| Russia | 192 |
| France | 143 |
| China | 137 |
| Italy | 107 |
| South Korea | 80 |
| Turkey | 71 |
| UK | 65 |

## HIGHEST-GROSSING FILMS OF ALL TIME

| FILM | YEAR OF RELEASE | WORLD GROSS INCOME $ |
|------|-----------------|----------------------|
| *Titanic* | 1997 | 1,749,900,000 |
| *Jurassic Park* | 1993 | 920,100,000 |
| *Independence Day* | 1996 | 811,200,000 |
| *Star Wars* | 1977 | 783,700,000 |
| *The Lion King* | 1994 | 766,900,000 |
| *E.T.: The Extra-Terrestrial* | 1982 | 704,800,000 |
| *Forrest Gump* | 1994 | 679,700,000 |
| *The Lost World: Jurassic Park* | 1997 | 614,100,000 |
| *Men in Black* | 1997 | 586,100,000 |
| *Return of the Jedi* | 1983 | 572,800,000 |
| *The Empire Strikes Back* | 1980 | 533,900,000 |

## MOST EXPENSIVE ITEMS OF FILM MEMORABILIA

This list excludes colour cels from animated films, which attain colossal prices: one cel from *Snow White* (1937) sold for $209,000. Prices are listed in American dollars – the currency in which they were bought.

| ITEM AND SALE | PRICE $ |
|---|---|
| Clark Gable's Oscar® for *It Happened One Night* Christie's, Los Angeles, 15 December 1996 | 607,500 |
| Vivien Leigh's Oscar® for *Gone with the Wind* Sotheby's, New York, 15 December 1993 | 562,500 |
| Poster for *The Mummy*, 1932 Sotheby's, New York, 1 March 1997 | 453,500 |
| James Bond's Aston Martin DB5 from *Goldfinger* Sotheby's, New York, 28 June 1986 | 275,000 |
| Clark Gable's personal script for *Gone With the Wind* Christie's, Los Angeles, 15 December 1996 | 244,500 |
| 'Rosebud' sled from *Citizen Kane* Christie's, Los Angeles, 15 December 1996 | 233,500 |

## FILMS TO WIN THE MOST OSCARS®

| FILM | YEAR | NOMINATIONS | AWARDS |
|---|---|---|---|
| *Ben-Hur* | 1959 | 12 | 11 |
| *Titanic* | 1997 | 14 | 11 |
| *West Side Story* | 1961 | 11 | 10 |
| *Gigi* | 1958 | 9 | 9 |
| *The Last Emperor* | 1987 | 9 | 9 |
| *The English Patient* | 1996 | 12 | 9 |
| *Gone With the Wind* | 1939 | 13 | 8 |
| *From Here to Eternity* | 1953 | 13 | 8 |
| *On the Waterfront* | 1954 | 12 | 8 |
| *My Fair Lady* | 1964 | 12 | 8 |

## TOP HOLLYWOOD STUDIOS

**COLUMBIA** Along with Tri-Star, Columbia is owned by Japanese company Sony. Among its blockbusters is *Men in Black* (1997).

**MGM** Among other films, Metro Goldwyn Mayer made the *Tom and Jerry* cartoons. It merged with United Artists in 1981.

**PARAMOUNT** Based on a studio founded in 1912, Paramount has earned huge amounts from the three Indiana Jones films, and in 1997 made *Titanic*, the highest-earning film to date.

**TWENTIETH CENTURY FOX** Founded in 1912, it is notable for smash hits such as *Independence Day* (1996).

**UNIVERSAL** Once the world's largest studio, Universal is most famous for *Jurassic Park* (1993) and *E.T.* (1982).

**WARNER BROS** Warner Brothers made the first sound film, *The Jazz Singer* in 1927. *Batman* (1989) is one of its highest-earning films ever.

## CINEMA MILESTONES

**1895** The cinema era begins when the Lumière brothers present a programme of films to a paying audience in the basement of a Paris café.

**1913** German film makers film stories of intrigue and mysterious death.

**1915** *The Birth of a Nation*, directed by D. W. Griffith, is released. It is the first "epic" film and is famous for its spectacular battle scenes.

**1920s** The first film studios in India spring up in Bombay, later known as "Bollywood".

**1927** *The Jazz Singer* is the first film to record spoken dialogue. The "talkies" revolutionize the cinema and silent films soon die out.

**1929** The Oscar® awards are presented for the first time. Today, the ceremony is a TV spectacular.

**1932** The Technicolor process is perfected. Colour films begin to replace black and white films.

**1940s** Song-and-dance musicals become popular.

**1953** Twentieth Century Fox's CinemaScope introduces wide-screen cinema.

**1977** *Star Wars* ushers in the era of the modern blockbuster.

**1996** *Toy Story* is the first full-length computer-generated film.

**❗ DID YOU KNOW?**
🔍 The Oscar® is so-called because the librarian at the Academy said that the statue reminded her of her Uncle Oscar. The name stuck!

ACADEMY FIRST AWARD
TO
CECIL BEATON
FOR COLOR COSTUME DESIGN OF
"MY FAIR LADY"

# FILM STARS

## YOUNGEST OSCAR® WINNERS

The Academy Awards ceremony usually takes place at the end of March in the year following that in which the film was released, so the winners are generally at least a year older when they receive their Oscar® than when they acted in their award-winning films.

| ACTOR/ACTRESS | AGE | AWARD | FILM | YEAR |
|---|---|---|---|---|
| Shirley Temple | 6 | Special Award | For all her films | 1934 |
| Margaret O'Brien | 8 | Special Award | *Meet Me in St Louis* | 1944 |
| Vincent Winter | 8 | Special Award | *The Little Kidnappers* | 1954 |
| Ivan Jandl | 9 | Special Award | *The Search* | 1948 |
| Jon Whiteley | 10 | Special Award | *The Little Kidnappers* | 1954 |

## OLDEST OSCAR®-WINNING ACTORS AND ACTRESSES

| ACTOR/ACTRESS | AGE | AWARD | FILM | YEAR |
|---|---|---|---|---|
| Jessica Tandy | 80 | Best Actress | *Driving Miss Daisy* | 1989 |
| George Burns | 80 | Best Supporting Actor | *The Sunshine Boys* | 1975 |
| Melvyn Douglas | 79 | Best Supporting Actor | *Being There* | 1979 |
| John Gielgud | 77 | Best Supporting Actor | *Arthur* | 1981 |
| Don Ameche | 77 | Best Supporting Actor | *Cocoon* | 1985 |

**DID YOU KNOW?**
Three-colour cameras for making Technicolor films were developed in 1932. *Becky Sharp* (1937) was the first Technicolor film.

## TOP FILMS WITH CHILD STARS

| FILM | DATE | CHILD STAR(S) |
|---|---|---|
| *Jurassic Park* | 1993 | Joseph Mazello, Ariana Richards |
| *E.T.: The Extra-Terrestrial* | 1982 | Drew Barrymore, Robert McNaughton, K.C. Martel |
| *The Lost World: Jurassic Park* | 1997 | Joseph Mazello, Ariana Richards |
| *Home Alone* | 1990 | Macaulay Culkin |
| *Mrs Doubtfire* | 1993 | Lisa Jakub, Matthew Lawrence, Mara Wilson |
| *Indiana Jones and the Temple of Doom* | 1984 | Jonathan Ke Quan |

## CLASSIC HOLLYWOOD FILM STARS (1920–1950)

**GRETA GARBO** One of Hollywood's most successful female stars, Swedish Greta Garbo captured the hearts of many men.

**CARY GRANT** British-born Cary Grant usually played the hero in light comedies, often with Katharine Hepburn.

**KATHARINE HEPBURN** The winner of four Oscars®, Katharine Hepburn often played strong female roles.

**INGRID BERGMAN** Winning an Oscar® in 1944 for her part in *Gaslight*, Swedish Ingrid Bergman was a leading lady.

**HUMPHREY BOGART** A star in the 1940s, Humphrey Bogart starred in many film noirs. His most famous film is *Casablanca*.

**MARILYN MONROE** A notorious Hollywood star, Monroe found fame in 1953. Her films include *Gentlemen Prefer Blondes*.

**JAMES DEAN** Dean became famous for his roles as a rebellious teenager, in films such as *Rebel Without a Cause*.

## FILMS WITH CASTS OF THOUSANDS (OF EXTRAS)

| FILM | COUNTRY | YEAR | EXTRAS |
|---|---|---|---|
| *Gandhi* | UK | 1982 | 300,000 |
| *Kolberg* | Germany | 1945 | 187,000 |
| *Monster Wang-magwi* | South Korea | 1967 | 157,000 |
| *War and Peace* | USSR | 1967 | 120,000 |
| *Ilya Muromets* | USSR | 1956 | 106,000 |

## ACTORS WHO HAVE PLAYED...

**ROBIN HOOD** A forest-dweller, who, with his band of Merry Men, stole from the rich and gave to the poor. Douglas Fairbanks (1922) • Errol Flynn (1938) • Russell Hicks (1948) • Jon Hall (1948) • Robert Clarke (1951) • Richard Todd (1952) • Don Taylor (1954) • Richard Greene (1960) • Barrie Ingram (1967) • Sean Connery (1976) • John Cleese (1981) Kevin Costner (1991) • Patrick Bergin (1991) • Cary Elwes (1993)

**SUPERMAN** A superhero with special powers. Kirk Alyn (1948, 1950) • George Reeves (1951, 1953–1957) Christopher Reeve (1978, 1980, 1983, 1987) • Dean Cain (1993–)

**TARZAN** A man reared by apes. Elmo Lincoln (1918–1921) • Johnny Weismuller (1932–1958) Buster Crabbe (1933) • Herman Brix (changed name to Bruce Bennett) (1935) • Lex Barker (1949–1952) • Gordon Scott (1955–1960) • Denny Miller (1959) • Jock Mahoney (1962–1963) Mike Henry (1966–1968) • Ron Ely (1970) Miles O'Keeffe (1981) • Christopher Lambert (1984)

**DRACULA** A vampire from Transylvania. Bela Lugosi (1931–1948) • Lon Chaney, Jr (1943) • John Carradine (1944–1979) • Christopher Lee (1958–1976) • David Niven (1975) George Hamilton (1979) • Frank Langella (1979) Gary Oldman (1992) • Leslie Nielsen (1995)

**JESUS** The son of God, according to Christian faith. Jeffrey Hunter (1961) • Luis Alvarez (1965) • Max Von Sydow (1965) • Victor Garber (1973) • Robert Powell (1977) • Kenneth Colley (1979) • Brian Deacon (1979) • John Hurt (1981) Willem Dafoe (1988)

**JAMES BOND** A British secret agent. David Niven (1967) • Sean Connery (1962–1983) • George Lazenby (1969) • Roger Moore (1973–1983) • Timothy Dalton (1987–1990) • Pierce Brosnan (1995–1997)

**DID YOU KNOW?** Pierce Brosnan was the favourite to replace Roger Moore in the James Bond series, but he was unavailable due to other acting obligations, so the role went to Timothy Dalton.

## MODERN COMEDY STARS

| STAR | FAMOUS FILM |
| --- | --- |
| Dan Ackroyd | *Ghostbusters* (1984) |
| Woody Allen | *Manhattan* (1979) |
| Jim Carrey | *The Mask* (1994) |
| Danny DeVito | *Get Shorty* (1995) |
| Whoopi Goldberg | *Sister Act* (1992) |
| Goldie Hawn | *Private Benjamin* (1980) |
| Steve Martin | *Parenthood* (1989) |
| Eddie Murphy | *Beverly Hills Cop* (1984) |
| Robin Williams | *Mrs Doubtfire* (1993) |

**DID YOU KNOW?** Stan Laurel, from the UK, and Oliver Hardy, from the USA, teamed up in 1926 and were to become one of the most famous comedy duos of all time.

## CARTOON CHARACTERS' FIRST SCREEN APPEARANCES

| CHARACTER | FILM | YEAR |
| --- | --- | --- |
| Felix the Cat | *Feline Follies* | 1919 |
| Mickey Mouse | *Steamboat Willie* | 1928 |
| Pluto | *The Chain Gang* | 1930 |
| Goofy | *Mickey's Review* | 1932 |
| Popeye | *Popeye the Sailor Man* | 1933 |
| Donald Duck | *The Wise Little Hen* | 1934 |
| Porky Pig | *I Haven't Got a Hat* | 1935 |
| Bugs Bunny | *Porky's Hare Hunt* | 1938 |
| Daffy Duck | *Porky's Hare Hunt* | 1938 |
| Tom and Jerry | *Puss Gets the Boot* | 1939 |
| Woody Woodpecker | *Knock Knock* | 1940 |
| Tweety Pie | *Birdie and the Beast* | 1944 |
| Sylvester the Cat | *Kitty Kornered* | 1945 |
| Road Runner | *Fast and Furry-ous* | 1948 |
| Speedy Gonzales | *Speedy Gonzales* | 1955 |
| Teenage Mutant Ninja Turtles | *Teenage Mutant Ninja Turtles* | 1990 |

# TOP FILMS

## TOP COP FILMS

Although films in which one of the central characters is a policeman have never been the most successful films of all time, many have done well at the box office.

| FILM | YEAR | ACTORS |
|------|------|--------|
| Die Hard III | 1995 | Bruce Willis |
| The Fugitive | 1993 | Harrison Ford |
| Se7en | 1995 | Brad Pitt |
| Lethal Weapon 3 | 1993 | Mel Gibson |
| Beverly Hills Cop | 1984 | Eddie Murphy |
| Beverly Hills Cop II | 1987 | Eddie Murphy |
| Speed | 1994 | Keanu Reeves |
| Lethal Weapon 2 | 1987 | Mel Gibson |

## TOP SCIENCE-FICTION FILMS

A science-fiction film is one that draws on scientific knowledge and speculation for its theme or setting.

*Jurassic Park* (1993)
*Independence Day* (1996)
*Star Wars* (1977) • *E.T.: The Extra-Terrestrial* (1982)
*The Lost World: Jurassic Park* (1997) • *Men in Black* (1997)
*The Empire Strikes Back* (1980)
*Terminator 2: Judgment Day* (1991) • *Return of the Jedi* (1983) • *Batman* (1989)

## TOP COMEDY FILMS

All of the films listed here have earned a total of more than $200,000,000 each worldwide.

*Forrest Gump* (1994) • *Home Alone* (1990) • *Ghost* (1990)
*Pretty Woman* (1990)
*Mrs Doubtfire* (1993)
*Flintstones* (1995) • *The Mask* (1994) • *Liar Liar* (1997)
*Look Who's Talking* (1989)
*Coming to America* (1988)
*My Best Friend's Wedding* (1997) • *Home Alone 2: Lost in New York* (1992)

## TOP MUSICAL FILMS

Traditional musicals (films in which the cast sing) and films in which a musical soundtrack is a major component of the film are included here.

| FILM | YEAR | FAMOUS SONG |
|------|------|-------------|
| Grease | 1978 | The One that I Want |
| Saturday Night Fever | 1977 | Stayin' Alive |
| The Sound of Music | 1965 | My Favourite Things |
| Footloose | 1984 | Let's Hear it for the Boy |
| American Graffiti | 1973 | That'll be the Day |
| Mary Poppins | 1964 | Supercalifragilistic… |
| Flashdance | 1983 | What a Feeling! |

**DID YOU KNOW?** The popular Disney films *Aladdin*, *The Lion King*, and *Pocahontas* have all won an Oscar® for "Best Original Song".

**DID YOU KNOW?** The first full-length Disney film was *Snow White and the Seven Dwarfs*, made in 1937.

## WHAT DOES "TOP" MEAN?

The lists here are about "top" films. This refers to the highest-earning films worldwide.

## ANIMATED FILMS

Animated films stand out among the leading money-makers of each decade, some earning more than $250,000,000 apiece.

**1930s** *Snow White and the Seven Dwarfs* (1937) was the second highest earning film of the 1930s (after *Gone With the Wind*).

**1940s** *Bambi* (1942) and *Fantasia* (1940), and through additional earnings from its re-release, *Pinocchio* (1940), were the most successful films of the 1940s.

**1950s** *Lady and the Tramp* (1955) was the second most successful film of the 1950s (after *The Ten Commandments*).

**1960s** *One Hundred and One Dalmatians* (1960) is the second most successful film of this decade (after *The Sound of Music*). It is followed by *Jungle Book* (1967).

**1970s** *The Aristocats* (1970) and *The Rescuers* (1977) were popular hits.

**1980s** *Who Framed Roger Rabbit*, a part animated, part live-action film (1988), was the most successful animated film of the 1980s, and is the fifth most successful animated film of all time.

**1990s** Eight of the top ten animated films were made in the 1990s: *The Lion King* (1994), *Aladdin* (1992), *Toy Story* (1995), *Beauty and the Beast* (1991), *Pocahontas* (1995), *The Hunchback of Notre Dame* (1996) *Casper* (part live-action – 1995), and *Hercules* (1997).

## TOP CHILDREN'S FILMS

This list is of non-animated films aimed at a young audience – though no doubt they are appreciated by parents!

| FILM | YEAR OF RELEASE |
| --- | --- |
| *Hook* | 1991 |
| *Space Jam* | 1996 |
| *Honey, I Shrunk the Kids* | 1989 |
| *Ace Ventura: When Nature Calls* | 1995 |
| *Teenage Mutant Ninja Turtles* | 1990 |
| *George of the Jungle* | 1997 |
| *The Karate Kid Part II* | 1986 |
| *Mary Poppins* | 1964 |
| *The Karate Kid* | 1984 |

**DID YOU KNOW?** Some of the most successful films of all time, such as *E.T.*, *Star Wars*, *Ghostbusters*, and *Home Alone* would top this list if it were based on "family audience" films.

## TOP DISASTER FILMS

| FILM | YEAR | DISASTER SUBJECT |
| --- | --- | --- |
| *Titanic* | 1997 | Sinking of ocean liner |
| *Twister* | 1996 | Tornadoes |
| *Die Hard III* | 1995 | Terrorists |
| *Apollo 13* | 1995 | Exploding space capsule |
| *Outbreak* | 1995 | Killer viruses |

## TOP HORROR FILMS

Horror films entertain or fascinate audiences by shocking or frightening, using an emphasis on bloodshed or supernatural forces.

| FILM | DATE | SCARY CHARACTER |
| --- | --- | --- |
| *Jaws* | 1975 | Shark |
| *Interview With the Vampire* | 1994 | Vampires |
| *Jaws II* | 1978 | Shark |
| *Bram Stoker's Dracula* | 1992 | Vampire |
| *The Exorcist* | 1973 | Evil spirit |
| *Mary Shelley's Frankenstein* | 1994 | Monster |

## TOP DINOSAUR FILMS

*Jurassic Park* (1993) • *The Lost World: Jurassic Park* (1997) • *Fantasia* (animated) (1940) • *The Land Before Time* (animated) (1988) • *Baby… Secret of the Lost Legend* (1985) • *One of Our Dinosaurs is Missing* (1975) • *Journey to the Centre of the Earth* (1959)

## MOST-FILMED STORIES OF ALL TIME

*Alice in Wonderland* (Lewis Carroll) • *A Christmas Carol* (Charles Dickens) • *Cinderella* (fairy story) • *Dr Jekyll and Mister Hyde* (Robert Louis Stevenson) • *Dracula* (Bram Stoker) *Frankenstein* (Mary Shelley) • *Hamlet* (William Shakespeare) *Julius Caesar* (William Shakespeare) • *Macbeth* (William Shakespeare) • *Oliver Twist* (Charles Dickens) • *Robinson Crusoe* (Daniel Defoe) • *Romeo and Juliet* (William Shakespeare)

## TOP WESTERNS

A western is a type of film that is set in the west of the USA in the 19th century.

*Dances with Wolves* (1990) • *Maverick* (1994) • *Unforgiven* (1992) • *Butch Cassidy and the Sundance Kid* (1969) *Jeremiah Johnson* (1972) • *How the West Was Won* (1962) • *Young Guns* (1988) • *Young Guns II* (1990) • *Pale Rider* (1985) • *Bronco Billy* (1980) *Little Big Man* (1970).

## TOP FILMS STARRING ANIMALS

This is a list of top non-animated films where an animal is acknowledged as the central, rather than a secondary character.

| FILM | YEAR | ANIMAL |
| --- | --- | --- |
| *Jaws* | 1975 | Man-eating shark |
| *101 Dalmatians* | 1996 | Dalmatian puppies |
| *Jaws II* | 1978 | Man-eating shark |
| *Free Willy* | 1993 | Orca whale |
| *Turner & Hooch* | 1989 | A bloodhound |

## TOP FILM SEQUELS OF ALL TIME

| ORIGINAL FILM | SEQUELS | CATEGORY |
| --- | --- | --- |
| *Star Wars* | *The Empire Strikes Back*, *Return of the Jedi* (1977–1997) | Sci-fi |
| *Jurassic Park* | *The Lost World: Jurassic Park* (1993–1997) | Sci-fi |
| *Batman* | *Batman Returns*, *Batman Forever*, *Batman & Robin* (1989–1997) | Sci-fi |
| *Raiders of the Lost Ark* | *Indiana Jones and the Temple of Doom*, *Indiana Jones and the Last Crusade* (1981–1989) | Action |

**DID YOU KNOW?** The original Hollywood sign read "Hollywoodland" and was lit up by 4,000 lights. A 120-m (400-ft) high replacement was erected in 1978, Hollywood's 75th anniversary.

# RADIO and TELEVISION

## FIRST TO HAVE TELEVISION

This lists the first to receive a high-definition regular public broadcasting service.

| COUNTRY | YEAR |
| --- | --- |
| UK | 1936 |
| USA | 1939 |
| USSR | 1939 |
| France | 1948 |
| Brazil | 1950 |
| Cuba | 1950 |
| Mexico | 1950 |
| Argentina | 1951 |
| Denmark | 1951 |

## RADIO RECORDS

**FIRST BROADCAST** The world's first radio broadcast took place on 24 December 1906. Canadian-born physicist Professor Reginald Augrey Fessenden played music and read from the Bible from Brant Rock, USA, to ships in the Atlantic Ocean.

**LARGEST AUDIENCE** The BBC World Service, which is broadcast in 41 languages, is estimated to have more than 140 million regular listeners around the world.

**MOST RADIO STATIONS** The USA has more than 12,000 authorized radio stations – more than any other country in the world.

**LONGEST-RUNNING RADIO PROGRAMME** *Rambling with Gambling*, aired six days a week on WOR radio in New York City, USA, was first broadcast in March 1925 and is still running.

**LONGEST-RUNNING RECORD PROGRAMME** BBC Radio's *Desert Island Discs* began in January 1942. In the programme, guests are asked to select the records they would take with them if stranded on a desert island.

**LONGEST-RUNNING SOLO PROGRAMME** Alistair Cooke has been presenting BBC's *Letter from America* since March 1946.

**LONGEST-RUNNING SOAP** First broadcast by the BBC in January 1951, *The Archers* remains a firm favourite today.

## TOP RADIO-OWNERS

| COUNTRY | RADIOS PER 1,000 POPULATION |
| --- | --- |
| USA | 2,093 |
| UK | 1,433 |
| Australia | 1,304 |
| Canada | 1,053 |
| Denmark | 1,034 |
| South Korea | 1,024 |
| Monaco | 1,019 |
| Finland | 1,008 |
| New Zealand | 997 |
| Germany | 944 |
| Netherlands | 937 |
| Japan | 916 |
| France | 895 |
| Lebanon | 891 |
| Sweden | 882 |
| Ukraine | 856 |
| Switzerland | 851 |
| Italy | 822 |

**DID YOU KNOW?** The top eight countries on this list have at least one radio per person.

**DID YOU KNOW?** The Australian serial *Blue Hill* was the world's longest running serial. During its 27-year run, 5,795 episodes were made, all written by the same scriptwriter, Ainsworth Harrison, alias Gwen Meredith. Its last show was broadcast in 1976.

## TV MILESTONES

**THE FIRST DAILY BROADCAST** The BBC, based in London, UK, made the first daily broadcast on 10 November 1936.

**THE FIRST TV COMMERCIAL** A 20-second commercial for a Bulova clock, which cost $9 to air, was broadcast by WNBT New York, during a game between the Brooklyn Dodgers and the Philadelphia Phillies, on 1 July 1941.

**THE FIRST SOAP OPERA ON TV** The first regular daytime serial, DuMont TV network's *A Woman to Remember*, began its run on 21 February 1947.

**THE FIRST BROADCAST OF A CURRENT AFFAIRS TV SHOW** NBC's *Meet the Press* was first broadcast on 6 November 1947.

**THE FIRST COMMERCIAL COLOUR BROADCAST** Hallmark's presentation of Gian Carlo Menotti's opera *Amahl and the Night Visitors*, aired on 24 December 1951, was the first colour broadcast.

**THE FIRST NETWORKED COAST-TO-COAST COLOUR TV SHOW** *The Tournament of Roses* parade at Pasadena, California, hosted by Don Ameche, was seen in colour in 21 cities across America on 1 January 1954.

## TV RECORDS

**WORLD'S LONGEST-RUNNING SHOW** NBC's *Meet the Press* was first transmitted on 6 November 1947 and it was shown weekly from 12 September 1948.

**LONGEST CONTINUOUS BROADCAST** GTV in Australia was on air between 19 and 26 July 1969 for a record 163 hours 18 minutes, whilst transmitting *Apollo XI's* Moon mission during which two men walked on the Moon for the first time in history.

**LONGEST-SERVING PRESENTER** The BBC's monthly *Sky at Night*, an astronomy show, has been presented by Patrick Moore without a break since 24 April 1957. It celebrated its 500th edition in April 1995.

**DID YOU KNOW?** The number of homes with TV sets is now more than 500 million worldwide.

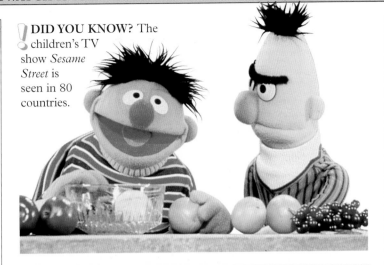

**DID YOU KNOW?** The children's TV show *Sesame Street* is seen in 80 countries.

## TV FIRSTS

**FIRST PRESIDENT TO APPEAR ON TV** The former American President Franklin D. Roosevelt was seen by US television viewers opening the World's Fair, New York, on 30 April 1939.

**FIRST CORONATION** The coronation of the British Queen, Elizabeth II in 1953, was broadcast live in the UK, and also in Germany, the Netherlands, and France.

**FIRST TELEVISED ATOMIC BOMB EXPLOSION** An "Operation Ranger" detonation at Frenchman Flats, Nevada, on 1 February 1951, was televised by KTLA, Los Angeles, USA.

**FIRST TV INTERVIEW** Irish actress Peggy O'Neil appeared on television at the Ideal Home Exhibition, UK, on 29 April 1930.

## TOP TV-OWNERS

| COUNTRY | TVS PER 1,000 POPULATION |
| --- | --- |
| USA | 805 |
| Monaco | 750 |
| Malta | 749 |
| Canada | 714 |
| El Salvador | 689 |
| Japan | 684 |
| Oman | 657 |
| France | 589 |
| Denmark | 574 |
| Germany | 564 |
| Finland | 519 |
| New Zealand | 514 |
| Austria | 497 |
| Netherlands | 497 |
| Australia | 495 |
| Czech Republic | 482 |
| Sweden | 478 |
| Latvia | 477 |
| Slovakia | 476 |
| Georgia | 468 |

## TOP BRITISH TV AUDIENCES OF ALL TIME

| PROGRAMME | DATE | AUDIENCE |
| --- | --- | --- |
| Royal Wedding of HRH Prince Charles to Lady Diana Spencer | 29 July 1981 | 39,000,000 |
| Brazil v England 1970 World Cup | 10 June 1970 | 32,500,000 |
| England v West Germany 1966 World Cup Final | 30 July 1966 | 32,000,000 |
| Chelsea v Leeds Cup Final Replay | 28 April 1970 | 32,000,000 |
| Funeral of Diana, Princess of Wales | 6 September 1997 | 31,000,000 |
| *EastEnders* Christmas episode | 26 December 1987 | 30,000,000 |

## MOST VIDEO RECORDERS

| COUNTRY | % OF HOMES | NUMBER OF VCRS |
| --- | --- | --- |
| USA | 89.6 | 86,825,000 |
| China | 13.3 | 40,000,000 |
| Japan | 80.4 | 34,309,000 |
| Germany | 71.8 | 26,328,000 |
| UK | 81.7 | 18,848,000 |
| Brazil | 37.2 | 15,488,000 |
| France | 70.4 | 15,483,000 |
| Italy | 60.2 | 13,161,000 |
| Russia | 20.6 | 10,315,000 |
| Mexico | 56.7 | 8,540,000 |
| Canada | 70.5 | 8,180,000 |
| Spain | 60.1 | 7,293,000 |

## VIDEO QUESTIONS AND ANSWERS

**WHO NAMED VIDEO?** The terms "video recording" and "videotape" were first used in the early 1950s by TV professionals.

**WHERE DOES VCR COME FROM?** VCR (Video Cassette Recorder) was used in the UK and USA in 1971.

**WHEN WAS VIDEO AVAILABLE?** The first domestic video recorders were sold in 1974, but were very expensive.

**WHEN WAS VHS LAUNCHED?** The VHS (Video Home System) was launched in 1976 in the USA and 1978 in Europe.

**HOW MANY PEOPLE OWN VIDEOS?** The number of homes with video recorders has increased 50-fold since 1980.

**WHICH IS THE BEST-SELLING VIDEO?** Disney's *Lion King* sold 20 million copies in the first six months of release.

**DID YOU KNOW?** The camcorder was invented in 1981. Its built-in recorder saves images onto a cassette. Today, you can buy a camcorder small enough to fit into the palm of your hand!

# WORLD SPORT

## SPORTING MISCELLANY

**DID YOU KNOW?** Sport hooliganism is not new. Roman writer Tacitus reported battles between rival team supporters in Pompeii's amphitheatre in the first century AD.

### COMMON SPORTS INJURIES

Even the fittest of athletes can injure themselves during strenuous training. The most common sports injuries are:

Bruising • Sprained ankle • Sprained knee • Lower back strain • Hamstring tear • Jumper's knee • Achilles tendinitis • Shin splints • Tennis elbow

### SPORTS INVOLVING ANIMALS OTHER THAN HORSES!

Not only horses are used for racing!

**PIGEON RACING** Homing pigeons are transported to a designated place and released to fly home. Several pigeons compete at a time, and the first to reach home is the winner.

**DOG-SLED RACING** This sport is popular in Alaska. Each sled is pulled by a team of dogs and is controlled by a driver called a musher. The most famous annual sled dog race is the 2,090-km (1,299-mile) Iditarod, from Anchorage to Nome.

**GREYHOUND RACING** Specially bred greyhound dogs chase an electric hare around a track over distances between 210 m (689 ft) and 1,100 m (3,609 ft). Races may involve six or eight dogs.

### SPORTING HEARTS

The more demanding a sport, the bigger the heart of the athlete. Here are the categories of athlete with the biggest hearts:

Tour de France cyclists • Marathon runners • Rowers • Boxers • Sprint cyclists Middle-distance runners •Weightlifters

### POPULAR SPORTING SUPERSTITIONS

**GENERAL** The number 13 is widely considered to be unlucky and no player wants to wear the number 13.

**TENNIS** It is bad luck to hold more than two balls at a time when serving.
• When switching sides, it is lucky to walk around the outside of the court.

**BASEBALL** It is lucky to spit into your hand before you pick up the bat.
• Never lend your bat to another player – it's considered to be unlucky.
• It is bad luck if a dog walks across the diamond before the first pitch.

**FISHING** Fish may not bite if a barefoot woman passes you on the way to the dock.
• Throw back your first catch for good luck.
• It's bad luck to change rods while fishing.
• Spitting on your bait before you cast your rod is said to make fish bite.

**BOWLING** If you are in the middle of a phase of winning, keep wearing the same clothes each time you play.

**GOLF** Start only with odd-numbered clubs.
• Carry coins in your pockets for good luck.
• Balls with a number higher than four are thought to be bad luck.

**ICE-HOCKEY** It is bad luck for hockey sticks to lie crossed.
• Players believe that they will win if they tap the goalie on his shin pads before a game.

### THE WORLD'S HIGHEST-EARNING SPORTSMEN

| NAME | SPORT | SALARY | ENDORSEMENTS | TOTAL |
|---|---|---|---|---|
| Michael Jordan | Basketball | 31,300,000 | 47,000,000 | 78,300,000 |
| Evander Holyfield | Boxing | 53,000,000 | 1,300,000 | 54,300,000 |
| Oscar De La Hoya | Boxing | 37,000,000 | 1,000,000 | 38,000,000 |
| Michael Schumacher | Motor racing | 25,000,000 | 10,000,000 | 35,000,000 |
| Mike Tyson | Boxing | 27,000,000 | — | 27,000,000 |
| Tiger Woods | Golf | 2,100,000 | 24,000,000 | 26,100,000 |
| Shaquille O'Neal | Basketball | 12,900,000 | 12,500,000 | 25,400,000 |
| Dale Earnhardt | Stock car racing | 3,600,000 | 15,500,000 | 19,100,000 |
| Joe Sakic | Ice-hockey | 17,800,000 | 100,000 | 17,900,000 |
| Grant Hill | Basketball | 5,000,000 | 12,000,000 | 17,000,000 |

This list gives the total annual income in US dollars of each sportsman during 1997. The total is, in each case, broken down into salary and endorsements, which is the money earned from sponsorship and royalties. All the sportsmen listed are American, with the sole exception of Michael Schumacher, who was born in Germany.

## TIMELINE OF SPORT

**c.3000–1500 BC**  Bull sports played in ancient Crete, Greece.

**c.1500 BC**  Wrestling, fighting, and running events in Egypt.

**c.776 BC**  First Olympic Games held at Olympia in Greece.

**c.200 BC**  Roman crowds watch gladiators fight to the death.

**c.20 BC**  Sumo wrestling develops in Japan from Chinese wrestling.

**c.AD 400**  Aztecs of Central America play *tlachtli*, a ball game.

**c.1100**  Jousting is popular with English and French knights.

**1200s**  Clergy and royalty of France play "real tennis"; skating is popular on frozen canals in Holland; bowls played in England.

**1400s**  *Calcio* (kick), a form of early football is played in Florence, Italy. Each side has 27 players.

**1636**  The game of lacrosse develops from baggataway, which is still played by the Huron people in present-day Ontario, Canada.

**1777**  British explorer Captain James Cook (1729–1779) observes people surfing off the Pacific islands of Tahiti and Oahu.

**1811**  First outdoor gymnasium opened by German teacher Friedrich Jahn (1778–1852), inventor of the rings and parallel bars.

**1823**  Rugby is born when William Webb Ellis, a pupil at Rugby School, England, picks up and runs with the ball in a soccer match.

**c.1829**  Baseball is first played in the USA.

**1839**  First Grand National steeplechase is held at Aintree, England.

**1843**  First cross-country ski race held in Tromso, Norway.

**1846**  Soccer rules drawn up at Cambridge University, England.

**1847**  Ten-pin bowling is born in Connecticut, USA.

**1861**  First hockey club formed in London.

**1865**  Gloved boxing develops from bare-knuckle fighting.

**1866**  First show-jumping event is held in Paris.

**1874**  American football develops from soccer and rugby.

**1876**  Modern badminton rules are drawn up in Poona, India.

**1877**  First cricket Test Match held in Melbourne, Australia; first Wimbledon lawn tennis championships held in England.

**1882**  Judo developed by Jigoro Kano (1860–1938) in Japan.

**1891**  Basketball invented in Massachusetts, USA.

**1895**  Volleyball devised by William G. Morgan in Massachusetts, USA. First motor race held, Paris–Bordeaux–Paris.

**1896**  First modern Olympic Games held in Athens.

**1903**  First Tour de France multi-stage cycle race.

**1924**  First Winter Olympics staged at Chamonix, France.

**1930**  Soccer's first World Cup is held in Uruguay.

**1960**  First Paralympics is held for disabled people in Rome, Italy.

**1980–1990s**  Regular mass marathons staged worldwide.

## SPORTING WOMEN OF THE 20TH CENTURY

**FANNY BLANKERS-KOEN**  Known as "The Flying Dutchwoman", this athlete won the 80 m hurdles, 100 m, 200 m, and the sprint relay at the 1948 Olympics in London.

**ZOLA BUDD**  In 1985, South African runner Zola Budd set a new world record of 14 min 48.07 sec for the 5,000 m race.

**NADIA COMANECI**  This Romanian gymnast was the first ever to score a perfect 10 at the 1976 Olympics.

**CHARLOTTE COOPER**  In 1900, this UK tennis player became first woman Olympic champion.

**DAWN FRASER**  This Australian swimmer won gold for the 100 m freestyle in three successive Olympic Games – 1956, 1960, and 1964.

**MARTINA NAVRATILOVA**  This Czech-born tennis player won her ninth Wimbledon singles title in 1990.

## SPORTING MEN OF THE 20TH CENTURY

**ROGER BANNISTER**  In 1954, this UK runner was the first to run a mile in under four minutes. His time was 3 min 59.4 sec.

**PRINCE BORGHESE**  In 1907, after 62 days, this Italian racer won the 12,872-km (8,045-mile) Peking to Paris motor race.

**DONALD BRADMAN**  This Australian cricketer set a Test match record on 12 July 1930 with a score of 334 runs in Leeds, UK.

**JOE LOUIS**  This heavyweight boxer was world champion from 1937 to 1949. He defended his title 25 times.

**DIEGO MARADONA**  Barcelona paid a record $7.5 million for Argentine footballer Maradona in 1982.

**JOE MONTANA**  This US footballer led his team, the San Francisco 49ers to victory in four Super Bowls in the 1980s.

**BABE RUTH**  This US baseball player of the Boston Red Sox was sold to the New York Yankees for $125,000 in 1920.

## MAXIMUM OFFICIAL BALL WEIGHTS

| BALL | WEIGHT | |
|---|---|---|
| | G | OZ |
| Table tennis ball | 2.53 | 0.09 |
| Squash ball | 24.60 | 0.87 |
| Golf ball | 45.93 | 1.61 |
| Tennis ball | 58.50 | 2.06 |
| Cricket ball | 163.01 | 5.74 |
| Ice-hockey puck | 170.00 | 5.98 |
| Pool ball | 170.10 | 5.99 |
| Volleyball | 280.00 | 9.86 |
| Rugby ball | 439.42 | 15.47 |
| Ten-pin bowling ball | 7,260.00 | 255.55 |

# BALL GAMES

## VOLLEYBALL FACTFILE

**WHAT IS THE GAME?** Players hit a ball over a high net using any part of their upper body. Play is usually on a hard court but can take place on the beach.

**NUMBER OF PLAYERS** Teams usually have six players each, but in beach volleyball teams of two compete. Six substitutions are allowed in each set.

**POSITIONS** Three players play from the front attack line. The remaining three cover the rear, with the right player acting as server. Positions are rotated at each change of service.

**RULES** The ball may not be caught. • A team has up to three hits to return the ball. • Service changes when a serve goes out or fails to clear the net.

## NETBALL FACTFILE

**WHAT IS THE GAME?** A female sport, played on a large hard court that is divided into thirds. Umpires control the game from the side of the court and blow whistles to start and stop play.

**AIM OF THE GAME** To score goals by throwing the ball into a ring placed at the opposing team's end of the court. Rings are fixed to the top of long poles.

**NUMBER OF PLAYERS** The game is played between two teams of seven players.

**POSITIONS** Goal shoot
Goal attack • Wing attack
Centre • Wing defence
Goal defence • Goalkeeper.

**RULES** Players must keep to their area. • Players must not move with the ball. • The ball cannot be held for over three seconds.

**SCORING** A goal is awarded when the ball is sent through the ring by a shooter or attacker.

## TOP OLYMPIC VOLLEYBALL MEDALLISTS

| COUNTRY | GOLD | SILVER | BRONZE | TOTAL |
|---|---|---|---|---|
| USSR | 7 | 4 | 1 | 12 |
| Japan | 3 | 3 | 2 | 8 |
| USA | 2 | 1 | 2 | 5 |
| Cuba | 2 | – | 1 | 3 |
| Brazil/China | 1 | 1 | 1 | 3 |
| Poland | 1 | – | 2 | 3 |
| Italy | – | 2 | 1 | 3 |
| Netherlands | 1 | 1 | – | 2 |
| East Germany | – | 2 | – | 2 |
| Bulgaria/ Czechoslovakia | | 1 | 1 | 2 |

## TOP OLYMPIC HANDBALL MEDALLISTS

Team handball was introduced at the 1936 Berlin Olympics as an 11-a-side outdoor game, played only by men. It was dropped from the Games until 1972, when it was reintroduced as a seven-a-side indoor game at the Olympics. It was first played at competition by women in 1976.

| COUNTRY | GOLD | SILVER | BRONZE | TOTAL |
|---|---|---|---|---|
| USSR | 5 | 1 | 2 | 8 |
| Yugoslavia | 3 | 1 | 1 | 5 |
| South Korea | 2 | 3 | – | 5 |
| Romania | – | 1 | 3 | 4 |
| East Germany | 1 | 1 | 1 | 3 |
| Sweden | – | 2 | – | 2 |
| Hungary | – | – | 2 | 2 |

## BOWLING GAMES

**TEN-PIN BOWLING** An indoor sport where players roll a ball down an alley aiming to knock down ten pins. It was first played in the USA in c.1850 as an alternative to the German game of nine-pins. World championships are held by the Fédération Internationale des Quilleurs (FIQ).

**BOWLS** In bowls, individuals roll bowls called woods along a flat green, aiming at a target ball called a jack. The rules of outdoor bowls were set out in 1848 by Scotsman William Mitchell. World Championships for outdoor and indoor bowls are held every four years.

**BOULES** Similar to bowls, the French game of boules is usually played on sandy ground. The metal bowls are lobbed at the target ball instead of rolled along the ground as they are in bowls.

## BASKETBALL FACTS
The basketball court measures 26 m (85 ft) long and 14 m (46 ft) wide. • The rim of the basketball net is positioned 3.05 m (10 ft) high. • The ball weighs 600 g (21 oz) and has a circumference of 75 cm (30 in).

## HANDBALL FACTFILE

**WHAT IS THE GAME?** One of the world's fastest team games, this Olympic sport is played between two teams on an indoor court. Goals are scored by shooting with the hands.

**AIM OF THE GAME** To score as many goals as possible by shooting into a 3-m (10-ft) wide goal. Players pass or bounce the ball using their hands, arms, head, or upper body.

**NUMBER OF PLAYERS** Up to seven may be in play at any time, but at least five must be on the court when the game begins.

**POSITIONS** All field players play both attack and defence. Each team has a goalkeeper.

**RULES** No part of the leg below the knee may be used in play. The ball must not be held for longer than three seconds. Only the goalkeeper is allowed in the goal area.

## TOP BASKETBALL TEAMS

**MOST GAMES PLAYED** Robert Parish has played 1,611 games in the National Basketball Association (NBA). This includes games played for the American Basketball Association (ABA), which folded in 1976. Parish gained this title on 6 April 1996, at the Gateway Arena, Cleveland, USA playing his 1,561st game.

**MOST NBA TITLES** The Boston Celtics have won no fewer than 16 NBA titles.

**TOP POINTS IN THE WNBA** In a game between the Utah Starzz and the Los Angeles Sparks, in the Women's National Basketball Association (WNBA), the score was 102–89 to the Starzz!

## BASKETBALL MILESTONES

**1891** Basketball is invented by Dr James Naismith at Springfield, Massachusetts, USA.

**1895** Five-a-side is agreed as the standard size of the basketball team.

**1898** The playing of professional basketball starts in the USA.

**1932** Basketball's world governing body, Fédération Internationale de Basketball (FIBA), is formed.

**1936** Basketball becomes an Olympic sport at the Berlin Olympics; won by USA.

**1939** NCAA Championships are held for the first time; won by Oregon, USA.

**1949** National Basketball Association (NBA) is formed when the National Basketball League and Basketball Association of America merge.

**1950** World Championship held for the first time at Buenos Aires; won by Argentina. Staged every four years.

**1953** World Championships for women basketball players are first held.

**1956** NBA "Most Valuable Player" is first awarded to Bob Petit, St Louis, USA.

**1982** NCAA Women's Championship are first held; won by Louisiana Tech.

**1989** 178 national federations have become members of FIBA.

**DID YOU KNOW?** A game very similar to basketball was played in Mexico in the tenth century BC, by the Olmec people.

**DID YOU KNOW?** Many basketball players are superstitious, and believe that the last person to shoot a basket during the warm-up will have good luck during the game!

## TOP POINTS-SCORERS IN AN NBA CAREER

| PLAYER | TOTAL POINTS |
| --- | --- |
| Kareem Abdul-Jabbar | 38,387 |
| Wilt Chamberlain | 31,419 |
| Michael Jordan | 29,277 |
| Karl Malone | 27,782 |
| Moses Malone | 27,409 |
| Elvin Hayes | 27,313 |
| Oscar Robertson | 26,710 |
| Dominique Wilkins | 26,534 |
| John Havlicek | 26,395 |
| Alex English | 25,613 |

## BASKETBALL FACTFILE

**WHAT IS THE GAME?** Popular in nearly 200 countries worldwide, players of this fast game bounce a large ball or throw it to each other as they move around a hard court.

**AIM OF THE GAME** To score points by putting the ball into a basket placed at the opposing team's end of the court. The high position of each basket favours taller players.

**NUMBER OF PLAYERS** Each team has five players and can substitute freely. Players may both attack and defend.

**POSITIONS** Forwards play near the sides and guards in the middle of the court. Centres are the tallest players and stay near the basket.

**TIME** A professional game lasts for four quarters of 12 minutes each. Teams can call a one minute "time out" to discuss tactics.

**RULES** Moving players may take one stride holding the ball, but can move freely while bouncing it. If an opponent is pushed, a personal foul is committed. Attacking players may stay in the free throw area for three seconds only.

## BASKETBALL WORLD CHAMPIONS

| YEAR | MEN | YEAR | WOMEN |
| --- | --- | --- | --- |
| 1978 | Yugoslavia | 1979 | USA |
| 1982 | USSR | 1983 | USSR |
| 1986 | USA | 1986 | USA |
| 1990 | Yugoslavia | 1990 | USA |
| 1994 | USA | 1994 | Brazil |

# SOCCER

## MAJOR SOCCER EVENTS

**INTERNATIONAL** World Cup (1930) Olympics (1908): both every four years World Club Championship (1960): annual

**EUROPE** European Championship (1960): every four years • European (Champions League) Cup (1956): annual • European Cup Winners' Cup (1961): annual • UEFA (Union des Associations Européennes de Football) Cup (1955): annual

**ENGLAND** FA (Football Association) Cup (1872) • Coca Cola (League) Cup (1961) • Auto Windscreens Shield • FA Vase (1975) • FA Trophy (1969) • Charity Shield (1898) • Women's FA Cup (1993) Women's League Cup (1993): all annual

**WALES** Welsh Cup (1950) • League of Wales Cup (1993): both annual

**SCOTLAND** Scottish Cup (1874) League Challenge Cup (1890): annual

**SOUTH AMERICA** Copa America (1910): every two years • Copa Libertadores (1960): annual

**AFRICA** African Nations Cup (1957): every two years

**DID YOU KNOW?** The first football boots were steel or chrome toe-capped. They were protective, but heavy!

## SOCCER MILESTONES

**1852** First inter-school football match takes place, Westminster v Harrow.

**1862** Notts County, oldest Football League club, is founded.

**1863** Football Association (FA) founded.

**1863** Rules first published.

**1867** Queen's Park, Scotland's oldest club, is founded.

**1874** Shinguards introduced.

**1876** First professional players.

**1878** Referee's whistle is first used.

**1888** Football League is founded.

**1889** "Soccer" (abbreviation for "Association") is first used.

**1890** Goal nets are invented.

**1891** Penalty kick is introduced.

**1899** Promotion and relegation introduced to Football League.

**1904** Fédération Internationale de Football Association (FIFA) is set up.

**1920** Third Division formed.

**1923** First Wembley Cup Final held.

**1930** First World Cup (Uruguay won 4–2 at home).

**1965** Substitutes first allowed.

**1991** First women's World Cup held.

**1998** Brazil's Denilson Oliveirá moves to Spain's Real Betis for a record transfer fee of $35 million.

**AMAZING FACT!** According to rumour, a coach full of Celtic supporters travelled from Glasgow, Scotland to Nuremberg in Germany to watch their team play, only to discover they had gone to the wrong venue!

## SOCCER HALL OF FAME

FIFA launched its first Hall of Champions on 12 January 1998. These players were the first ten retired players inducted into the Hall "for sporting success that contributed to the positive image of the game".

Franz Beckenbauer (Germany) • Bobby Charlton (England) • Johan Cruyff (Holland) • Alfredo di Stefano (Argentina) • Eusebio (Portugal) Stanley Matthews (England) • Pelé (Brazil) • Michel Platini (France) • Ferenc Puskas (Hungary) • Lev Yashin (USSR)

## CLUBS WITH THE MOST FA CUP WINS

| TEAM | FIRST WIN | LAST WIN | TOTAL |
|---|---|---|---|
| Manchester United | 1909 | 1996 | 9 |
| Tottenham Hotspur | 1901 | 1991 | 8 |
| Arsenal | 1930 | 1998 | 7 |
| Aston Villa | 1887 | 1957 | 7 |
| Blackburn Rovers | 1884 | 1928 | 6 |

## SOCCER FACTFILE

**AIM OF THE GAME** The aim is to score goals by hitting the ball into the opponents' goal. Shots are usually attempted with the feet or head.

**NUMBER OF PLAYERS** Each team is made up of 11 players, but play continues with fewer if one is sent off.

**POSITIONS** Attacking players, called strikers, are the main goal-scorers. Defenders make it difficult for opponents to shoot. Midfielders act as links between attack and defence. Each team has one goalkeeper who tries to prevent balls from entering the goal.

**RULES** No player, except the goalkeeper, may handle the ball with the arms or hands. Fouls are committed if players trip, obstruct, or hold opponents. Yellow and red cards indicate a player is cautioned or dismissed.

## DID YOU KNOW?
Aged only 18, England's Michael Owen scored two goals in the 1998 World Cup.

## TOP COUNTRIES IN THE WORLD CUP

Scoring in the World Cup is calculated as follows: four points for winning the tournament, three points for runner-up, two points for third place, and one point for fourth place.

| COUNTRY | WIN | RUNNER-UP | THIRD | FOURTH | TOTAL |
| --- | --- | --- | --- | --- | --- |
| Brazil | 4 | 2 | 2 | 1 | 27 |
| Germany/West Germany | 3 | 3 | 2 | 1 | 26 |
| Italy | 3 | 2 | 1 | 1 | 21 |
| Argentina | 2 | 2 | – | – | 14 |
| Uruguay | 2 | – | – | 2 | 10 |

## BIGGEST WORLD CUP ATTENDANCES

As is apparent from these figures, many South Americans have a passion for football, either as players or spectators. Brazil's team has won the World Cup more times than any other team.

| MATCH | VENUE | YEAR | ATTENDANCE |
| --- | --- | --- | --- |
| Brazil v Uruguay | Rio de Janeiro | 1950 | 199,854 |
| Brazil v Spain | Rio de Janeiro | 1950 | 152,772 |
| Brazil v Yugoslavia | Rio de Janeiro | 1950 | 142,409 |
| Brazil v Sweden | Rio de Janeiro | 1950 | 138,886 |
| Mexico v Paraguay | Mexico City | 1986 | 114,600 |
| Argentina v West Germany | Mexico City | 1986 | 114,590 |
| Mexico v Bulgaria | Mexico City | 1986 | 114,580 |
| Argentina v England | Mexico City | 1986 | 114,580 |

## WORLD CUP WINNERS

| YEAR | WINNERS | BEAT | SCORE |
| --- | --- | --- | --- |
| 1930 | Uruguay | Argentina | 4:2 |
| 1934 | Italy | Czechoslovakia | 2:1 |
| 1938 | Italy | Hungary | 4:2 |
| 1950 | Uruguay | Brazil | 2:1 |
| 1954 | West Germany | Hungary | 3:2 |
| 1958 | Brazil | Sweden | 5:2 |
| 1962 | Brazil | Czechoslovakia | 3:1 |
| 1966 | England | West Germany | 4:2 |
| 1970 | Brazil | Italy | 4:1 |
| 1974 | West Germany | Holland | 2:1 |
| 1978 | Argentina | Holland | 3:1 |
| 1982 | Italy | West Germany | 3:1 |
| 1986 | Argentina | West Germany | 3:2 |
| 1990 | West Germany | Argentina | 1:0 |
| 1994 | Brazil | Italy | 3:2 |
| 1998 | France | Brazil | 3:0 |

## DID YOU KNOW?
The lowest-scoring World Cup competition ever was Italia 1990, which produced 115 goals from 52 matches – an average of just 2.21 per game.

## AMAZING FACT!
In the 1994 World Cup, Oleg Salenko, playing for Russia, scored a record five goals for his team in one game, against Cameroon!

## YOUNGEST BRITISH SCORERS

| PLAYER | YEAR | OPPONENTS | AGE YRS | DAYS |
| --- | --- | --- | --- | --- |
| Michael Owen | 1998 | Romania | 18 | 190 |
| Tommy Lawton | 1938 | Wales | 19 | 16 |
| Jimmy Greaves | 1959 | Peru | 19 | 86 |
| Joe Baker | 1959 | Northern Ireland | 19 | 123 |
| Jimmy Brown | 1882 | Ireland | 19 | 172 |
| Jackie Robinson | 1937 | Finland | 19 | 238 |

*British goal scorers in the World Cup*

# AMERICAN FOOTBALL and RUGBY

## SUPER BOWL WINNERS AND LOSERS

The Super Bowl is the annual championship American football game between the best team of the National Football Conference (NFC), and that of the American Football Conference (AFC). Together, the NFC and AFC form the National Football League (NFL). The Super Bowl is the climax of the football season.

| YEAR | WINNERS | LOSERS | SCORE | VENUE |
|---|---|---|---|---|
| 1990 | San Francisco 49ers | Denver Broncos | 55–10 | Superdome, New Orleans |
| 1991 | New York Giants | Buffalo Bills | 20–19 | Tampa Stadium |
| 1992 | Washington Redskins | Buffalo Bills | 37–24 | Metrodome, Minneapolis |
| 1993 | Dallas Cowboys | Buffalo Bills | 52–17 | Rose Bowl, Pasadena |
| 1994 | Dallas Cowboys | Buffalo Bills | 30–13 | Georgia Dome, Atlanta |
| 1995 | San Francisco 49ers | San Diego Chargers | 49–26 | Joe Robbie Stadium, Miami |
| 1996 | Dallas Cowboys | Pittsburgh Steelers | 27–17 | Sun Devil Stadium, Tampa |
| 1997 | Green Bay Packers | New England Patriots | 35–21 | Superdome, New Orleans |
| 1998 | Denver Broncos | Green Bay Packers | 31–24 | Qualcomm Stadium, San Diego |

**DID YOU KNOW?** Each American football team has up to 40 players, but only 11 may play at one time.

## LARGEST NFL STADIUMS

The first professional American football game was played in Pennsylvania, in 1895. Today, the sport is immensely popular, as the seating capacities of the stadiums below illustrate.

| STADIUM | HOME TEAM | CAPACITY |
|---|---|---|
| Pontiac Silverdrome | Detroit Lions | 80,368 |
| Rich Stadium | Buffalo Bills | 80,091 |
| Arrowhead Stadium | Kansas City Chiefs | 79,101 |
| Jack Cooke Stadium | Washington Redskins | 78,600 |
| Giants Stadium | New York Giants | 78,148 |
| Mile High Stadium | Denver Broncos | 76,078 |

## SUCCESSFUL AMERICAN FOOTBALL TEAMS

The winner of a Super Bowl is awarded two points; the runner-up receives one. Wins take precedence over runners-up in determining ranking.

| TEAM | WINS | RUNNERS-UP | POINTS |
|---|---|---|---|
| Dallas Cowboys | 5 | 3 | 13 |
| San Francisco 49ers | 5 | 0 | 10 |
| Pittsburgh Steelers | 4 | 1 | 10 |
| Washington Redskins | 3 | 2 | 8 |
| Green Bay Packers | 3 | 1 | 7 |
| Oakland/ Los Angeles Raiders | 3 | 1 | 7 |
| Miami Dolphins | 2 | 3 | 7 |
| Denver Broncos | 1 | 4 | 6 |

## AMERICAN FOOTBALL FACTFILE

**AIM OF THE GAME** Two teams of 11 players score points by carrying the ball over the opponents' goal line or kicking it between their goal posts.

**POSITIONS** Quarterback Punter • Kicker • Running back Defensive back • Centre Lineback • Defensive linesman Offensive guard • Tackle Wide receiver • Tight end

**TIME** Playing time consists of four 15-minute quarters. Each team is allowed three "time-outs", of 90 or 270 seconds duration, per half. Half-time lasts 15 minutes.

**RULES** The attacking team has four attempts ("downs") to advance the ball 10 yd (9.1 m). If they fail, their opponents get the ball. Each down must start with a snap – a backward pass through the legs of a player.

**SCORING** A touchdown is scored by crossing the goal line with the ball, or gaining possession within the end zone. A field goal is scored by kicking the ball through the goal posts.

## MOST CAREER POINTS

In American football, a touchdown scores six points and a field goal scores three. Individual points are made up of a combination of these.

| PLAYER | POINTS |
|---|---|
| George Blanda | 2,002 |
| Nick Lowery | 1,711 |
| Jan Stenerud | 1,699 |
| Gary Anderson | 1,681 |
| Morten Andersen | 1,641 |

## MOST CAREER TOUCHDOWNS

In American football, players earn six points for their team by scoring a touchdown. This is when a player is in possession of the ball on, above, or behind the opponents goal line.

| PLAYER | TOUCHDOWNS |
|---|---|
| Jerry Rice | 166 |
| Marcus Allen | 145 |
| Jim Brown | 126 |
| Walter Payton | 125 |
| Emmitt Smith | 119 |

## TOP POINTS-SCORERS IN MAJOR RUGBY INTERNATIONALS

| PLAYER | COUNTRY | YEARS | POINTS |
|---|---|---|---|
| Michael Lynagh | Australia | 1984–1995 | 911 |
| Gavin Hastings | Scotland | 1986–1995 | 667 |
| Grant Fox | New Zealand | 1985–1993 | 645 |
| D. Dominguez | Italy | 1991–1998 | 609 |
| Neil Jenkins | Wales | 1991–1998 | 594 |
| S. Bettarello | Italy | 1979–1988 | 483 |
| Rob Andrew | England | 1985–1997 | 396 |
| T. Lacroix | France | 1989–1997 | 367 |
| A.P. Mehrtens | New Zealand | 1995–1997 | 364 |

## RUGBY UNION WORLD CUP WINNERS

| YEAR | VENUE | WINNING TEAM |
|---|---|---|
| 1987 | Australia and New Zealand | New Zealand |
| 1991 | British Isles and France | Australia |
| 1995 | South Africa | South Africa |

## MOST-CAPPED RUGBY UNION PLAYERS

When a player is selected for a representative team, in this case, for a national squad, he is "capped".

| PLAYER | COUNTRY | YEARS | CAPS |
|---|---|---|---|
| Philippe Sella | France | 1982–1995 | 111 |
| David Campesi | Australia | 1982–1996 | 101 |
| Serge Blanco | France | 1980–1991 | 93 |
| S.B.T. Fitzpatrick | New Zealand | 1986–1997 | 92 |
| Rory Underwood | England | 1984–1996 | 85 |
| Will Carling | England | 1988–1997 | 72 |
| Ieuan Evans | Wales | 1987–1998 | 72 |
| Rob Andrew | England | 1985–1997 | 71 |
| I.D. Jones | New Zealand | 1990–1997 | 70 |
| Mike Gibson | Ireland | 1964–1979 | 69 |

## RUGBY UNION AND LEAGUE FACTFILE

**WHAT IS THE GAME?** This highly physical sport is divided into two forms – Union and League. Rules and scoring differ between the two types, but the aim in both is to score points by placing a ball on or over the opponents' touchline (goal line), or by kicking it over the crossbar of their goal.

**NUMBER OF PLAYERS** Union rugby is played between two teams of 15 players; League features two teams of 13.

**POSITIONS** Prop forward • Hooker • Lock forward Flank forward • Number 8 forward • Scrum half back • Fly half Left wing • Left centre • Right centre • Right wing • Full back

**RULES** The ball may not be passed forward to a team-mate. The player scoring a try must be touching the ball when it meets the ground. Games start with a place kick from the centre point.

**SCORING** In Union, a try (five points) is scored by grounding the ball on or over the touchline. Kicking the ball over the crossbar scores differently if it follows a try (two points), occurs during play (three points), or is a penalty (three points). In League, a try scores three points, and a conversion or a penalty goal both score two.

## AUSTRALIAN FOOTBALL FACTS

**WHAT IS THE GAME?** Contested on an oval field, this sport originated in the Australian state of Victoria. The aim is to score points by kicking a ball between posts placed at either end of the field. The 18 players per team kick, "mark", or "handball" the ball.

**POSITIONS** Full back • Back pocket • Halfback flank • Centre half back • Follower • Rover Wing • Centre • Half forward flank • Centre half forward Forward pocket • Full forward

**RULES** One player may "shepherd" another using the hip and shoulder if he or she is within 5 m (16 ft) of the ball. A running player must touch the ball on the ground every 10 m (33 ft).

**SCORING** Kicking the ball cleanly between the two central posts scores a goal worth six points. A "behind" – worth one point – is scored if the ball passes between the behind post and the goal post.

**DID YOU KNOW?** In 1932, a rugby ball was kicked a distance of 82 m (270 ft).

# STICK GAMES

## TEAM STICK AND BALL GAMES AND EVENTS

| GAME | MAIN COMPETITIONS | ESTABLISHED |
|------|-------------------|-------------|
| Bandy | World Championships | 1957 |
| Croquet | The Croquet Championship | 1867 |
| | President's Cup | 1934 |
| | World Championships | 1989 |
| Hockey (field) | FIH World Cup: | |
| | Men's Cup | 1971 |
| | Women's Cup | 1974 |
| Hurling | All Ireland Championship | 1887 |
| Lacrosse | World Championship | 1967 |
| Roller hockey | World Championships | 1936 |
| Shinty | Camanachd Association Challenge Cup | 1896 |
| Softball | World Championship: | |
| | Women's Championship | 1965 |
| | Men's Championship | 1966 |
| | US National Fast Pitch Championship | 1950 |
| | Slow Pitch Championship: | |
| | Men's Championship | 1953 |
| | Women's Championship | 1962 |

## TOP OLYMPIC HOCKEY MEDALLISTS

In this list, Great Britain includes England, Ireland, Scotland, and Wales, which competed separately in the 1908 Olympics. Germany competed as a combined team in 1956; West Germany competed separately from East Germany in 1972 and 1984.

| COUNTRY | GOLD | SILVER | BRONZE | TOTAL |
|---------|------|--------|--------|-------|
| India | 8 | 1 | 2 | 11 |
| Great Britain | 3 | 2 | 5 | 10 |
| Netherlands | 2 | 2 | 5 | 9 |
| Pakistan | 3 | 3 | 2 | 8 |
| Australia | 2 | 3 | 2 | 7 |
| Germany | 2 | 2 | 2 | 6 |
| Spain | 1 | 2 | 1 | 4 |
| South Korea | – | 2 | – | 2 |
| USA | – | – | 2 | 2 |
| USSR | – | – | 2 | 2 |

DID YOU KNOW? Field hockey first appeared as an event in the 1908 London Olympics. More than 70 years later, women's hockey qualified as an Olympic event, making its debut at the 1980 Olympic Games held in Moscow.

DID YOU KNOW? Early Greek wall carvings from about 500 BC show hockey-like games, while curved-stick games appear on Egyptian tomb paintings from about 2050 BC.

## HOCKEY FACTFILE

AIM OF THE GAME To shoot a cork ball into an opponents' goal using a hooked stick.

NUMBER OF PLAYERS Each team has 11 players, including a captain and a goalkeeper. Up to three players may be substituted during the game.

POSITIONS Field players serve as attack and defence. Goalkeepers stand guard in front of each goal. They wear protective clothing – including helmets and leg guards – to shield them from injury by the ball, which can move at great speeds.

TIME There are two halves of 35 minutes each. Teams change ends at half-time, when there is an interval lasting 10 minutes. Time lost during play is added to the end of the second half of the game.

RULES Players may play the ball with the flat side of the stick only. A player must not raise the stick above the shoulder. Goal shots must only be attempted from within the shooting circle.

SCORING A goal is scored when the ball completely crosses the goal line between the goalposts and under the crossbar. The team with the greater number of goals at the end of the game wins the match.

DID YOU KNOW? There are several different weights of hockey stick available.

## WORLD CUP HOCKEY

The men's World Cup hockey event has been contested since 1971, and the women's since 1974. These are the winners of the men's competition since the event began.

| TEAM | NO. OF WINS |
|------|-------------|
| Pakistan | 4 |
| Netherlands | 3 |
| India | 1 |
| Australia | 1 |

DID YOU KNOW? Although its origins are ancient, the earliest mention of hockey dates back to 1527, when a Scottish law described the game as "the horlinge (hurling) of litill balle with stickes or staves" – and banned it!

## CHAMPION LACROSSE TEAMS

The lacrosse World Championships for men are now contested every four years. These are the results since the Championships began in 1967.

| COUNTRY | NO. OF WINS |
| --- | --- |
| USA | 7 |
| Canada | 1 |

The Women's World Cup was formerly the World Championship. These are the results since the World Cup started in 1982.

| COUNTRY | NO. OF WINS |
| --- | --- |
| USA | 4 |
| Australia | 1 |

## WINNERS OF TOP GOLF TOURNAMENTS

**JACK NICKLAUS (b.1940)** US golfer Nicklaus has won 70 PGA Tours and 14 internationals. He is the winner of the most Majors, and was named "Player of the Century" in 1988.

**GREG NORMAN (b.1955)** Australian player Norman has won 18 PGA Tours, 57 internationals, and is the all-time highest-earning golfer.

**TIGER WOODS (b.1975)** High-ranking American golfer Woods has played golf professionally since 1996. He has seven PGA Tour wins, two internationals, and was voted the 1997 Player of the Year.

**SEVE (SEVERIANO) BALLESTEROS (b.1957)** Top Spanish golfer Ballesteros has won the PGA Tour on six occasions, and was captain of the winning European Ryder Cup team in 1997.

**NICK FALDO (b.1957)** British golfer Faldo has six PGA Tour wins, 33 internationals, including three British Opens, and was the first non-American to be named Player of the Year in 1990.

## GOLF FACTFILE

**AIM OF THE GAME** To knock a small, dimpled ball into holes that are set far apart. The game is played on a landscaped area of grass that features obstacles, such as streams, sand bunkers, bushes, and uneven ground.

**EQUIPMENT** There are three types of club: woods, irons, and putters. Woods send the ball the farthest and are used for the first shot; irons are used along the course; and putters are used at the hole.

**NUMBER OF PLAYERS** Individuals or teams of up to four usually compete. In the biennial Ryder Cup competition, European and American teams of 12 men play individually and in pairs.

**RULES** The ball must be played from the position it lies in on the course. The ball must be struck with the club's head, not pushed. A player may use a maximum of 14 clubs.

**SCORING** The score is calculated from the number of strokes above or below par that it takes to play a hole.

## LACROSSE FACTFILE

**AIM OF THE GAME** To send a ball into a goal placed at the opponents' end of the field, using a stick with a netted head to throw, catch, and carry it.

**NUMBER OF PLAYERS** Women's teams have a maximum of 16 players, including four substitutes. Men's teams have ten players and are permitted up to 13 substitutes in international competition.

**POSITIONS** Men's teams consists of three defenders, three midfielders, three attackmen, and a goalkeeper. Each team must keep four players in its own half and three in its opponents' half at all times.

**TIME** Men's matches last four 25-minute quarters; each team is allowed two 90-second time-outs per half. Women's matches consist of two 25-minute halves; during the first 23 minutes, the clock is stopped after every goal.

**RULES** Women players may not kick the ball or engage in physical contact. Men players are permitted shoulder-to-shoulder contact and body-checking. No attacking player may enter the goal crease. A goal is scored when the ball passes completely over the goal line.

## GOLF WORDS AND THEIR MEANINGS

**PAR** The standard score for a hole or round (18 holes) on a course, based on what a top player would be expected to shoot, and allowing for two putts.

**BIRDIE** A score of one stroke under par for a hole.

**BOGEY** A score of one stroke over par for a hole.

**EAGLE** A score of two strokes under par for a hole.

**HOLE** A complete section, from tee to putting green; the round hole into which the ball is played.

**TEE** The ground that marks the start of a hole; a peg on which the ball is put for the first stroke of a hole.

**ALBATROSS** Holing out in three under par on a hole.

**BUNKER** A sandpit on a course, known in the USA as a trap.

**FAIRWAY** A course between the tee and the green.

**GREEN** The cut grass area around the hole used for putting.

## GOLF TOURNAMENTS

| TOURNAMENT | FIRST HELD |
| --- | --- |
| British Open | 1860 |
| US Open | 1895 |
| US PGA | 1916 |
| US Masters | 1934 |
| Ryder Cup (male team event) | 1927 |
| Curtis Cup (female team event) | 1932 |

**DID YOU KNOW?** During a golf match in America held in the early 1900s, one of the entrants drove her ball into a river at the 16th hole. She finally completed the hole in 166 shots after going out in a boat to retrieve the ball!

# RACKET GAMES

## TENNIS MILESTONES

**c.1050** French monks play *jeu de paume* – hitting the ball with the palm of the hand.

**c.1500** Long-handled racket introduced – the start of "real tennis", which is still played today as a separate sport.

**1793** "Field tennis" mentioned in British *Sporting Magazine*.

**1873** Lawn tennis, called *sphairistike* (Greek for "ball game") invented.

**1874** First tennis rules published.

**1875** All-England Croquet Club, Wimbledon, builds first tennis courts.

**1877** First Wimbledon Championships held (men only). Standard size of singles court and height of net agreed.

**1881** US Championship inaugurated.

**1896** Tennis included in first Olympics (dropped 1934).

**1900** Davis Cup first contested.

**1923** Wightman Cup (female UK and US competition) first contested.

**1925** French Championships started.

**1925** Australian Championships begin.

**1926** First professional tennis players.

**1938** Don Budge (USA) first to achieve Grand Slam.

**1968** Start of open era (amateurs and professionals in same events).

**1988** Tennis reintroduced at Olympics.

## WOMEN WITH THE MOST WIMBLEDON TITLES

| PLAYER | COUNTRY | YEARS | SINGLES | DOUBLES | MIXED | TOTAL |
|---|---|---|---|---|---|---|
| Billie Jean King | USA | 1961–1979 | 6 | 10 | 4 | 20 |
| Elizabeth Ryan | USA | 1914–1934 | 0 | 12 | 7 | 19 |
| Martina Navratilova | Czechoslovakia/USA | 1976–1995 | 9 | 7 | 3 | 19 |
| Suzanne Lenglen | France | 1919–1925 | 6 | 6 | 3 | 15 |
| Louise Brough | USA | 1946–1955 | 4 | 5 | 4 | 13 |
| Helen Wills-Moody | USA | 1927–1938 | 8 | 3 | 1 | 12 |

## MEN WITH THE MOST WIMBLEDON TITLES

| PLAYER | COUNTRY | YEARS | SINGLES | DOUBLES | MIXED | TOTAL |
|---|---|---|---|---|---|---|
| William Renshaw | UK | 1880–1889 | 7 | 7 | 0 | 14 |
| Lawrence Doherty | UK | 1897–1905 | 5 | 8 | 0 | 13 |
| Reginald Doherty | UK | 1897–1905 | 4 | 8 | 0 | 12 |
| John Newcombe | Australia | 1965–1974 | 3 | 6 | 0 | 9 |
| Ernest Renshaw | UK | 1880–1889 | 1 | 7 | 0 | 8 |
| Tony Wilding | New Zealand | 1907–1914 | 4 | 4 | 0 | 8 |
| Wilfred Baddeley | UK | 1891–1896 | 3 | 4 | 0 | 7 |

## TENNIS FACTFILE

**WHAT IS THE GAME?** A racket game played on a marked clay, grass, or synthetic court.

**AIM OF THE GAME** To hit the ball over the net so it lands in the correct area of the court and cannot be returned by the opponent.

**NUMBER OF PLAYERS** Individuals play singles competitions, while pairs play in doubles matches. In mixed doubles, each pair consists of a man and a woman.

**EQUIPMENT** Rackets are made of lightweight artificial materials, such as graphite. Balls are made of rubber and covered with a woolly material that makes them less slippery.

**RULES** The ball being served must clear the net and bounce once in the opponent's service court before being returned by the opponent.

**SCORING** Each rally won is worth a point; a score of four points wins the game. A player must win at least six games, and have a two-game lead, to win the set. A match lasts the best of five sets for men and the best of three for women.

## DID YOU KNOW?

Wimbledon, the world's oldest tennis championship, takes place every June. It has become traditional for spectators to eat strawberries and cream during their visit.

## FASTEST TENNIS SERVES

| NAME | COUNTRY | YEAR | KM/H | MPH |
|---|---|---|---|---|
| Mark Philippoussis | Australia | 1997 | 229 | 142 |
| Steve Denton | USA | 1984 | 222 | 138 |
| Brenda Schulz-McCarthy | Netherlands | 1996 | 196 | 123 |
| Jana Novotna | Czech Republic | 1993 | 185 | 115 |

## HISTORY OF INTERNATIONAL RACKET GAMES

**JAI ALAI** In this fast-moving game, of which several forms exist around the world, players hit the ball with a wicker basket, called a *cesta*, attached to a glove.

**RACKETS** Originally a medieval ball and racket game for two or four players, rackets was popular in 18th-century England.

**RACKETBALL** There are two versions of this squash-like game: in the USA it is called racquetball, and in Britain, it is called racketball. The original game was invented in 1949 by Joe Sobek of the USA, when he sawed half the handle off a tennis racket!

**REAL TENNIS** A forerunner of modern tennis, real tennis is played only in France, UK, USA, and Australia. The World Championship began in c.1740 and is the oldest of any sport.

**SQUASH** First played in 1817 at Harrow School, UK, squash was used as a means of practising rackets with a softer, "squashy" ball.

**TABLE TENNIS** First played in the UK in the 1880s, table tennis is commonly called ping pong. It is now played worldwide.

## WINNERS OF MEN'S GRAND SLAM TENNIS SINGLES TITLES

| PLAYER | COUNTRY | A | F | W | US | TOTAL |
|--------|---------|---|---|---|----|-------|
| Roy Emerson | Australia | 6 | 2 | 2 | 2 | 12 |
| Bjorn Borg | Sweden | 0 | 6 | 5 | 0 | 11 |
| Rod Laver | Australia | 3 | 2 | 4 | 2 | 11 |
| Pete Sampras | USA | 2 | 0 | 4 | 4 | 10 |
| Jimmy Connors | USA | 1 | 0 | 2 | 5 | 8 |
| Ivan Lendl | Czechoslovakia | 2 | 3 | 0 | 3 | 8 |

*A – Australian Open; F – French Open; W – Wimbledon; US – US Open*

**GRAND SLAM?** The world's four major tournaments are known as "grand slam" tournaments. For a player to achieve the grand slam itself, he or she must win all four major titles within a season.

## WINNERS OF WOMEN'S GRAND SLAM TENNIS SINGLES TITLES

| PLAYER | COUNTRY | A | F | W | US | TOTAL |
|--------|---------|---|---|---|----|-------|
| Margaret Court | Australia | 11 | 5 | 3 | 5 | 24 |
| Steffi Graf | Germany | 4 | 5 | 7 | 5 | 21 |
| Helen Wills-Moody | USA | 0 | 4 | 8 | 7 | 19 |
| Chris Evert-Lloyd | USA | 2 | 7 | 3 | 6 | 18 |
| Martina Navratilova | Czechoslovakia/ USA | 3 | 2 | 9 | 4 | 18 |
| Billie Jean King | USA | 1 | 1 | 6 | 4 | 12 |
| Maureen Connolly | US | 1 | 2 | 3 | 3 | 9 |
| Monica Seles | Yugoslavia/USA | 4 | 3 | 0 | 2 | 9 |

**DID YOU KNOW?** Martina Navratilova holds most Wimbledon singles titles – nine, which she won between 1978 and 1990.

## TOP BALL SPEEDS

Jai alai 302 km/h (188 mph) • Squash 232 km/h (144 mph) Tennis 229 km/h (142 mph) • Badminton 200 km/h (124 mph) • Table tennis 170 km/h (106 mph)

## SQUASH FACTFILE

**WHAT IS THE GAME?** A fast racket game for two, occasionally four people, played using all four walls of an enclosed court.

**EQUIPMENT** A small, round-headed racket; hollow rubber ball, colour-coded to indicate its speed.

**RULES** The server must first hit the ball onto the front wall above the cut line, but below the out-of-court-line. The ball must be returned before it bounces twice.

**SCORING** A match consists of the best of five games. The winner of a game is the first player to reach nine points.

## TABLE TENNIS FACTFILE

**WHAT IS THE GAME?** An indoor game for two or four players, who use small wooden bats faced with pimpled rubber to hit a lightweight plastic ball over a low net across a table.

**RULES** The ball must always bounce before being returned over the net. When serving, the ball is thrown vertically from the flat hand to avoid spin.

**SCORING** The first side to score 21 points wins the game, but if the score reaches 20-all, the game continues until one side has a two-point lead. A match is decided by the best of three or five games.

## BADMINTON FACTFILE

**WHAT IS THE GAME?** Players use a long-handled racket to hit a feathered shuttlecock over a high net. Games take place indoors on a court that provides a non-slip surface for play.

**AIM OF THE GAME** To hit the shuttlecock over a high net so it lands in the opponent's area of the court. Players serve underhand, but may return with an overhead swing.

**NUMBER OF PLAYERS** Singles matches take place between individuals. Pairs of players compete in doubles competitions. The rules of service are different for singles and doubles play.

**EQUIPMENT** The racket is made of lightweight metal or carbon graphite, and is strung with gut. The shuttlecock has a cork base, which contains a ball-bearing to add weight and is circled by 16 feathers.

**TIME** A match lasts the best of three games. An interval of five minutes between the second and third games of a set is permitted in international competitions.

**RULES** A player must return the shuttle before it touches the ground. When serving the player must hit the shuttle below waist level. A player may not strike the shuttle with two successive shots.

**SCORING** Doubles and men's matches have 15 points; women's have 11. Only the server can score points. Service is passed to the other side when the server commits a fault.

# CRICKET and BASEBALL

## CRICKET FACTFILE

**WHAT IS THE GAME?** A bat-and-ball game played by two teams of 11 on a pitch with a large outfield.

**AIM OF THE GAME** In each "innings" the batting side defends the "wicket" and scores runs by hitting the ball bowled by a bowler. The fielding side gets the batting side out by dismissing the batsmen.

**NUMBER OF PLAYERS** There are two teams of 11 players. The fielding side has all 11 players on the field. The batting side has only two batsmen on the field at the same time.

**POSITIONS** The two batsmen each stand in front of their wickets. The fielders take up different positions on the field.

**TIME** Test matches are two-innings games played over five days. Limited-overs cricket is a one-day, one-innings game.

## TEST COUNTRIES

Test matches are internationals between major cricket-playing countries. These currently include the following:

| | |
|---|---|
| Australia | England |
| India | New Zealand |
| Pakistan | South Africa |
| Sri Lanka | West Indies |
| Zimbabwe | |

## MOST TEST CENTURIES

When a cricketer scores 100 runs it is called a century. A century scored in a Test match is called a Test century.

| PLAYER (COUNTRY) | CENTURIES |
|---|---|
| Sunil Gavaskar (India) | 34 |
| Don Bradman (Australia) | 29 |
| Allan Border (Australia) | 27 |
| Gary Sobers (West Indies) | 26 |
| Greg Chappell (Australia) | 24 |
| Viv Richards (West Indies) | 24 |
| Javed Miandad (Pakistan) | 23 |

## MAIN WAYS OF BEING OUT IN CRICKET

**BOWLED** The ball breaks the batsman's wicket.

**CAUGHT** A fielder catches the ball after it has hit the batsman's bat or gloves.

**HIT WICKET** The batsman breaks his wicket while playing a shot.

**LEG BEFORE WICKET (LBW)** The batsman obstructs a delivery that would have otherwise touched the wicket, without previously playing the ball with his bat.

**RUN OUT** The wicket is broken by the fielding team before the batsman reaches the popping crease (a line that marks the limit of a batsman's approach when hitting the ball).

**STUMPED** The wicketkeeper breaks the batsman's wicket while the batsman is outside his ground when receiving a ball.

**HANDLING THE BALL** The batsman touches the ball in play.

**TIMED OUT** The batsman takes too long to reach the crease.

## HIGHEST INNINGS TOTALS IN TEST CRICKET

| MATCH | VENUE | YEAR | SCORE |
|---|---|---|---|
| Sri Lanka v India | Colombo, Sri Lanka | 1997–1998 | 952–6d |
| England v Australia | London, UK | 1938 | 903–7d |
| England v West Indies | Kingston, Jamaica | 1929–1930 | 849d |
| West Indies v Pakistan | Kingston, Jamaica | 1957–1958 | 790–3d |

*d = innings declared closed by the batting side's captain*

## CRICKET MILESTONES

**1646** First recorded cricket match at Coxheath, Kent, England. At this time, wickets were up to 1.8 m (6 ft) wide.

**1676** First overseas cricket game recorded in Aleppo, Syria.

**1709** First match between two English counties (Kent v Surrey), at which there is also evidence of betting on the sport.

**1729** Oldest surviving cricket bat made – now on show in the pavilion at The Oval, London, UK.

**1744** Standard 22-yard (20.12-m) pitch introduced; first laws of cricket published.

**1775** First six-seamed ball made of crimson leather around an interior of cork; third stump introduced.

**1786** First use of two bails for each wicket. Early wickets carried only one – sometimes several feet long!

**1853** Modern bat, with a willow blade and cane handle invented.

**1877** First Test Match (Australia v England).

**1887** First women's cricket club.

**1890** First professional women cricketers.

**1934** First women's Test match (England v Australia).

**1972** Benson & Hedges Cup (one-day match) started.

**1973** First women's World Cup.

**1975** First World Cup – a one-day international tournament.

## CRICKET SCORES LIST

| RUNS | HOW RUNS ARE GAINED |
|---|---|
| 1 | The two batsmen pass each other to reach opposite wicket |
| 1 | No ball: bowler steps outside batting creases or throws, rather than bowls the ball |
| 1 | Wide: a delivery is too high or wide of the stumps for the batsman to play the ball |
| 4 | Ball reaches boundary after touching ground |
| 6 | Ball reaches boundary without touching ground |

## GREAT BASEBALL PLAYERS

**TY (TYRUS RAYMOND) COBB (1886–1961)** He played for Detroit between 1905 and 1926, and was regarded as the greatest offensive player of all time. His records for "career batting average" and "most runs in a career" stand to this day.

**LOU GEHRIG (1903–1941)** This New York Yankees player hit 49 home runs in 1936, and was the only player to hit 14 home runs against one opponent in a season.

**WILLIE MAYS (b.1931)** Mays was a Giants centrefielder, who scored 660 home runs. He was the youngest player to achieve 50 home runs in a season, which he did in 1955, at the age of just 24.

**PETE ROSE (b.1941)** Nicknamed "Charlie Hustle", Rose played for Cincinnati and scored a record 4,256 hits in his career.

**"BABE" (GEORGE HENRY) RUTH (1895–1948)** Yankees outfielder who, at his retirement, was holder of more than 50 records. He is regarded as baseball's greatest player.

**"HONUS" (JOHN PETER) WAGNER (1874–1955)** Baseball's most popular player prior to Ruth, and was considered the game's greatest shortstop.

**"CY" (DENTON TRUE) YOUNG (1867–1955)** Pitcher record-holder after whom the coveted pitching award is named. He played 22 seasons between 1890 and 1911.

## BASEBALL FIELDING POSITIONS

The nine fielding positions are:

Pitcher • Catcher • First baseman • Second baseman • Third baseman • Shortstop • Left fielder • Center fielder • Right fielder

## FIRST PITCHERS TO THROW PERFECT GAMES

In all, only 14 pitchers have ever thrown perfect games, which means that they allow the opposition no hits, no runs, and do not allow a player to reach first base.

| PLAYER | MATCH | DATE |
|---|---|---|
| Lee Richmond | Worcester v Cleveland | 12 June 1880 |
| Monte Ward | Providence v Buffalo | 17 June 1880 |
| Cy Young | Boston v Philadelphia | 5 May 1904 |
| Addie Joss | Cleveland v Chicago | 2 October 1908 |
| Charlie Robertson | Chicago v Detroit | 30 April 1922 |

## WHO'S HIT FOUR HOME RUNS IN ONE GAME?

A home run is when the batter hits the ball so far that he or she manages to run around all four bases in one go.

| PLAYER | CLUB | DATE |
|---|---|---|
| Rocky Colavito | Cleveland | 10 June 1959 |
| Willie Mays | San Francisco | 30 April 1961 |
| Mike Schmidt | Philadelphia | 17 April 1976 |
| Bob Horner | Atlanta | 6 July 1986 |
| Mark Whitten | St Louis | 7 September 1993 |

**DID YOU KNOW?**
When the pitcher pitches the ball it can travel at more than 145 km/h (90 mph).

## WORLD SERIES STARS

The World Series is a post-season event played between American League and National League teams on a best-of-seven basis to determine the major league baseball champions.

| TEAM | WINS |
|---|---|
| New York Yankees | 23 |
| St Louis Cardinals | 9 |
| Philadelphia/Kansas City/Oakland Athletics | 9 |
| Brooklyn/Los Angeles Dodgers | 6 |
| New York/San Francisco Giants | 5 |
| Boston Red Sox | 5 |
| Cincinnati Reds | 5 |
| Pittsburgh Pirates | 5 |
| Detroit Tigers | 4 |

*Teams separated by / show changes of franchise and are regarded as the same team for record purposes.*

## BASEBALL FACTFILE

**WHAT IS THE GAME?** Baseball is a bat-and-ball game played by two teams of nine players. Each team takes turns to bat and field. It is the official national sport of the USA.

**AIM OF THE GAME** The batting side scores runs by hitting the ball and running around four bases, touching or "tagging" each base in turn.

**RULES** The pitcher throws the ball at a height between the batter's armpits and knees – the "strike zone". The batter is out if he misses three strikes in a row, the ball is caught, or he is "tagged".

**TIME** There are nine periods called "innings". An innings ends when three members of the batting team are out.

# ATHLETICS and GYMNASTICS

## OLYMPIC TRACK AND FIELD EVENTS

**DECATHLON** Ten events (men): 100 m, long jump, shot put, high jump, 400 m, 110-m hurdles, discus, pole vault, javelin, 1,500 m.

**DISCUS** Thrown from a circle, it must land within a 40° arc.

**HAMMER THROW** Like the discus, the hammer is thrown from a circle and must fall within a 40° arc.

**HEPTATHLON** Seven events (women): 100-m hurdles, high jump, shotput, 200 m, long jump, javelin, 800 m.

**HIGH JUMP** Competitors have three jumps to clear the bar. As the bar is raised, jumpers are eliminated until the winner is left.

**HURDLING** Races have ten hurdles and are run over 110 m (100 for women) and 400 m.

**JAVELIN** The javelin is thrown from behind a curved line at the end of a run-up track and must land within a 29° arc.

**LONG JUMP** Athletes take a fast run-up to launch themselves.

**MARATHON** These long-distance runs over 26 miles 385 yd (42,195 m) are run on roads but start and end in the stadium.

**POLE VAULT** Athletes jump over a bar with the aid of a long pole.

**RELAY RACING** The major events are the 4 x 100 m and 4 x 400 m. Each athlete runs with the baton and passes it to the next runner.

**RUNNING** Races are run over distances of 100 m, 200 m, 400 m, 800 m, 1,500 m, 5,000 m, and 10,000 m.

**SHOT PUT** Athlete throws, or "puts", a heavy ball.

**TRIPLE JUMP** This consists of a hop, step, and jump starting with a run-up to the take-off board and finishing in the sand pit.

**WALK** The men's walking race is held over a distance of 20 km and 50 km, and the women's is over 10 km.

**DID YOU KNOW?** Rhythmic gymnastics is performed by women only, using hand apparatus.

## ATHLETICS AND GYMNASTICS RECORDS

**FOUR-MINUTE MILE** Roger Bannister, UK, broke through this barrier with 3 min 59.4 secs on 16 May 1954. The current world record of 3 min 44.39 secs has been held by Noreddine Morceli (Algeria) since 5 September 1993.

**GYMNASTICS** Larisa Latynina (USSR) won an unbeaten record of nine gold (six individual, three team) five silver, and four bronze medals in the Olympics in the 1956, 1960, and 1964 Games.

**DISCUS** The women's record of 76.80 m (252 ft), by Gabriele Reinsch, is greater than the men's 74.08 m (243 ft) held by Jürgen Schult, both of East Germany. The men's discus is twice as heavy!

**HIGH JUMP** In 1993, Javier Sotomayor of Cuba broke his own record with a jump of 2.45 m (8 ft).

**JAVELIN** Jan Zelezny (Czech Republic) set the record of 98.48 m (323 ft 1 in) on 25 May 1996.

**LONG JUMP** Mike Powell (USA) set the world record of 8.95 m (29 ft 4 in) on 30 August 1991.

**SHOT PUT** The world men's record of 23.12 m (75 ft 10 in) was set by Randy Barnes of the USA on 20 May 1990.

## LONGEST LONG JUMPS

| ATHLETE | COUNTRY | YEAR | DISTANCE | | |
|---------|---------|------|----|----|-----|
| | | | M | FT | IN |
| Mike Powell | USA | 1991 | 8.95 | 29 | 4.3 |
| Bob Beamon | USA | 1968 | 8.9 | 29 | 2.4 |
| Carl Lewis | USA | 1991 | 8.87 | 29 | 1.2 |
| Robert Emmiyan | USSR | 1987 | 8.86 | 29 | 0.7 |

## HIGHEST HIGH JUMPS

| ATHLETE | COUNTRY | YEAR | HEIGHT | | |
|---------|---------|------|----|----|-----|
| | | | M | FT | IN |
| Javier Sotomayor | Cuba | 1993 | 2.45 | 8 | 0 |
| Patrik Sjöberg | Sweden | 1987 | 2.42 | 7 | 11.2 |
| Igor Paklin | USSR | 1985 | 2.41 | 7 | 10.8 |
| Rudolf Povarnitsyn | USSR | 1985 | 2.40 | 7 | 10.4 |

## LONGEST-STANDING OUTDOOR EVENT RECORDS

| EVENT | HOLDER | TIME/DISTANCE | DATE SET |
|---|---|---|---|
| 4 × 1500 m relay | West Germany | 14:38.7 | 17 August 1977 |
| 4 × 200 m relay | East Germany | 1:28.15 | 9 August 1980 |
| 25,000 m | Toshihiko Seko (Japan) | 1:13:55.8 | 22 March 1981 |
| 30,000 m | Toshihiko Seko (Japan) | 1:29:18.7 | 22 March 1981 |
| 1 hour* | Silvana Cruciata (Italy) | 18,084 m | 4 May 1981 |
| 1000 m | Sebastian Coe (UK) | 2:12.18 | 11 July 1981 |
| 4 × 800 m relay | UK | 7:03.89 | 30 August 1982 |
| 800 m* | Jarmila Kratochvilová (Czechoslovakia) | 1:53.28 | 26 July 1983 |
| 4 × 800 m relay* | USSR | 7:50.17 | 5 August 1984 |

*Denotes women's races*

**DID YOU KNOW?** UK athlete Sebastian Coe's 800 m world record of 1:41.73, set on 10 June 1981, was matched exactly by Wilson Kipketer of Denmark on 7 July 1997. This was the first time since records have been kept to one-hundredths of a second that a world outdoor record had been exactly equalled. However, Kipketer finally succeeded in breaking the world record on 24 August 1997.

## FASTEST TIMES FOR THREE WORLD MARATHONS

| COMPETITOR | COUNTRY | EVENT | YEAR | HR:MIN:SEC |
|---|---|---|---|---|
| Boston Marathon | Kenya | Cosmas Ndeti | 1994 | 2:07:15 |
| Boston Marathon | Germany | Uta Pippig* | 1994 | 2:21:45 |
| London Marathon | Spain | Abel Anton | 1998 | 2:07:56 |
| London Marathon | Norway | Ingrid Kristiansen* | 1985 | 2:21:06 |
| New York Marathon | Tanzania | Juma Ikangaa | 1989 | 2:08:01 |
| New York Marathon | Australia | Lisa Ondieki* | 1992 | 2:24:40 |

*Denotes best women's times*

**DID YOU KNOW?** The marathon originated in ancient Greece in 490 BC when a messenger called Pheidippides ran 39 km (24 miles) to report the Athenian victory over the Persians at the Battle of Marathon. Today, marathons are standardized at 26 miles 385 yards (42,195 m). Many of the world's major cities have hosted marathon events for members of the public who are sponsored for money which goes to different charity organizations.

## HIGHEST POLE VAULTS

| ATHLETE | COUNTRY | YEAR | HEIGHT | | |
|---|---|---|---|---|---|
| | | | M | FT | IN |
| Sergey Bubka | Ukraine | 1994 | 6.14 | 20 | 1.6 |
| Okkert Brits | S. Africa | 1995 | 6.03 | 19 | 9.4 |
| Igor Trandenkov | Russia | 1996 | 6.01 | 19 | 8.6 |
| Rodion Gataullin | USSR | 1989 | 6.00 | 19 | 8.1 |

**DID YOU KNOW?** The men's javelin weighs 800 g (28.22 oz) and the women's javelin 600 g (27.74 oz).

**DID YOU KNOW?** There are two Olympic gymnastic events: rhythmic gymnastics for women only, and artistic gymnastics, which includes rings, parallel bars, horse vault, asymmetric bars, and floor routines.

## FASTEST MEN OVER 100 METRES

| ATHLETE | COUNTRY | YEAR | SEC |
|---|---|---|---|
| Donovan Bailey | Canada | 1996 | 9.84 |
| Leroy Burrell | USA | 1994 | 9.85 |
| Carl Lewis | USA | 1991 | 9.86 |
| Frank Fredericks | Namibia | 1996 | 9.86 |
| Linford Christie | UK | 1993 | 9.87 |
| Ato Boldon | Trinidad | 1997 | 9.89 |

**DID YOU KNOW?** In 1984, Carl Lewis (b.1961) won Olympic golds in the 100 m, 200 m, 4 × 100 m relay, and the long jump. He won five more golds in later Olympics, and retained his long-jump title three times (1988–1996), becoming only the second athlete in history to win four golds in one event.

## FASTEST WOMEN OVER 100 METRES

| ATHLETE | COUNTRY | YEAR | SEC |
|---|---|---|---|
| Florence Griffith Joyner | USA | 1988 | 10.49 |
| Merlene Ottey | Jamaica | 1996 | 10.74 |
| Evelyn Ashford | USA | 1984 | 10.76 |
| Irina Privalova | Russia | 1994 | 10.77 |
| Dawn Sowell | USA | 1989 | 10.78 |
| Marlies Göhr | East Germany | 1983 | 10.81 |
| Gail Devers | US | 1992 | 10.82 |
| Gwen Torrence | US | 1994 | 10.82 |
| Marita Koch | East Germany | 1983 | 10.83 |
| Juliet Cuthbert | Jamaica | 1992 | 10.83 |

## TOP PENTATHLON COUNTRIES

Both men and women compete in the Modern Pentathlon, though only men compete in the Olympics. It covers five events: fencing, swimming, pistol shooting, cross-country running, and riding.

| COUNTRY | GOLD | SILVER | BRONZE | TOTAL |
|---|---|---|---|---|
| Sweden | 9 | 8 | 5 | 22 |
| Hungary | 8 | 6 | 4 | 18 |
| USSR/Russia | 5 | 7 | 6 | 18 |
| USA | 0 | 5 | 3 | 8 |
| Italy | 2 | 2 | 3 | 7 |

# THE OLYMPIC GAMES

## OLYMPIC GAMES SUMMER VENUES

The modern Olympic Games, which began in 1896, were the brainchild of French scholar Pierre de Coubertin, who had been inspired by stories of the ancient Greek games. Every four years, athletes from all over the world meet to compete in the Summer Olympic Games. The only pauses since 1896 came in 1916, 1940, and 1944 when the games were cancelled as a result of war. Today, over 10,000 competitors take part in more than 20 sports.

| YEAR | LOCATION |
| --- | --- |
| 1896 | Athens, Greece |
| 1900 | Paris, France |
| 1904 | St Louis, USA |
| 1906 | Athens, Greece |
| 1908 | London, UK |
| 1912 | Stockholm, Sweden |
| 1920 | Antwerp, Belgium |
| 1924 | Paris, France |
| 1928 | Amsterdam, Netherlands |
| 1932 | Los Angeles, USA |
| 1936 | Berlin, Germany |
| 1948 | London, UK |
| 1952 | Helsinki, Finland |
| 1956 | Melbourne, Australia* |
| 1960 | Rome, Italy |
| 1964 | Tokyo, Japan |
| 1968 | Mexico City, Mexico |
| 1972 | Munich, Germany |
| 1976 | Montreal, Canada |
| 1980 | Moscow, USSR |
| 1984 | Los Angeles, USA |
| 1988 | Seoul, South Korea |
| 1992 | Barcelona, Spain |
| 1996 | Atlanta, USA |
| 2000 | Sydney, Australia |
| 2004 | Athens, Greece |

*Equestrian events held in Stockholm, Sweden*

## LONGEST-STANDING CURRENT OLYMPIC TRACK AND FIELD RECORDS

| EVENT | DISTANCE/ TIME/SCORE | COMPETITOR | COUNTRY | DATE |
| --- | --- | --- | --- | --- |
| Men's long jump | 8.90 m (29 ft 2.4 in) | Bob Beamon | USA | 18 October 1968 |
| Men's javelin | 94.58 m (310 ft 4 in) | Miklos Nemeth | Hungary | 25 July 1976 |
| Women's shot | 22.41 m (73 ft 6 in) | Ilona Slupianek | GDR | 24 July 1980 |
| Women's 800 m | 1 min 53.43 sec | Nadezhda Olizarenko | USSR | 27 July 1980 |
| Women's 4 x 100 m | 41.60 sec | Team names | GDR | 1 August 1980 |
| Men's 1500 m | 3 min 32.53 sec | Sebastian Coe | GB | 1 August 1980 |
| Women's marathon | 2 hr 24 min 52 sec | Joan Benoit | USA | 5 August 1984 |
| Men's 800 m | 1 min 43 sec | Joaquim Cruz | Brazil | 6 August 1984 |
| Decathlon | 8,847 points | Daley Thompson | GB | 9 August 1984 |
| Men's 5000 m | 13 min 05.59 sec | Said Aouita | Morocco | 11 August 1984 |

In the 1968 Olympics at Mexico, Bob Beamon added a staggering 55.25 cm (21.75 in) to the old long jump record, and won the competition by a lead of 72.39 cm (28.5 in). His jump of 8.90 m (29 ft 2.4 in) was the first beyond both 28 and 29 feet (8.53 and 8.84 m). The first 8.53 m (28 ft) jump in the Olympics was not until 1980, 12 years later.

## FAMOUS OLYMPIC COMPETITORS

**GENERAL PATTON** George Patton (1885–1945), US World War II general, took part in the Modern Pentathlon at the 1912 Stockholm Games, coming fifth in the event. He might have won, but for the fact that shooting was his weakest sport!

**DR SPOCK** A member of the winning US rowing eights team at the 1924 Paris Olympics was Benjamin Spock (1903–1998), who later became famous as the author of *The Common Sense Book of Baby and Child Care* (1946), one of the bestselling books of all time.

**TARZAN** Johnny Weismuller (1904–1984), winner of swimming gold medals at the 1924 Paris Olympics and 1928 Amsterdam Olympics, went on to appear as Tarzan in numerous films.

## LAST APPEARANCES OF OLYMPIC SPORTS

Each Olympic Games includes different, new sports. However, as new ones arrive, other sports are discontinued.

| SPORT | LAST APPEARANCE |
| --- | --- |
| Cricket | Paris, 1900 |
| Croquet | Paris, 1900 |
| Golf | St. Louis, 1904 |
| Lacrosse | London, 1908 |
| Motor boating | London, 1908 |
| Tug-of-war | Antwerp, 1920 |
| Rugby | Paris, 1924 |
| Polo | Berlin, 1936 |

## OLYMPIC DECATHLON EVENTS

The decathlon event, in which men only compete, has been included in every Olympic games since 1904. Ten different events make up the decathlon:

100 m • Long jump • Shot put • High jump • 400 m • 110 m hurdles • Discus • Pole vault • Javelin • 1500 m

**AMAZING FACT!** A number of decathletes have gone on to become film actors. Floyd Simmons, who was a bronze medallist in Helsinki in 1952, appeared in *South Pacific* (1958), and Bruce Jenner, a gold medallist in Montreal in 1976, found fame through his role in *Can't Stop the Music* (1980).

## TOP INDIVIDUAL MEDAL WINNERS IN A SUMMER OLYMPICS CAREER

| MEDALLIST | COUNTRY | SPORT | YEARS | GOLD | SILVER | BRONZE | TOTAL |
|---|---|---|---|---|---|---|---|
| Larissa Latynina | USSR | Gymnastics | 1956–1964 | 9 | 5 | 4 | 18 |
| Nikolay Andrianov | USSR | Gymnastics | 1972–1980 | 7 | 5 | 3 | 15 |
| Edoardo Mangiarotti | Italy | Fencing | 1936–1960 | 6 | 5 | 2 | 13 |
| Takashi Ono | Japan | Gymnastics | 1952–1964 | 5 | 4 | 4 | 13 |
| Boris Shakhlin | USSR | Gymnastics | 1956–1964 | 7 | 4 | 2 | 13 |
| Sawao Kato | Japan | Gymnastics | 1968–1976 | 8 | 3 | 1 | 12 |
| Paavo Nurmi | Finland | Athletics | 1920–1928 | 9 | 3 | 0 | 12 |
| Viktor Chukarin | USSR | Gymnastics | 1952–1956 | 7 | 3 | 1 | 11 |
| Vera Cáslavská | Czechoslovakia | Gymnastics | 1964–1968 | 7 | 4 | 0 | 11 |
| Carl Osborn | USA | Shooting | 1912–1924 | 5 | 4 | 2 | 11 |
| Mark Spitz | USA | Swimming | 1968–1972 | 9 | 1 | 1 | 11 |

**AMAZING FACT!** The only event at which outstanding gymnast Larissa Latynina did not win a medal between 1956 and 1964 was the beam, in 1956. She came fourth!

**DID YOU KNOW?** The Olympic symbol is made up of five interlocking rings, standing for the continents of Europe, Asia, Africa, Australasia, and America.

## MOST SUMMER OLYMPICS MEDALS

| COUNTRY | GOLD | SILVER | BRONZE | TOTAL |
|---|---|---|---|---|
| USA | 815.5 | 622 | 534 | 1,971.5 |
| USSR | 395 | 319 | 295 | 1,009.0 |
| UK | 165 | 215.5 | 213 | 593.5 |
| France | 161 | 172 | 187.5 | 520.5 |
| Germany | 147.5 | 173 | 178 | 498.5 |

**AMAZING FACT!** "Half medals" result when nationality is uncertain and they are shared between two countries.

## MOST SUMMER OLYMPICS COMPETITORS

| CITY | YEAR | COUNTRIES | COMPETITORS |
|---|---|---|---|
| Atlanta | 1996 | 197 | 10,310 |
| Barcelona | 1992 | 172 | 9,364 |
| Seoul | 1988 | 159 | 9,101 |
| Munich | 1972 | 122 | 7,156 |
| Los Angeles | 1984 | 141 | 7,058 |
| Montreal | 1976 | 92 | 6,085 |
| Mexico City | 1968 | 112 | 5,530 |

## ONE-OFF OLYMPIC EVENTS

As well as sports such as cricket, croquet, golf, lacrosse, polo, and rugby, which remain popular in many countries but are no longer included in the Olympics, there are a number of "oddity" sports that have appeared once or twice, but never again:

**100 M SWIMMING FOR SAILORS** Only members of the Greek navy could enter this event, included in the 1896 Athens Olympics.

**JUMPING ON HORSEBACK** Both long jump and high jump on horseback were included in the Paris Olympics in 1900.

**UNDERWATER SWIMMING** In this event, which appeared only once, in the 1900 Paris Olympics, contestants received extra points for the length of time they managed to stay submerged.

**WATER OBSTACLE RACE** In this unusual race, held at the Paris Games, 1900, swimmers had to swim under and climb over boats.

**DUELLING** Duelling pistol shooting was included in the Athens Games, 1906.

**ARCHERY** At Antwerp, 1920, archers used live birds as targets.

## PARALYMPICS FACTS

**WHAT ARE THE PARALYMPICS?** The Paralympic Games are the Olympics for athletes with disabilities. They are held every four years, after the Olympic Games, and always at the same venue.

**WHEN DID THEY START?** The first Paralympics were held in Rome in 1960, with about 400 athletes from 23 countries. Until 1972, they were restricted to athletes with spinal injuries, but now include those with other disabilities. Winter Paralympics have been held since 1976.

**NUMBER OF ATHLETES** At the 1996 Atlanta Paralympics, 4,000 athletes from 118 countries competed.

**CHAMPION GOLD MEDALLIST** Louise Sauvage (Australia) won four gold medals at the 1996 Atlanta Games. She also won the Boston Wheelchair Marathon in both 1997 and 1998.

**YOUNGEST COMPETITOR** LeAnn Shannon (US) is the youngest person ever to compete in the Paralympic Games. Aged 13 at the time of the 1996 Atlanta Games, she won three gold medals and one silver, and holds the world record in the 400, 800, and 1,500 m wheelchair events.

# WINTER SPORTS

## TOP ALPINE SKIING WORLD CUP TITLES

The Alpine Skiing World Cup, comprising a series of slalom and downhill events, has been staged annually since 1967. Points are awarded for race performances worldwide during the winter.

| NAME | COUNTRY | YEARS | TITLES |
|------|---------|-------|--------|
| Annemarie Moser-Proll | Austria | 1971–1979 | 6 |
| Marc Girardelli | Luxembourg | 1985–1993 | 5 |
| Gustavo Thoeni | Italy | 1971–1975 | 4 |
| Pirmin Zurbriggen | Switzerland | 1984–1990 | 4 |
| Ingemar Stenmark | Sweden | 1976–1978 | 3 |
| Phil Mahre | USA | 1981–1983 | 3 |

**DID YOU KNOW?** Downhill races are the fastest races in which skiers follow a set route down the mountain. Competitors regularly reach speeds of more than 100 km/h (62 mph)

## SPORTS INCLUDED IN THE WINTER OLYMPICS

**BIATHLON** Introduced into the Olympics in 1960, this combined event involves cross-country skiing and shooting at targets.

**BOBSLEIGHING** The sport dates from 1888 and has been part of the Olympics since 1924. Sleds are four- and two-man.

**CURLING** A bowls-like game played with big stones on ice, curling dates back to the 1600s or earlier. It entered the Olympics in 1998.

**ICE-HOCKEY** Fast and furious game, in the Olympics since 1920.

**FIGURE SKATING** First included in the 1908 Olympics.

**LUGE** The modern luge, which is a small one- or two-person sled on which contestants lie back, was included in the 1964 Olympics.

**SKIING** Alpine skiing, introduced in the 1948 Olympics, includes downhill, slalom, and freestyle. Nordic skiing includes cross-country and ski-jumping.

**SKI-JUMPING** Introduced into the Olympics in 1924, jumps have become progressively longer; the men's world men's record now stands at 204 m (669 ft).

**SNOWBOARDING** The development of high-tech boards has made this snowboarding one of the most popular snow-sports. It was first included in the 1998 Winter Olympics.

**SPEED SKATING** An Olympic sport since 1924. Speed skaters are the fastest self-propelled humans on a level surface. Short track speed skating was introduced in 1992.

## VENUES FOR THE WINTER OLYMPIC GAMES

Until 1992, the Winter Games were held in the same year as the Summer Games. They are now held two years after the Summer Games.

| YEAR | LOCATION | COUNTRY |
|------|----------|---------|
| 1924 | Chamonix | France |
| 1928 | St. Moritz | Switzerland |
| 1932 | Lake Placid | USA |
| 1936 | Garmisch-Partenkirchen | Germany |
| 1948 | St. Moritz | Switzerland |
| 1952 | Oslo | Norway |
| 1956 | Cortina d'Ampezzo | Italy |
| 1960 | Squaw Valley | USA |
| 1964 | Innsbruck | Austria |
| 1968 | Grenoble | France |
| 1972 | Sapporo | Japan |
| 1976 | Innsbruck | Austria |
| 1980 | Lake Placid | USA |
| 1984 | Sarajevo | Yugoslavia |
| 1988 | Calgary | Canada |
| 1992 | Albertville | France |
| 1994 | Lillehammer | Norway |
| 1998 | Nagano | Japan |
| 2002 | Salt Lake City | USA |

**DID YOU KNOW?** The Winter Olympics that were planned to take place in Japan, Switzerland, and Germany in 1940, and at Cortina d'Ampezzo, Italy, in 1944 had to be cancelled due to World War II.

## COUNTRIES WITH THE MOST WINTER OLYMPICS MEDALS 1924–1998

| COUNTRY | GOLD | SILVER | BRONZE | TOTAL |
|---------|------|--------|--------|-------|
| Norway | 83 | 89 | 67 | 239 |
| Russia (ex USSR) | 78 | 57 | 59 | 194 |
| USA | 60 | 59 | 42 | 161 |
| Austria | 39 | 53 | 54 | 146 |

## ICE-HOCKEY FACTFILE

**WHAT IS THE GAME?** Ice-hockey is a fast, six-a-side game played on an iced surface surrounded by wooden boards, with a goal net at each end. It originated as the winter version of hockey.

**AIM OF THE GAME** The object of the game is to hit a frozen rubber disc, called a puck, into the opposing team's net with an ice-hockey stick. The team scoring most goals wins.

**NUMBER OF PLAYERS** Ice-hockey is played six-a-side with up to 14 substitutes. Substitutions are allowed at any time during the game. Teams are sometimes forced to continue short-handed when penalized players are serving time in the penalty box.

**POSITIONS** The rink is divided into the defending, neutral, and attacking zones. Players may move with the puck and pass it to one another but may not pass it more than two zones across the rink markings.

**TIME** Each game consists of three periods of 20 minutes, divided by breaks of 15 minutes, when the ice is resurfaced.

**RULES** The game begins when the referee drops the puck between the sticks of two players from opposing teams, who "face off". After a foul, the game is restarted by a "face off" in the nearest circle.

**SCORING** A goal is scored when the puck crosses the goal-line between the posts and under the crossbar of the goal.

## TOP POINTS-SCORERS IN A NATIONAL HOCKEY LEAGUE CAREER

Founded in 1917, the major professional competition in North America is the National Hockey League. Players win points by scoring goals and by helping to score goals (assists).

| PLAYER | SEASONS | GOALS | ASSISTS | TOTAL POINTS |
|---|---|---|---|---|
| Wayne Gretzky (still playing) | 19 | 885 | 1,910 | 2,795 |
| Gordie Howe | 26 | 801 | 1,049 | 1,850 |
| Marcel Dionne | 18 | 731 | 1,040 | 1,771 |
| Mark Messier (still playing) | 19 | 597 | 1,015 | 1,612 |
| Phil Esposito | 18 | 717 | 873 | 1,590 |

## FASTEST SPEED SKATERS

| EVENT | MEN | COUNTRY | MIN:SEC | WOMEN | COUNTRY | MIN:SEC |
|---|---|---|---|---|---|---|
| 500 m | H. Shimazu | Japan | 0:34.82 | C. Le May | Canada | 0:37.55 |
| 1000 m | J. Wotherspoon | Canada | 1:10.16 | C. Witty | Canada | 1:14.96 |
| 1500 m | A. Sondral | Norway | 1:46.43 | M. Timmer | Netherlands | 1:57.58 |
| 3000 m | B. Veldkamp | Belgium | 3:48.91 | G. Niemann | Germany | 4:01.67 |
| 5000 m | G. Romme | Netherlands | 6:21.49 | G. Niemann | Germany | 6:58.63 |
| 10000 m | G. Romme | Netherlands | 13:15.33 | No women's event | | |

## TOP OLYMPIC BOBSLEIGH MEDALLISTS

| COUNTRY | GOLD | SILVER | BRONZE | TOTAL |
|---|---|---|---|---|
| Switzerland | 9 | 9 | 8 | 26 |
| Germany/West Germany | 5 | 5 | 7 | 17 |
| USA | 5 | 4 | 5 | 14 |
| East Germany | 5 | 6 | 2 | 13 |
| Italy | 4 | 4 | 3 | 11 |
| UK | 1 | 1 | 2 | 4 |

**DID YOU KNOW?** Ice-hockey is the fastest team game in the world. The puck, which is usually black and made of toughened rubber is hit at speeds of up to 190 km/h (118 mph).

## TEAMS WITH MOST STANLEY CUP WINS

The Stanley Cup is North America's most prestigious ice-hockey trophy. It is named after Sir Frederick Arthur Stanley who was Governor General of Canada from 1888 to 1893 and who presented the first Cup.

| TEAM | WINS |
|---|---|
| Montreal Canadiens | 23 |
| Toronto Maple Leafs | 13 |
| Detroit Red Wings | 8 |
| Boston Bruins | 5 |
| Edmonton Oilers | 5 |
| New York Islanders | 4 |
| New York Rangers | 4 |
| Chicago Black Hawks | 3 |
| Philadelphia Flyers | 2 |
| Pittsburgh Penguins | 2 |

**DID YOU KNOW?** Cross-country races have no steep slopes but are a test of stamina, covering up to 50 km (155 miles). Nordic skis are lighter and narrower than Alpine skis.

## FIGURE SKATING FACTS

**OLYMPIC COUNTRIES** The USA and Russia (formerly USSR) have each won 40 Olympic medals, but Russia has 20 golds compared with the USA's 12.

**MOST OLYMPIC GOLDS** Gillis Grafstöm (Sweden), Sonja Henie (Norway), and Irina Konstantinovna (USSR) each won three gold medals in consecutive Olympic Games.

**MEN'S WORLD TITLES** Ulrich Salchow (Sweden) won ten skating titles between 1901 and 1905 and 1907 and 1911.

**WOMEN'S WORLD TITLES** Sonja Henie (Norway) won ten titles between 1927 and 1936. She later became a Hollywood film star.

**MOST POINTS** Jayne Torvill and Christopher Dean (UK) were awarded maximum points in the 1984 Olympic ice-dance event.

# WATER SPORTS

## WATER SPORTS

**BOARDSAILING** A sailboard is steered by moving the position of the sail. The three main types of competition are wave performance, course racing, and slalom.

**CANOEING AND KAYAKING** There are two types of competition canoe. A kayak has a closed top and the canoeist sits inside, with legs outstretched. The paddle has a blade at each end. A Canadian canoe is usually open and the canoeist sits or kneels. The paddle has only one blade. Canoe races may be sprints, long-distance, or white water, the latter including slalom racing.

**DIVING** There are two divisions of diving: highboard and springboard. Snorkelling, scuba diving, and skin diving are all underwater leisure sports.

**POWERBOAT RACING** The two main types of powerboat racing are inshore and offshore. There are several classes, depending on size and type of engine.

**ROWING** This is a racing sport for lightweight, narrow boats of up to eight rowers, often with a cox to steer. In sculling, each rower uses two oars instead of one. All boats have the same basic design made of reinforced plastic or wood, but length varies. Rowers sit on sliding seats for extra power.

**SURFING** Most competition boards are tri-fins, with three fins on the tail. Surfers paddle out to sea on lightweight boards and "ride" the waves back to shore. Judges assess style and timing.

**SWIMMING** This includes individual and team racing events, as well as synchronized swimming in which swimmers perform movements to music.

**WATER POLO** This game is played seven-a-side in water. Only the goalkeeper can stand to play the ball, touch it with both hands, or punch it.

**WATER SKIING** Water skiers, towed behind a motorboat, compete in slalom, trick, and jumping events.

**YACHTING** Apart from the Olympics, major competitions are the biennial Admiral's Cup in the UK and the Americas Cup.

## WATER SPORT COMPARISONS

| SPORT | TOP SPEED | |
| --- | --- | --- |
| | KM/H | MPH |
| Canoeing | 20 | 12 |
| Rowing | 21 | 13 |
| Sailing | 69 | 43 |
| Windsurfing | 82 | 51 |
| Powerboat racing | 166 | 103 |
| Water-skiing | 230 | 143 |

**SPEED DATA!** The top rowing speed of 21 km/h (13 mph) is the average Olympic record speed for an eight over 2 km (1.24 m). The fastest Olympic powerboat speed is 166 km/h (103 mph), but much faster records have been set by boats that have been specially designed to break the record. The top canoeing speed is the average Olympic record speed for a K4 over 1 km (0.62 miles).

## TOP OLYMPIC ROWING MEDALLISTS

| COUNTRY | GOLD | SILVER | BRONZE | TOTAL |
| --- | --- | --- | --- | --- |
| USA | 30 | 23 | 16 | 69 |
| East Germany | 33 | 7 | 8 | 48 |
| Germany/West Germany | 19 | 13 | 13 | 45 |
| Russia/USSR | 12 | 20 | 12 | 44 |
| UK | 17 | 15 | 7 | 39 |
| Italy | 13 | 10 | 8 | 31 |
| France | 4 | 14 | 12 | 30 |
| Canada | 4 | 12 | 9 | 25 |
| Romania | 10 | 6 | 6 | 22 |

## TOP OLYMPIC CANOEING MEDALLISTS

| COUNTRY | GOLD | SILVER | BRONZE | TOTAL |
| --- | --- | --- | --- | --- |
| Hungary | 10 | 23 | 20 | 53 |
| Russia/USSR | 30 | 13 | 10 | 53 |
| Germany/West Germany | 19 | 18 | 14 | 51 |
| East Germany | 15 | 7 | 10 | 32 |
| Romania | 9 | 10 | 12 | 31 |
| Sweden | 14 | 4 | 10 | 48 |

**DID YOU KNOW?** Canoeing was not recognized as an official Olympic sport until 1936 at the games in Berlin, Germany, although it first appeared as a demonstration sport at the 1924 Olympics in Paris, France.

## ROWING FACTFILE

**WHAT IS THE SPORT?** Boats are raced through water by individuals or crews using bladed sticks called oars. Rowers use a single oar each; scullers have two oars each.

**AIM OF THE SPORT** The aim is to be the first boat to finish, or, in the case of processional events, the quickest.

**TEAM SIZES** Boats seat two, four, or eight, sometimes with a cox. Scullers race as singles, doubles, or quadruples.

**POSITIONS** Rowers sit one behind the other. The cox, who steers and directs the boat, sits at the stern (back).

**RACES** Championship races, or regattas, take place in lanes over 2 km (1.24 miles). In processional races crews start at intervals and race against the clock.

**DID YOU KNOW?** Canoes and kayaks originated among the Native Americans and Inuit of eastern North America.

## SWIMMING AND DIVING FACTFILE

**ABOUT SWIMMING** Swimmers race in pools over a pre-set distance in one of four recognized strokes. The aim is to be the first to finish the race.

**NUMBER OF COMPETITORS** Swimming is both an individual and a team sport.

**TIMING** Swimmers are timed to one-thousandth of a second by touching sensitive electronic pads at the end of the race.

**SWIMMING RULES** Swimmers must not start before the gun or, in relays, until the previous swimmer has touched the pad. Rules govern each stroke (except for freestyle), including turns made.

**ABOUT DIVING** Divers perform a set number of dives in springboard and highboard events. There are six main diving styles. The aim is to score the highest number of points.

**COMPETITORS** Diving is an individual sport, but teams compete in international events.

**SCORING** A panel of judges awards points according to the style and degree of difficulty of the dive being performed.

**DID YOU KNOW!** Developed and promoted in the 19th century, the front crawl is sometimes called the "American crawl". It is the fastest competition stroke.

## OLYMPIC YACHT CLASSES

| CLASS | LENGTH | | |
|---|---|---|---|
| | **M** | **FT** | **IN** |
| Soling | 8.20 | 26 | 9 |
| Star | 6.92 | 22 | 8 |
| Tornado | 6.09 | 20 | 0 |
| 470 | 4.70 | 15 | 5 |
| Finn | 4.54 | 14 | 9 |
| Laser | 4.23 | 13 | 9 |
| Mistral | 3.72 | 12 | 2 |
| Europe | 3.35 | 11 | 0 |

## TOP OLYMPIC SWIMMING MEDALLISTS

This prize table includes medals for the diving and water polo events that form part of the Olympic swimming programme.

| COUNTRY | GOLD | SILVER | BRONZE | TOTAL |
|---|---|---|---|---|
| USA | 231 | 176 | 136 | 543 |
| Australia | 41 | 37 | 47 | 125 |
| Germany/West Germany | 22 | 44 | 49 | 115 |
| Russia/USSR | 29 | 34 | 40 | 103 |
| East Germany | 39 | 34 | 25 | 98 |
| UK | 18 | 23 | 30 | 71 |
| Hungary | 29 | 23 | 19 | 71 |
| Sweden | 13 | 20 | 21 | 54 |

## YACHTING RACES

**INSHORE RACING** takes place off the coast on predetermined courses marked by buoys.

**OFFSHORE RACING** takes place across the ocean. There are different classes of yachts based on size.

**ONE-DESIGN EVENTS** are for boats of the same class.

**HANDICAP EVENTS** are for boats of different designs.

## TOP OLYMPIC YACHTING MEDALLISTS

| COUNTRY | GOLD | SILVER | BRONZE | TOTAL |
|---|---|---|---|---|
| USA | 16 | 18 | 15 | 49 |
| Great Britain | 15 | 10 | 9 | 34 |
| Sweden | 9 | 12 | 9 | 30 |
| Norway | 15 | 11 | 3 | 29 |
| France | 10 | 6 | 9 | 25 |
| Denmark | 10 | 8 | 4 | 22 |

**DID YOU KNOW?** Paul Elvström of Denmark became the first person to win gold medals at four consecutive games (1948, 1952, 1956, and 1960), and went on to compete in a further four Games.

## SWIMMING STROKES

**BREASTSTROKE** In breaststroke, used recreationally and for competitions, the arms and legs remain under water, and leg movement is frog-like. The sidestroke, with a scissor leg action, developed from breaststroke.

**FRONT CRAWL** Also called freestyle, front crawl has an up-and-down leg motion and alternate arm movements.

**BACKSTROKE** Swimmers lie on their back, move their arms "windmill" style, and kick with their legs.

**BUTTERFLY** In butterfly, the arms enter the water simultaneously and the legs perform a "dolphin kick". It first appeared in the 1930s.

## TAKE A DIVE

Competitive springboard and highboard diving began in the 1890s and have featured in the Olympic Games since 1904 for men and 1912 for women. The main dives are:

**FORWARD** Performed from a run-up or a standing position, the feet are kept together with body as straight as possible.

**BACKWARD** With straight body and head up, arms are swung upwards just before diving.

**REVERSE** The diver starts facing forward and rotates in mid-air.

**ARMSTAND** The diver does a hand-stand on the platform and dives off.

**INWARD** The diver faces the board and rotates forward while diving.

**SAFETY TIP!** Always check the depth of the water before you dive – serious injuries may result from diving into shallow water.

# EQUESTRIAN SPORTS

## MAJOR HORSE RACES

| RACE | TYPE | COURSE | DISTANCE | FIRST RUN |
|---|---|---|---|---|
| St Leger | Flat | Doncaster, UK | 1 mile 6 furlongs 132 yd | 1776 |
| Oaks | Flat | Epsom, UK | 1 mile 4 furlongs | 1779 |
| Derby | Flat | Epsom, UK | 1 mile 4 furlongs | 1780 |
| Ascot Gold Cup | Flat | Ascot, UK | 2 miles 4 furlongs | 1807 |
| 2,000 Guineas | Flat | Newmarket, UK | 1 mile | 1809 |
| 1,000 Guineas | Flat | Newmarket, UK | 1 mile | 1814 |
| Grand National | Steeplechase | Aintree, UK | 4 miles 4 furlongs | 1837 |
| Melbourne Cup | Flat | Melbourne, Australia | 3,200 m | 1861 |
| Irish Sweeps Derby | Flat | The Curragh, Ireland | 1 mile 4 furlongs | 1866 |
| Kentucky Derby | Flat | Churchill Downs, USA | 1 mile 2 furlongs | 1875 |
| Prix de l'Arc de Triomphe | Flat | Longchamp, France | 2,400 m | 1920 |

**DID YOU KNOW?** There are two types of horse race: flat or with jumps. Flat races are for horses aged two or more years and cover between 5 furlongs (1 km) and 2 miles (3 km). Races with low hurdles are for three-year-old horses upwards; steeplechases have ditches, water jumps, and large fences, and are for horses aged four or more years. A furlong is equal to 220 yd (201 m).

### DID YOU KNOW?
Cushioned saddles were invented in China in c.AD 25–220

## POLO FACTS

**ORIGIN** Polo originated from Persia (now Iran) in about 600 BC. British soldiers in India discovered the game in the mid-19th century.

**FIRST UK AND US MATCHES** Polo was first played in the UK in the 1870s. It was promoted in the USA by James Gordon Bennett.

**THE GAME** Four mounted players on each team. Play is divided into periods called "chukkas". The 274.32-m (900-ft) pitch is the largest of any sport.

## EQUESTRIAN EVENTS FACTFILE

**WHAT IS THE SPORT?** Races and trials that test the abilities of a horse and its rider.

**SHOW JUMPING** Horse and rider must negotiate jumps, and are penalized for errors. Those with fewest faults win.

**EVENTING** Tests of show jumping, speed and endurance, and dressage.

**DRESSAGE** Horse and rider carry out a variety of paces, figures, and movements. Marks are given for quality.

**RACING** Flat or fenced courses that test speed and agility.

## TOP OLYMPIC EQUESTRIAN MEDALLISTS

These figures include the medal totals for both individual and team disciplines: Show Jumping, Three-Day Event, and Dressage.

| COUNTRY | GOLD | SILVER | BRONZE | TOTAL |
|---|---|---|---|---|
| West Germany/ Germany | 31 | 17 | 20 | 68 |
| Sweden | 17 | 8 | 14 | 39 |
| USA | 8 | 17 | 13 | 38 |
| France | 11 | 12 | 11 | 34 |
| Italy | 7 | 9 | 7 | 23 |
| Great Britain | 5 | 7 | 9 | 21 |

**DID YOU KNOW?** US jockey Bill Shoemaker won a record 8,833 out of 40,350 races during his career (1949–1990).

**DID YOU KNOW?** The fastest-ever racehorse is *Big Racket*, who ran at 69.62 km/h (43.26 mph) in Mexico City, 1945.

# COMBAT SPORTS

## BOXING WEIGHT DIVISIONS

Divisions according to the bodyweight of a boxer were introduced into the sport during the mid-19th century. Today there are 17 weight divisions, as listed below:

| WEIGHT DIVISION | LIMIT | |
|---|---|---|
| | KG | LB |
| Heavyweight | 86+ | 190+ |
| Cruiserweight | 86 | 190 |
| Light-heavyweight | 79 | 175 |
| Super-middleweight | 76 | 168 |
| Middleweight | 73 | 160 |
| Junior-middleweight, Super-welterweight | 70 | 154 |
| Welterweight | 67 | 147 |
| Junior-welterweight, Super-lightweight | 65 | 140 |
| Lightweight | 61 | 135 |
| Junior-lightweight, Super-featherweight | 59 | 130 |
| Featherweight | 57 | 126 |
| Junior-featherweight, Super-bantamweight | 55 | 122 |
| Bantamweight | 54 | 118 |
| Junior-bantamweight, Super-flyweight | 52 | 115 |
| Flyweight | 51 | 112 |
| Junior flyweight, Light-flyweight | 49 | 108 |
| Straw-weight, Mini-flyweight | 48 | 105 |

## DID YOU KNOW?

The earliest record of gloves for boxing is in a painting from c.1520 BC, but boxing did not become a legal sport until 1901.

8 OZ / 227 GR

## BOXING FACTFILE

**WHAT IS THE SPORT?** Boxing is a combat sport in which two contestants, wearing padded leather gloves, aim to punch each other on the head or upper body while avoiding each other's blows. The contest takes place in a raised, square "ring" bounded by ropes.

**DURATION OF CONTEST** Amateur boxing is staged over three three-minute rounds. Professional fights last up to 12 rounds (15 in title fights).

**SCORING** Fights are won by a knock-out, by the referee calling time, or on points.

## COMBAT AND STRENGTH SPORTS

**AIKIDO** Martial art similar to judo.

**BOXING** A carefully controlled, but dangerous combat sport.

**FENCING** Evolved from sword-fighting, and held since the first Olympics.

**JUJITSU** Based on a range of throws, kicks, and punches. World Championships were first staged in 1984.

**JUDO** Dating from the 1880s, judo has been in the Olympics since 1964. World Championships were first held in 1956.

**KARATE** A Japanese martial art. World Championships were first held in 1970.

**KENDO** Japanese sword art. World Championships have been held since 1970.

**WEIGHTLIFTING** Has always been in the Olympics. Like boxing, it is competed for in a range of weight classes.

**WRESTLING** One of the oldest of all combat sports, a feature of both the ancient and modern Olympics. The first World Championship was staged in 1921.

## FASTEST KNOCKOUTS IN WORLD TITLE FIGHTS

| BOXERS (WINNERS FIRST) | WEIGHT | DATE | DURATION IN SECONDS |
|---|---|---|---|
| Gerald McClellan v Jay Bell | Middleweight | 7 August 1993 | 20 |
| James Warring v James Pritchard | Cruiserweight | 6 September 1991 | 24 |
| Lloyd Honeyghan v Gene Hatcher | Welterweight | 30 August 1987 | 45 |

## FENCING FACTFILE

**WHAT IS THE SPORT?** The sport of fencing takes place between opponents on a narrow "piste". They use three sword types – the foil, épée, and sabre – all designed with safety in mind.

**AIM OF THE SPORT** Competitors try to touch target areas on their opponent with their sword. The winner is the one who scores the greatest number of "hits".

**NUMBER OF COMPETITORS** Two.

**POSITIONS** Attack, parry, and riposte.

## MARTIAL ARTS FACTFILE

**WHAT ARE THEY?** Martial arts originate in the East and are used in self-defence.

**JUDO** Aim is to display superior holding and throwing technique to the opponent.

**KARATE** Relies on high-energy punches, strikes, and kicks aimed at the opponent.

**AIKIDO** Uses flowing, defensive techniques to throw opponent off balance.

**JUJITSU** Forerunner of judo and aikido.

**KENDO** "Sword"-fight with bamboo sticks.

## TOP OLYMPIC JUDO MEDALLISTS

Judo made its debut at the 1964 Tokyo Olympics, but for men only. Women's judo was not introduced until 1992.

| COUNTRY | GOLD | SILVER | BRONZE | TOTAL |
|---|---|---|---|---|
| Japan | 19 | 10 | 11 | 40 |
| France | 8 | 3 | 15 | 26 |
| South Korea | 6 | 9 | 9 | 24 |
| USSR | 5 | 5 | 13 | 23 |
| Cuba | 3 | 5 | 9 | 17 |

# Wheeled Sports

## SPORTS ON WHEELS

**BICYCLE RACING** Olympic cycle events include road racing, off-road racing, and track racing. Bicycles are lightweight and streamlined to maximize speed. Cycling has been an Olympic sport since 1896.

**DRAG RACING** Dragster cars are very light, with powerful engines, and much larger tyres on the back than the front. Races are won on speed. Drag racing is most popular in the USA.

**KARTING** Small, open karts race on indoor and outdoor circuits.

**MOTORCYCLE RACING** The first motorcycle race was held in 1897. World Championships started in 1949 and consist of a range of grand prix races for bikes of different engine sizes. The Isle of Man TT races, first held in 1907, are a main event.

**MOTOCROSS** The cross-country branch of motorcycle racing, where riders must negotiate steep climbs and drops, difficult bends, and muddy water.

**INDYCAR RACING** Streamlined, super-fast cars race on oval circuits in the USA.

**MOUNTAIN BIKING** This became an Olympic event in 1996. It includes trials and cross-country racing.

**RALLY DRIVING** Enhanced saloon cars race over public roads, often for thousands of miles in stages. The aim is to achieve the fastest time.

**SPEEDWAY** Motorcycle racing on dusty tracks. Four riders race for four laps. The annual World Championships were first held in 1936 in London.

**ROLLER SKATING** Invented in 1760, roller skating is a popular leisure activity as well as a competitive sport. Competitions include speed, figure, and dance.

## CYCLING FACTFILE

**WHAT IS THE SPORT?** In cycle sports, cyclists ride specially designed bicycles in races held on tracks, roads, and cross-country circuits. Races range from sprints to multi-stage events that last several weeks and cover hundreds of kilometres (miles).

**OFF-ROAD RACING** The original form of cross-country cycling is cyclocross, where riders carry their bikes over obstacles and may have to run up hills. Mountain biking is now the most popular off-road cycle sport.

**ROAD RACING** Road races take place on courses set along ordinary roads. They are either single stage races or multi-stage events in which aggregate, or total, time decides the finishing positions.

**TRACK RACING** Track races take place on wooden indoor tracks, with banked sides, or flat asphalt outdoor tracks. Races include sprints, where riders make a dash for the line on the last lap, and pursuits, where the winner is the fastest rider.

## TOP TOUR DE FRANCE WINNERS

The Tour de France is the world's top multi-stage road race, held over three weeks every summer.

| RIDER (COUNTRY) | WINS |
| --- | --- |
| Jacques Anquetil (France) | 5 |
| Eddy Merckx (Belgium) | 5 |
| Bernard Hinault (France) | 5 |
| Miguel Indurain (Spain) | 5 |
| Philippe Thys (Belgium) | 3 |
| Louison Bobet (France) | 3 |
| Greg LeMond (USA) | 3 |
| Lucien Petit-Breton (France) | 2 |
| Firmin Lambot (Belgium) | 2 |
| Ottavio Bottecchia (Italy) | 2 |
| Nicholas Frantz (Luxembourg) | 2 |
| André Leducq (France) | 2 |
| Antonin Magne (France) | 2 |
| Gino Bartali (Italy) | 2 |
| Sylvere Maës (Belgium) | 2 |
| Fausto Coppi (Italy) | 2 |
| Bernard Thevenet (France) | 2 |
| Laurent Fignon (France) | 2 |

**DID YOU KNOW?** You can tell the leaders in the Tour de France from their tops: yellow is the race leader, red polka dots is the rider with most points from climbs, and green is the rider with most points from sprints.

## TOP OLYMPIC CYCLING MEDALLISTS

There are five Olympic cycling events: sprint, pursuit, points race, time trial (men only), and team pursuit (men only). Women's events only began in 1984.

| COUNTRY | GOLD | SILVER | BRONZE | TOTAL |
| --- | --- | --- | --- | --- |
| France | 32 | 18 | 21 | 71 |
| Italy | 30 | 15 | 6 | 51 |
| Great Britain | 8 | 21 | 16 | 45 |
| Germany | 7 | 12 | 14 | 33 |
| Holland | 10 | 12 | 5 | 27 |
| USSR/Russia | 12 | 5 | 9 | 26 |

## MOTORCYCLING FACTFILE

**WHAT IS THE SPORT?** In motorcycling, riders race around circuits on powerful motorcycles. There are competitions for different types of bike. Motocross, or scrambling, is held over a cross-country course.

**RACING BIKES** Racing motorcycles are powerful machines designed for speed. Classes range from 125cc upwards, with a special class for sidecars.

**GRAND PRIX RACING** The world's leading drivers and manufacturers compete in 12 or more grands prix each season for world championships in several classes: 500cc, 250cc, 125cc, and sidecar. Points are awarded for the first 15 home in each grand prix – 25 points for first, 20 for second, down to one point for 15th.

**MOTOCROSS** In big motocross events as many as 40 riders race over several laps of a winding, muddy, hilly course. Motocross bikes are light but strong.

**RACING SIDECARS** Sidecars are attached to the motorcycle to make one unit. The driver and passenger work together as a team, the latter leaning over behind the driver to balance the bike when cornering.

## RALLY AND INDYCAR RECORDS

**MOST FAMOUS INDYCAR CIRCUIT** The Indianapolis track, home to Indycar racing, is 4 km (2.5 miles) long.

**TOP DRIVING FAMILY** Al Unser from the USA, has won the Indy 500 four times; his brother Bobby three times, and son Al Jr twice.

**LONGEST RALLY** In 1977, the London to Sydney Rally race covered a distance of 31,107 km (19,329 miles).

**LONGEST ANNUAL RALLY** The Safari Rally, held annually in Kenya, Africa.

**DID YOU KNOW?** The fastest ever Indycar speed is 385 km/h (239 mph)!

## MOTOR RACING FACTFILE

**FORMULA ONE** Streamlined, Formula One cars compete in 16 worldwide races.

**INDYCAR RACING** Mostly USA-based, on oval circuits.

**DRAG RACING** Dragsters race along a 400-m (440-yd) "drag strip". The fastest can reach 485 km/h (300 mph). Parachutes slow them down.

**KARTING** Karts are like miniature racing cars. The simplest have 60cc or 100cc engines and no gear box.

**RALLY DRIVING** "Souped-up" saloon cars compete on regular roads, country roads, and tracks. Drivers lose points for exceeding set times.

## FORMULA ONE GRAND PRIX CIRCUITS

In Formula One, teams of car manufacturers and drivers compete for the World Championship title, in a series of worldwide races.

| COUNTRY | LOCATION | LAPS NO. | KM | MILES |
|---|---|---|---|---|
| Argentina | Buenos Aires | 72 | 4.259 | 2.646 |
| Australia | Melbourne | 58 | 5.303 | 3.295 |
| Austria | Al-Ring | 71 | 4.319 | 2.684 |
| Belgium | Spa-Francorchamps | 44 | 6.968 | 4.330 |
| Brazil | Interlagos | 72 | 4.292 | 2.667 |
| Canada | Gilles Villeneuve | 69 | 4.421 | 2.747 |
| France | Magny-Cours | 71 | 4.250 | 2.641 |
| Germany | Hockenheim | 45 | 6.823 | 4.240 |
| Hungary | Hungaroring | 77 | 3.972 | 2.468 |
| Italy | Monza | 53 | 5.770 | 3.585 |
| Japan | Suzuka | 53 | 5,864 | 3.643 |
| Luxembourg | Nürburgring | 67 | 4.556 | 2.831 |
| Monaco | Monaco | 78 | 3.367 | 2.092 |
| San Marino | Enzo e Dino Ferrari | 62 | 4.930 | 3.063 |
| Spain | Catalunya | 65 | 4.728 | 2.938 |

## DRIVERS WITH THE MOST GRAND PRIX WINS

| DRIVER | NATIONALITY | YEARS | WINS |
|---|---|---|---|
| Alain Prost | France | 1981–1993 | 51 |
| Ayrton Senna | Brazil | 1985–1993 | 41 |
| Nigel Mansell | UK | 1985–1994 | 31 |
| Jackie Stewart | UK | 1965–1973 | 27 |
| Jim Clark | UK | 1962–1968 | 25 |
| Niki Lauda | Austria | 1974–1985 | 25 |
| Michael Schumacher | Germany | 1992–1997 | 25 |
| Juan Manuel Fangio | Argentina | 1950–1957 | 24 |
| Nelson Piquet | Brazil | 1980–1991 | 23 |

*Up to and including 1997 season*

**DID YOU KNOW?** Ferrari has taken part in the World Championships since 1950 and boasts 113 wins to date – more wins than any other Formula One team!

## YOUNGEST FORMULA ONE WORLD CHAMPIONS

| DRIVER | NATIONALITY | YEAR | AGE YEARS | MONTHS |
|---|---|---|---|---|
| Emerson Fittipaldi | Brazil | 1972 | 25 | 9 |
| Michael Schumacher | Germany | 1994 | 25 | 10 |
| Jacques Villeneuve | Canada | 1997 | 26 | 5 |
| Niki Lauda | Austria | 1975 | 26 | 7 |
| Jim Clark | UK | 1963 | 27 | 7 |
| Jochen Rindt | Austria | 1970 | 28 | 6 |

If a driver has won the World Championship more than once, only his youngest age is considered in this list.

# ULTIMATE LISTS

# EVENTS of the 20TH CENTURY

## 1900s

**1900** Umberto I, king of Italy, is shot by an anarchist in Milan.

**1903** US brothers Orville and Wilbur Wright make first powered flight.

**1902** Boer War ends in South Africa.

**1904** Double-sided records produced for the first time in the USA.

**1904** Japanese torpedo the Russian fleet following tension over control of China.

**1905** Russian troops fire on workers' demonstration in "Bloody Sunday" attack.

**1906** Women aged over 24 get the vote in Finland.

**1906** San Francisco, USA, is razed to the ground by a violent earthquake.

**1907** New Zealand becomes independent from British rule.

**1907** Over a million emigrate to the USA.

**1908** Two-year-old Pu Yi becomes Emperor of China.

## 1910s

**1910** In Portugal, republican revolutionaries overthrow King Manuel II.

**1912** The ocean liner *Titanic* sinks after hitting an iceberg in the North Atlantic.

**1913** Grand Central Station, New York's new railway terminus opens.

**1914** France, Russia, and Britain declare war on Germany and Austria-Hungary at the start of World War I.

**1914** Western Front truce halts the war for Christmas Day.

**1916** Irish nationalists stage the Easter Uprising in Dublin.

**1917** Russian Tsar Nicholas II abdicates.

**1917** US troops enter World War I.

**1917** Lenin seizes power in Russia.

**1918** The Russian royal family is executed by revolutionaries in the Urals.

**1918** Arab forces capture Damascus.

**1918** World War I ends.

## 1920s

**1920** Prohibition (ban) of the making and selling of alcohol begins in the USA.

**1920** 29 countries attend the first meeting of the League of Nations.

**1920** US women win right to vote.

**1921** Chinese communist party founded.

**1921** Famine devastates Russia.

**1922** Tutankhamun's tomb is discovered in Valley of the Kings, Egypt.

**1922** Indian nationalist Mohandas Gandhi is imprisoned by the British.

**1923** German currency collapses.

**1927** US pilot Charles Lindbergh is the first to fly solo across the Atlantic.

**1927** Chinese communist coup crushed.

**1929** St Valentine's Day massacre in Chicago, USA.

**1929** Wall Street Crash in USA leads to world financial crisis.

## 1930s

**1930** Stalin declares all farmland in USSR "collectively owned".

**1931** German Danatbank goes bankrupt.

**1931** Spain declares itself a republic.

**1931** In the USA, the General Electric Building is finished.

**1933** Hitler becomes German Chancellor.

**1934** US gangsters Bonnie and Clyde are gunned down.

**1935** Hitler's Nuremberg decrees deprive German Jews of citizenship.

**1935** Italy, under Mussolini, invades the north African kingdom of Abyssinia,

**1935** In China, the communists' long march, led by Mao Zedong, ends.

**1936** In the UK, 200 men go on the Jarrow Crusade to protest unemployment.

**1936** Civil war breaks out in Spain.

**1936** German troops enter the French-controlled cities of the Rhineland.

**1939** After the invasion of Poland, Britain and France declare war on Germany, marking the start of World War II.

## 1940s

**1940** Charles de Gaulle sets up Free French National committee.

**1941** Japanese attack US Pacific Fleet Base at Pearl Harbor.

**1943** Soviet women fly bomber aircraft.

**1943** Italian dictator Mussolini resigns.

**1944** Launch of the German V-1, "flying bomb", the first cruise missile.

**1944** Allied troops land in northern France and go on to liberate Paris.

**1945** Hitler commits suicide in Berlin.

**1945** Germany surrenders and Europe celebrates VE day.

**1945** Japan surrenders after USA drop atom bombs at Hiroshima and Nagasaki.

**1946** The United Nations is established.

**1948** Mahatma Gandhi is assassinated.

**1948** Jewish leaders declare the new Jewish state of Israel.

**1949** NATO (North Atlantic Treaty Organization) is formed.

## 1950s

**1950** North Korea invades South Korea in an attempt to unify the peninsula.

**1952** Crown Prince Hussein becomes King of Jordan.

**1953** New Zealander Edmund Hillary and Sherpa Tenzing Norgay climb Everest.

**1956** Egyptian president Nasser seizes control of the Suez Canal.

**1956** Pro-democracy protesters rebel against Soviet forces in Hungary.

**1957** USSR launches *Sputnik 1*, the first artificial satellite in space.

**1957** Six countries – France, West Germany, Italy, Belgium, Holland, and Luxembourg – form the European Common Market.

**1957** Francois Duvalier is elected president of Haiti.

**1958** Iraq's Faisal II is assassinated.

**1958** General Charles de Gaulle is elected President of France.

**1959** Fidel Castro takes control of Cuba.

## 1960s

**1960** In South Africa 69 blacks are killed as they demonstrate for their rights.

**1960** Sirimarvo Bandaraniake of Ceylon is the first woman Prime Minister.

**1961** East Germans build wall to separate east and west Berlin.

**1965** The USA sends troops to Vietnam.

**1968** US black civil rights leader Martin Luther King is assassinated.

**1969** US *Apollo 11* lands on the Moon.

### ! DID YOU KNOW?
US President John F. Kennedy was assassinated in Dallas in 1963.

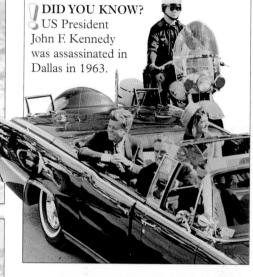

## 1970s

**1970** King Hussein of Jordan and Yassir Arafat of the PLO sign a truce to end war.

**1973** The Vietnam ceasefire is signed in Paris, but the war does not end.

**1973** President Allende of Chile is assassinated.

**1974** US President Nixon resigns.

**1975** The Vietnam war ends.

**1975** Civil war breaks out in Angola.

**1976** White police fire on black children in Soweto, South Africa.

**1976** China's Chairman Mao Zedong dies.

**1977** Thousands flee Vietnam in boats to escape communist regime.

**1979** Nuclear accident at Three Mile Island, USA.

## 1990s

**1991** Coup in the USSR topples Premier Gorbachev.

**1993** Terrorists explode bomb under World Trade Center in New York.

**1993** Israeli Prime Minister Yitzhak Rabin and PLO leader Yassir Arafat sign peace accord in the USA.

**1994** New South African flag is raised, marking the end of white rule.

**1994** Serb troops bomb Sarajevo in Bosnia, killing 68 people.

**1994** Conflict between Tutsi rebels and the Hutu government in Rwanda erupts.

**1995** Israel's prime minister Yitzhak Rabin is assassinated.

**1995** Talks are held to bring peace to war-torn Bosnia.

**1997** Diana, Princess of Wales dies in a car crash in Paris, France.

## 1980s

**1980** The Iran-Iraq war escalates.

**1981** Nobel Peace Prize winner President Sadat of Egypt is assassinated.

**1984** Famine in Ethiopia.

**1984** Scientists warn of global warming.

**1984** Discovery of virus that causes AIDS.

**1985** Live Aid concert is watched by 1.5 million people, raising £40 million ($60 million) for African famine relief.

**1986** Space Shuttle *Challenger* explodes 73 seconds after lift-off.

**1986** The Ukraine suffers the effects of a major nuclear accident at the Chernobyl power plant.

**1987** US President Reagan and Soviet Premier Gorbachev sign treaty to cut nuclear arsenal.

**1988** Bangladesh is hit by terrible floods.

**1988** More than 100,000 people die when Armenia in the USSR is hit by an earthquake.

**1989** The wall dividing East and West Berlin, in East Germany, is torn down.

# DEAD ENDS

**DID YOU KNOW?** Halley's Comet appeared in 1835, the year American writer Mark Twain was born. He believed that he would die when it next appeared. The comet appeared again on 20 April 1910, and the following day, Twain died.

## WEIRD DEATHS OF FAMOUS PEOPLE

**AESCHYLUS** A dramatist known as the "Father of Greek Tragedy", Aeschylus died in 456 BC. It is said that a prediction that he would be killed by a blow from heaven came true, when an eagle dropped the tortoise it was carrying on his head.

**FRANCIS BACON** This Elizabethan philosopher died on 9 April 1626 after he caught a chill while experimenting with deep-freezing a chicken by stuffing it with snow.

**HILAIRE BELLOC** This French-born English writer and Liberal MP died on 16 July 1953, after a burning coal fell out of his fire and set him ablaze.

**HARRY HOUDINI** The Hungarian-born American escapologist, whose real name was Erich Weiss, died on 31 October 1926, after being punched in the stomach.

**THOMAS MAY** This English poet was strangled to death by the cloth he used to support his double chin, on 13 November 1650.

## FAMOUS PEOPLE WHO DIED YOUNG

| NAME | AGE AT DEATH |
|---|---|
| Anne Frank, German diarist, in concentration camp, 1945 | 15 |
| Lady Jane Grey, Queen of England, executed, 1554 | 16 |
| Ritchie Valens, American rock singer, plane crash, 1959 | 17 |
| Joan of Arc, French heroine, burned at the stake, 1431 | 19 |
| Buddy Holly, American rock singer, plane crash, 1959 | 22 |

## FAMOUS PEOPLE WHOSE BODIES WERE MOVED

**CHARLIE CHAPLIN** The British-born film actor died in 1977 and was buried in Switzerland. His body was stolen and held to ransom, but the thieves were apprehended, and the body reburied in a concrete vault.

**ELVIS PRESLEY** Presley died of heart failure in 1977, and was buried at Memphis Forest Hill cemetery. He was reburied at Graceland, his home, after threats of body-snatching.

**SITTING BULL** Sitting Bull was a Native American chief who died in 1890, and whose remains were stolen in 1952. They were reburied under concrete in Sitting Bull Park, South Dakota, USA.

## FAMOUS PEOPLE WHO COMMITTED SUICIDE

**THOMAS CHATTERTON** A British poet who poisoned himself on 24 August 1770.

**KURT COBAIN** The lead singer of rock group Nirvana, he shot himself on 8 April 1994.

**GEORGE EASTMAN** American multi-millionaire, founder of Kodak, and philanthropist, who committed suicide on 14 March 1932.

**ERNEST HEMINGWAY** An American author, he committed suicide (as had his father and brother), with a shotgun on 2 July 1961.

**MARILYN MONROE** In 1962, the famous American actress was found dead by her housekeeper with a bottle of sleeping pills by her side.

**DID YOU KNOW?** Many believe that Marilyn Monroe was the victim of murder.

## EUPHEMISMS FOR "DEAD"

A euphemism is a polite or pleasant way of saying something rude or unpleasant. Few words have as many euphemisms as "dead" – these are just a few of them:

Answered the final summons • Bit the dust • Breathed one's last Called away • Croaked • Crossed over • Departed • Expired Fallen (used of soldiers) • Gone for a Burton • Gone to meet one's Maker • Gone to the happy hunting ground • Hopped off the twig • Is no more • Joined one's ancestors • Kicked the bucket Laid to rest • Made one's final exit • Passed on • Perished Pushing up the daisies • Six feet under • Turned up one's toes

## ASHES TO ASHES: ENDS FOR THE REMAINS OF CELEBRITIES

**ALBERT EINSTEIN** The German-born mathematician died in Princeton, New Jersey, in 1955. His ashes were scattered in the Delaware River, Trenton, New Jersey.

**D H LAWRENCE** A British author who died in France and was buried there in 1930, but was exhumed and cremated in 1935. His ashes were mixed in concrete to form part of the altar in the memorial chapel at Taos, New Mexico.

**VIVIEN LEIGH** A British actress, who died in London in 1967. Her ashes were dispersed in the lake at her home.

## FAMOUS PEOPLE KILLED IN TRANSPORT ACCIDENTS

**JOHN JACOB ASTOR III** A millionaire and science-fiction author, who went down with the *Titanic* on 15 April 1912.

**RUDOLPH DIESEL** A German engineer and inventor of the diesel engine, who fell off a steamer in the English Channel on 29 September 1913. His body was found by fishermen who threw it back, after which it was never recovered.

**LORD KITCHENER** A British soldier famed for his image on the "Your Country Needs You" World War I recruitment posters, who was killed when HMS *Hampshire* struck a mine off Orkney on 5 June 1916.

**DENNIS WILSON** A singer with the Beach Boys, Wilson drowned while diving to a sunken boat off the California coast on 28 December 1983.

**MARC BOLAN** The lead singer of the British group T. Rex died when a Mini driven by his American girlfriend, Gloria Jones, crashed into a tree at Barnes Common, London, UK, on 16 September 1977. The tree is now a shrine for T. Rex fans.

**ALBERT CAMUS** A French Nobel Prize-winning author, who was killed in a car accident, along with his publisher Michel Gallimard on 4 January 1960.

**EDDIE COCHRAN** An American rock star, who died following a taxi crash in Wiltshire, UK, on 17 April 1960. The first policeman to arrive on the scene was 16-year-old cadet, Dave Dee, who later fronted the group Dave Dee, Dozy, Beaky, Mick & Tich. Cochran's first posthumous single was *Three Steps To Heaven*.

**DIANA, PRINCESS OF WALES** The British princess died from injuries caused by a car crash in Paris on 31 August 1997.

**ISADORA DUNCAN** An American dancer, who was strangled on 14 September 1927, when her scarf caught in the wheel of the Bugatti in which she was a passenger.

**GRACE KELLY** A former American film actress, who became Princess Grace of Monaco, and was killed when her car overturned near Monte Carlo on 14 September 1982.

## FAMOUS PEOPLE KILLED BY ANIMALS

**KING ALEXANDER OF GREECE** Died in 1920 after being bitten by his pet monkey.

**ELLEN BRIGHT** A British animal entertainer known as the "Lion Queen", was savaged to death by a tiger in 1850.

**RUPERT BROOKE** An English poet who died in 1915 following a mosquito bite.

**EMILY DAVISON** An English suffragette who killed herself by running under Amner, a horse owned by the King, during the Derby in 1913.

**GENGHIS KHAN** A Mongol ruler, who died after falling from his horse in 1227.

**WILLIAM III** An English king who died in 1701 after a fall when his horse stumbled over a molehill.

**ROY KINNEAR** A British comedy actor who died in Spain after falling from a horse during the filming of *The Return of the Musketeers* in 1988.

**🛈 DID YOU KNOW?**
Hannah Beswick of Manchester, UK, was "buried" above ground in a glass coffin. Her corpse was regularly visited from the time of her death in 1758, until 1868.

## COUNTRIES WITH MOST CREMATIONS

| COUNTRY | % OF DEATHS | CREMATIONS |
|---|---|---|
| China | 35.20 | 2,830,000 |
| Japan | 98.70 | 938,777 |
| USA | 21.31 | 492,434 |
| UK | 71.28 | 445,934 |
| Germany | 37.76 | 333,373 |

## HEARTS THAT ARE NOT IN THE RIGHT PLACE

**ANNE BOLEYN** The second queen of Henry VIII was executed at the Tower of London on 19 May 1536. Her heart, secretly buried in a church near Thetford, UK, was found in 1830 and reburied.

**LORD BYRON** An English poet, who died in Greece on 19 April 1824. His body was buried at Hucknall Torkard, Nottingham, UK, and his heart and brains were placed in a nearby urn.

**FRÉDÉRIC CHOPIN** A Polish composer who died on 17 October 1849. Before his burial in Paris, his doctor, Jean Cruveilhier, removed his heart and sent it to Poland, where it was buried in the wall of the Church of the Holy Cross, Warsaw.

**THOMAS HARDY** The ashes of this British writer who died on 11 January 1928 were buried in Westminster Abbey, but there is evidence that his heart, supposedly buried at St Michael's, Stinsford, UK, was in fact seized and devoured by his sister's cat!

## FAMOUS LAST WORDS

**JULIUS CAESAR** The Roman emperor was assassinated in 44 BC. He is supposed to have said "Et tu, Brute?" ("You as well, Brutus?"). Brutus was Caesar's friend, who betrayed him by joining the conspirators who stabbed him.

**DOUGLAS FAIRBANKS SNR** An American film actor who died in 1939. His last words were "I've never felt better".

**VISCOUNT PALMERSTON** A British Prime Minister who died in 1865. He said "Die, my dear doctor? That's the last thing I shall do."

**ANNA PAVLOVA** A Russian ballerina who died in 1931. Her last words were "Get my swan costume ready".

**OSCAR WILDE** There are two versions of the Irish author's last words in 1900: "Either these curtains go/that wallpaper goes, or I do," or "I am dying as I have lived – beyond my means."

# LAST LISTS

**DID YOU KNOW?** After 1999, Neptune, not Pluto, will be farthest from Earth, due to a change in orbits.

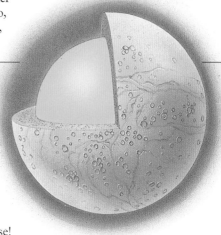

## FAMOUS LASTS

**CUSTER'S LAST STAND** The name given to the final battle fought by American General George Custer, against an army of Sioux Indians, at Little Bighorn, USA, 25 June 1876.

**THE LAST JUDGEMENT** The name given to the prophesied final day, when God judges all Christians.

**THE LAST NIGHT OF THE PROMS** The final night of a series of classical music concerts held every year in London, UK, and broadcast around the world.

**THE LAST OF THE RED-HOT MAMAS** The stage nickname of American singer Sophie Tucker (1884–1966), derived from the title of a song she first performed in 1928.

**THE LAST SUPPER** The final meal eaten by Jesus and his disciples, and the title of Leonardo da Vinci's famous painting of the subject, a mural on the wall of the refectory of Santa Maria delle Grazie, Milan, painted between 1495 and 1498.

**THE LAST POST** The name of the music traditionally played by buglers at military funerals.

**DID YOU KNOW?** A bugle is played on the 11th hour of the 11th day of the 11th month to remember the war dead.

## LAST BOOKS

**CHARLES DICKENS** *The Mystery of Edwin Drood* was published in monthly episodes, but Dickens died in 1870, leaving it unfinished.

**SHERLOCK HOLMES** Sir Arthur Conan Doyle's *The Adventure of Shoscombe Old Place* was published in 1927.

**ROALD DAHL** *Esio Trot* appeared in 1990, the year Dahl died. *The Minpins* and *The Vicar of Nibbleswick* were both published a year later.

## LAST STRUCTURES

**LAST OF THE SEVEN WONDERS** Built in 280 BC, the 136-m (445-ft) Pharos (lighthouse) of Alexandria, Egypt, was partly demolished by invaders and eventually destroyed by an earthquake.

**LONDON BRIDGE** Between 1831 and 1832, after 600 years, the old bridge of houses and shops was demolished and the new bridge opened alongside it.

**LAST NIGHT OF CRYSTAL PALACE** This glass building in London – the world's largest – caught fire in November 1936. The blaze was seen for 80 km (50 miles).

## SPACE LASTS

**LAST MONTH WITHOUT A FULL MOON** This occurred in February 1866. The next will not occur for 2.5 million years – until the year 2,501,991 to be precise!

**LAST PLANET TO BE DISCOVERED** Pluto was discovered by American amateur astronomer Clyde Tombaugh in 1930. The name Pluto, after the Roman god of the underworld, was suggested by an English schoolgirl, Venetia Burney.

**THE FIRST SATELLITE'S LAST DAY** The USSR's *Sputnik 1*, the first ever satellite, burned up on its re-entry to Earth on 4 January 1958, three months after its launch on 4 October 1957.

**LAST MEN ON THE MOON** US *Apollo 17* astronauts Eugene A. Cernan and Harrison H. Schmitt spent three days on the Moon, blasting off on 14 December 1972.

**LAST TIME HALLEY'S COMET WAS SEEN** Halley's Comet returns to Earth every 76 years. It was last visible to the naked eye in 1986, but was seen by astronomers in Chile as late as 1991. It is scheduled to return in 2061.

## THEATRE AND FILM LASTS

**WILLIAM SHAKESPEARE'S LAST PLAY** *The Tempest*, written in 1611, is the last known play by William Shakespeare. The playwright died in 1616, and the play was first published in 1623.

**LAST YEAR WHEN ALL FILMS WERE SILENT** Films were silent in the early years of the industry, with 1926 being the last year in which films lacked sound. *The Jazz Singer*, starring Al Jolson, which premiered at the Warner Theatre in New York on 6 October 1927, was the first full-length feature film containing vocal sound (although it actually contained very little dialogue – its two spoken sequences contain a total of just 354 words). Thereafter, most films had sound.

**LAST BLACK AND WHITE FILM TO WIN A "BEST PICTURE" OSCAR®** *Schindler's List*, directed by Steven Spielberg, contains colour, but is predominantly a black and white film. Its moving re-enactment of ammunition factory director Oscar Schindler's courageous attempt to save Jewish people from Nazi Germany won the 1993 "Best Picture" Oscar®.

**MOLIÈRE'S LAST PLAY** French actor-playwright Jean-Baptiste Molière died dramatically on 17 February 1673 after collapsing on stage. He was performing the lead role in *Le Malade Imaginaire* (*The Hypochondriac*).

## CRIME LASTS

**LAST LIVING WITNESS TO THE ASSASSINATION OF ABRAHAM LINCOLN** As a five-year-old boy, Samuel Seymour saw John Wilkes Booth shoot Abraham Lincoln on 14 April 1865. Seymour lived until 1956.

**LAST BOW STREET RUNNERS** Invented by Henry Fielding in 1750, the Bow Street Runners were London's first police force. In September 1829, they were replaced by the Metropolitan Police, but some Runners continued in the force until 1839.

**LAST PUBLIC HANGING IN THE UK** Michael Barrett was hanged outside Newgate Prison, London, UK, on 26 May 1868 for the murder of Sarah Ann Hodgkinson, one of several victims of a bomb he had planted.

**LAST DUEL** The last to take place in the UK was in 1852, between two Frenchmen, when M. Barthélemey shot M. Cournet in Surrey.

## MUSIC LASTS

**LAST STRADIVARIUS VIOLIN** Antonio Stradivarius (c.1644–1737) is considered the greatest violin-maker of all time. Between 1666 and 1733, when he made his last violin, he is reckoned to have made more than 1,000 instruments, of which over 700 survive.

**BEETHOVEN'S LAST SYMPHONY** Ludwig van Beethoven's 9th Symphony was his last before his death in 1827. He promised the London Philharmonic Society that he would write his 10th Symphony for them, but died before he could begin work on it.

**LAST BEATLES' CONCERT** The Beatles last played in public at Candlestick Park, San Francisco, USA, on 29 August 1966. The only occasion on which the three surviving members have sung together since then was at a memorial service for Paul McCartney's wife Linda in 1998, when they sang *Let it Be*.

## SPORT LASTS

**LAST ANCIENT OLYMPIC GAMES** The Olympic Games were held at Olympia, on the Greece-Macedonia border, every four years from 776 BC. The 293rd and last was held in AD 392, after which they were banned. The modern Olympics began in 1896.

**LAST BAREKNUCKLE BOXING MATCHES** Boxing gloves and strict rules were introduced during the 1870s, but bareknuckle fighting lingered in the UK until 1885, and in the USA until 1889.

**LAST OLYMPICS FOR MEN ONLY** The 1904 St Louis Olympics continued the men-only tradition established in 1896, but it was the last such competition: the 1908 Games held in London included women in the tennis events. Thereafter, women competed in more Olympic sports.

## TRANSPORT LASTS

**STAGECOACH** After carrying passengers and mail around Britain for two centuries, stagecoaches were gradually replaced by trains during the 19th century. Coaches continued in use in the USA until the country's rail networks were developed.

**HORSE-DRAWN LONDON BUS** The last was taken out of service in 1911.

**VOYAGE OF THE TITANIC** The first and last voyage of the luxury ocean liner *Titanic* ended on 15 April 1912, when it struck an iceberg and sank, with the loss of 1,517 lives.

**LAST MODEL T FORD** After almost 20 years' production, the 15,007,033rd Model T rolled off the US production line on 26 May 1927.

**LAST AIRSHIP** In 1937, an explosion destroyed the airship *Hindenburg* at Lakehurst, New Jersey, USA, heralding the end of passenger-carrying airships.

## ROYAL LASTS

**LAST ROMAN EMPEROR** Romulus Augustulus was about 14 years old when he was deposed, in AD 476, and the Roman empire split.

**LAST AZTEC EMPEROR** Montezuma II was deposed by Spanish invaders and killed in June 1520.

**LAST KING OF FRANCE** Louis Philippe (1773–1850), was ousted in 1848. He escaped to England disguised as "Mr Smith".

**LAST EMPEROR OF CHINA** Hsüan T'ung abdicated in 1912. His life is depicted in the film *The Last Emperor*.

**LAST TSAR** Nicholas II was murdered during the Russian Revolution of 1917.

**! DID YOU KNOW?**
The baker of the *Titanic* survived because he had been drinking whisky and the alcohol in his blood kept him alive in the icy water.

**! DID YOU KNOW?**
The *Titanic* was the world's biggest passenger ship.

# INDEX

# ACKNOWLEDGEMENTS

**DID YOU KNOW? THIS IS THE 1001ST LIST IN THIS BOOK – NOW TRY COUNTING THEM!**

## AUTHOR'S THANKS

The author would like to thank the following individuals, organizations, and publications for their help in preparing the lists in this book:

Academy of Motion Picture Arts and Sciences; *Amusement Business*; Amusement & Music Operators Association; *Annual Abstract of Statistics*; Art Sales Index; Caroline Ash; Associated Press; Audit Bureau of Circulations; BMI; *The Bookseller*; BPI; *BP Statistical Review of World Energy*; Richard Braddish; British Broadcasting Corporation; British Library; British Rate & Data; Cameron Mackintosh Ltd; Carbon Dioxide Information Analysis Center; Central Intelligence Agency; Channel Swimming Association; Christian Research Association; Christie's; *Classical Music*; Luke Crampton; Cremation Society; *Crime in the United States*; *Criminal Statistics England & Wales*; Death Penalty Information Center; Diamond Information Centre; Dr Stephen Durham; Euromonitor; Federal Bureau of Investigation; Feste Catalogue Index Database/Alan Somerset; *Financial Times*; *Flight International*; Food and Agriculture Organization of the United Nations; *Forbes*; Christopher Forbes; Ford Motor Company Ltd; *Fortune*; Geological Museum, London; Gold Fields Mineral Services Ltd; Russell E. Gough; Higher Education Statistics Agency; Duncan Hislop; Home Office; Indianapolis 500; Institute of Sports Medicine; International Atomic Energy Agency; International Civil Aviation Organization; International Monetary Fund; International Union for the Conservation of Nature; International Union of Geological Sciences Commission on Comparative Planetology; Interpol; Alan Jeffreys; Robert Lamb; Jackie Lane; Library Association; Lloyds Register of Shipping/MIPG/PPMS; Dr Benjamin Lucas; Meteorological Office; MORI; Ian Morrison; MRIB; NASA; National Basketball Association (NBA); National Football League (NFL); NCAA; Niagara Falls Museum; Nua Ltd; Office of National Statistics; *Oxford English Dictionary*; P&O Cruises; Patent Office; Phobics Society; *Playbill*; Popular Music Database; Professional Golf Association (PGA); Public Library Association; Pullman Power Products Corporation; *Railway Gazette International*; Really Useful Group; Recording Industry Association of America (RIAA); Adrian Room; Royal Aeronautical Society; Royal Opera House; Science Museum, London; *Screen Digest*; Shakespeare Birthplace Trust; Siemens AG; Sotheby's; *Spaceflight*; Sports Council; *Statistical Abstract of the United States*; James Taylor; *Theatre World*; Tidy Britain Group; UNESCO; *Uniform Crime Statistics*; United Nations; Universal Postal Union; US Bureau of the Census; USCOLD; US Department of Justice; US Geological Survey; US Social Security Administration; *Variety*; Tony Waltham; Arthur H. Waltz; World Bank; World Health Organization; World Resources Institute; World Tourism Organization

## PICTURE CREDITS

The publishers would like to thank the following for their kind permission to reproduce their photographs:

b = below; c = centre; l = left; t = top; r = right

Allsport: 174 tr, 177 tl
Bridgeman Art Library, London/New York: Louvre, Paris, France 150 tr; Private collection 150 bc; British Museum, London, UK 50 bl
Beaulieu Motor Museum: 66–67
Boosey and Hawkes: 154 bl
British Library, London: 124–125 b, 146 tl, 147 tr
British Museum London: 106 c, 126 br
The Buddha Pidipa Temple, Wimbledon 118 tc
City of London Police: 138–139
Peter Clayton Associates: 198 br
Corbis UK Ltd: Bettman/UPI 199 cr; NASA 1991
Danish National Museum: 122 tl
Mary Evans Picture Library: 72 tr, 73 c, 74 bl, 132 bl, 146 b
Glasgow Museums: 119, 122 c
Ronald Grant Archive; 167 br
Sonia Halliday Photographs: 125 tr
Robert Harding Picture Library: 153 r; Tony Gervis; 62 tc; Geoff Renner 16–17
Hulton Getty: 44 bl, 73 bl, 200 cr
Hutchison Library: Goycolea 164 l
Impact: David Palmer 18
Imperial War Museum: 132 tr
INAH: 127 tr
Louisiana National Guard: 58 c
N.A.S.A. JPL 13 br
National Maritime Museum, Greenwich, UK: 51, 55r, 64–65 b, 127 bc, 134 b
National Railway Museum, York: 70 tl
Natural History Museum, London: 29
NSE 12–13
QA Photos Ltd: 70–71 b
Rex Features: 98 tl; SIPA Press 123 tr
Royal Geographical Society Picture Library: Hillary 103
Kevin Salt, Pegasus Stables, Newmarket: 194 b
Science Museum, London: 58–59 b, 70 cl, 72 c, 158 tl
Science Photo Library: David Nunuk 10 tr; Library of Congress 12 cl; Simon Fraser 116
Frank Spooner Pictures: Buu Alain 101
St Bride Printing Library: 148 tl
The Stock Market: 75 b, 84 cl
Tony Stone Images: Doug Armand 15 tr; Fred Ravendam 90 tl; D E Cox 77 bc; Jodeph Pobereskin 85; Stephen Studd 84 tr; Darryl Torckler 20–21
Tintin Shop, Covent Garden, London; 149

DK special photography: John Bulmer 171 b; Mark Hamilton 100; Barnabas Kindersley 120 tl, 121 br, 121 tl; Alex Wilson 97 cl; Jerry Young 40–41 b

## PAGE*One*'s THANKS

PAGE*One* would like to thank the following people for their help during the making of this book: Martin Redfern and Kathleen Bada at Dorling Kindersley for their diligent and speedy editorial research; Robert Graham for supplying endless reference material; Tina Borg, Cathy Chesson, and Darren Holt for design assistance; Charlotte Stock for extra editorial help.